FROMMER'S
EasyGuide
TO
CROATIA

By
Jane Foster

Easy Guides are ✦ **Quick To Read** ✦ **Light To Carry**
✦ **For Expert Advice** ✦ **In All Price Ranges**

FrommerMedia LLC

Published by
FROMMER MEDIA LLC

Copyright © 2015 by Frommer Media LLC. All rights reserved. No part of this publication may be reproduced, stored in a retrieval system, or transmitted in any form or by any means, electronic, mechanical,
photocopying, recording, scanning or otherwise, except as permitted under Sections 107 or 108 of the
1976 United States Copyright Act, without the prior written permission of the Publisher. Requests to the
Publisher for permission should be addressed to support@frommermedia.com.

Frommer's is a registered trademark of Arthur Frommer. Frommer Media LLC is not associated with any
product or vendor mentioned in this book.

ISBN 978-1-62887-116-6 (paper), 978-1-62887-117-3 (e-book)

Editorial Director: Pauline Frommer
Editor: Ethan Wolff
Production Editor: Carol Pogoni
Cartographer: Liz Puhl
Indexer: Maro Riofrancos

For information on our other products or services, see www.frommers.com.

Frommer Media LLC also publishes its books in a variety of electronic formats. Some content that
appears in print may not be available in electronic formats.

Manufactured in the United States of America

5   4   3   2   1

AN IMPORTANT NOTE

The world is a dynamic place. Hotels change ownership, restaurants hike their prices, museums
alter their opening hours, and busses and trains change their routings. And all of this can occur
in the several months after our authors have visited, inspected, and written about, these hotels,
restaurants, museums and transportation services. Though we have made valiant efforts to keep
all our information fresh and up-to-date, some few changes can inevitably occur in the periods
before a revised edition of this guidebook is published. So please bear with us if a tiny number
of the details in this book have changed. Please also note that we have no responsibility or liability for any inaccuracy or errors or omissions, or for inconvenience, loss, damage, or expenses suffered by anyone as a result of assertions in this guide.

CONTENTS

ABOUT THE AUTHOR

Jane Foster is a freelance travel writer (with a background in architecture), specializing in Croatia and Greece. Based in Split on the Dalmatian coast, she has traveled extensively through Croatia and neighboring countries, and has seen the region go through many changes since 1998. She writes for various U.K. and U.S. guidebooks, websites, newspapers, and in-flight magazines. She enjoys hiking, cycling, sailing, discovering hidden beaches, camping, drinking red wine, and cooking and eating with the seasons. For more information, see www.jane-foster.com.

ABOUT THE FROMMER'S TRAVEL GUIDES

For most of the past 50 years, Frommer's has been the leading series of travel guides in North America, accounting for as many as 24 percent of all guidebooks sold. I think I know why.

Although we hope our books are entertaining, we nevertheless deal with travel in a serious fashion. Our guidebooks have never looked on such journeys as a mere recreation, but as a far more important human function, a time of learning and introspection, an essential part of a civilized life. We stress the culture, lifestyle, history, and beliefs of the destinations we cover and urge our readers to seek out people and new ideas as the chief rewards of travel.

We have never shied from controversy. We have, from the beginning, encouraged our authors to be intensely judgmental, critical—both pro and con—in their comments, and wholly independent. Our only clients are our readers, and we have triggered the ire of countless prominent sorts, from a tourist newspaper we called "practically worthless" (it unsuccessfully sued us) to the many rip-offs we've condemned.

And because we believe that travel should be available to everyone regardless of their incomes, we have always been cost-conscious at every level of expenditure. Although we have broadened our recommendations beyond the budget category, we insist that every lodging we include be sensibly priced. We use every form of media to assist our readers and are particularly proud of our feisty daily website, the award-winning Frommers.com.

I have high hopes for the future of Frommer's. May these guidebooks, in all the years ahead, continue to reflect the joy of travel and the freedom that travel represents. May they always pursue a cost-conscious path, so that people of all incomes can enjoy the rewards of travel. And may they create, for both the traveler and the persons among whom we travel, a community of friends, where all human beings live in harmony and peace.

Arthur Frommer

THE BEST OF CROATIA

Until recently, Croatia's tourist season ran from July through August, and belonged almost exclusively to Europeans, who clogged border crossings in their annual migration to the country's endless coastline and clear blue sea. Finally, however, the rest of the world has discovered Croatia's charms: its wealth of Roman ruins, medieval hilltop castles, and staggering cache of natural wonders. Even though the summer season now runs longer and the crowds are larger and more diverse, it is still possible to find a secluded pebble cove, or a family-run winery where time seems to have stood still. Every town and village has at least one restaurant where the locals hang out and where the slice of life you get with your meal is the best dessert there is. When all the big modern hotels are filled, there is always a room waiting in a private home where the landlord welcomes you like a long-lost friend.

This chapter is a "road map," directing you to some of my favorites. I know you'll add to the list when you find some of your own.

THE best TRAVEL EXPERIENCES

- **Arriving in Vis Town by Sailboat** (Vis): There's no better way to explore Croatia's myriad islands than by private boat. If you charter a yacht in Split, you can arrive on the distant island of Vis in approximately 5 hours (depending on the wind), passing the more visited islands of Brač and Hvar on the way. Vis Town sits in a sheltered bay, where you can moor up on the seafront and step ashore for a dinner of fresh fish and locally produced organic wine. See p. 176.
- **Exploring Brijuni National Park** (Istria): Rising from the turquoise-blue Adriatic, the meticulously kept islet of Veli Brijuni boasts lawns, parkland, pinewoods, Roman ruins, exotic animals, and a small museum to the former president of Yugoslavia, Tito, who entertained glamorous friends like Liz Taylor and Richard Burton here each summer. See p. 80.
- **Listening to the Sea Organ** (Zadar): Waves create music as they move water through this organ's undersea pipes. Add a set of white stone steps leading into the crystal water above, and beams of light shooting from sister installation **Greeting to the Sun** on Zadar's Riva, and the result is a matchless venue for enjoying a multimedia symphony courtesy of the sea and sky. See p. 130.

o **Reaching the Top of Mount Biokovo** (Makarska): Rising behind the seaside town of Makarska, rocky Biokovo is Croatia's second highest mountain. From Sveti Jure, at the top (1,762m/5,780 ft.), you get stunning views down onto the deep blue Adriatic and the Dalmatian islands of Brač, Hvar, and Korčula. Looking inland, to the east, you can see the rugged mountains of Bosnia/Herzegovina, which often remain snow-covered into April. See p. 159.

o **Sea-Kayaking Round the Elafiti Islets** (Dubrovnik): One of Croatia's top draws is its varied choice of adventure sports activities. Near Dubrovnik, the tiny car-free Elafiti Islets are ideal for exploring by sea kayak, as they lie close together. While you're at it, kayaking does wonders for your torso. See p. 195.

o **Visiting the Museum of Broken Relationships** (Zagreb): Love and separation are universal themes. Croatia knows plenty about them, having once been a member of Yugoslavia before fighting a bitter war for independence. This internationally acclaimed museum has found a fitting home in Zagreb, with each exhibit connected to a love story that went wrong, accompanied by a brief written explanation. The concept is simple but the results are multifaceted, making this many people's favorite museum in all Croatia. See p. 38.

o **Walking Dubrovnik's Walls** (Dubrovnik): Walk a complete circuit of the magnificent medieval walls that protect Dubrovnik's Old Town for fantastic views over the terracotta rooftops and down onto the deep blue Adriatic. Allow at least one hour, and be sure to bring a camera and a bottle of water.

o **Watching the Sunrise Over Hvar Town's Harbor** (Hvar): After a night of partying, buy a take-away coffee and find a place to sit overlooking Hvar Town's harbor—the perfect vantage point for witnessing the sunrise. At night, once the bars and restaurants have closed, everything is dark and silent. Then, just before dawn, the scene is painted in liquid gold. Pinks and blues are next, and finally the buildings and sea come into focus in silver, turquoise, and red. It's an idyllic way to start a new day, even if you haven't slept.

THE best NATURAL WONDERS

o **Kornati National Park** (part of the Zadar Archipelago): Kornati's 140 islands are really the tops of mountains that were above sea level 20,000 years ago but now are mostly submerged. One side of each island is rocky and lightly blanketed with vegetation (a few grapevines and olive trees). The other side, facing the sea, is a sheer rock wall known as a "crown" that plunges almost 76m (250 ft.) straight into the water. Sixty-nine species of butterflies live here. Perhaps the most interesting part of the park is Kornati's underwater landscape, with offshore rock formations supporting flourishing flora and fauna. See p. 139.

o **Krka National Park** (less than half an hour from Šibenik): This park was formed to protect the Krka River, which runs from its source near Knin to the sea near Šibenik. The river has created a series of spectacular gorges, waterfalls, lakes, and rapids on its trip through the mountains. The jaw-droppingly steep Skradinski Buk and Roški Slapovi are the most impressive of the falls. Between the two are Lake Visovac and Visovac Island, home to a Franciscan monastery. See p. 141.

o **Paklenica National Park** (btw. Zadar and Karlobag): Paklenica's raw beauty is best appreciated by hikers and nature lovers. But even motorists respect the imposing Velebit peaks because the limestone cliffs that soar above deep gorges and dense vegetation are visible for miles from nearby highways. Even from afar you can see cave openings and imagine what's inside. See p. 133.

○ **Plitvice Lakes National Park** (145km/90 miles southwest of Zagreb): Plitvice is Croatia's best-known natural wonder. The park's 16 crystal-clear turquoise lakes and countless waterfalls put on a great show. The lakes flow into one another and tumble over deposits of travertine, creating waterfalls that drop a few feet or plunge as much as 64m (210 ft.). All this beauty is set in a dense forest accessed via footpaths and populated by bears and wild boar. See p. 52.

THE best OPEN-AIR MARKETS

○ **Dolac** (Zagreb): This urban market, above the main square at the foot of Old Town, is more than just a place to buy fruits and veggies. Dolac is a crossroads where people come to see and be seen; to trade gossip; and to relax with a cup of coffee. Morning is the best time to visit because that's when the bread is freshest, the displays the prettiest, and the people the most interesting. See p. 36.

○ **Pazar** (Split): Pazar is reminiscent of a Turkish bazaar in looks, sounds, and smells. Stalls vending colorful seasonal fruits and vegetables set up each morning at sunrise, as small holders from the hills bring their own produce, including eggs and cheeses, into town. In addition, booths and tables line both sides of Hrvojeva Street outside the east wall of Diocletian's Palace from the Riva to the Silver Gate, selling clothes, sunhats, and beach bags. See p. 148.

○ **Placa** (Rijeka): On the seafront, close to Rijeka's port, the city market is made up of three pavilions selling meat, dairy, and fish. Out front, open-air stalls are piled high with fresh seasonal fruit and vegetables, while to one side, in front of the Croatian National Theater, you'll find a small and colorful flower market. See p. 106.

THE best SMALL HOTELS & INNS

○ **Art Hotel Kalelarga** (Zadar): In the heart of Zadar's historic center, on a car-free peninsula, this old stone building was carefully renovated to open as a chic boutique hotel in 2012. Rooms have wooden floors and are decorated in subtle earthy shades of cream, beige, and brown, but the highlight for most visitors is the ground-floor restaurant, which serves an indulgent cooked-to-order breakfast, and has sliding doors that open onto Zadar's main pedestrian thoroughfare. See p. 130.

○ **Bevanda** (Opatija): A sophisticated retreat overlooking the Kvarner Gulf, Bevanda started out as a gourmet seafood restaurant, then expanded to include this small luxury hotel in 2013. The rooms feature lots of contemporary woodwork, reminiscent of Scandinavian design. All have sea views, spacious bathrooms with Jacuzzis, and well-stocked bars. See p. 108.

○ **Bračka Perla** (Brač): Set in a garden with a pool and overlooking a small bay, this peaceful hotel is the perfect retreat for families. Apartments, which are color-themed and named after local plants, come with a double room plus a living room with a sofa bed that sleeps two. You also have your own kitchen and a stone terrace for eating out in the garden. See p. 163.

○ **Hotel Boškinac** (Novalja, Pag Island): Boškinac is in the middle of nowhere even for Pag, but that's part of its charm. This country-chic hotel is surrounded by gardens, olive groves, vineyards, and forest, far from the madding weekenders who descend on nearby Novalja all summer long. Boškinac's restaurant is one of the most creative in Croatia, and the wines from its vineyards are prized all over the country. See p. 138.

○ **Hotel San Rocco** (Brtonigla, near Poreč): San Rocco's location deep in Istria adds to the romance of its lovingly restored stone buildings and grounds. Flowers, olive groves, and an assortment of ruins comprise the hotel's sensual "curb appeal." But it's really the beautifully put together guestrooms, with their mélange of antique and modern touches, the inviting pool, and the magnificent gourmet restaurant that seal the deal. See p. 90.

○ **Hotel Vestibul Palace** (Split): The Roman Empire meets the 21st century at the Palace, where most rooms share at least part of a wall built by Diocletian. Gourmet delights align with history to make this one of the best hotel experiences in Croatia. Each room has a personality of its own, complete with cleverly designed windows carved into the stone walls to reveal views of various aspects of Old Town. See p. 150.

○ **Lešič Dimitri Palace** (Korčula): Each of the five pieds-à-terre in this lavishly renovated medieval stone palace has a personality of its own. Privacy, elegance, and whimsy are built into each unit, any of which would be a fitting home for royalty in Manhattan or Marrakesh. There's also a gourmet restaurant, a small spa with Thai masseuses, and two hotel boats available for private excursions. See p. 174.

○ **Palmižana** (Hvar): Not really a hotel, this is more a blissful back-to-nature escape, with bungalows and small villas set amid an overgrown botanical garden on a tiny car-free islet. The owner is an art collector, and each building is decorated with colorful paintings and quirky sculptures by contemporary Croatian artists. There's a small beach, two excellent restaurants, and taxi-boat service to trendy Hvar Town. See p. 168.

THE best BIG LUXURY HOTELS

○ **Hilton Imperial** (Dubrovnik): This is the U.S. chain's first foray into Croatia; rather than build a hotel from scratch, Hilton had the wisdom to restore what was salvageable from Dubrovnik's historic 19th-century Imperial and graft a modern hotel onto its base. Every detail has been taken care of and you'll be treated as an honored guest here. See p. 195.

○ **Hotel Amfora** (Hvar): Reopened in 2008 after a complete renovation, this vast 1970s building opens onto a terraced garden, with a series of cascading turquoise pools and artificial islets with palm trees. Beyond the garden lies the Bonj "les bains" beach club, giving way to the glistening Adriatic. A 10-minute walk along the coast leads to trendy Hvar Town, with its centuries-old stone buildings and fishing harbor filled with yachts. Amfora also makes a fine all-around choice for families with kids. See p. 168.

○ **Iadera** (Petrčane, near Zadar): Home to one of the biggest and most luxurious spas in Croatia, the ultra-modern Iadera stands on a small peninsula. Rooms are spacious, light, and airy, with oak floors and discreet details in royal blue and turquoise, subtly suggesting a maritime theme (fitting given there's sea on three sides here). An infinity pool out front is lit with ever-changing colored lights at night, and the a la carte restaurant serves fresh seafood on a terrace in the garden, with the Adriatic rising on the horizon. See p. 130.

○ **Monte Mulini** (Rovinj): Truly luxurious, even the lowest-priced room at Monte Mulini has a huge glamour bathroom with a separate shower and an array of designer toiletries. MM's world-class restaurants, services, and people-centric staff cater to guests' every whim. The spa is the ultimate in decadence, with a floating bath filled with water of such a high concentration of salt that you stay suspended in water no matter how hard you try to touch bottom. As of summer 2014, MM has a beach, too. See p. 85.

○ **Radisson BLU** (Orašac): Orašac is 12km (7½ miles) from Dubrovnik and an idyllic spot for getting away from it all without going too far. The nice thing about the BLU is that you never have to leave its lavishly landscaped grounds. You can veg out right here and still experience Dalmatia's natural beauty, fine food, and hospitality—all while being environmentally responsible. See p. 196.

o **The Regent Esplanade** (Zagreb): The oldest continually operating luxury hotel in Croatia compares favorably with 5-star hotels in New York and Paris—for a fraction of the cost. From rich furnishings in the guestrooms to a concierge who is a gallant repository of Croatian history, a stay at the Esplanade is an experience you'll never forget. See p. 43.

THE best ROMAN RUINS

o **Diocletian's Palace** (Split): Diocletian built his estate on a scale so grand it was converted into a city after he died. What remains of the palace and what's been built on its footprint is now Split's Old Town. If you walk around, through, and under it enough, you'll begin to understand the enormity of Diocletian's ego. See p. 148.

o **Pula Amphitheater** (Pula): Smaller than Rome's Colosseum but in much better shape, this amphitheater is more accessible to tourists than its Rome counterpart. In summer it hosts the Pula Film Festival, plus various open-air concerts. If you're in town when there's something on, get a ticket no matter who is headlining. See p. 77.

o **Salona** (Solin): The grandeur that was Rome is still evident in the crumbling buildings and foundations of this former outpost of the empire. It isn't difficult to imagine what Salona looked like in its prime, but it is tough to imagine why Salona was left to sink into the earth for centuries. See p. 154.

THE best BEACHES

o **Baška** (Krk Island): This coastal village has more than 30 beaches of varying size and a promenade that skirts most of them. The shore is a stretch of fine pebble, which gently curves around a southeast-facing bay, making this former fishing village a sun worshipper's paradise. See p. 113.

o **Novalja** (Pag Island): Any cove off Novalja can be a private beach. The water offshore is so clear you can see the white, sandy bottom 6m (20 ft.) below. If you have a boat, drop anchor for a while, take a dip, and let your stress float away. Partygoers come here specifically to swim, drink, and dance on Zrće beach, just outside town, which is also known for its open-air summer music festivals. See p. 137.

o **Orebić** (Pelješac Peninsula): Orebić is a civilized place where families linger together. At the end of the day, Mom brings covered bowls full of fruit down to kids who don't want to leave their sand castles and snorkels. The water is warm, the sun is constant, and the people are as nice as they come. See p. 206.

o **Zlatni Rat** (Brač Island): Visit this beach just so you can say you did. This is the famous strip that appears in all the Croatia ads, usually in an aerial view. From above, it resembles a green finger rimmed with sand and tipped with a curling tendril extending into the sapphire sea. From ground level, it is a sun-blasted, pebbled landscape covered with a huge international crowd soaking up the rays. It also happens to be Croatia's top windsurfing destination. See p. 162.

THE best CHARMING RUSTIC VILLAGES

o **Čigoć** in Lonjsko Polje is known as the "Stork Place" because of the long-legged birds that perch atop the village roofs. The storks are the hook that gets tourists to stop in the middle of the marsh, but the historic cabins and natural surroundings keep them here for hours. See p. 64.

o **Hum** (Istria): It calls itself the smallest town in the world, and population-wise, it might be. But so many people visit this village high in the Istrian interior that it always seems crowded. The village fathers have done a wonderful job of restoring the buildings to make it an appealing, tourist-friendly destination. See p. 100.

o **Kumrovec** in the Zagorje region is like a Croatian Williamsburg, Virginia, with restored cabins and barns furnished as they were when Croatia's most famous son, Josip Broz Tito, was born in the late 19th century. Some of the rustic buildings in this open-air museum contain photos and displays, while others feature docents in traditional costumes who explain weaving, candle making, and other crafts of the times. See p. 56.

THE best CATHEDRALS & CHURCHES

o **Cathedral of St. James** (Šibenik): On a raised piazza above the harbor, this Gothic-Renaissance cathedral has a distinctive trefoil facade with a beautifully carved portal. It's considered to be the masterpiece of 15th-century architect Juraj Dalmatinac. Inscribed on the UNESCO World Heritage list, it is also notable for its elegant cupola and vaulted roof, which were highly innovative for their time. See p. 141.

o **Church of St. Mary** (Beram): This chapel in the woods is so small and so remote that you would never notice it if it weren't in a guidebook. But St. Mary's remoteness is what protected the eye-popping frescoes that dance on its walls. You'll need to pick up one of the church's keepers in Beram and drive her to the chapel in the woods so she can unlock the doors. See p. 95.

o **Euphrasian Basilica Complex** (Poreč): A must-see sight in this city of superlatives, this UNESCO World Heritage church is the last of four that were built on top of each other. Euphrasius is not just one church, but a series of church buildings, each with its own story. One of the basilica's premier attractions is its collection of Byzantine mosaics. See p. 89.

o **St. Donatus** (Zadar): Notable for its unusual shape (it's circular inside), this monumental 9th-century Byzantine church stands on the Roman Forum. Although no longer used for Mass, its great acoustics make it a favored venue for classical concerts. Like other churches of its era (9th c.), Donatus is one of several buildings in an intriguing clerical complex. See p. 129.

THE best CASTLES

o **Pazin Kaštel** (Istria): One of the best-preserved castles in Istria, this is a surprising attraction in the interior. Pazin Kaštel is next to one of the scariest-looking gorges you'll ever see, a feature that was conveniently utilized as a dumping ground (literally) for enemies of whomever controlled the castle. What may be Croatia's best ethnographic museum is inside. See p. 95.

o **Stari Grad** (Varaždin): This Gothic Renaissance defensive complex includes a castle and the Varaždin Town Museum. It's also this Baroque town's best attraction. The museum is an excellent showcase for artwork and historical items, and the multilingual docents are happy to help visitors. See p. 59.

o **Trakošćan Castle** (near Varaždin): North of Zagreb is one of Croatia's most visited sites and one of its most impressive castles—from the outside. The grounds are extensive and the structure is everything you'd expect a storybook castle to be, with stone walls, turrets, and a drawbridge. Inside, renovations have been less than meticulous, and sometimes border on tacky. Trakošćan is worth the trip if for no other reason than to ponder the plastic deer mounted on the walls outside the entrance. See p. 58.

o **Veliki Tabor** (Zagorje Region): North of Zagreb is this imposing, solid brick fortress that looks like the place where Rapunzel let down her hair. Veliki Tabor has its own legends, including murder, mayhem, and a ghost. While the exterior of the 12th-century structure looks like it could withstand a nuclear attack, the inside is still under partial renovation. See p. 56.

THE best RESTAURANTS

o **Bevanda** (Opatija): This highly regarded seafood restaurant dates from 1971, though the building was totally restructured in 2013, with floor-to-ceiling windows affording romantic sea views. A six-course degustation menu includes delights such as tuna carpaccio with avocado and raw quail egg, and black ravioli in a prawn reduction with white truffle shavings. See p. 108.

o **Boškinac** (Novalja, Pag Island): Boškinac has a knack for turning fresh produce and local ingredients like Pag lamb and Pag cheese into dishes that surprise the palate. Whether it's a Saturday lunch on the sunny terrace or a gala dinner in the elegant dining room, Boškinac's creations are always sublime. It's worth the detour to get here. See p. 139.

o **Konoba Lambik** (Milna, near Hvar Town): In a magical garden with flickering candles, olive trees, lavender bushes, and a big stone barbecue area, this tavern is a very special place where you can experience the way local people used to eat and live on the islands. The owner-cook prepares authentic regional dishes using his own homegrown vegetables, locally caught fresh fish, and home-cured meats. He also serves his own wine. See p. 171.

o **Konoba Mate** (Pupnat, near Korčula Town): Up in a village in the hills, this farmhouse eatery serves truly outstanding local dishes, made from homegrown produce. Expect ravioli filled with goat's cheese, or a wild asparagus and smoked ham omelette. Be sure to try the local wine, a crisp white Pošip, served by the carafe. See p. 175.

o **Mala Hiža** (Mažkovec): Mala Hiža is one of the finest restaurants in the country. The building dates from 1887 and once stood outside Zagreb—it was deconstructed, moved, and reassembled in this gorgeous garden close to Čakovic. The menu is full of creative interpretations of regional Croatian cuisine, and the chef will prepare any old-time recipe if you call ahead with a request. See p. 62.

o **Pelegrini** (Šibenik): On stone steps leading off the square, overlooked by Šibenik Cathedral, this restaurant could well be the place you experience your best meal in Croatia. The owner-chef runs a tight ship, with highly professional young waiters and a crack sommelier. Expect exquisite seafood presented with creative flair and occasionally flavored with pungent truffles among other unexpected delights. See p. 142.

o **Zigante** (Livade): Behold truffle king Giancarlo Zigante's gourmet palace. Almost everything on the extensive menu here utilizes the truffle, the precious fungus with which Zigante made his fortune. The restaurant is not a gimmick: Everything on the menu is expertly prepared and informed by creativity. See p. 98.

CROATIA IN DEPTH

"The Mediterranean As It Once Was," "Europe's Summer Home," "Ethnic Battlefield," "War-Torn Nation." Croatia has been labeled all these things, but which identity is correct, and is the country worth visiting when there are so many exciting but less controversial destinations vying for a traveler's time and dollars?

The answer is that Croatia is a little of each but not dominated by any, and that's part of its allure.

Where else can you spend the night in a room on a working farm, then spend the day poking around an intact Roman amphitheater? How many places let you walk atop a massive fortification in the footsteps of a guard on the lookout for invaders from the sea, then sip martinis at midnight watching models strut down a runway in a square surrounded by churches and remnants of the Renaissance? Is there another destination where you can hike through a forest to the tempo of water rushing from falls too numerous to count, then dress for dinner on a candlelit terrace where passengers from the Orient Express once mingled during a layover?

Italians, Austrians, Hungarians, Germans, and other Europeans know Croatia as the sun-drenched land where their ancestors spent more than a century of August vacations frolicking in the sea and dining on just-caught seafood. Other foreigners know Croatia as the site of one of the most vicious wars in European history. For Croatians, the country is simply home and heritage, and they are proud of who they are, what they have endured, and who they have become.

Contemporary Croatia is a product of its history, its present, and even its future aspirations. It is a country that is embracing the challenges of the 21st century, but hasn't forgotten its past. That's no different from the histories of Italy, France, Germany, or any other popular destination. The difference is that Croatia's struggles are more recent and have not yet faded to black.

My advice is to put aside labels and preconceived notions about Croatia and plan to experience the country "as is." Seek out experiences that appeal to you as you read this book, then be prepared to be surprised, stay open to a change of plans, and don't be afraid to pursue your own discoveries. Head for the coast and bask in the sun, but take a day to explore villages in the inland hills, too. Book a room in a slick design hotel, but carve out time to have lunch at a family-run inn in the country. You might wander a bit in Croatia, but you'll never feel lost.

CROATIA TODAY

On July 1, 2013, Croatia finally became a member of the European Union (EU), following years of preparations, which included economic reforms, a concerted attempt to eradicate corruption in both the public and private sectors, and Croatia's cooperation with the International Criminal Tribunal for the former Yugoslavia regarding war crimes.

In January 2012, the country had held a referendum asking the electorate if they were for or against EU membership. The outcome saw 66 percent in favor of joining. However, given the ongoing global economic crisis and the harsh austerity measures that the EU has imposed on other floundering member countries, like Greece, Croatia remains skeptical as to the benefits it will reap from EU membership.

On top of this, some 20 years after the end of the War of Independence, Croatia is still rebuilding its image as a tourist destination following the collapse of tourism during the hostilities.

Up until 2009 and the onset of the global crisis, the mood had been one of relative optimism. Although in the years since there has been a noticeable downturn in most sectors of the economy, Croatia continues to attract an ever-increasing number of foreign visitors, due largely to the growing number of budget airlines flying to the country from other parts of Europe, making it infinitely more accessible. Coupled with this, the tourist infrastructure has been upgraded to include refurbished hotels, restaurants serving contemporary takes on regional cuisines, vineyards open to the public for wine tasting, and adventure-sports companies offering well-organized activities on both land and sea.

The December 2011 general election saw the country choose the center-left Social Democratic Party (SPD) to form the government, with Zoran Milanović as Prime Minister. The income per capita in Croatia is now higher than that of several other EU members, namely Bulgaria, Romania, and Latvia. (In 1989, while still part of Yugoslavia, the unemployment rate in Croatia was 8 percent, but this figure soared during the war when the country was thrown into chaos.) Unemployment has risen steadily since 2009, reaching 22.5 percent by February 2014. Croatia's economy has been in recession since 2009, but there are hopes that the situation will improve in 2015. Tourism is doing its part: It contributed 15 percent of Croatia's GDP in 2013.

LOOKING BACK AT CROATIA

Prehistory

At the turn of the 20th century (1899), the remains of a type of Neanderthal who lived in caves some 130,000 years ago were discovered at Krapina, a tiny town north of Zagreb. These early cave dwellers' bones were dubbed "Krapina Man," and they established a time line that put humans in Croatia in the middle of the Stone Age. Traces of other prehistoric cultures also have been found in Vukovar in eastern Croatia, but none is more significant than Krapina Man.

Illyrians

Recorded Croatian history begins around 1200 B.C., when the people occupying the region that is now Croatia, Bosnia, Albania, and Serbia began to form a coalition of tribes known as the Illyrians. Illyrian lifestyles had similarities, such as dwelling designs and burial customs, but there is no concrete evidence that any tribe was assimilated by any other. In fact, the tribes were known by different names according to where they settled, and at least some of them became regional powers and established cities that survive today.

The Greek Colonists

The Greeks began colonizing the Adriatic coast of Croatia in the 4th century B.C., beginning with Issa (Vis), a colony founded by residents of Syracuse (a seaport in Sicily). Other settlements followed, including Paros (Hvar) and Tragurion (Trogir). The Illyrians traded oil, wine, salt, metals, and other commodities with the Greeks but nonetheless tried to get rid of foreign settlements. In the 3rd century B.C., the Illyrians attempted to form an independent state under the leadership of one of their pirate tribes. The Greeks were alarmed by this turn of events, and in 229 B.C. asked the Romans for help in containing Illyrian lawlessness. When the Romans sent messengers to negotiate peace with the Illyrian Queen Teuta, she had them executed. This touched off a series of wars that lasted more than 60 years, ending with the defeat of the Illyrians and the creation of the Roman province of Illyricum.

The Roman Occupation

The spread of Roman colonies across Croatia continued until A.D. 9, when the Adriatic coast and interior lands were annexed by the Emperor Tiberius to create three Roman provinces: Dalmatia (Adriatic seacoast), Noricum (northern territory/Austria), and Pannonia (Hungary). The Romans built fortresses, roads, bridges, aqueducts, and sparkling new cities that overtook Illyrian culture or drove it away. The main Roman cities of that time were Pola (Pula), Jader (Zadar), Salona (Solin) near Split, and Epidaurum (Cavtat). The Roman propensity for building roads linked northeast Italy to Byzantium and opened lines of communication that facilitated trade and troop movements and the spread of Roman culture.

Those same roads brought Christianity to the area, and with it persecution, primarily by Emperor Diocletian, whose "retirement home" at Split is one of Croatia's best-preserved vestiges of the Roman era, which flourished until the end of the 4th century.

From about A.D. 395 until the 7th century, Croatia suffered a series of invasions by the Ostrogoths, Slavs, and other barbarians. But it was the Avars, a warlike Asian tribe, who allegedly attracted the Slavic Croats—ancestors to today's Croatians—to the area. According to the 10th-century Byzantine emperor Constantine Porphyrogenitus, Emperor Heraclius asked the Croats to get rid of the Avars and to protect Rome's interests, though the Croats didn't stop at saving the Roman occupation.

The Croat Migration

Porphyrogenitus's account has been disputed, partly because it was written 300 years after the fact. Other accounts differ about the Croats' appearance in southeastern Europe. Some experts say the Croats came from the Ukraine; others pinpoint Poland; and some say the Croats migrated from Iran because the name "Hvrat" has Persian origins. The trail leading back to the Croats is further clouded because "Hvrat" was used by other Slavic tribes of the times (White Croats in Poland; Croats in the Czech Republic area; and other groups from nearby Slovenia, Slovakia, and Macedonia). It is likely that there were several waves of Croat migration, with the first group settling the part of the Roman province of Pannonia that is now southern Hungary. Later migrations settled land all the way to Dalmatia.

Eventually, the Croat émigrés organized into two dukedoms and began to accept Roman-rite Christianity and Roman culture. The existence of two distinct centers of culture—Mediterranean (Dalmatia) and central European (Pannonia)—served to form a dueling Croatian psyche, which lingers today. Croats continued to live under a series of foreign and Croatian administrations until A.D. 924, when the country was united under the leadership of Tomislav I, the first king of Croatia.

Medieval Croatia

When Tomislav was crowned around A.D. 924, he united the Pannonian and Dalmatian duchies, which included much of present-day Slavonia, Dalmatia, Istria, and Bosnia/ Herzegovina. Tomislav died about A.D. 928, but no one disputes that he had a profound effect on Croatia in his short rule. He was succeeded by a series of monarchs who enjoyed relative stability for almost the next two centuries. Among them were King Petar Krešimir IV (1058–74) and King Dmitar Zvonimir (1075–89). Zvonimir's reign is notable because he entrenched Catholicism in Croatia and strengthened the country's relationship with the Roman Church. His reign is immortalized on the Baška Tablet, a kind of Croatian Rosetta stone engraved with the oldest known Croatian text. The tablet is on display in Zagreb's archaeological museum.

Hungary & Venice

After Zvonimir's death in the 11th century, the monarchy withered, and Croatia and Hungary formed a common kingdom guided by a parliament (Sabor). During this time, the wealth and power of the landed nobility grew, and an increase in the feudal obligations of the agrarian population followed.

Free cities (Dubrovnik, among others) were founded along the coast, increasing trade and political strength in the region. Many made trade agreements with Venice, which by now was a contender for control of Croatia's ports.

Trade increased, and northern Croatian cities also saw rapid development, but a Tatar invasion in 1242 diverted the government's attention to the country's defense as invaders razed Zagreb and everything else in their path. Ultimately, Hungarian King Bela IV outmaneuvered the Tatars and retained control, but Croatia's growing strength from its alliance with Hungary fueled Venice's determination to control Istria and Dalmatia and ultimately access to the sea.

Venice began a long-term campaign to take over the Croatian coast early in the 13th century: They captured Zadar in 1202 and Dubrovnik in 1205. For the next century, the Venetian influence along the coast increased until they achieved their objective. During the period of Venetian acquisition, the counts of Anjou came to the Croatian throne, and in 1358 they reasserted Hungarian control of Dalmatia thanks to Louis of Anjou. King Louis expelled the Venetians, but disarray in the House of Anjou ultimately resulted in the sale of rights over Dalmatia back to the Venetians in 1409.

Ottomans & Hapsburgs

During the 15th century, the Ottoman Turks advanced on Croatian lands, taking Bulgaria and Bosnia and leaving the rest of Croatia vulnerable. During the battle against the Turks at Mohács, Hungarian King Louis II was killed in action, leaving the Turk Sultan Suleyman the Magnificent in control of much of southern Croatia. Louis did not have an heir, and the throne went to his designated successor, Ferdinand I of Hapsburg, a move that put Croatia in the Hapsburg Empire.

The first Hapsburg rulers were determined to defend Croatia against the Turks, who continued to gobble up Croat land until the mid-17th century despite efforts to contain them. During this time, Croatia lost 75 percent of its territory and people, but by the mid-17th century the Hapsburgs had retaken Croatia and pushed the Turks out of the region. Subsequently, Hapsburg armies gradually drove the Turks out of the rest of central Europe (except for Bosnia and Herzegovina).

The decrease in Turk strength opened the door for the Venetians to once again surge in Dalmatia.

In 1671, the Croats made a push for self-rule, but the Hapsburgs would have none of it and quashed the movement. During the next century, the Hapsburgs gradually squeezed out Croatian authority, which further made Croatia a takeover target.

By this time many Orthodox Serbs who were living in Catholic Croatia and Russia began to show an interest in the region. This raised the question of who would take control, Catholic Austria or Orthodox Russia. Thus began the so-called Eastern Question, which was one of the precipitators of World War I.

The Napoleon Effect

During the 18th century, Austria, Hungary, and Venice all continued to vie for pieces of Croatia and for imposition of their own cultures. The Hapsburgs pushed to install German customs and language; the Hungarians proposed that Hungarian be accepted as the official language and claimed that Slavonia belonged to Hungary; the Venetians extended their territories to the Dinara mountains and beyond, thanks to the Treaty of Požarevac; and the Turks retained control of Bosnia and Herzegovina. The Požarevac treaty made it difficult to define Croatia's geography, but in 1808 Napoleon "solved" the problem by capturing coastal towns, uniting Dalmatia with parts of Slovenia and Croatia, and renaming the joint territories the Illyrian Provinces. Napoleon's influence was profound but short-lived. He promoted agriculture and commerce, raised the status of the Orthodox population, and started a reawakening of Croatian nationalism. But with his defeat in 1815 at the hands of the English navy, control of Dalmatia once again reverted to the Hapsburgs, who immediately reasserted authority over Croatia.

Illyrianism

After the fall of Napoleon, Austria created the Kingdom of Illyria, an administrative unit designed to thwart Hungarian nationalism and unification of the South Slavs. Dalmatia, however, was not part of this reorganization, as Austria decided to keep this goldmine as its vacation playground. Eventually, the Hapsburgs' attempts to exert absolute control over every aspect of Croatian life backfired. Croatian leaders began stirring up nationalism by promoting the Croatian language and culture, as well as formation of a Slavic kingdom, right under the Hapsburgs' noses. In 1832, Ljudevit Gaj, a Croatian noble, tried to elbow the Hungarians aside by addressing the Sabor in the Croatian language, which was daring for the time. Gaj, who was a journalist and linguist, pushed a South Slavic literary language, engineered a Latin-based script, and in 1836 founded an anti-Hungarian journal that called for cultural and political unity. The Hungarians were understandably angered by these developments and tried to impose Hungarian as the official language of Slavonia. The Croatians responded by sending any correspondence written in Hungarian back to Hungary unread.

Austro-Hungarian Rule

In 1848, Hungary challenged Austria during the revolution that was sweeping across Europe. Croatians, who feared another wave of domination from Hungary and who had hoped for unification, sided with Austria and began to call for self-determination. Austria yielded to Croatian pressure and raised Josip Jelačić to the position of *ban* (viceroy) of Croatia. Jelačić immediately convened the Croatian Sabor to consolidate his support. He suspended relations with Hungary and declared war, but his Austrian allies reasserted their authority over Croatia after defeating the Hungarians with Jelačić's help.

Austria ended absolute rule over Croatia in 1860, and in 1866 the Austro-Hungarian empire was near collapse. In order to save it, Emperor Franz Joseph united Austria and Hungary in a dual monarchy. In a Sabor dominated by pro-Hungarian officials, a compromise on Croatia was reached that acknowledged the country as a distinct political entity within the empire.

Croatia increased its autonomy within the empire and in 1868 established a political/cultural base in Zagreb. However, the Croatian leadership was divided between those advocating a South Slav union and those favoring a Greater Croatia. In addition, animosity between the Croats and Serbs was on the rise. Bishop Josip Strossmayer attempted to reduce the religious differences between the Croats and Serbs to defuse the growing tensions.

Ante Starčević represented the opposition to Strossmayer's initiatives and was suspicious of any conciliatory moves directed at the Serbs. Both movements were sabotaged by Ban Károly Khuen-Hédervary when he ignored a compromise that allowed home rule for Croatia and promoted Hungarian language and culture by provoking conflict between Croats and Serbs.

Despite Hédervary's treachery, in 1906, Serbs and Croats again came together to create the Croat-Serb Coalition, which immediately came under attack from Vienna, which feared a loss of Austrian influence.

World War I

In 1908, Austria-Hungary annexed Bosnia and its diverse population of Catholic Croats, Orthodox Serbs, and Muslims. This move set back the Serb goal of creating a Serbian state and reignited tensions between Croats and Serbs. Thus, when Hapsburg heir Franz Ferdinand visited the Bosnian capital of Sarajevo in 1914, the mood of the city was hostile.

On June 28, Bosnian Serb Gavrilo Princip assassinated Franz Joseph and his wife, and a month later Austria-Hungary declared war on Serbia. Germany sided with Austria; Russia, France, and Great Britain countered by forming an alliance of their own, thus drawing a line in the sand for World War I.

For a time, the Croats sided with the Hapsburg contingent, but on December 1, 1918, after the Austro-Hungarian empire had been defeated, Serb Prince Aleksandar Karadordević broke rank and created the Kingdom of Serbs, Croats, and Slovenes. The unification seemed reasonable in theory, but it did not allow for autonomy of any of the nations nor did it provide any guidelines to facilitate cooperation among diverse people suddenly thrown together under a single umbrella.

Only one high-profile Croat raised an alarm about the ramifications of unification. Stjepan Radić, leader of the Croatian Peasant's Party, urged caution, but his pleas went unheeded. After the new Croatian government failed to move in the direction of autonomy, in 1927 Radić and Serbian Svetozar Pribićević of the Independent Democratic Party joined forces to unite the Serbs and Croats. However, on June 20, 1928, extremists from Belgrade fatally shot Radić and two members of the Peasant's Party while parliament was in session. Fearing that the assassination would incite further ethnic violence, King Aleksandar dissolved parliament, established a dictatorship, and changed the name of the state to the Kingdom of Yugoslavia (South Slavia).

World War II

Aleksandar's dictatorship resembled a police state in which 90 percent of the police and government officials were Serbian, a situation that invited trouble. As a reaction to this state of affairs, in 1929 Croat Ante Pavelič founded the Ustaše, an organization dedicated to the overthrow of Aleksandar's state. Five years later, in 1934, the Ustaše, with Italy's help, assassinated the king in Marseilles, an act that threw Yugoslavia into turmoil and made it vulnerable to Nazi exploitation.

Yugoslavia tried to remain neutral at the start of World War II, but pressure to support the Axis side was great, and on March 25, 1941, Yugoslavia's Prince Pavle aligned the country with the fascists. Within two days the prince was overthrown and the pact nullified, but the Nazis would not let the nullification stand. On April 6, they bombed Belgrade and invaded Yugoslavia. It took the Nazis just 10 days to defeat the Yugoslav army. Shortly after that, the Ustaše formed the Independent State of Croatia (Nezavisna Država Hrvatska, NDH), leaving the rest of Yugoslavia isolated.

The Ustaše at first attempted to drive the Serbs out of Croatia, but when that proved impossible, they set up several concentration camps, the most infamous being the camps at Jasenovac, about 97km (60 miles) south of Zagreb on the Sava River. No one knows how many people died in Jasenovac at the hands of the Ustaše, but acts of inhumanity and barbarism in the camps were chronicled. Not all Croats condoned the Ustaše and their methods.

The Resistance Movement

A resistance movement to counter the Ustaše was organized almost immediately after Germany invaded in 1941, but it was divided between the pro-Serbian Četniks and the pro-Communist Partisans led by Josip Broz "Tito." Committed as these groups were, they were not very effective in combating the Ustaše because they were more intent on competing with and killing each other. However, the Allies recognized Tito's Partisans as the official resistance at the Tehran Conference and funneled all aid to the Communist group, which helped liberate Belgrade.

Ironically, the internal conflict between opposing resistance groups in Yugoslavia helped the Allied victory because it tied up hundreds of thousands of Axis troops, who then were unavailable to fight the Allies. Even so, when the war ended in 1944, more than 1.7 million Yugoslavs had died as a result of the fighting, a number that represented 10 percent of the country's population.

Postwar Yugoslavia

After the war, Tito's Communist Party won the Yugoslav election with 90 percent of the vote. The country became known as the Socialist Federal Republic of Yugoslavia, modeled on the Soviet Union, with Tito as President. However, in 1948 Tito broke off relations with Stalin and began to create his own variation of Socialism. In 1962, together with the leaders of India, Burma, Indonesia, Egypt, and Ghana, Tito founded the Non-Aligned Movement, which aimed to find a middle way between the world's dominant powers, the communist East and the capitalist West.

Nonalignment was a double-edged sword for Yugoslavia. On the one hand, the country had to endure a Soviet blockade in the 1950s as a result of Tito's nonconformity, but on the other, Tito's independent position helped tourism flourish along the Adriatic coast. His approval of site management allowed competition and created efficiencies in the workplace. He also gave each of Yugoslavia's six republics—Croatia, Serbia, Slovenia, Bosnia/Herzegovina, Macedonia, and Montenegro—control over its own internal affairs.

Tito's largesse had its limits. In 1967 the Croatian economy was booming, which buoyed national sentiment. The first expression of renewed nationalism surfaced in the cultural realm: The Croatian intelligentsia, worried by attempts to create a single Serb-Croat literary language, issued a declaration stating that Croatian was a language distinct from Serbian. Croatia's Serbs retorted that they had a right to their own language, too, and that they wanted to use the Cyrillic script. Tito quickly suppressed both sides of the argument, which curbed the nascent nationalist movement dubbed the "Croatian Spring."

For a while, other efforts at liberalization—demands for autonomy, student strikes, calls for government reform—were attempted, but in 1971 Tito cracked down on those reformers, too, effectively putting an end to the Croatian Spring once and for all. Tito's hard line had a chilling effect on reform efforts not only in Croatia but also in the rest of Yugoslavia, though his iron hand didn't stop Yugoslavs outside the country from criticizing his style of government.

Yugoslavia in Turmoil

On May 4, 1980, after decades of balancing Communist ideology with Western capitalism in Yugoslavia, Josip Broz "Tito" died at the age of 88. His funeral in Belgrade was attended by thousands of Yugoslavs and more than 100 heads of state.

Unfortunately, as with many authoritarian leaders, Tito had not developed a plan of succession, which left the Yugoslav state without a strong leader. To complicate matters, the region's economy was deteriorating in the wake of the 1970s oil crisis, a huge national debt, and the disappearance of foreign credit sources. The republics once again became restless, and old problems resurfaced.

The first hot spot was Kosovo, a region in southwest Serbia with a large Muslim Albanian population that in 1981 aspired to republic status after having enjoyed a modicum of autonomy. Six years later, the emboldened Serb minority in Kosovo took the position that the Albanians there were a threat to them. That inspired Serbs in Croatia to almost simultaneously express the same sentiment about the Croats. A collective angst spread, cracking Yugoslavia along national, religious, and ethnic lines.

In 1987, a relatively unknown Serb politician named Slobodan Milošević began to proclaim Serb superiority while working toward installing a Communist government in Yugoslavia. Two years after Milošević's debut as a champion of Serbs, the Berlin Wall came down, leaving him holding an unpopular position while the rest of Europe raced off in the opposite ideological direction.

War in Croatia

Despite Milošević's efforts to expand his bloc of followers, Croatia and other Yugoslav republics were trying to make the transition to democracy. In May 1989, the Croatian Democratic Union (HDZ), led by former general and historian Franjo Tuđman, became one of the first non-Communist organizations in Croatia, and in less than a year began campaigning for Croatia's secession from Yugoslavia. By April, free elections were held in Croatia and Tuđman was sworn in as president the next month. He promptly declared Croatian statehood, a preliminary stage before independence. At the same time, Stjepan Mešić was chosen as Croatia's first post-Communist prime minister, and a constitution was written that declared Serbs in Croatia a national minority rather than a nation within the republic.

This classification fomented outrage in the Serb community. In 1991, Milošević, seeing that the breakup of Yugoslavia was inevitable, began gathering support for a Greater Serbia, which would include all the areas of Croatia and Bosnia/Herzegovina where Serbs were in residence. Worse, Milošević developed a plan to "ethnically cleanse" eastern Croatia of any Croats living there. Under such conditions, civil war was imminent.

Hostilities broke out in 1991 with Milošević pulling Serb forces into Croatia from all over Yugoslavia. During the violence, cities such as Vukovar and Dubrovnik suffered heavy damage, thousands of Croatians were forced to leave their homes, and thousands more were killed. The fighting also spread to other republics in Yugoslavia—most notably Bosnia—as Milošević and the Serbs kept advancing and pressuring Croats and Muslims in Bosnia to fight each other.

Finally, fighting on Croatian soil stopped following Operation Storm, a massive military offensive staged over three days in August 1995, which saw an estimated 200,000 Croatian-Serbs flee the country, leaving Croatia's Serb-occupied territories deserted. Hostilities in Bosnia/Herzegovina also came to an end with the signing of the Dayton Agreement in December 1995.

Postwar Croatia

Croatia's economy was a shambles as the war drew to a close: Unemployment was hovering at 20 percent; industry was almost nonexistent; agricultural output was drastically low; and some companies were unable to pay workers the depressed average monthly wage of $400.

In 2000, Tuđman died, paving the way for the election of Stjepan Mesić, who had opposed Tuđman's war policies in Bosnia/Herzegovina. Mesić served as President of Croatia up until 2010, when mild-mannered law professor and classical music composer Ivo Josipović took over.

The bad memories from the Croat-Serb civil war haven't completely disappeared, and many people are trying to recover from the horrors of ethnic cleansing, poverty, and loss. In April 2001, Slobodan Milošević, architect of the campaign to "cleanse" certain areas of all but Serbs, was arrested and charged with corruption after a 26-hour armed standoff with police at his Belgrade home. Two months later Milošević was turned over to the United Nations and charged with committing crimes against humanity in Kosovo and Croatia.

In November 2001, the United Nations War Crimes Tribunal charged Milošević with genocide stemming from his alleged activity during the 1992–95 Bosnian war. He was the first head of state to face an international war-crimes court. He died on March 12, 2006, while in custody at The Hague. His trial was in progress, and a verdict was never reached.

Serbs who fled Croatia during Operation Storm are gradually returning to their homes or at least selling their old properties so as to be able to build new lives somewhere else. Croatia has been put under pressure to help these people either resettle or to find some sort of economic compensation.

In July 2009, without explanation, Croatia's longtime Prime Minister Ivo Sanader withdrew from politics. Sanader had been leader of the Croatian Democratic Union (HDZ) since the death of wartime President, Franjo Tuđman, in 2000. As the story unraveled, Sanader fled the country for Austria, only to be extradited and put on trial for multiple corruption charges. He was eventually sentenced to 10 years in prison in November 2012 (the sentence was later reduced by 18 months). The scandal lead to public disenchantment with the HDZ, which further increased with the harsh economic measures imposed by Sanader's successor, Jadranka Kosor.

In the December 2011 general election, voters chose the center-left SDP (Social Democratic Party) to lead the country into the future, ousting the much-maligned HDZ from power, and finally closing the final chapter in Croatia's post-war recovery.

CROATIA'S ART & ARCHITECTURE

Croatian art and architecture are largely unknown outside the Balkans. That's understandable, given the country's size and the restrictions imposed by past dictators. Croatia's art phases follow a time line that parallels the nation's history, with tastes informed by the serial occupiers who controlled the country in waves through the centuries.

Prehistoric to 1 B.C.

The remains of cave dwellers have been found in Vukovar, on Vis, and most famously in Krapina in the northwestern part of the country, where archaeologists found the bones of the 130,000-year-old Krapina Man. Specimens of primitive art—pottery, tools, even jewelry—usually are part of any such find, but the most famous Croatian *objet d'art* discovered in these ancient time capsules is the ceramic **Dove of Vučedol** (2000 B.C.), which was found during an archaeological dig in Vučedol, 4.8km (3 miles) outside of Vukovar. The Vučedol Dove has become the symbol of Vukovar and a popular totem of Croatian nationalism, available in many souvenir renditions.

Illyrian, Roman & Byzantine (1st–6th c.)

There is almost nowhere in Croatia that is without a collection of art or architecture from at least one of these cultures, usually items that were found nearby. Vestiges of the Illyrians and Greeks who settled Vis (Issa) are scarce inland, but beautiful examples of sculpture, textiles, metalwork, and architecture are on display in Vis's archaeological museum and in situ. Go there just to see a perfect sculpture of the **head of the goddess Aphrodite** (or Artemis) from the 4th century B.C., as well as **the remains of a Roman theater** that held 3,500. There's also the mosaic floor of a **Roman bathhouse** that is still being excavated.

The Romans completely infiltrated Croatia, and there are few places along the country's coast, on its islands, or even inland that are without something the Romans brought or built there. Pula, which was a Roman outpost called Pietas Julias, is home to one of the largest **Roman amphitheaters** still standing. The 1st-century beauty was built to hold more than 20,000 spectators, and though now reduced in size, it's in terrific shape thanks to restoration. The remains of **Diocletian's Palace** in Split, numerous **Roman summer homes** *(villa rusticate)* on the islands and along the coast, and the remains of **Salona,** the former Roman seat of power outside Split, are just a few examples of the mark the Romans left on Croatia. And of course, smaller, more portable Roman leavings, such as **amphorae, funerary art,** and **statues,** have been found all over Croatia. They are on display in most of the country's museums.

Enter the barbarians and the fall of Rome. Just as Roman influence was receding in its provinces, including Croatia, the influence of Byzantium was creeping in, thanks to the Emperor Justinian, who was educated in Constantinople and served as consul there. It is almost impossible to distinguish between Rome as it declined and the Byzantine Empire of Constantinople because both were part of the same political institution, the Roman Empire. Byzantium's capitol, Constantinople, had been founded as the capital of Rome by the emperor Constantine, and while it was a solid part of the Roman Empire, it had Greek influences, too. One of the best architectural examples of this transition is the 6th century **Basilica of Euphrasius** in Poreč, with its mosaics set on a gilded background. The basilica is on the UNESCO World Heritage list.

Romanesque to Renaissance (7th–17th c.)

There is some controversy about where the Croats originated, but there is agreement that they arrived in Croatia in the 7th century. Whatever its origins, this migrating group brought along its art and introduced a signature design *(pleter)* that resembles stylized Celtic knots. The design found its way onto the stone ornamentation of almost every medieval church in Croatia, including the first built by this new group of immigrants, **Nin's Holy Cross Church.**

As with all art movements, this one segued into another style, the Romanesque phase, but not until **St. Donat's in Zadar** was built with three apses, a soaring rotunda, and remnants of Roman architectural ornamentation.

CROATIA IN BOOKS, FILM & MUSIC

A good introductory read on Croatia is "Croatia: Travels in Undiscovered Country" (University of Alberta Press, 2003), an account of author Tony Fabijančić's travels through the country in search of his father's roots. The people he meets and the situations he encounters enlighten more than any travelogue ever could.

"Croatia: Aspects of Art, Architecture, and Cultural Heritage" (Frances Lincoln, 2009) puts Croatia's art and architecture in the context of its history. It is a scholarly look at the monuments, grand houses, art collections, Roman influence, and Gothic leavings that embody the story of Croatia. Essays and anecdotes from American, English, and Croatian experts predominate.

Rebecca West's "Black Lamb and Grey Falcon: A Journey Through Yugoslavia" (Penguin Books, 1994) is a classic, graceful history/travel journal that portrays Croatia in a Balkan context. West, who was a journalist, novelist, and critic, undertook her research in the Balkans with the idea of writing a travel book, but the final seminal product turned out to illuminate the tangled history of the former Yugoslavia.

"Croatia: A Nation Forged in War" by Marcus Tanner (Yale University Press, 2001) is also a history of Croatia, but Tanner's book goes from the beginning of Croatia's history in A.D. 800 through the start of the millennium and includes the 1991–95 War for Independence.

Robin Harris's "Dubrovnik: A History" (SAQI, 2003) is an excellent historical overview of the former Republic of Ragusa and helps shed light on how Dubrovnik came to be the "Pearl of the Adriatic."

Listen to the CD "Songs of Croatia," a collection of traditional Dalmatian songs by Klapa Cambi (www.cambi.hr), for an introduction to *klapa*. A form of harmony singing without instrumental accompaniment, klapa is unique to Dalmatia; the lyrics of its songs recount stories of unrequited love, the beauties and perils of the sea, and the drinking of copious amounts of wine; all timeless themes close to the heart of every Dalmatian.

"Harrison's Flowers" is a 2001 film, available on DVD, set in Croatia during the War for Independence. It is the story of a woman searching for her photojournalist husband in Vukovar and elsewhere in the war zone in the middle of battle. While the plot is fictional, the setting is not, and the film gives some context to the situation in Croatia during the hostilities.

EATING & DRINKING IN CROATIA

Traditional Croatian cuisine reflects widely diverse cultural and geographic influences. Some are a result of Croatia's proximity to the sea and fertile farmland, and some are the result of foreign occupiers who imported their tastes and recipes. Croatians are very proud of their gastronomic traditions, and while there are regional differences, you'll find that freshness, grilling, and daily baking are consistent across the country.

Until recently, there was little menu variety within the region. By summer 2009, it had become clear that a new breed of chefs had infiltrated Croatia's dining scene with food-forward trends and preparations. In cities large and small, menus offering dishes made with local produce, meats, and fish were being prepared using sophisticated methods like sous vide, infusion, and vertical presentations. In cities like Dubrovnik and Zagreb, there has been an explosion of ethnic restaurants offering Croatians the opportunity to sample global cuisines including Thai, Mexican, Japanese, and even Southern American. The new culinary outlook has given new life to Croatia's dining scene, which is now innovative and exciting. In Istria, the development of the country's first quality rating system for wine and olive oil production has opened the way for new export possibilities.

These are long overdue accomplishments, and they're making a significant contribution to the development of a new Croatian culinary tradition.

Meals & Dining Customs

Croatia's *old* dining tradition is still strong, but it is changing as citizens shift their work hours, eating habits, and culinary awareness.

BREAKFAST & GABLEC   Western-style breakfast (*doručak:* eggs, pastries, meats, cereals) is served at larger hotels and restaurants throughout Croatia. In smaller towns and in homes, a glass of *rakija* (fruit brandy), a cup of coffee, and bread or a roll hot from the local bakery comprise the usual early-morning meal.

Around 10am Croatians who farm or start work early often stop for *gablec* (*marenda* on the coast), literally "breakfast eaten with cutlery." This meal is a smaller version of lunch, Croatia's main meal, but it sometimes substitutes.

Gablec was common in the former Yugoslavia because back then people started work and school around 6 or 7am, which didn't allow time for breakfast. They were hungry around midmorning and a meal of homestyle food and *sarma* (stuffed sour cabbage) or *gulaš* (goulash) were customarily offered in factories, schools, and local restaurants.

LUNCH   Lunch (*ručak*) generally is Croatia's main meal. It often begins with a bowl of soup followed by an entree of roasted meat, vegetable or salad, potatoes or noodles, and dessert. Croatians eat lunch anywhere from noon to late afternoon, and if they eat dinner at all, it usually is a light meal.

DINNER   Dinner (*večera*) for Croatians often consists of a very thin-crusted pizza or a shared plate of snacks, such as *čevapi* (spicy grilled sausage), *pršut* (smoked ham) and cheese, or grilled sardines, usually served well after 8pm. If they aren't eating at home, Croatians most frequently dine at **restorans** or **konobas,** both of which serve a wide range of dishes but differ in levels of formality, with *restorans* being the fancier of the two.

COFFEE & ICE CREAM   Drinking coffee is a social event in Croatia. People sipping espresso are a common sight on almost every street in every town at every time of day. Sometimes Croatian coffee shops are cafes attached to restaurants or pastry shops, and sometimes they are freestanding shops that serve only drinks (alcoholic or nonalcoholic). Ice cream shops—almost as ubiquitous as coffee shops—serve coffee and mostly nonalcoholic beverages, plus a huge array of frozen concoctions ranging from basic cones to multilayered sundaes, as well as a selection of cakes and pastries.

TIPPING   Tipping in Croatia is becoming more commonplace, especially in upscale restaurants. In the past, tipping was welcome but not expected. Today, an extra 10 or 15 percent is the norm in upscale establishments and big cities. Tipping is rare and not expected in informal restaurants and in smaller towns, but most people leave any coins they receive in change for the waiter. Croatian waiters do not depend on tips for living wages.

COUVERT   Adding a *couvert* to the bill is a relatively new practice in Croatian restaurants and it is not uniformly imposed. The *couvert* is a "cover charge" that is a prima facie charge for bread, which is brought to the table automatically in most places. Menus usually list the couvert and its cost, which can range from 5kn to 20kn or more.

Regional Specialties

Dining is a national sport in Croatia. Generally, food is surprisingly good in all regions of the country. Beyond the ever-present offerings of pizza and grilled meat and fish from north to south, each part of the country prides itself on specific traditional dishes.

CONTINENTAL CROATIA (ZAGREB, BILOGORA, ZAGORJE, PODRAVINA, MEĐIMURJE)   Food traditions in this region have roots in seasonal climate, fertile farmland, and the rural lifestyle of the common people, plus the lavish gastronomy of the nobility (Austro-Hungarian) who lived in castles dotting the terrain.

Consequently, cuisine in this part of Croatia is more substantial than in other regions. For example, the need to store meat safely inspired *lodrica ili tiblica* (big wooden bowl), baked meats kept in bowls full of lard in cool places for later use. Smoking and drying, also methods used to preserve meats, extended to cheese *(prgica),* still a popular item in regional markets. *Žganci,* a kind of grits topped with cheese, sour cream, yogurt, or bacon, is a common breakfast dish. Turkey or duck with *mlinci* (baked noodles), *sarma* (ground meat in cabbage leaves), and *krvavice* (blood sausage with sauerkraut) are popular mains.

Favorite desserts in this region are *štrukle* (phyllo filled with fresh cheese, apples, cherries, or other fruit) and *palačinke* (crepes filled with honey and walnuts or jam). *Knedle sa šljivama* (potato dumplings stuffed with plums) are on almost every restaurant menu. In Međimurje, *prekmurska gibanica* (yeast cake layered with fresh cheese, apples, walnuts, poppy seeds, and raisins) is a must-try sweet after dinner.

GORSKI KOTAR & LIKA   The area southwest of central Croatia (including Plitvice Lakes National Park) is a combination of forests, hills, and pastures where winters are long and summers short. The food is similar to that of continental Croatia, with a few notable additions. You'll see a lot of roadside stalls selling homemade cheeses and fruit brandies as well as spit-roasted lamb and pork. Look for *janjetina* (lamb) or *janjetina* baked under a *peka* (a metal, bell-shaped lid). *Lika*-style sauerkraut is another specialty that consists of marinated cabbage and smoked sausage served with potatoes boiled in their skins. *Pijane pastrve* (drunken trout) is fish cooked in wine sauce and served with potatoes and veggies, while *lički lonac* (Licki pot) is a stew of cabbage, potatoes, root vegetables, and meat.

SLAVONIA & BARANJA   Cuisine in the eastern part of continental Croatia has a Hungarian influence: The food is quite heavy and seasoned with a lot of paprika. Specialties include *čobanac* (meat goulash seasoned with hot paprika, garlic, and bay leaves), *ribli paprikaš* (paprika-based stew with a variety of fish), *punjene paprike* (paprika peppers stuffed with minced pork, rice, and bacon), and freshwater fish grilled on a spit over an open fire. *Kulen* (spicy paprika sausage), and *rezanci* (broad egg noodles topped with sweetened walnuts or poppy seeds) are other regional delights. And the red stuff served with meat is called *ajvar,* a kind of red-pepper tapenade that can be mild or hot. The most popular wine in Slavonia is the white *Graševina.*

KVARNER & ISTRIA   These two regions offer the most diverse cuisine in Croatia, perhaps because they combine both inland and coastal tastes. Here stews prepared using a *peka* (domed metal lid) are slow-cooked under hot ash. In the Kvarner, try *Creska janjetina* (lamb from the island of Cres) and *škampi* (shrimp cooked under the peka); or try game stews infused with bay leaves that come from the mountainous part of Cres island.

In Lovran and along Kvarner Bay, *maruni* (chestnuts) are used in almost everything, including *kroštule* (fried strips of dough made with flour, eggs, lemon zest, and grape brandy). On Pag, try *Paški sir* (Pag cheese), lamb, and *pršut* (Dalmatian ham), all infused with a distinct Pag flavor because of the animals' diet of local herbs.

Istria has the most refined cuisine in Croatia, and it is also the source of some of the country's best wines. Try *riblja juha* (fish soup), *riblji složenac* (fish stew), *kuhane kozice* (boiled prawns), *crni rižoto sa plodovima mora* (black and white seafood risotto), and any dish with *tartufe* (truffles), including *Istarski fuži sa tartufima* (Istrian fuzi with truffles). A special *Istarski fuži sa gulasom od divljači* (fuzi with game goulash) is worth trying. Wines from this region are *Malvazija* and *Vrbnička žlahtina* (whites); and *Teran* (red).

DALMATIA   Freshness and simplicity are the watchwords that most aptly characterize Dalmatian cuisine. Main meals typically start with *pršut* and *Paški sir,* both often scattered with olives that have different flavors, depending on the Dalmatian village that grows and processes them. Oysters *(kamenice)* from Ston on the Pelješac Peninsula are also prized, as is anything from the sea. *Riba na žaru* (fish grilled with olive oil) and served with *blitva* (boiled Swiss chard and potatoes) is a common main course, as is *školjke i škampi na buzaru* (shellfish and shrimp stew). There are as many recipes and spellings for *buzara* as there are restaurants, but common ingredients in this sauce are olive oil, garlic, parsley and wine. *Pašticada* (beef stewed in red wine with prunes) is another good choice.

Wines to seek out in this region include *Bogdanuša, Pošip, Grk* and *Vugava* (whites); and *Plavac* and *Babić* (reds).

CROATIA REGIONS & SUGGESTED ITINERARIES

3

Croatia is such a diverse country that it is difficult to make any touring plan of action to cover all its important places without leaving out many "must-sees." Consequently, I've divided itineraries into two parts: routes for those who enter the country at Zagreb, and routes for those who start in Dubrovnik. These include my favorite places and allow for time frames of varying lengths.

Note: If you plan to spend 2 weeks in Croatia, simply follow two 1-week itineraries, in whichever order you prefer.

THE REGIONS IN BRIEF

There are many ways to designate Croatia's regions—coastal and inland, islands and mainland, northern and southern—and the best way to get a feel for the diverse charms of its geography is to look at each from a variety of perspectives.

Dalmatian Coast Croatia's Dalmatian Coast is characterized by extremes. From **Zadar** in the north to **Dubrovnik** in the south, the terrain that extends westward from the dramatic backdrop of the rugged Dinaric mountain range becomes a sun-washed 3-D mosaic of red-tiled roofs, graceful bell towers, lush vegetation, and shimmering beaches as the land rolls toward the sea. The coast is also a repository of history, with very visible Roman and Venetian influences. Add to that a mild Mediterranean climate that supports a thriving fishing industry and an agricultural economy rich in olives and grapes, and you have the formula for tourism gold. Offshore, Croatia's many islands (1,168 to be exact, if you include all the islets and reefs, although only 47 are inhabited) lure boating and watersports enthusiasts, sun worshipers, Europeans on vacation, and celebrities trying to get away from it all. They are part of Dalmatia's mystique and some of its most valuable assets.

The picture isn't so rosy on the Dinaric's eastern side. There the sun's rays become harsh spotlights that emphasize the landscape's stark and rocky personality, a struggling economy, and the lingering effects of war.

Inland Croatia This area reflects a melting pot of cultures, each distinct, but all Croatian. The country's largest city, **Zagreb**, is here, a thriving

SHIPWRECK diving

Croatia's 5,830km-long (3,625-mile) coast-line and the waters around its scattered islands are a diver's paradise. Marine life, reefs, parts of sunken cities, and rock formations abound, but shipwrecks are often the biggest lure for deep-sea explorers. For complete information on diving opportunities in Croatia, go to www. ronjenjehrvatska.com, which has English texts and a complete list of diving centers and sites. Some of Croatia's most popular submerged wrecks and their locations are listed below.

VIS

USAF Boeing B-17: This World War II military plane settled on the ocean floor off the island's south coast in 1943 at a depth of almost 75m (250 ft.). The aircraft's fuselage and engines were damaged in a bombing raid on Maribor, and it sank while attempting a landing on Vis. For experienced divers.

"Vassilios T": This Greek cargo ship went down in a storm in 1939 and is now at rest off the coast of Komiža at depths of 20m to 55m (66 ft. to 180 ft.). The ship's coal cargo is visible in the cargo holds and around the vessel. Underwater lamps are a plus for viewing the ship's interior. For intermediate divers.

BRAČ

"Meja": This ship is located in 40m (130 ft.) of water off Brač, east of the isle of Mrduja. Diving is possible in the cabin section, and there is a sunken wall that can be visited on the return from the wreck. For experienced divers.

PULA

"Baron Guatsch": A torpedo took out this Austro-Hungarian passenger ship in 1914 just north of the Brijuni Islands. It has four decks and is at rest 40m (130 ft.) down on a sandy bottom. Only two of the decks are available for exploration, but the ship has become a habitat for a variety of fish, shells, and plants. For experienced divers.

CAVTAT

Greek cargo ship flotsam and jetsam: The 2,000-year-old shipwrecks are long gone, but their cargo is strewn over a large area off Cavtat. Amphorae are plentiful and marine life is rich and diverse. There is a "newer" cargo ship from A.D. 400, 30m (100 ft.) down, but it is protected by a steel cage. For beginners diving with a registered club.

metropolis of more than one million people. Zagreb is the economic and political center of this part of Croatia, which is a gateway to the spectacular natural wonders of the south and to the hilly, winegrowing regions of the north. The extreme northern part of the country is home to many Hapsburg-inspired towns and castles set at regular intervals across the rolling farmland east of Zagreb, through Slavonia, and all the way to the Danube. The countryside here flattens out into farmland and historic towns and villages that have been the subject of battles for centuries (the area was severely affected by the 1991 war).

Istria Istria is a peninsula that hangs off the northwestern end of Croatia into the northern Adriatic. Istria is Croatia's de facto league of nations: It is the part of the country that abuts Western Europe, and it has a complex identity thanks to cultural osmosis and a long history of occupation by Romans, Venetians, Austro-Hungarians, Italians, and Yugoslavs prior to becoming part of independent Croatia. Part of Istria's charm is its foresight in letting the region's coastal towns and interior medieval

Croatia

AUSTRIA

Klagenfurt

Mura R.

Mursko
Središče

Drava R.

Maribor

Tarvisio

Velenje

Čakovec

Varaždin

Prelog

Ivanec

Ludbreg

Kranj

Celje

Krapina

ITALY

Sava R.

Bedekovčina

Križevci

Ljubljana

Oroslavje

Vrbovec

Udine

SLOVENIA

Zaprešić

ZAGREB

Dugo Selo

Gorizia

Samobor

Čazma

Monfalcone

Velika
Gorica

Portogruaro

Sisak

Trieste

Kupa R.

Karlovac

Petrinja

Koper

RISNJAK
N.P.

Delnice

Duga
Resa

Glina

Pt. Savudrija

Umag

Opatija

Rijeka

Ogulin

Bosanski
Novi

Novigrad

Lovran

Kraljevica

Poreč

Pazin

Crikvenica

ISTRIA

Krk

Rovinj

Labin

Cres

Krk

Senj

Vodnjan

Prvić

Otočac

Bihać

BRIJUNI N.P.

Pula

Rab

Rab

SJEVERNI
VELEBIT
N.P.

Una R.

Medulin

Cres

PLITVICE
LAKES N.P.

Pt: Kamenjak

Unije

Gospić

Kvarner

Kvarnerić

Pag

Mali Lošinj

Pag

PAKLENICA
N.P.

Silba

Olib

Velebit Mountains

Premuda

Privlaka

Molat

Ugljan

Zadar

Benkovac

Knin

Dugi
Otok

Sukošan

Pašman

Biograd

KRKA
N.P.

Drniš

ADRIATIC

Kornat

Murter

Vodice

Šibenik

KORNATI
N.P.

Žirje

Trogir

ITALY

SEA

Šolta

Vis

Biševo

0   20 mi

0   20 km

24

settlements retain their personalities through the centuries. These places still possess unique customs and architecture that are a strong draw for people both outside and within Croatia. Istria knows how to be an excellent host to visitors, who have been flocking to the region's seaside resorts and Roman ruins from Western Europe (and now from everywhere) for more than a century. Istria also is known as one of Croatia's food and wine capitals thanks to the excellent vintages produced in its vineyards, the rich supply of truffles found in its forests, and the refined cuisine served in its restaurants, a mix that reflects the region's cultural past, present, and future.

Kvarner Gulf   The Kvarner Gulf is home to some of Croatia's largest islands and biggest resorts. Croatia's largest port, and one of the country's biggest transportation hubs (**Rijeka**) are also here, as is one of its most developed holiday cities (**Opatija**). The entire area skirts the Kvarner Gulf, which lies between Istria and Dalmatia. It is a mélange of stark island landscapes, sophisticated resorts, excellent beaches, and some of the most forbidding mountains in Croatia. The islands of **Krk, Cres, Lošinj, Pag,** and **Rab** are easily accessed from Rijeka and other points on the mainland, and they're especially busy with tourists during the summer months. Croatia's wild and wooly northeastern wind *(bura)* is the only deterrent to enjoying this part of the country. When the *bura* blows, tourism goes.

A WEEKEND IN & AROUND ZAGREB

Zagreb makes a great base of operations for exploring Inland Croatia. Take a hike in the forest of Mount Medvednica (the "Bear Mountain"), book a tour or drive to Plitvice National Park, or head north of the city to castle country. The 3-day itinerary that follows may be short in duration, but it's long on discovery.

Day 1: Mount Medvednica

You don't need a car or an organized tour to visit **Sljeme** (p. 42), the highest peak in the Zagrebačka highlands, or to poke around **Medvedgrad,** a 13th-century castle 4km (2½ miles) south of Sljeme. You can catch the no. 14 tram at Trg Jelačić in Zagreb, ride it to the end of the line at Mihaljevac, and then transfer to the bus to the **Tomislavov Dom** hotel on Sljeme. (Note that the old cable car is no longer functioning.) From Tomislavov Dom, a network of marked trails lead through the surrounding woodland, one running straight to medieval Medvedgrad. Along the way, there are plenty of allocated spots for picnicking, with wooden tables and benches, so you can bring your own packed lunch. *Note:* If you drive, be aware that the road up to Sljeme is one way up and one way down; there is another road that leads to the backside of the mountain, where the Zagorje region begins. You'll have plenty of time when you get back to Zagreb to stroll **Tkalčićeva Street** and have an upscale dinner at **Dubravkin Put** (p. 46) to celebrate your achievements.

Day 2: Plitvice National Park

Plitvice (Plitvička Jezera; www.np-plitvicka-jezera.hr) is second only to the Adriatic coast when it comes to tourist visits in Croatia. Once you get here, you can choose among sightseeing loops that take between 2 and 8 hours to complete and vary in difficulty. The park itself comprises 16 lakes, countless waterfalls, and a wide array of flora and fauna. Hiking is the usual way to see everything, but Plitvice also uses environmentally friendly hiker assists like small ferries and

Suggested Croatia Itineraries

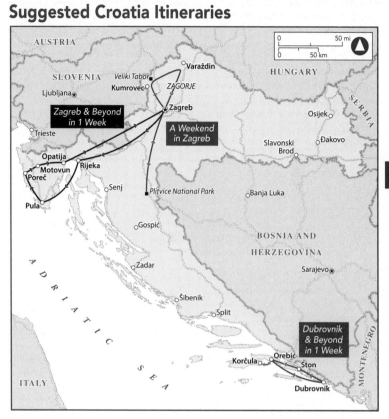

electric buses to move people through the park, which is open from 7am to 7pm daily in summer (shorter hours in the other seasons). Park entry in peak season (July–Aug) costs 185kn and includes a map on the back of your ticket. Get there independently by bus, or on an organized day trip, which you can book through numerous tourist agencies or at most large hotels in Zagreb. You also can rent a car and drive there. The trip from Zagreb takes about 2 hours each way. *Tip:* If you drive, you can stop for authentic Lička cuisine at **Restoran Degenija** (p. 55), in the village of Drežničko Selište, 5km (3 miles) north of the park.

Day 3: Castle Country

The Zagorje region northwest of Zagreb is Hansel and Gretel country. In a single day you can visit **Kumrovec** and the open-air ethno museum that was **Josip Broz Tito's birthplace** (p. 56), investigate the imposing 12th-century **Veliki Tabor Castle** (p. 56) and its resident ghost, and have lunch at **Grešna Gorica** (p. 57), a homey restaurant that appears to have been plopped down in the middle of a farmyard. Daily buses run from Zagreb to Kumrovec, but if you want to also see Veliki Tabor and anything else, you can book a tour at the Zagreb Tourist Bureau or rent a car and set your own course. This is a day trip that can be either a half- or full-day adventure. To pack a tighter schedule, you can continue a little further north and include the fairy-tale white hilltop castle of **Trackošćan** (p. 58) or the Baroque town of **Varaždin** (p. 58).

ZAGREB & BEYOND IN 1 WEEK

If you are flying to Croatia directly from North America, chances are you will land in Zagreb. That means that even if your plan is to move on to somewhere else, you will have at least half a day to explore the Croatian capital—just enough time to scratch the surface. You may want to consider giving yourself more time to explore. A full week will let you get familiar with the city while also providing time to get to know the surrounding area.

Day 1: Zagreb

Pick up your rental car or catch the shuttle to town at the Zagreb airport. Settle into your hotel, then catch the tram to **Jelačić Trg** (p. 34), the central square at the foot of the old town. Explore Zagreb's historic center and discover trendy bars, a tiny gastro-eatery, a museum dedicated to broken relationships, and an atelier filled with 20th-century sculpture.

Days 2 & 3: Rijeka & Pula

Take the fast *autocesta* (highway) from Zagreb to **Rijeka** and you'll arrive on the coast in approximately 2 hours. On your way, be sure to make a stop at **Trsat** just outside town, to explore the castle (p. 107) and Marian shrine (p. 107) there. From **Rijeka,** you'll cross into Istria. Follow the road that goes south along Istria's eastern coast to **Pula.**

If you want to be based right in the center of town, arrange to stay at family-run **Hotel Scaletta** (p. 79), just a few blocks from Pula's 2nd-century **amphitheater** (p. 77) and the sea. Alternatively, reserve a room at **Vela Nera** (p. 79), a boutique hotel with a highly regarded restaurant, in the village of Šišan, 5km (3 miles) east of Pula.

On **Day 3,** spend the morning exploring the amphitheater and the rest of Pula's cache of Roman ruins. Then head toward **Rovinj** (p. 83) around 2pm. That should give you plenty of time to stop in **Vodnjan** to see its mummies (p. 82) and still get to Rovinj for dinner. Arrange to stay the night at either the design-conscious **Hotel Lone** (p. 84), complete with its own beach, or at **Casa Garzotto** (p. 86), furnished with antiques, in the Old Town. Spend the evening having dinner at **Monte** (p. 87) at the foot of the hill leading to **St. Euphemia Church.** Then walk off the calories by strolling down **Grisia Street,** peeping in the ateliers and souvenir shops as you go. Round off the evening with a drink at romantic waterside **Valentino's** (p. 88) on the Old Town peninsula.

Days 4 & 5: Poreč

Take a morning walk to Rovinj's market near the dock and stop at any cafe for coffee and a roll. Be sure to photograph this part of town in the morning light. Collect your things and head north to **Poreč.** Once you settle into the **Grand Hotel Palazzo** (p. 90) at the harbor or in the private accommodations that you booked on the way into town, head for the city's walled Old Town, which is laid out in a geometric design popular with the Romans. Poreč is very attuned to tourists' needs; there are multilingual signs and captions in front of every important building. **Trg Marafor** (p. 89) used to be the site of Poreč's Forum and a temple dedicated to Jupiter, Juno, and Minerva. You still can see the ruins of that ancient house of worship. You'll want to reserve a full hour to view the **Basilica of Euphrasius** (p. 89), its art, and its fabulous mosaics. Once you're finished, take a pre-dinner promenade through Old Town, which probably has more jewelry shops per capita (followed closely by the number of *gelaterias*) than any other place in Croatia. You'll have to resist their siren songs if you want to see anything historic.

Plan to spend **Day 5** out of town. Poreč is an excellent jumping-off point for a trip to **Pazin** and its **castle-museum and chasm** (p. 95). From there, you can meet up with the local woman who guides visitors to the frescoes at **St. Mary's in Beram** (p. 95) as well as the **Church of St. Nicholas** (p. 95). If you didn't catch the **Vodnjan mummies** on the way into Poreč, now is the time. Spend the night in Poreč.

Days 6 & 7: Motovun & Opatija

Leave Poreč after breakfast for Istria's medieval hilltop towns. These are fairly close together, but the roads are narrow, steep, and winding, so the trip through this part of Istria takes longer than you might think. You'll start by going toward **Pazin,** but about halfway there you'll veer north to **Motovun,** which is about 16km (10 miles) northwest of Pazin. As you approach Motovun you'll see two parking lots, one at the top of the hill just outside the old town, and one lower down (not that the upper one is often full). Wear decent shoes, as the cobbled alleys can be hard on your feet. The effort to walk will be worth it, as the views of the valley are stunning. From Motovun, continue north through seemingly endless vineyards to **Livade,** stopping for lunch at **Zigante** (p. 98), one of Croatia's best restaurants. The meal may be pricey, but you'll get an education on truffles. From Livade, head a few more miles north to **Grožnjan** and take time to soak up its heady atmosphere. If you're lucky, there will be music in the air. Finally, start back to Zagreb via **Glagolitic Alley** and its sculpture garden displaying ancient Croatian symbols; **Roč** and its very low fortification wall; and **Hum,** supposedly the world's smallest town. Get back on the main road and drive through the **Učka Tunnel** toward **Opatija** and spend the night at **Bevanda** (p. 108), an upmarket seafood restaurant with an adjoining boutique hotel overlooking the Kvarner Gulf.

Start **Day 7** with a swim off one of Opatija's concrete beaches and then drive to **Lovran** to inspect the countryside and **Mount Učka** (p. 110). Return to Opatija for a 2.4km (1½-mile) walk along the waterfront promenade (you can drive there, too) to **Volosko,** where **Plavi Podrum** (p. 110) restaurant serves a fabulous lunch. You'll know at this point that you haven't had enough time in Opatija, but to keep to your schedule, you must now head toward Zagreb. You should be back in time for dinner.

DUBROVNIK & BEYOND IN 1 WEEK

If you are visiting Dubrovnik, you may have arrived by air, or by car after an overnight train to Split, or by ferry from Rijeka or Italy. Whichever way you arrived at this spectacular city in southern Dalmatia, you'll want to make the most of every moment inside—and outside—its walls.

Days 1 & 2: Dubrovnik

Settle into your hotel, take a swim, and catch the bus to the **Pile Gate** (or walk there if you happen to be staying at the **Imperial Hilton**). Just before you get to the gate, stop at the tourist office (across the street from the Hilton) and pick up a map of Dubrovnik's Old Town. Next, check the time. If it's between 11am and 5pm, kill time by strolling the **Stradun:** Explore the Old Town's churches and museums; stop for lunch, perhaps at **Proto;** and wait until the sun is low in the sky before you start your **walk on the walls.** Grab a bottle of water and head for the Pile Gate entrance to the stairs leading to the top of the stone fortification. Doing the entire 2km (1¼-mile) circuit atop the walls is a nonnegotiable must-do if you are physically able. After all, you've traveled all the way to Dubrovnik and this is the ultimate Dubrovnik experience.

Allow a minimum of 1 hour for this trek, more if you are prone to oohing and aahing at spectacular scenery, or if you want to make a splash jumping off the rocks directly outside the seaward walls before or after your trek. By the time you've come down to earth, the promenade on the Stradun will have begun. You'll be ready for a break, a swim, and a glass of wine, so head to **Buža** (p. 201), where you'll get amazing views of the sun setting over the sea.

Spend **Day 2** in Dubrovnik exploring everything Old Town has to offer, including the streets that radiate from the **Stradun.** You'll find some interesting surprises here, including the second-oldest synagogue in Europe, galleries, restaurants, and a shop or two. This is the day to "do" the churches, museums, and palaces in Old Town. Be sure to check out **War Photo Ltd** (p. 190), too. In the afternoon, take a taxi-boat to the tiny islet of **Lokrum** and have a swim, or ride the **Dubrovnik Cable Car** (see p. 184) to the peak of Mount Srdj for amazing views down on the fortified Old Town. Have dinner in **Otto** (see p. 199) overlooking the port on the edge of **Lapad,** but make it an early night because Day 3 will be busy.

Days 3 & 4: A Day Trip from Dubrovnik

An ideal side trip from Dubrovnik is a visit to the **Pelješac Peninsula.** You can take a self-guided tour or sign up at Atlas or another agency for an escorted tour of the Pelješac vineyards and wineries. If you drive yourself, take the coastal highway north.

The first stop is **Ston,** the Pelješac town closest to the mainland. Ston's obvious draw is the 5km (3 mile) **14th-century defensive wall** (see p. 210) that stretches above the town from both sides and forms a horseshoe in the hills above it. You'll want to climb this mini–Great Wall of China with a friend just so you can get your picture with the wall behind you. This is not an easy climb (there are lots of stairs), and parts of the wall are still under renovation. Ston and its twin settlement **Mali Ston** up the road are both known for their oyster and mussel beds, and both have restaurants that serve fabulous versions of these shellfish—savor them for lunch at **Kapetenova Kuća** (p. 211). You can walk the salt pans outside town to see how this ancient salt collection method works (you'll probably have the place to yourself). Stop at the ticket kiosk at the entrance and buy a few bags of souvenir sea salt from Ston.

The Pelješac Peninsula runs for about 64km (40 miles) from Ston to **Lovišće** and measures from 2.4 to 6.8km (1½ to 4¼ miles) wide at various points. However, these parameters are deceptive as Pelješac is quite mountainous, and the end-to-end drive usually takes more than 2 hours. It will be midafternoon by the time you finish with Ston, and you'll want to visit some of Pelješac's wineries, which are scattered all over the peninsula.

Day 5: Orebić

From Ston, you'll head to low-key **Orebić** toward the far end of the peninsula, where you'll spend the night at **Hotel Adriatic** (see p. 207) or in the private accommodations you arranged in Dubrovnik.

Orebić is a lively town from dawn to dusk; people stay on the beach and in the sea well after dark. At night the promenade along the waterfront is alive with families walking to and from restaurants and cafes. However, for a truly memorable dinner, drive up the hillside behind town to eat at **Panorama** (p. 208)—try to arrive in the early evening so you can enjoy the amazing view of the sun setting over the sea before your meal.

Days 6 & 7: Korčula

From Orebić, it is a half-hour's boat ride to the island of **Korčula** and the medieval-walled **Korčula Town** where Marco Polo was supposedly born. Korčula Town is a nice, relaxing day trip, with its majestic cathedral, cobbled alleys, and quaint eateries, though you might well be tempted to stay a night if you look up the luxurious **Lešič Dimitri Palace** (p. 174). If you have a car or rent a scooter, you can venture into the island's hilly interior, and have lunch at **Konoba Mate** (p. 175) in Pupnat. You'll return to Orebić to spend the night and prepare for the trip back to Dubrovnik.

The trip back to Dubrovnik takes about 3 hours if you drive straight through, but you may end up stopping at more wineries along the way. Once back in Dubrovnik, you can reprise your favorite experiences or see the things you missed when you arrived.

ZAGREB

There is a new spirit in Zagreb, a city that travelers regarded as more a stopover than a destination as far back as the days of the Orient Express. No more. Zagreb's attractions aren't as famous as Paris's, or as numerous as Rome's, but it's still impossible to experience all the city's delights on just an overnight stay.

Zagreb has always played a pivotal role in the life of Croatia, mostly because of its location at the crossroads where western and eastern Europe meet. This is not a glitzy city, but one of history, culture, and purpose, informed by war and natural disasters. Zagreb is still finding itself after nearly a millennium of foreign domination, but it is changing and growing, and emerging as a destination in its own right.

Nowadays, Zagreb's squares fill every summer with people speaking a variety of languages. New restaurants, attractions, and entrepreneurial ventures are sprouting everywhere. As so often happens with travel, much of how one experiences Zagreb can come down to luck—being here at the right moment. On rainy Sundays, central Zagreb is deserted: Stores are closed and restaurants and museums are empty. If a visitor has just a day and is forced to see the city from under an umbrella, Zagreb seems a sad, gray place. But if that same visitor is lucky enough to be in the city center on a sunny Saturday, Zagreb is a vital metropolis, pulsating with color and buzzing with energy. On a day like that, Zagreb hums with chatter as fashionistas haggle with wizened old ladies in black at the colorful **Dolac Market,** and the city becomes a backdrop for curious tourists, for friends sipping wine at sidewalk cafes, and for anyone listening to the street musicians that fill **Trg Ban Jelačić** with beautiful noise.

Weekdays, Zagreb is alive with serious hustle and bustle, and what seem like endless hordes sipping coffee at sidewalk cafes or carrying briefcases or bags of bread and flowers. Evenings, Zagreb is all softness and laughter, as diners linger over dessert at the newly restored **Gradska Kavana,** head for open-air cocktail bars, or just stroll the cobblestone streets.

The city's blend of old and new, of country and cosmopolitan, is a yin-yang combo that somehow works. This is not a city that instantly takes your breath away, but—given enough time—Zagreb will wiggle its way into your heart and tempt you to stay a while.

ESSENTIALS

Arriving

BY PLANE   There are no direct flights to Croatia from the U.S., Canada, or Australia, but Croatia Air, the national airline, connects Zagreb with several major European hubs as well as with other cities in Croatia. **Pleso International Airport** (www.zagreb-airport.hr; ☏ **01/456-22-22**) is about 16km (10 miles) south of the city center. A shuttle bus (www.plesoprijevoz. hr) between the airport and Zagreb bus station coincides with incoming and outgoing flights; tickets cost 30kn, and the ride takes ½ hour. Taxi fares to the city center run between 150kn and 200kn.

BY BUS Zagreb Bus Station (Autobusni Kolodvor) is a bright, efficient hub with restaurants, shops, a post office, ATMs, luggage storage (*garderoba*), and regular trams to the city center. Frequent bus connections link Zagreb and all of Croatia's main cities, which in turn hook up with local lines that run to virtually every village in the country. International connections link Zagreb to an increasing number of European cities.

BY TRAIN Zagreb Train Station (Glavni Kolodvor) is a proud 19th-century building, overlooking Trg Kralja Tomislava on the city's Green Horseshoe. It lies a 10-minute walk south of the main square (Trg Bana Josip Jelačić), which is also served by regular trams. The train station has a restaurant, fast-food kiosks, ATMs, and coin-operated luggage lockers.

BY CAR Driving in Zagreb can be stressful. Most streets are marked only at intersections by small ornamental signs on plaques affixed to buildings, so you can't see the sign until you're past it. Many buildings in Zagreb do not display street numbers at all, or if they do, they can't be read unless you're on top of them. There is also a tangled network of one-way and pedestrian streets, perpetual street construction, and a parking dearth, all of which add up to a driver's nightmare inside the city limits.

Visitor Information

The **Zagreb Tourist Information Center** at Trg Bana Jelačić 11 (www.zagreb-tourist info.hr; ✆ **01/481-40-51**) is open 8:30am to 8pm Monday to Friday, 9am to 6pm Saturday, and 10am to 4pm Sunday and holidays. The information center provides maps, directions, and brochures, and it has a selection of books about Zagreb and Croatia as well as some souvenirs.

    Zagreb County Tourist Association at Preradovićeva 42 (www.tzzz.hr; ✆ **01/487-36-65**) is useful for information about excursions from Zagreb. Hours are 8am to 4pm Monday to Friday.

City Layout

The city of Zagreb is nestled between Mount Medvednica and the Sava River. It is a sprawling metropolis, but almost every attraction of note is within 2.4km (1½ miles) of **Trg Bana Jelačić,** the city's main square (commonly known as Trg Jelačić). The area north of the main square includes **Gornji Grad (Upper Town)** and its Gradec and Kaptol neighborhoods, which are Zagreb's most picturesque areas. **Donji Grad (Lower Town)**, south of Trg Jelačić, includes Zagreb's famous **Green Horseshoe** and runs south to the main train station. You can walk to most points of interest from Trg Jelačić. Further afield, **Mount Medvednica Nature Park** and its **Sljeme Peak** in the hills north of town can be accessed by tram from the main square, followed by a bus to **Tomislav Dom Hotel** on Sljeme (note that the cable car is out of order and looks unlikely to start working again in the near future). **Mirogoj Cemetery** is also north of the center and can be reached by bus from the cathedral. **Novi Zagreb (New Zagreb)** is an area of modern apartment blocks and industry south of the Sava; here you'll find **Jarun Lake,** just north of the river, and the **Museum of Contemporary Art,** both served by tram. You'll also find **Pleso International Airport,** served by the airport bus.

The Neighborhoods in Brief

Zagreb is easy to navigate via public transportation if you have a good map and know a few key Croatian terms for deciphering directional signs on the trams and buses. You can also walk to almost everything of note. Most of Zagreb's attractions are in the city center, which is divided into "neighborhoods," each connected by the city's main square, Trg Jelačić, with distinct characters of their own. Gornji Grad (Upper City), the area north of the square, is Zagreb's heart. It is divided along historical lines into Kaptol and Gradec, territory that was halved by a stream that is now Tkalčićeva Street, home to a string of open-air cafes, chic designer shops, and artists' ateliers.

Kaptol is both a neighborhood and a street in modern Zagreb. In medieval times, Kaptol was a town of its own, dominated by the clergy (neighboring Gradec was a lay settlement). Today, Zagreb's neo-Gothic cathedral and church buildings are still situated in Kaptol. North of the cathedral, Kaptol is becoming a trendy enclave where well-heeled young professionals shop, drink, and dine.

Gradec is a hilly residential area dotted with stately mansions and leafy squares as well as some of the city's best galleries and museums. It is a good place to see ornate homes built by Zagreb's 19th-century aristocrats, as well as the only surviving city gate. Here you will find the **Croatian Sabor** (Parliament), as well as several foreign embassies and consulates, and a few upscale restaurants.

Trg Bana Jelačić, ringed by proud 19th-century Austro-Hungarian buildings, is Zagreb's fulcrum: It seems that everything begins and ends in this plaza dominated by a statue of Ban Josip Jelačić, seated on a confident horse with its tail in the air. Ban Jelačić was a 19th-century governor of Croatia who was much beloved by the people for his bravery. His statue is a focal point of the square and the space "under the tail" is a popular rendezvous spot. The square is a wonderful place to start any city tour because many tram routes crisscross here, and it is within easy walking distance of Kaptol and Gradec, Dolac Market, and Tkalčićeva Street.

Donji Grad (Lower Town) is south of Gradec, and it might seem like a solid block of buildings broken up by a few green spaces. Donji Grad begins at Trg Jelačić and includes Ilica Street, where designer shops are increasing in number every day. The neighborhood ends at the main train station to the south. Draškovićeva is Donji Grad's eastern border, and Republika Austria the western border. In the middle of this section of the city, a U-shaped series of adjacent parks runs roughly from Trg Bana Jelačić south to the main train station; from there to the western end of the Botanical Gardens; and north to the end of Trg Marsala Tita. Known as the "Green Horseshoe," or Lenuci's Horseshoe, these public green spaces are dotted with galleries, museums, and schools.

Getting Around

ON FOOT   Walking is by far the best way to see Zagreb. Crime in the city is low, and on foot you can safely get to almost any museum or restaurant in the central town within half an hour.

BY TRAM OR BUS   Zagreb's electric tram system is quick, clean, efficient, and reliable, and it runs 24/7, although the frequency is reduced in the wee hours. New, air-conditioned, Croatian-made cars were added in 2007 on most routes, and they make riding public transportation comfortable. Tram routes cover central Zagreb and connect to buses that run to outlying areas and suburbs. Most lines go to the main train station, Trg Ban Jelačić, or both.

Tickets for both can be purchased at Tisak news kiosks for 12kn or on board for 15kn. Tickets are good for 90 minutes each way and must be validated with a time stamp at the orange machines on board. There are no conductors checking tickets, but there are random control checks. If you are caught without a ticket or with an unstamped ticket, the fine is 150kn on the spot, more if you don't have the money immediately.

There are maps of all tram and bus routes at stops and on most city maps, but if you aren't familiar with the city or the language, it can be difficult to figure out whether a given vehicle goes to your destination because only the final destination and a stop or two are listed on the tram or bus itself.

BY TAXI Taxis are quite expensive in Zagreb, though prices have dropped somewhat in recent years with the founding of a number of private taxi companies. The most popular companies include **Eko Taxi** (www.ekotaxi.hr; ✆ **060/77-77**), **Radio Taxi Zagreb** (www.radio-taksi-zagreb.hr; ✆ **060/800-800**), and **Taxi Cammeo** (www.taxi-cammeo.hr; ✆ **1212**). Although prices vary slightly from company to company, you can expect to pay around a 10kn flat fee plus 6kn for every kilometer (⅗ mile). A surcharge is added on Sundays and at night.

[FastFACTS] ZAGREB

ATMs & Banks There are numerous ATMs (Bank-omats) in central Zagreb where you can withdraw cash using American Express, Diners Club, Maestro/MasterCard, and Visa. Most banks open Monday to Friday 8am to 7pm and Saturday 8am to noon.

Dentists **Dental Emergency** at Perkovčeva 3 (✆ **01/480-32-00**) is open 24/7 and takes walk-ins.

Doctors & Hospitals Zagreb's **main hospital** is Klinička Bolnica "Sestre Milosrdnice" at Vinogradska Cesta 29, ✆ **01/378-71-11.** For medical emergencies, you can also try the **Emergency Center** at Draškovićeva 19 (✆ **01/469-70-00**) near the Sheraton. It's open 24 hours. **KB Dubrava** (✆ **01/290-24-44**) at Avenija Gojka Šuška 6 makes house calls to most parts of town.

Embassies & Consulates The **U.S. Embassy** is at Thomasa Jeffersona ulica 2 (www.zagreb.usembassy.gov; ✆ **01/661-22-00**).

The **Canadian Embassy** is at Prilaz Gjure Deželića 4 (✆ **01/488-12-00**).

The **United Kingdom Embassy** is at I. Lučića 4 (www.gov.uk/government/world/organisations/british-embassy-zagreb; ✆ **01/600-91-00**).

The **Irish Consulate** is at Miramarska 23 (✆ **01/631-00-25**).

The **Australian Embassy** is at Centar Kaptol, Nova Ves 11/III (✆ **01/489-12-00**).

The **New Zealand Consulate** is at Vlaška 50a (✆ **01/461-20-60**).

Emergencies For police dial ✆ **192;** for an ambulance, ✆ **194;** and to report a fire, ✆ **193.** For road assistance from the **Croatian Auto Club,** dial ✆ **1987** (www.hak.hr).

Internet Access Almost every hotel and hostel now offers free Internet access to guests, as do many cafes.

Mail & Postage You can mail letters at any yellow Posta box, but if you need to buy stamps or send a package, the Central Post Office (✆ **072/303-304**) is at Branmirova 4, next to the train station, open daily 7am to midnight. The post office will tell you that it takes

roughly 2 weeks for regular mail to reach the U.S. from Croatia. (Our experience is that mail to the U.S. takes 4 weeks or more.) A letter home to the U.S. will cost 8kn per 50gr and a postcard 3.50kn. If you are in a hurry, go to DHL at Utinjska 40, in Novi Zagreb (www.dhl.hr; ✆ **01/665-11-11**). It's open Monday to Friday 7:30am to 8pm, Saturday 8am to noon.

Pharmacies Need an aspirin? In Zagreb (and all of Croatia) you'll have to go to a pharmacy (*ljekarna*) to buy some. No drugs of any kind are sold anywhere except at a pharmacy. There are several 24-hour ljekarna in Zagreb. Two are at Trg Jelačić 3 (✆ **01/481-61-59**) and at Ilica 301 (✆ **01/375-03-21**).

Safety Zagreb enjoys relatively low crime rates. It's perfectly safe to ride public transportation at night and to walk through high-traffic areas. The police presence on Zagreb streets is subtle and you'll rarely see a uniformed officer, but they're there. Exercise the same precautions you'd take in any big city.

WHAT TO SEE & DO

The best—and in some cases the only—way to see Zagreb is on foot, with the occasional tram or bus ride. Almost everything in the city center is pedestrian-accessible, as are some of the sites farther afield. Gornji Grad (Upper Town) is flush with historical buildings and churches, restaurants, boutiques, monuments, and entertainment venues. Donji Grad (Lower Town) is strong on museums, parks, historic architecture, and shopping. Other attractions are a short ride from the center of town. Anton Dominik Fernkorn's statue of Ban Josip Jelačić is the centerpiece of **Trg Bana Jelačić (Jelačić Square).** The statue was installed on the square in 1866 and it stood there until World War II, when the square was renamed Republic Square. The statue was removed and stored in pieces because the powers-that-be determined it had become a rallying point for Croatian nationalists, who were seen as a threat to the ruling Communist Party. It wasn't until 1990 that the statue was restored to its original home, and the square to its original name. Today Jelačić Square is ringed by cafes and shops; other smaller plazas radiate out from it.

Kaptol

Cathedral of the Assumption of the Virgin Mary ★★
An earlier cathedral on this site dated from the 12th century, but was largely destroyed during the Tartar invasion in 1242. What you see today dates from between the 13th and 16th centuries; the elegant neo-Gothic facade and twin spires were added by Austrian architect Herman Bollé in the late 19th century. Inside, behind the main altar, note the sarcophagus of the former Archbishop Alojzije Stepinac, which bears a relief by sculptor Ivan Meštrović. Stepinac remains a controversial figure in Croatia due to his alleged collaboration with the extreme right during World War II.

Kaptol 31. ℂ **01/481-47-27.** Free admission. Open for sightseeing Mon–Sat 10am–5pm; Sun 1–5pm. Masses are at 7am, 8am, 9am, and 6pm weekdays; and at 7am, 8am, 9am, 10am, 11:30am, and 6pm Sun.

Dolac Market ★★★
Immediately north of Jelačić Square, this market is affectionately known as the "Belly of Zagreb." Each morning at daybreak, on the open-air piazza, vendors set up their stalls with fresh seasonal fruit and vegetables. Down below, the covered market has separate halls dedicated to meat, fish, and cheese. There's also an area of stalls selling local craftwork, such as wooden toys, basketry, and lace.

Dolac bb. Mon–Fri 6am–2pm; Sat 6am–3pm; Sun 6am–noon.

Tkalčićeva ★★★
From the northwest corner of the main square, this pedestrian-only cobblestone street winds uphill into Gornji Grad (Upper Town). It is lined with pastel-colored 19th-century mansions, many now hosting popular cafes, bars, restaurants, boutiques, and galleries at ground level. Zagrebians come here to drink coffee in the morning or beer after dark. On a summer evening, the outdoor tables are packed with clientele from all walks of life.

West of Dolac Market.

Gradec

Gradec is the second arm of central Zagreb's civic neighborhood triumvirate. Less commercial than Kaptol, Gradec is packed with some of the city's most interesting museums and monuments.

What to See & Do in Zagreb

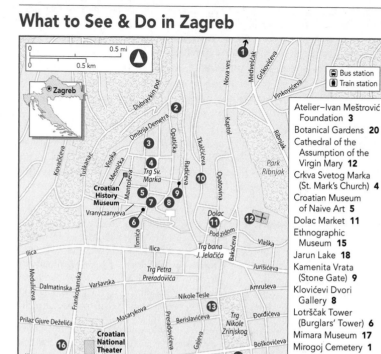

0	0.5 mi	
0	0.5 km	

Bus station
Train station

Atelier–Ivan Meštrović Foundation **3**
Botanical Gardens **20**
Cathedral of the Assumption of the Virgin Mary **12**
Crkva Svetog Marka (St. Mark's Church) **4**
Croatian Museum of Naive Art **5**
Dolac Market **11**
Ethnographic Museum **15**
Jarun Lake **18**
Kamenita Vrata (Stone Gate) **9**
Klovićevi Dvori Gallery **8**
Lotršćak Tower (Burglars' Tower) **6**
Mimara Museum **17**
Mirogoj Cemetery **1**
Mount Medvednica **1**
The Museum for Arts & Crafts **16**
Museum of Broken Relationships **7**
Museum of the City of Zagreb **2**
Museum of Contemporary Art **19**
Strossmayer Gallery of Old Masters **14**
Tkalčićeva Ulica **10**
Zagreb Archaeological Museum **13**

Crkva Svetog Marka (St. Mark's Church) ★

The vivid red, white, and blue tiled roof on this church can't be missed. It depicts the coats of arms of Zagreb and the Kingdom of Croatia, Dalmatia, and Slavonia. The roof was added in 1880, though the church itself dates to the 13th century. In comparison, its interior is rather plain and austere. Opening hours vary and the church is often kept locked outside Mass hours.

Trg Svetog Marka 5. ⓒ **01/485-16-11.** Free admission. Open for Masses at 7:30am and 6pm weekdays and Sun at 10am, 11am, and 6pm.

The Croatian Museum of Naïve Art ★

Unique to Croatia, the so-called Hlebine School was made up of farmers from the village of Hlebine in north Croatia. Although they had no formal art education, their work attracted considerable interest, and became known as Croatian Naïve Art. Besides working on canvases, they often painted on glass, employing bright, garish colors and depicting farm animals and scenes from rural life. On display in this Baroque mansion you can see pieces by noted naïve artists, such as Ivan Generalić and Ivan Lacković.

Ćirilometodska 3. www.hmnu.org. ℂ **01/485-19-11.** Admission 20kn. Tues–Fri 10am–6pm; Sat–Sun 10am–1pm.

Kamenita Vrata ★★   From Tkalčićeva, a long flight of wooden stairs leads up to Radićeva. From there, a steep winding cobblestone path brings visitors to Kamenita Vrata, the Stone Gate. After a devastating 1731 fire, a painting of the Virgin and Child was found here in the ashes, totally undamaged. The image was declared miraculous and housed in a dedicated shrine. Today locals still come here to pray, in a dark grotto, with several pews and dozens of flickering candles. The walls bear countless tiny stone plaques saying "*hvala*" (thank you), in gratitude to the Virgin.

Kamenita bb. Open 24 hr.

Klovićevi Dvori Gallery ★★   Built by the Jesuits in the 17th century, this building was turned into an art gallery in 1982. It is used to stage big international exhibitions, generally running for three months. Recent major shows include Picasso in 2013 and Degas, Tiziano, Tintoretto, and Veronese in 2012. There's a peaceful courtyard cafe and a gift shop.

Jezuitski Trg 4. www.galerijaklovic.hr. ℂ **01/485-19-26.** Admission fees are variable, depending on the current exhibition. Tues–Sun 11am–7pm.

Kula Lotrščak (Lotrščak Tower) ★★   Overlooking the lovely Strossmayer Promenade, with amazing views over the city rooftops, Lotrščak Tower dates from the 13th century. Each day at noon, a cannon is fired from here to commemorate Croatia's success in fending off the Ottoman Turks in the early 16th century. The tower now functions as a gallery, under the management of Klovićevi Dvori, hosting temporary exhibitions. You can climb to the top for views over the entire city and south across the River Sava.

Strossmayerovo Šetalište 9. www.galerijaklovic.hr. ℂ **01/485-17-68.** Admission 20kn. Mon–Fri 9am–5pm; Sat–Sun 10am–3pm.

Meštrović Atelier ★★★   The former home and studio of Dalmatian sculptor Ivan Meštrović is set in a charming 17th-century townhouse, where he lived and worked from 1924 to 1942. Inside, you can see a vast array of his output, including preparatory sketches and sculptures of famous people and religious figures. Meštrović fled the country during World War II, and ended up living in the United States, where he worked as a professor of sculpture at the University of Notre Dame. He died in 1962, regarded as Croatia's greatest 20th-century sculptor.

Mletačka 8. www.mdc.hr/mestrovic/atelijer/index-en.htm. ℂ **01/485-11-23.** Admission 20kn. Tues–Fri 10am–6pm; Sat–Sun 10am–2pm.

Museum of Broken Relationships ★★★   This museum, opened in 2010, asks the question "What is the role of love tokens once a relationship has ended?" The idea is very simple, but it has generated a fascinating and complex collection. Visitors here find an extraordinary array of personal possessions connected to love stories that went wrong. Each exhibit has been donated by someone who endured a failed relationship, and is accompanied by a text explaining the significance of the object. The current

IVAN MEŠTROVIĆ (1883–1962)

Ivan Meštrović was Croatia's greatest sculptor of religious art since the Renaissance. He worked in various materials—marble, wood, and bronze—to create realist sculpture, usually exploring religious themes. Meštrović was born in Vrpolje (Slavonia) to a peasant family on August 15, 1883, and spent most of his childhood in Otavice, a tiny, impoverished village in the mountainous interior of Dalmatia west of Šibenik. When he was 16, Meštrović was apprenticed to a stonecutter in Split, where he developed his skills by reproducing the city's Roman works of art. After just 9 months in Split, a wealthy Viennese patron sponsored a place for him at the Academy of Fine Arts in Vienna. There, Meštrović met French sculptor Auguste Rodin, who became a strong influence on the young artist and encouraged him to broaden his artistic vision through travel. Meštrović took Rodin's advice and spent time working in Paris, Belgrade, and eventually Rome, where he won a first prize for sculpture at the World Exhibition of 1911. In the early 1920s,

Meštrović settled in Zagreb, where he transformed a 17th-century house (**Meštrović Atelier,** see above) into his home and studio. In 1942 he was imprisoned by the Ustaše, but released thanks to intervention by Pope Pius XII. After World War II, he emigrated to the U.S., where he became a professor of sculpture at Syracuse University and later at Notre Dame. There are a few of Meštrović's works in Zagreb, most notably the "Well of Life" (1950) in front of the Croatian National Theater. In addition to the atelier, I recommend a visit to the **Meštrović Gallery** (a villa he designed himself, where he spent his summers) in Split, for travelers who are heading to Dalmatia after the capital. Meštrović's best known public work in Split is the colossal bronze statue of "Grgur Ninski," which stands just outside the walls of Diocletian's Palace, close to the Zlatna Vrata. Travelers continuing down to the Dubrovnik area might want to check out the elegant white stone **Račić Mausoleum** in Cavtat, also designed by Meštrović.

collection was arranged in January, 2014. This is probably Zagreb's most-loved museum. It has a pleasant cafe for drinks, plus an amusing gift shop.

Ćirilmetodska 2. www.brokenships.com. ℂ **01/485-10-21.** Admission 25kn. Jun–Sept daily 9am–10:30pm; Oct–May daily 9am–9pm.

Museum of the City of Zagreb ★ This museum is housed in the former convent of the Order of St. Clare and it's worth a quick look in as an introduction to Zagreb's history. Tracing the centuries from medieval times to the present, objects on display include weapons, religious paraphernalia, furniture, and scale models of the city at various stages of its development.

Opatička 20. www.mgz.hr. ℂ **01/485-13-61.** Admission 20kn. Tues–Fri 10am–6pm; Sat 11am–7pm; Sun 10am–2pm.

Donji Grad (Lower Town)

Botanical Gardens ★ The Botanical Gardens opened in 1894 and lie a 10-minute walk west of the Hotel Esplanade. Offering a peaceful retreat from urban chaos, they feature a lush arboretum, two ponds, and an ornamental bridge.

Trg Marka Marulića 9a. ℂ **01/489-80-60.** Free admission. Apr–Oct Mon–Tues 9am–2:30pm; Wed–Sun 9am–7pm; winter, closed.

heart OF THE MATTER

The shiny red hearts on display in nearly every Zagreb souvenir shop are actually *licitar*, a honey dough similar to gingerbread that is shaped in wooden molds, hardened, coated with edible red lacquer, and decorated with trim, flowers, and swirls. Young men traditionally gave the colorful hearts to their girlfriends as an expression of love. Today, the decorated cookies are still given as a sign of affection, but they also are used as special occasion gifts or as remembrances.

Personalized hearts are sometimes wedding favors, toys, or Christmas ornaments. The hearts have even been immortalized in a ballet, "Licitarsko Srce" ("Gingerbread Hearts"), by Croatian composer Krešimir Baranović. Today, these gingerbread hearts are used as hospitality tokens by the Croatia National Tourist Board—they are rarely eaten, but instead saved and displayed as instantly recognizable symbols of Croatia.

Ethnographic Museum ★★   This museum displays folk costumes from Croatia's various regions, with a vast array of different colors and decorative styles. There are carefully embroidered scarves and aprons, and intricate lacework from the island of Pag. Also on display is traditional farming equipment, with an emphasis on wine and olive oil production, showing how people once toiled to work the land.

Mažuranićev Trg 14. www.emz.hr. ℂ **01/482-62-20.** Admission 20kn. Tues–Thurs 10am–6pm; Fri–Sun 10am–1pm.

Mimara Museum ★   There's very little Croatian artwork on display here. In fact, it is the private collection of just one man, Ante Topić Mimara, who was born in Dalmatia and spent most of his life abroad but left everything to his country when he died. Here you can see paintings spanning several centuries and movements, by artists as disparate as Paolo Veneziano, Diego Velazquez, John Constable, and Edouard Manet, as well as a vast hoard of glass, ceramics, and textiles from all over the world. You'll find the collection in a neo-Renaissance building, a 10-minute walk southwest of the main square.

Rooseveltov Trg 5. www.mimara.hr. ℂ **01/482-81-00.** Admission 40kn. Jul–Sept, Tues–Fri 10am–7pm, Sat 10am–5pm, Sun 10am–2pm; Oct–Jun, Tues–Wed and Fri–Sat 10am–5pm, Thurs 10am–7pm, Sun 10am–2pm.

The Museum for Arts and Crafts ★★   This light and spacious 19th-century building was designed by Herman Bollé, who was also responsible for the facade of Zagreb Cathedral. Inside you'll find a vast array of period furniture, clocks, and light fittings, displayed in chronological order from the Baroque period up to the 20th century, giving some idea of how people's homes once looked. I'd recommend it for those interested in design and design history, who could easily while away a couple of hours here.

Trg Maršala Tita 10. www.muo.hr. ℂ **01/488-21-11.** Admission 30kn. Tues–Sat 10am–7pm; Sun 10am–2pm.

Strossmayer Gallery of Old Masters ★★   Former Bishop of Đakovo Josip Juraj Strossmayer (1815–1905) was an avid collector of religious art. At any one time you can see some 300 pieces from his 4,000-piece collection at this gallery on the upper floors of the Croatian Academy of Sciences and Arts. Most of the works were made by European masters between the 14th century and the early-20th century, represented by the likes of Italian Renaissance painter Vittore Carpaccio, Cretan Mannerist El Greco, and Flemish Renaissance artist Pieter Bruegel. In the lobby on the ground floor, note the renowned Baška Tablet, an 11th-century stone slab, engraved in medieval Glagolitic script, unique to Croatia. Originally in a tiny church near the village of Baška on the island of Krk, it was moved here for safekeeping in 1934.

Trg Nikole Šubića Zrinskog 11. ℂ **01/489-51-17.** Admission 30kn. Tues 10am–7pm; Wed–Fri 10am–4pm; Sat–Sun 10am–1pm.

Zagreb Archaeological Museum ★ This museum traces the centuries from prehistoric times up to the Tartar invasion of Europe in 1242. Pride of place here goes to the "Zagreb Mummy," wrapped in bandages which are covered in a curious text written in Etruscan script. It was purchased as a souvenir in Egypt in the 19th century and is believed to date from 250 B.C. There's also a collection of funerary items, including the Vučedol Dove, a three-legged ceramic vessel in the form of a bird which was found in Vukovar in eastern Croatia and dates back to the fourth millennium B.C.

Trg Nikole Šubića Zrinskog 19. www.amz.hr. ℂ **01/487-30-00.** Admission 20k. Tues–Wed and Fri–Sat 10am–6pm; Thurs 10am–8pm; Sun 10am–1pm.

Farther Afield

Jarun Lake ★★ Jarun was a swamp until 1987, when it was turned into an artificial lake and watersports center. Lying 4km (2½ miles) southwest of the city center and ringed by footpaths, it's a popular venue for rowing and sailing. In summer locals come here to sunbathe and swim. It's also home to some of the capital's liveliest bars and discos—being so far from the center, noise is not a problem here. Each year in July, Jarun Lake hosts the three-day INmusic Festival, with past performers like the Pixies and Iggy Pop. It is served by tram no. 17 from Jelačić Square.

Free entrance to Jarun.

Mirogoj Cemetery ★★ This stunning cemetery dates back to 1879. Designed by architect Herman Bollé (of Zagreb Cathedral fame), it incorporates arcades and pavilions, trees and flowers, and bouquets and candles. There are many impressive tombs, some created by eminent sculptors such as Ivan Meštrović (see p. 39), Antun Augustinčić, and Dušan Đamonja. Reflecting the multicultural land that Yugoslavia once was, here you'll see graves marked by Christian crosses, Jewish six-point stars, socialist five-point stars, and elegant Muslim headstones. Among the well-known personalities buried in Mirogoj are former NBA basketball player Dražen Petrović, abstract painter Edo Murtić, and Croatia's wartime President Franjo Tuđjman. To get to Mirogoj, take the no. 106 bus from Kaptol opposite the cathedral.

Mirogoj, about 2.4km (1½ miles) northeast of the city center. Apr–Sept daily 6am–8pm; Oct–Mar daily 7:30am–6pm.

Mount Medvednica ★★★ A favorite Sunday outing for Zagrebians, Medvednica has been set aside as a nature park. From spring through autumn locals come here to walk and cycle (there is a network of well-marked paths), and in winter they come to ski. There are several cozy mountain huts, serving hearty fare for hikers, as well as ski-rental shops. There's also a medieval fortress, Medvedgrad, which is open to the public. Medvedgrad (ℂ **01/457-20-71**) was built on the slopes of Mt. Medvednica in the 13th century as a strategic lookout point to protect Zagreb after the Mongol invasion of 1242. However, it was badly damaged in an earthquake in 1590, and consequently abandoned. Outside standard opening hours (May–Oct Tues–Sun 11am–7pm

LENUCI'S horseshoe

The U-shaped block of parks and gardens that runs from Trg Bana Josip Jelačić to the main train station and back is known as Lenuci's Green Horseshoe, a flowing, tree-lined series of grassy areas, fountains, flower beds, monuments, and pavilions dotted with museums and galleries. According to Lenuci's 19th-century plan, the green strips and stately cultural palaces are strategically placed to break up the visual monotony of the blocks and blocks of gray apartments and office buildings that characterize this part of town. The horseshoe cuts a green pattern through Lower Town and is home to such landmarks as the neo-Renaissance **Academy of Sciences and Art,** the neo-Baroque **Croatian National Theater,** and the **Botanical Gardens.**

and Nov–Apr Tues–Sun 11am–4pm; admission 15kn), it hosts occasional classical music concerts. The highest peak in the park is Sljeme (1,033m/3,390 ft.), which is a 20-minute drive from Zagreb. If you are using public transport, take tram no. 14 from the main square to the end of the line (Mihaljevac), and then a bus to Tomislav Dom Hotel on Sljeme. Note that the cable car is no longer functioning.

15km (9 miles) north of the city center. www.pp-medvednica.hr. ℰ **01/458-63-17.**

Museum of Contemporary Art ★★★ Art lovers should put a half day aside to visit this excellent museum located south of the city center in Novi Zagreb. Housed in a light and airy concrete building, opened in 2009, the permanent collection features over 600 paintings, sculptures, and installations created between 1950 and the present, mainly by Croatian artists. It also hosts very good temporary exhibitions. There is a small ground floor cafe and a gift shop with a selection of art books. Admission is free on the first Wednesday of each month. To reach the museum, take tram no. 6 from either the main square or the train station to its terminus, Sopot.

Avenija Dubrovnik 17. www.msu.hr. ℰ **01/605-27-00.** Admission 30kn. Tues–Sun 11am–6pm; Sat 11am–8pm.

Especially for Kids

Exploring Zagreb with children in tow can be challenging on a number of fronts. Ushering little ones across the open tram tracks, up and down steep cobbled streets, and through churches and museums that appeal mainly to adults can put a strain on parents and kids alike. Most of Zagreb's hotels and sights don't have any special extras for kids, though many do offer rate reductions for the younger set. Unlike hotels in Croatia's resort towns, Zagreb hotels have no all-day programs to keep kids entertained. Very few restaurants have children's menus or highchairs, though most will do what they can for customers with children.

One of the best bets for keeping kids amused in Zagreb is **Jarun Lake** (see p. 41), south of the center. Besides a beach, Jarun has paddle boats, playground equipment, and often sports competitions like beach volleyball to keep kids entertained. Children might also enjoy Zagreb's **cinemas**—most show films in their original versions (usually English) with Croatian subtitles, so kids won't have any trouble understanding what's going on. Out of town, a day exploring **Mount Medvednica** (see p. 41), walking the hiking trails and stopping for a picnic, should appeal to most kids, and also result in a good night's sleep for all.

WHERE TO STAY

Zagreb's hotels are generally of a high standard and offer comfortable rooms with private bathrooms; however, except at the top end, they tend to be somewhat bland. Many of the better hotels offer special rates at weekends, over the Internet, or for multiday stays, but you have to ask. Otherwise, hotel rates in the city are generally not subject to seasonal changes or cash discounts. Note that breakfast is included in the prices shown below unless otherwise stated. There is a slight dearth of good low-cost hotels in Zagreb, but as of 2010 several cleverly designed, rather quirky hostels have opened in the center, some offering private rooms as well as dorm beds, making them an interesting option for gregarious travelers.

Expensive

Best Western Premier Hotel Astoria ★   Just a 5-minute walk from the train station, and a similar distance from the main square in the opposite direction, this smart, peaceful hotel was fully renovated in 2005. The bar area has comfy leather sofas and polished wood paneling. The restaurant decor is slightly less inspiring, but it does a delicious and very filling buffet breakfast. Guests from the U.S. might consider the rooms small, but they provide everything one might want on a short stay. Interconnected rooms are available, as are cribs, baby food, and highchairs, making this a fine choice for families traveling with kids.

Petrinjska Ulica 71. www.hotelastoria.hr. ℓ **01/480-89-00.** 102 units. From 162€ double. **Amenities:** Restaurant; bar; smoke-free rooms; rooms for those w/limited mobility; limited free parking; Wi-Fi (free).

Hotel Esplanade ★★★   Lovers of old-fashioned luxury will appreciate the opulent Esplanade, which dates to 1925, when it was built as a stopover for passengers on the Orient Express (hence its proximity to the train station). From the elegant Art Deco lobby, sweeping marble stairs lead up to the rooms and suites, which are spacious and furnished in classic style, with fabrics and carpets in muted cream and beige tones, and marble bathrooms complete with double sinks, separate showers and bathtubs, and L'Occitane toiletries. A generous buffet breakfast, with smoked salmon eggs Benedict, omelets and pancakes cooked to order, and proper coffee, is served at outdoor tables on the patio in summer. The restaurant has a halal certificate. Former guests include Louis Armstrong, Orson Welles, and Woody Allen. *Tip:* If you're thinking of traveling with a canine companion, check out the Esplanade's Very Important Dog (VID) scheme, which includes a dog menu and specially designed beds.

Mihanovićeva 1. hotel.esplanade.hr. ℓ **01/456-66-66.** 208 units. From 155€ double. **Amenities:** 2 restaurants with terraces; bar; concierge; fitness center; room service; sauna; smoke-free rooms; valet service; Wi-Fi (free).

Hotel President Pantovčak ★★   This stylish little boutique hotel lies on a peaceful side street off Ilica, Zagreb's busiest shopping street, a 10-minute walk west of the main square. Opened in 2008, it has seven airy rooms and suites with wooden floors. The restaurant overlooks a lush garden, with sliding glass doors that open onto a terrace. Expect a mix of antique furniture and contemporary art, personalized service, and a sumptuous (but rather pricey) breakfast with a choice of cooked-to-order menus.

Pantovčak 52. www.president-zagreb.com. ℓ **01/488-14-80.** 7 units. Doubles from 119€; breakfast from 15€ per person. Parking 19€ per day. **Amenities:** Restaurant; bar; room service; Wi-Fi (free).

Moderate

Hotel Dubrovnik ★   Overlooking the main square, Hotel Dubrovnik occupies two adjoining buildings, one from 1929 and the other from 1982 (with a slightly garish glass and aluminum facade). Although marketed primarily for business travelers, the hotel's central location makes it a fine choice for tourists, too. The renovation, started in 2011 and completed in summer 2014, has made for fewer rooms than before, but they are more spacious, modern, and luxurious, and come with slick new bathrooms. Facilities include the Dubrovnik Café, with its Art Deco interior, a popular meeting place for hotel guests and non-guests alike.

Gajeva 1. www.hotel-dubrovnik.hr. ⓒ **01/486-35-55.** 222 units. From 115€ double. **Amenities:** 2 restaurants; cafe; room service; smoke-free rooms; valet; rooms for those w/limited mobility; limited free parking; Wi-Fi (free).

Hotel Jadran ★   Ideally located, just a 5-minute walk east of the main square, this 3-star hotel was renovated in 2013. Functional and very reasonably priced, the rooms here are rather small, but modern and tastefully decorated in shades of cream and chocolate brown. The best ones have views of the cathedral's twin spires. The staff is friendly and helpful, and the hotel does a decent breakfast. Parking is free.

Vlaška 50. www.hotel-jadran.com.hr. ⓒ **01/455-37-77.** 49 units. From 76€ double. **Amenities:** Restaurant; limited free parking; Wi-Fi (free).

Hotel Jagerhorn ★★   This is Zagreb's oldest continually running hotel, dating back to 1827. It lies hidden away in a courtyard off Ilica, the city's main shopping street, just a 5-minute walk west of the main square. Fully renovated in 2011, it now has 18 cozy rooms, plus a bar in the walled garden at the back, where breakfast is served on sunny mornings. This is an unpretentious retreat for couples, especially suited to a romantic winter city break.

Ilica 14. www.hotel-jagerhorn.hr. ⓒ **01/483-38-77.** 18 units. From 120€ double. **Amenities:** Restaurant; terrace; bar; limited free parking; Wi-Fi (free).

Hotel Palace ★★   Lying between the train station and the main square, overlooking a leafy square, this heritage hotel dates from 1907. It was renovated in 2013, but has retained its old-fashioned charm, with a retro-chic look. Facilities include a Viennese-style ground floor cafe, a restaurant serving traditional local cuisine, and a wellness center offering massage, sauna, and beauty treatments. This is a good choice for families, as the hotel provides free extra beds for kids and can arrange babysitting.

Trg JJ Strossmayera 10. www.palace.hr. ⓒ **01/489-96-00.** 123 units. From 105€ double. **Amenities:** Restaurant; bar; babysitting; room service; smoke-free rooms; limited free parking; Wi-Fi (free).

Inexpensive

Hotel Jarun ★   Located in a leafy residential neighborhood close to Lake Jarun (a 20-min. tram ride south of the city center), this modern, 3-star hotel provides a very reasonably priced, comfortable, and peaceful retreat. Rooms are spacious and well-designed, with bamboo floors, modern minimalist furniture, and a big black-and-white photo of the city covering the wall above the bed. The bathrooms have walk-in showers and a generous selection of toiletries. There is no restaurant, but the hotel does serve breakfast.

Hrgovići 2. www.hotel-jarun. ⓒ **01/369-11-11.** 30 units. From 62€ double in Aug. **Amenities:** Bar; room service; smoke-free rooms; free parking; Wi-Fi (free).

Where to Stay & Dine in Zagreb

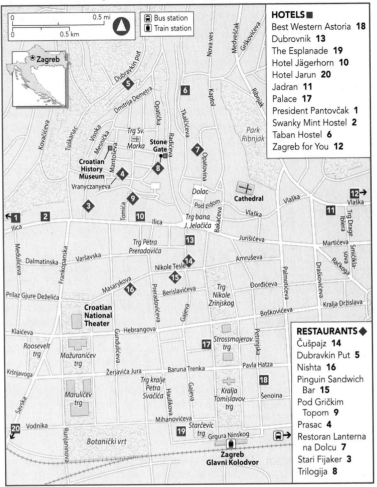

HOTELS ■
Best Western Astoria **18**
Dubrovnik **13**
The Esplanade **19**
Hotel Jägerhorn **10**
Hotel Jarun **20**
Jadran **11**
Palace **17**
President Pantovčak **1**
Swanky Mint Hostel **2**
Taban Hostel **6**
Zagreb for You **12**

RESTAURANTS ◆
Čušpajz **14**
Dubravkin Put **5**
Nishta **16**
Pinguin Sandwich Bar **15**
Pod Gričkim Topom **9**
Prasac **4**
Restoran Lanterna na Dolcu **7**
Stari Fijaker **3**
Trilogija **8**

ZAGREB | Where to Stay

4

Swanky Mint Hostel ★★★ In a renovated 19th-century dry cleaning and textile-dye factory, this funky hostel combines its former industrial identity with recycled furniture and an eco-friendly atmosphere. There's a choice of beautifully designed self-catering apartments, private rooms with en suite bathrooms, and dorms with bunks built from chipboard. There's also a bar which hosts concerts and art events, a sunny garden with outdoor seating (a favorite meeting place for local architecture students), and a fully equipped kitchen. The hostel is just a 5-minute walk west of the main square.

Ilica 50. www.swanky-hostel.com. ✆ **01/400-42-48.** 55 beds. From 11€ per person. **Amenities:** Cafe with terrace; kitchen; Wi-Fi (free).

45

Taban Hostel ★★　On car-free, cobbled Tkalčićeva Street, known for its busy open-air cafes and restaurants, this welcoming hostel has a total of 50 beds divided between single, double, and family rooms, and 6-bed dorms. The friendly ground floor bar stages regular concerts and DJ nights, making it popular with visitors and locals alike (it has excellent soundproofing, so you can't hear the music when you're upstairs). A great choice for budget accommodation, the hostel sits in Gornji Grad, just a 10-minute walk north of the main square.

Tkalčićeva 82. www.tabanzagreb.com. ☏ **01/553-35-27.** 50 beds. From 11€ per person. **Amenities:** Bar with terrace; laundry service; Wi-Fi (free).

Zagreb for You ★　This 1930s fire station was converted into a small hotel in 2012, decorated throughout in minimalist white, grey, and charcoal shades. Lying a 20-minute walk east of the main square (three tram stops), it is run by a young, friendly staff. Each of the nine double rooms comes with a private bathroom with shower, A/C, flat-screen TV, and free Wi-Fi. There is no dining room, but breakfast (extra) is served in a nearby restaurant. The hotel runs a Gastro Tour for those wishing to learn more about traditional Croatian food and cooking. Parking is free.

Fijanova 6. www.zagreb-accommodation.com. ☏ **091/213-70-16.** 9 units. From 52€ double (not including breakfast). **Amenities:** Lounge; free parking; Wi-Fi (free).

WHERE TO DINE

While Croatia in general offers a rather narrow choice of cuisines (predominantly traditional and local), in Zagreb the selection is far more varied. Besides the region's hearty meat dishes, you'll encounter a new wave of up-and-coming young chefs, who create contemporary dishes by reinterpreting traditional recipes with a refined touch. Pizzerias remain the most common type of casual dining spots around the city, and Croatian pizza is remarkably good and inexpensive, but restaurants offering a wide range of ethnic cuisines (Thai, Istrian, Bosnian, Mexican, Middle Eastern) are making inroads. Traditional fast food is the Bosnian *burek* (phyllo pastry filled with either cheese or meat), although there are also kiosks vending pizza by the slice and baguette sandwiches. For sweets, the city's ubiquitous cafes and *slastičarnicas* (ice-cream/pastry shops) provide indulgent treats.

Very Expensive

Dubravkin Put ★★★ SEAFOOD　Generally regarded as Zagreb's best seafood restaurant, Dubravkin Put is modern, light, and airy, set amid lush greenery on the edge of Tuškanac Park, just a 10-minute walk from the main square. Popular dishes include Dalmatian *brodet* (fish stew with fresh herbs) and tagliatelle with white truffles. To try a bit of everything, opt for the elaborate degustation menu, which combines both fish and meat and includes Adriatic sea bass, scallops from Novigrad, goose liver with sour cherries, fresh trout from Gacka, and veal fillet. The service is attentive and professional, and a sommelier will recommend wines to accompany the dishes you choose.

Dubravkin Put 2. dubravkin-put.com. ☏ **01/483-49-75.** Degustation menu 465kn; fish and seafood priced by weight. Mon–Sat 11am–midnight.

Prasac ★★★ CREATIVE MEDITERRANEAN　Run by owner-chef Dino Galvagno, this tiny gastro-eatery lies in a romantic location close to Lotrščak Tower in Gornji Grad. The menu changes with the seasons, offering a choice of just three appetizers, three main courses, and three desserts at any one time. Expect tasty dishes like creamy celery soup, trout tartar, tuna steak, and stuffed zucchini flowers. Some people complain that the portions are small and the service a little arrogant, but the food is undeniably sublime. Only 20 diners are seated at any time, so reservations are strongly recommended.

Vranicanijeva 6. www.prasac.hr. 𝄞 **01/485-14-11.** Entrees 90kn–140kn. Mon–Fri 6–11pm; Sat noon–3pm and 6–11pm.

Expensive

Pod Gričkim Topom ★★ CROATIAN   In Gornji Grad, at the foot of Lotrščak Tower, this restaurant has a small terrace with potted geraniums and hanging flower baskets, plus amazing panoramic views over the city's rooftops, making it an impressive venue for a special meal. Popular with both businesspeople and tourists, the menu combines Croatian and international dishes, with house specialties like shrimp risotto, charcoal-grilled lamb chops, and veal escalopes with mushrooms. Reservations are strongly recommended.

Zakmardijeve stube 5. www.restoran-pod-grickim-topom.hr. 𝄞 **01/483-36-07.** Entrees 70kn–130kn; fish and seafood priced by weight. Mon–Sat 11am–midnight.

Trilogija ★★ CREATIVE MEDITERRANEAN   Hidden away in a vaulted brick cellar opposite Kamenita Vrata in Gornji Grad, this much-loved eatery seats just 40 diners. The kitchen specializes in Mediterranean cuisine with a contemporary twist. The menu changes daily, depending on the best fresh ingredients to be found at the morning market. The offerings are chalked up on a blackboard: Expect tempting dishes such as *rižoto od kozica* (prawn risotto) or *svinjski lungić s pireom ob buće* (pork tenderloin with pumpkin purée). There's an excellent wine list, too, with most wines available by both the glass and the bottle.

Kamenita 5. www.trilogija.com. 𝄞 **01/485-13-94.** Entrees 70kn–150kn. Mon–Thurs 11am–midnight; Fri–Sat 11am–1am.

Moderate

Nishta ★★ VEGETARIAN   Opened in January, 2014, this is the sister restaurant to the very popular Nishta in Dubrovnik. Its lies a 5-minute walk southwest of the main square, in a spacious dining room with wooden floors and red and white checkered tablecloths. The menu offers a tasty choice of vegetarian, vegan, and gluten-free dishes, such as pumpkin soup with sour cream and toasted walnuts, a Waldorf mousaka with celery, apples, and walnuts, and daikon canelloni stuffed with sun-dried tomatoes and almonds.

Masarykova 11/1. www.nishtarestaurant.com. 𝄞 **01/889-74-44.** Entrees 48kn–60kn. Mon–Sat 11am–11pm.

Restoran Lanterna na Dolcu ★ TRADITIONAL CROATIAN   Close to the Dolac open-air market, on the north side of the main square, this restaurant occupies a vaulted brick cellar, with less than a dozen tables and subtle lighting creating an intimate atmosphere. The menu includes old traditional Croatian recipes, served in generous portions, with an emphasis on meat. Look out for main dishes such as *medaljoni Opatovina* (veal medallions in a truffle sauce), *maksimirska rolada* (chicken stuffed with fresh arugula and prosciutto), and *gornjogradski medaljoni* (pork medallions cooked in prunes and red wine).

Opatovina 31. 𝄞 **01/481-90-09.** Entrees 55kn–85kn. Tues–Sun 11am–midnight.

Stari Fijaker ★ TRADITIONAL CROATIAN   Close to Britanski trg, off Ilica, this old-fashioned eatery specializes in traditional Zagrebian dishes. The dining room, with its tile floor and heavy wooden furniture, reflects the rustic hearty meals on offer, such as *punjena paprika* (stuffed peppers), *sarma* (cabbage leaves stuffed with rice and minced meat), *purica s mlincima* (roast turkey with a delicious pasta-like side dish), and *gulaš od divljači* (venison stew with gnocchi).

Mesnička 6. www.starifijaker.hr. ℰ **01/483-38-29.** Entrees 35kn–80kn. Mon–Sat 11am–11pm; Sun 11am–10pm.

Inexpensive

Čušpajz ★★ SOUPS   Ideal for a warming and inexpensive lunch, this eatery specializes in soups. A 5-minute walk south of the main square, it is owned and run by Leonarda Boban, wife of 1990s Croatian footballer Zvonimir Boban. The menu changes daily, depending on what Leonarda finds at the morning market, but she always offers a choice of three hearty soups, including at least one vegetarian option, as well as freshly baked bread.

Ljudevit Gaj 9. Soups 38kn. Mon–Sat 11am–5pm.

Pinguin Sandwich Bar ★ FAST FOOD   A popular spot for a late-night post-clubbing snack, Pinguin dates from 1987. A wide range of freshly made sandwiches are served, with a firm favorite being the *Toplo-Hladno* (Hot-Cold), which combines grilled chicken and mushrooms in a ciabatta bun with olives. The place looks like a dive, but locals recommend it for an inexpensive quick bite.

Nikola Tesle 7. Sandwiches 15kn–33kn. Mon–Sat 10am–4am; Sun 6pm–2am.

ZAGREB AFTER DARK

Zagreb nightlife revolves primarily around the student population, meaning plenty of lively cafes and bars with outdoor seating, plus venues offering cultural events such as concerts and film screenings. At the other end of the scale are Zagreb's young professionals, who tend towards cocktail and chic wine bars. For late-night clubbing, the place to go is **Jarun Lake,** which lies far enough from the center to mean that noise is not a problem and the music can play at full volume till sunrise.

Cocktail Bars

Maraschino ★   A 5-minute walk from the main square, just off Ilica behind the Orthodox church, this bar has a small, dark interior, with a DJ playing both funky and mainstream music. Named after a cherry-based liqueur from Zadar, it's popular with the young urban crowd.

Margaretska 1. ℰ **095/866-52-94.** Daily 8am–2am.

Melin ★★   This legendary bar works as a cafe during the day, turning into a small club after dark, with occasional live jazz on weekends. The subtle lighting and mismatched retro wooden furniture give it a friendly, unpretentious atmosphere. You'll find it set back slightly off Tkalčićeva Street, with several benches out front. Melin is a 10-minute walk uphill from the main square.

Kožarska 19. www.melin.hr. ℰ **01/488-02-98.** Daily 10am–2am.

Live Music Venues

Bacchus ★★   On the square directly in front of the train station, Bacchus occupies a cavernous vaulted space. A shelf filled with books functions as the bar, and trinkets, old typewriters, and radios are on display. Live jazz is hosted Wednesday to Saturday evenings. Entrance is through a pleasant courtyard garden.

Trg Kralja Tomislava 16. ℂ **01/492-22-18.** Mon–Sat 11am–midnight.

Tvornica ★★ This grungy club hosts some of Zagreb's best live concerts, with an emphasis on rock and alternative music. Gogol Bordello, the Pixies, Patti Smith, the Violent Femmes, and Public Image Limited have all played here. It's open for coffee during the day. The location is close to Zagreb bus station, in a former factory (after which Tvornica takes its name).

Šubićeva 2. www.tvornicakulture.com. ℂ **01/457-83-89.** Cafe Mon–Sat 8am–11pm; club Mon–Sat 11pm–4am.

Nightclubs

Aquarius ★★ South of the city center, on the shores of Lake Jarun, this popular, vibrant club extends over two floors, playing commercial dance music with occasional theme nights and live concerts. In summer, Aquarius moves out to the seaside, for all-night clubbing on Zrće Beach on the island of Pag in North Dalmatia.

Matije Ljubeka, Jarun. www.aquarius.hr. ℂ **01/369-32-48.** Cafe daily 9am–9pm; nightclub Fri–Sat 10pm–6am.

Hemingway's ★★ On the edge of Tuškanac Park, in an 1838 building which was formerly used as a cinema, Hemingway is part of a chain of clubs, with additional venues in Rijeka, Opatija, and Split. People come here to see and be seen, either sipping one of a vast array of (rather expensive) cocktails, or dancing to mainstream DJ music.

Tuškanac 1. www.hemingway.hr. ℂ **01/483-49-56.** Mon–Sat noon–5am.

Pubs & Beer Halls

Oliver Twist ★★ Oliver Twist is hugely popular and always busy. Outdoor tables are arrayed on a spacious stone terrace below green awnings, backed by a vine-covered facade. Inside, Irish draught beers, whiskies, and cocktails are served from the wooden bar area to a soundtrack of predominantly foreign music.

Tkalčićeva 60. ℂ **01/481-22-06.** Daily 9am–4am.

Pivnica Medvedgrad Ilica ★ Medvedgrad was founded outside the city center as a microbrewery back in 1994. In 2009, the brewery opened this beer hall, just a 5-minute walk from the main square, with tables and benches on an open-air terrace. Five different beers are served, ranging from a dark stout to a light lager, plus hearty pub food. Occasional live music is staged as well. You'll find a smaller sister venue, Pivnica Mali Medo Tkalčićeva, at Tkalčićeva 36.

Ilica 64. www.pivnica-medvedgrad.hr. ℂ **01/484-69-22.** Mon–Sat 10am–midnight; Sun noon–midnight.

Wine Bars

Wine Bar Basement ★★★ In a vaulted brick cellar in a side alley off Ilica Street (close to the funicular), this sophisticated but cozy wine bar is the ideal place to sample Croatian regional wines by the glass, accompanied by platters of cheese and cured meats. The staff is friendly, knowledgeable, and attentive. Reservations are recommended on weekends.

Tomićeva 5. www.basement-bar.net. ℂ **01/777-45-85.** Mon–Sat 9am–2am; Sun 10am–midnight.

EXCURSIONS FROM ZAGREB

Most visitors to Croatia know something about its sophisticated capital, Zagreb, and the country's stunning Adriatic coastal scenery, but they know little about what lies beyond. There is much less traveler chatter about Croatia's inland towns—both close to Zagreb and farther away—than there is about the coast, even though these interior regions provide rich alternatives to sun-and-fun culture. Croatia away from Zagreb and the coast dances to a much less frenetic beat than its glamorous siblings. The atmosphere in the cool, green hills is more down-to-earth and less commercial. Working towns and farms are juxtaposed with castles and medieval fortresses, built centuries ago to protect the country from foreign invaders.

5

The northern regions of the Zagorje and Međimurje are where many of Croatia's heroes were born, and where many patriots died fighting for Croatia's freedom. There, hilltop towers stand sentry, as if to protect the land against harm, and tiny *klets* stand between crop rows to provide shelter for farmers and their tools.

Towns among the rolling hills and flatlands outside Zagreb are beginning to actively court tourists as the capital spreads outward to meet fields of yellow sunflowers waving in the wind. So get out of town and take a trip to the country, where the roads less traveled will lead you to the "real" Croatia and the genuine people who live there.

ORIENTATION

You don't have to take a long road trip to sample Croatia's northern heartland: Many of the castles, wineries, historical sites, and natural wonders within a 161km (100 mile) radius of **Zagreb** can be visited on day trips. Excursions such as a day of hiking the trails at **Plitvice Lakes National Park,** with its waterfalls and gorges, or exploring the shops, cafes, and castle in the Baroque town of **Varaždin,** are within easy reach of Zagreb. Whether you want to spend a few days driving through the Međimurje wine country in extreme northern Croatia, or if you have just half a day to wander around Tito's childhood village at **Kumrovec** in the **Zagorje,** you can do it without spending a lot of time in transit. Check with the **Zagreb County Tourist Association** (www.tzzz.hr; ✆ 01/487-36-65) at Preradovićeva 42 for excursion possibilities. To get information on exploring the territory north of Zagreb in the Zagorje or Međimurje regions, contact the **Tourist Board of Međimurje County** (www.tzm.hr; ✆ 040/374-064) in Čakovec at R. Boškovića 2.

Excursions from Zagreb

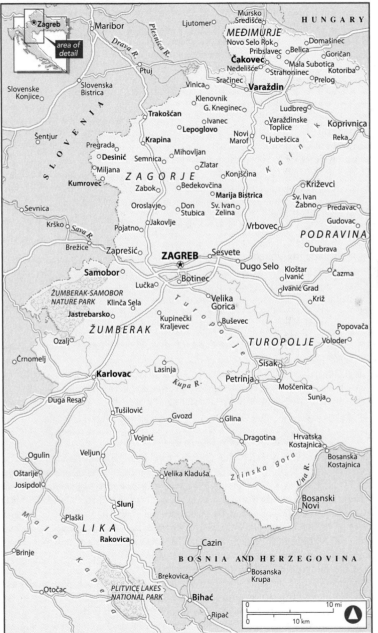

Getting There & Getting Around

From Zagreb, all of the destinations below can easily be reached by car. Alternatively, visitors can travel by train; for schedules, go to **Croatian Railways** (www.hzpp.hr; ℂ **060/333-444**). Buses leave from **Zagreb Bus Station** (www.akz.hr; ℂ **060/313-333**). No matter how you arrive, your adventure will involve walking, as these destinations are compact, and some are even pedestrian-only.

EXCURSIONS SOUTH OF ZAGREB

Undoubtedly the most rewarding day trip south of the capital is to **Plitvice Lakes National Park,** Croatia's most visited inland destination. A lush wonderland of rocky slopes covered with dense pine forests, with a succession of turquoise-blue lakes and thundering waterfalls, it appeals to both young and old. Depending on levels of fitness and stamina, visitors can appreciate it at a slow, relaxed pace, contemplating the glorious vistas and natural wonders, or explore it with a vengeance, packing a picnic and hiking marked trails from dawn to dusk.

Essentials

VISITOR INFORMATION   Just about every tourist office in every city throughout Croatia offers tours of Plitvice Lakes. Tourist offices in Zagreb in particular have racks of maps, brochures, and information on most attractions and events within 161km (100 miles) of the city. In addition, most towns in Croatia have city tourist offices with more localized information, plus commercial tourist agencies that run excursions and handle private accommodations.

GETTING THERE & GETTING AROUND   Plitvice Lakes National Park (Plitvička Jezera) ★★★ can be accessed via the Zagreb-Rijeka *autocesta* (highway). It lies a 2-hour drive from Zagreb, and you'll want to allow plenty of time for exploring the trails and gazing at the countless waterfalls—in fact, if you have the time, an overnight stay in Plitvice is well worth considering. Plitvice can be reached by bus from Zagreb, but a rental car provides more freedom in planning an itinerary.

Plitvice Lakes National Park

The **Plitvice Lakes National Park** is Croatia's most touted natural wonder: Its majestic waterfalls, lakes, and forests have earned it a place on the UNESCO register of world natural heritage sites and make it Croatia's second-biggest tourist attraction, after the Adriatic coast and islands. The park's most compelling features are the waterfalls that interconnect its 16 turquoise lakes, which are set amid soaring rock formations in dense forests of beech, fir, and spruce. The park's 4,856-hectares (12,000 acres) break down into 3,642 hectares (9,000 acres) of forest, 1,133 hectares (2,800 acres) of grassy areas and villages, and 36 hectares (88 acres) of water. Everywhere the water is crystal-clear thanks to the deposits of travertine (powdery white limestone rock, see "Waterfall Chemistry," below) under the water. The regular distribution of travertine creates the underwater mounds responsible for the waterfalls. The park is also rich with caves, springs, flowering meadows, the source of the River Korana (a gorge that looks like a green branch of the Grand Canyon), and several animal species including deer, wolves, wild boar, and the increasingly rare brown bear (though these animals rarely make an appearance during the hours when the park is open to visitors).

Plitvice became a national park in 1949. One of the Serb-Croat war's first casualties was a park policeman who was killed in an incident that is sometimes cited as one of the flashpoints for the 1991 war. The park was occupied for most of the war by Serb troops, who stayed until 1995. During that time, park offices and hotels were trashed, but the park itself was undamaged. Since then, the hotels and other buildings have been restored, and visitors have returned to the park in droves. Plitvice now lures nearly a million visitors annually, with acreage crisscrossed by well-marked gravel paths and boardwalks that allow visitors to wander for anywhere from 2 to 8 hours per outing, depending on how they structure their routes.

Park signs at the trailheads suggest itineraries and lengths of time each would take, but in reality, you can make your own path and stay as long or as short a time as you like—provided you don't take a wrong turn and miss one of the bus or ferry stops (the in-park transportation system runs on eco-friendly fuel, whisking visitors between sights).

ESSENTIALS

VISITOR INFORMATION The national park (www.np-plitvicka-jezera.hr; ✆ **053/751-015**) has two entrances, Ulaz 1 and Ulaz 2, each of which has a tourist info office, gift shop, and snack shop. Both entrances are open daily 7am to 7pm mid-Apr to mid-Sept, and 9am to 4pm mid-Oct to mid-Apr. Tickets are 185kn July to August; 110kn April to May and September to October; and 55kn November to March per person. There are reduced rates for children and seniors. There is also a separate **Plitvice Tourism Office** (www.tzplitvice.hr; ✆ **053/776-798**) in Korenica at Trg Sveti Jurja 6 for further information.

GETTING THERE Plitvice is on the old road (E71) between Split and Zagreb, but you don't need a car because almost every town and hotel in the country either runs tours or connects visitors with tours that include Plitvice.

BY CAR To get to Plitvice by car from Zagreb (trip time about 2 hr.), take the Zagreb-Rieka *autocesta* to Karlovac. From there, follow the signs to Plitvice via the old road to Split (E71).

BY BUS There are several buses per day from the main bus station in Zagreb (2½ hr.). You can check schedules online at www.akz.hr, but you should visit the bus station at Avenue Marin Držića 4 to make a reservation or get a ticket. Make sure your bus stops at Plitvice and that it doesn't take the new highway and bypass the park on the way to Split.

GETTING AROUND The best place to begin your tour is at Ulaz 2 (Entrance 2), as this puts you in the middle of the property and gives you more options for exploring. Ulaz 2 is also the site of the park's hotels (p. 54), for travelers who want to stay near the park and weren't lured by the ubiquitous SOBE ("rooms") signs on the roads leading to and from Plitvice.

WHAT TO SEE & DO

Plitvice is a hiker's paradise, but even couch potatoes can see most of the park's features by combining some walking with rides on the Plitvice ferries and buses. Ulaz 2 is roughly in the middle of the park, so if you start there, you can easily get to **Prošćansko,** the highest and largest lake in the park, which is ringed by a hilly green landscape. (No waterfalls here, as you're at the top of the cascade.) From Ulaz 2, it's a quick downhill walk to a ferry which will take you toward paths flanked by waterfalls which you can almost reach out and touch. *Tip:* Don't try this: Swimming is forbidden, as is walking on the travertine.

WATERFALL chemistry

Visitors to Plitvice can't help wondering why the water is so clear, why each lake seems to have a different jewel-like color, and what the heck is travertine (park signs forbid visitors from stepping on the stuff). The official park map explains that over thousands of years, super-pure water pouring into Plitvice from the mountains eroded the surrounding limestone rocks. Moss and algae acted as catalysts to turn the dissolved rock (calcium carbonate) into the porous stone known as travertine, which then was deposited in the water. Nature is still "manufacturing" travertine at Plitvice, and the dissolve-and-deposit process is responsible for creating the park's waterfalls and for the lakes' vivid blue-green color. (As the travertine sinks to the lake floor, it coats vegetation and the lake's floor in white mineral "dust," which creates a bottom that reflects sunlight and sky—thus the brilliant colors.) As the travertine accumulates on the bottom, it also builds to the point that it creates barriers between the lakes. These barriers eventually get tall enough to create the waterfalls that are the essence of Plitvice's constantly shifting landscape.

You can also follow the signs here to the foot of **Veliki Slap (Big Waterfall),** where slender streams of water zoom off a vertical granite face into **Korana Gorge.** Veliki Slap is the most dramatic waterfall in the park and sometimes it seems that everyone is rushing to get there. However, there are falls in other parts of the park that are almost as impressive.

WHERE TO STAY

There are three hotels within the park, where groups touring by bus tend to stay. In nearby villages, you'll also find local homes renting out rooms to visitors.

Hotel Degenija ★★ Lying in lush rolling countride north of Plitvice National Park, this modern 4-star hotel has 20 spacious rooms and suites. Interiors feature wooden floors, fabrics in muted cream and beige tones, and immaculate tiled bathrooms with bathtubs. The hotel serves a generous buffet breakfast, and the staff is friendly and efficient. Information about visiting the park is readily available and there are bicycles for hire.

Drežničko Selašte 59, Rakovica. www.hotel-degenija.com. © **047/782-143.** 20 units. Off-season from 45€; July–Aug 120€ double. **Amenities:** Restaurant; terrace; rental bikes; Wi-Fi (free).

Hotel Jezero ★ Ideally located within the national park, this big hotel is inevitably popular with tour groups. Dating from the 1970s, it is somewhat impersonal, but the rooms are spacious and comfortable, and the best ones have balconies and views over the lake. Some rooms are interconnected, making them great choices for families with kids. Food at the restaurant is basic but adequate, and additional facilities include a gym, sauna, whirlpool massage, and tennis court.

Plitvička Jezera bb. www.np-plitvicka-jezera.hr. © **053/751-500.** 210 units. Off-season from 43€; July–Aug 114€ double. **Amenities:** Restaurant; bar; pool; gym; sauna; tennis court; 2 rooms for those w/limited mobility; Wi-Fi (free).

WHERE TO DINE

Hundreds of dining spots pepper the road to and from Plitvice, most offering spit-roasted lamb or pig and other local specialties. You can stop for a bite, or buy your roasted meat by the kilo and picnic in the woods. There are a few sandwich concessions within the park itself in addition to the hotel restaurants. There also used to be an excellent restaurant within the park called Lička Kuča, but sadly it burnt down in 2012.

Bistro Vila Velebita ★ CROATIAN   One of the numerous local eateries with lamb and pigs roasting on spits out front, Vila Velebita lies 10km (6 miles) south of Plitvice National Park. The menu includes tasty homemade cream of mushroom soup, roast lamb (served by the kilo), and barbecued chicken skewers (with bacon, peppers, and onions). On sunny days, guests sit on the terrace at rustic wooden tables and benches with red and white checkered tablecloths.

Rudanovac 12a, Korenica. www.vila-velebita.com. ✆ **053/755-040.** Entrees 40kn–80kn. Daily 11am–11pm.

Restoran Degenija ★★ CROATIAN   Next door to Hotel Degenija (under the same management), this highly regarded restaurant serves authentic regional dishes, with an emphasis on meat. Local trout and brick-oven pizza are additional highlights. In summer, you can dine outside on the terrace, with flowers in hanging baskets and views over the surrounding countryside. The restaurant lies just 5km (3 miles) from the park and is generally acknowledged as the best eatery in the area.

Drežničko Selašte 59, Rakovica. www.restoran-degenija.hr. ✆ **047/782-060.** Entrees 50kn–85kn. Daily 7am–11pm.

EXCURSIONS NORTH OF ZAGREB

The verdant, rolling landscape of the Zagorje and Međimurje regions north of Zagreb could have been patterned on illustrations from "Grimm's Fairy Tales." This is Croatia's storybook land, where each new vista reveals another gentle swell of green topped with cream-colored hilltop churches and gingerbread-brown brick cottages. In the troughs between, the villages of rural Croatia remain repositories of the nation's early culture and customs, a source of larger-than-life heroes and historic events that helped shape the country and its unique character.

Visitors can see **Kumrovec,** Tito's rural birthplace, which now looks like a Croatian version of Williamsburg, Virginia, with blacksmiths forging iron, costumed guides explaining exhibits, and townspeople selling homemade *rakija* (brandy) and local honey. Other notable attractions include the medieval fortresses of **Veliki Tabor** and **Trakošćan,** and the Baroque town of **Varaždin** and its museums and castle. In the north of the country, close to the Slovenian border, lies the town of **Čakovec,** in a rural area of Međimurje, where family vineyards abound, and everyone from grandma to the smallest of children pitches in to harvest the grapes.

The people of the Zagorje and Međimurje are known throughout Croatia as some of the nation's most industrious and frugal citizens. They also have reputations for generous hospitality, for serving exceptional meals made with local produce, and for loving their land and the fruit of their trees and vines. Just like the winegrowers in France's Beaujolais region who celebrate *le vin nouveau* on the third Thursday in November, the people in northern Croatia also have a designated November day (Nov. 11, St. Martin's Day) to taste and tout their new vintage. On that day, the wine is blessed and the whole area takes part in a festival of food, wine, and merrymaking, a celebration of a season's work that lasts well into the night, ending only with morning and the beginning of a new cycle of life.

Kumrovec & Veliki Tabor

The route north from Zagreb past Mount Medvednica and through the Stubica Valley leads to the Zagorje region, home to some of Croatia's most beautiful vistas and the best castles in the country. On the way, you'll be immersed in the Zagorje's appealing rural atmosphere, which hasn't changed much over the centuries. History buffs will make beelines for the ethno village of **Kumrovec (Staro Selo),** where Josip Broz Tito was born, and **Veliki Tabor,** one of Croatia's oldest castles.

ESSENTIALS

VISITOR INFORMATION   The **Kumrovec Tourist Board** (www.kumrovec.hr; ✆ **049/553-728**) is at Ulica Josipa Broza 12.

GETTING THERE   You can see both **Kumrovec (Staro Selo)** and **Veliki Tabor** in a day if you are driving, but it will take longer if you are using public transport, which is available from Zagreb and other parts of Croatia. Several public buses run daily to Kumrovec. To get to Veliki Tabor, however, you'll have to take one of several buses to Desinič and walk almost 3.2km (2 miles) to the castle from the bus stop. See "Orientation," p. 50, for bus schedule contact information.

GETTING AROUND   Once you reach your destination, walking or biking are the only ways to explore this area. You can drive up to Veliki Tabor, but you must park outside the limits of Staro Selo and explore the village on foot.

WHAT TO SEE & DO

It's possible to fashion a castle tour, a winery tour, or even a Croatian culture tour to take in the numerous sites here. It's difficult to do justice to these beautiful areas without your own transportation or a focused, organized tour, because while public transportation is available, the time spent in transit and making connections is out of proportion to the time you need to see some of the sites.

Kumrovec ★★   Deep in the heart of rural Zagorje, 40km (25 miles) from Zagreb, Staro Selo (Old Village) is best known as the birthplace of Josip Broz Tito (1892–1980), the much-loved President of Yugoslavia, who ruled the country from the end of World War II until his death. A cluster of 25 cottages and numerous farm buildings have been restored to look just as they would have when Tito was a boy, some complete with period furnishing. On weekends, local craftsmen give displays of traditional skills like blacksmithing, carpentry, weaving, and candle-making. The house where Tito was born is easy to spot—there's a larger-than-life bronze sculpture of the man himself, standing in the garden.

Staro Selo. www.mdc.hr/kumrovec/eng/index.html. ✆ **049/225-830.** Admission 20kn. Apr–Sept daily 9am–7pm; Oct–Mar daily 9am–4pm.

Veliki Tabor ★   Dating back to the 12th century, this imposing hilltop fortress reopened to the public in 2011, following a four-year restoration project. Although the main body of the building is medieval, the fortress was reinforced with extra towers during the 16th century. It is built around a central courtyard, overlooked by three floors of colonnaded galleries. Besides an exhibition of period weaponry, paintings, and ceramics, the fortress hosts medieval archery displays.

Kośnićki Hum 1, Desinić. www.veliki-tabor.hr. ✆ **049/374-970.** Admission 20kn. Apr–Sept Tues–Fri 9am–5pm, Sat–Sun 9am–7pm; Mar and Oct Tues–Fri 9am–4pm, Sat–Sun 9am–5pm; Nov–Feb Tues–Sun 9am–4pm.

HER NAME WAS veronika

According to legend, Veronika of Desinić was a beautiful girl who lived in the village at the foot of Veliki Tabor during the 15th century. During that time, the castle was owned by Count Herman II of Celje, a powerful Croatian governor who had a son named Friederich. One day while out riding, Friederich spotted the lovely village maiden and fell in love at first sight. However, Herman didn't approve of the liaison and forbade his son to see the lowborn Veronika. As the young are wont to do, the couple defied Herman and eloped, but their time together was short. When the count found out what Veronika and his son had done, he had his soldiers hunt them down. Friederich was captured immediately and whisked away to a solitary cell where he was imprisoned for four years. Veronika was not so lucky. The count's minions found her and had her brought to Veliki Tabor, where she was jailed and tried as a witch. The judges found Veronika guilty of nothing more sinister than love and ordered her set free. However, Herman was still enraged at being defied and he ordered his servants to drown Veronika in a bucket of water before she left the courtroom. He then had Veronika's body bricked into the walls of the castle's pentagonal tower. In 1982, a female skull was found behind a Veliki Tabor wall during renovation, but there is no proof that it is Veronika's. The skull now resides in Veliki Tabor chapel. It is said that on stormy winter nights, a woman's screams can be heard at the castle.

WHERE TO DINE & STAY

There is no shortage of restaurants in the Zagorje area, though most are very small, family-run affairs. Wherever you stop, it's almost impossible to get a bad meal, especially if you stick to local specialties.

Grešna Gorica ★★ REGIONAL CROATIAN   On a hillside overlooking the medieval castle of Veliki Tabor, you can eat like a lord at this countryside *klet* (tavern). The setting is informal and rustic, with ingredients provided by local farmers. Look for hearty regional dishes like *zagorski štrukli* (baked cheese dumplings), *pečena teletina* (roast veal), and *gulaš od jelena* (venison goulash), all served in generous portions with side salads. You can eat outside in summer, and there's a play area for kids. Note that it's cash only.

Taborgradska 35, Desinić. www.gresna-gorica.com. ℂ **049/343-001.** Entrees 42kn–78kn. Daily 10am–9pm.

Zelenjak ★★ REGIONAL CROATIAN   In a lovely setting on the banks of the River Sutla, this family-run restaurant dates from 1936, and is well known for serving up traditional Zagorje home cooking. Regional favorites, including local trout, veal, and turkey, are highlights. This is a popular venue for wedding parties and excursion groups, and there's a large garden with a playground for kids. The restaurant also has seven basic but comfortable double rooms, so you can even stay overnight.

Risivica 1, Kumrovec. www.zelenjak.com. ℂ **049/550-747.** Entrees 40kn–80kn. Daily 8am–11pm.

Trakošćan

There are many interesting side trips possible along the road between Varaždan and Trakošćan. The sights require a few detours, and perhaps venturing onto winding back roads, but they help complete the picture of the real Croatia.

ESSENTIALS

VISITOR INFORMATION   Information, maps, and lists of events in this region can be obtained at the **Varaždin County Tourist Association** (www.turizam-vzz.hr; ℰ **042/210-096**).

GETTING THERE   There are no direct public buses from Zagreb to Trakošćan. However, even if you don't have your own transport, you can access Trakošćan by taking a bus to Varaždin and backtracking to Trakošćan.

GETTING AROUND   As with most sites in Croatia, walking is the method of choice here.

WHAT TO SEE & DO

Majestic **Trakošćan Castle** is the main draw in this part of northern Croatia.

Trakošćan Castle & Park ★★★   Like a vision from a fairy tale, this dreamy white hilltop castle has pointed turrets and a drawbridge. There's been a castle here since the 13th century, when the fortification served as an observation point over the surrounding valleys, but it was largely remodeled in Romantic style in the 19th century, when it became a place of pure whimsy. Inside, on the first floor, wood-paneled rooms are furnished as they would have been in the 1800s, and walls are hung with portraits of the former owners, the Drašković family. On the upper floors, you can see medieval weaponry and a couple of tapestries. The landscaped parkland below the castle is a lovely place to wander on a sunny afternoon. It's especially beautiful in fall, when the trees take on russet hues. The park centers on an artificial lake, which freezes over in winter.

Near Krapina. www.trakoscan.hr. ℰ **042/796-281.** Castle admission 30kn. Castle open Apr–Oct daily 9am–6pm; Nov–Mar daily 9am–4pm.

Varaždin

Eighteenth-century churches, houses, and public buildings are just some of the charms that make Baroque Varaždin a popular excursion from Zagreb. **Stari Grad** is

HILLTOP wonders

Croatia is world-renowned for its beautiful Adriatic seacoast. Less well known is the treasure trove of mountaintop castles scattered throughout the country. You can find castles in every part of Croatia, from Dalmatia to Istria to Slavonia to Zagorje (the area north and west of Zagreb). Most are in various stages of ruin, although a few have been restored. All of them are fascinating both historically and architecturally—no two castles are the same—and all have spectacular views of the surrounding countryside.

Most Croatian castles served not only as medieval residences but also as fortresses. They were built in the 12th or 13th centuries to defend against the Tartars (Mongols). In the 16th century, they were expanded and refortified as bulwarks against Ottoman Turk invasions. The Turks succeeded in capturing many of the castles, but some were so inaccessible or impenetrable that they held out. Still others experienced much fighting and changed hands several times. By the 17th century, advances in military technology had rendered castle fortresses obsolete. Besides, by that time noble ladies were refusing to live in isolated, damp, drafty stone structures. Those castles not destroyed in battle were abandoned in favor of more luxurious, comfortable manor houses in the valleys.

—Courtesy of Tocher Mitchell

Varaždin's magnificent 12th-century castle, and the centerpiece of any visit to the former Croatian capital, which today is one of northern Croatia's main cultural and economic centers. Varaždin owes its character and its title of "Baroque Capital of Croatia" to an unfortunate 1776 fire that destroyed most of the town (though not its historic center)—a tragedy the town turned to its advantage when the ruined buildings were rebuilt as they appear today.

Trg Kralija Tomislava is Varaždin's main square and it's lined with the best Baroque facades in town, conveniently identified with plaques that explain their lineage. Start at the 15th-century **Town Hall (Gradska Vijećnica),** with its 18th-century clock tower. From there, go south to the **Cathedral of the Assumption,** the town's first Baroque building. The cathedral was built in the mid-18th century by the Jesuits, who also built a monastery among their other contributions to Varaždin.

Every year since 1971, from late September into early October, the town has hosted **Varaždin Baroque Evenings** (www.vbv.hr), a festival of after-dark concerts that attract Baroque music enthusiasts from Croatia and beyond.

Most recently, "The New York Times" listed Varaždin as one of "52 Places to Go in 2014."

ESSENTIALS
VISITOR INFORMATION   Varaždin's **Tourist Association** (www.tourism-varazdin. hr; ✆ **042/210-987**) is at Ivana Padovca 3. The office is open Monday to Friday 8am to 4pm and Saturday 10am to 1pm. The very helpful and friendly staff distribute maps and brochures, and can give suggestions about dining and accommodations in town. They also have information about the region, including Međimurje to the north.

GETTING THERE   Varaždin is about 1 hour's drive northeast from Zagreb along a well-marked highway. The town is also linked to the capital by frequent bus and train service.

GETTING AROUND   Varaždin's central district is a pedestrian area, so you'll have to park on the outskirts of Trg Ban Jelačića north of the sights and walk in. Stari Grad (castle) is a 5-minute walk from the center of town.

WHAT TO SEE & DO
Besides its stunning architecture, Varaždin has several good museums and interesting churches. Restoration is ongoing, but Varaždin is visitor-friendly, with plenty of historical and directional information, as well as a large number of cafes, restaurants, and shops.

Cathedral of the Assumption ★★   Built by the Jesuits between 1642 and 1646, this Baroque cathedral originally incorporated both a church and a Jesuit College. The interior is adorned with frescoes and woodcarvings, and focuses on a monumental main altar, decorated with gilt, marble, statues, and a painting of the Assumption of the Blessed Virgin Mary. Because of its great acoustics, many concerts scheduled during the Varaždin Baroque Evenings (www.vbv.hr) are held here.

Pavlinska 5. ✆ **042/320-180.** Free admission. Mon–Sat 9am–6pm; open for Mass Mon–Sat 7:30am, 9am, and 7pm; Sun 7:30am, 9am, 11am, and 7pm.

Stari Grad ★★★   Set in a green park just a 5-minute walk from the center of town, Gothic-Renaissance Stari Grad is Varaždin's top attraction. Built on the site of an earlier medieval castle, Stari Grad as you see it today dates largely from the 16th century, when the round towers were added to further defend it against the Ottoman Turks. In 1925, the privately owned castle became the Town Museum. Inside, 10 rooms are devoted to a display of period furniture, as well as glassware, ceramics, and clocks, giving you some idea of how the local aristocracy once lived.

Šetalište J.J. Strossmayera 7. www.gmv.hr. ✆ **042/658-754.** Admission 25kn. Tues–Fri 9am–5pm; Sat–Sun 9am–1pm.

Town Cemetery ★ Although it was originally founded in 1773, in 1905 the town cemetery was given a complete makeover. Planted with some 7,000 trees, including ash, birch, cedars, cypresses, magnolias, maples, and red beeches, it would be more like an arboretum than a graveyard were it not for the beautifully carved tombstones and fresh flowers that adorn this peaceful resting place.

West of Varaždin Castle. Free admission. May–Sept 7am–9pm; Mar–Apr and Oct 7am–8pm; Dec–Feb 7am–7pm.

Town Hall ★ On the main square, the Town Hall dates from 1523, and is one of the oldest continually serving buildings of its type in Europe. Through the centuries its appearance has been modified, with its most striking feature, the central clock tower, added in 1791. From mid-May to mid-October, every Saturday between 11am and noon you can see the Varaždin Civil Guards parade in front of the building in bright blue period uniforms.

Trg Kralja Tomislava 1 (better known by locals as the "Korzo").

WHERE TO STAY

Varaždin accommodations are mostly in pensions and private homes, though there is a fairly modern hotel within a few blocks of the town center and others on the town's periphery.

Hotel Istra ★★ On a pedestrian-only street just off the main square, this hotel originally opened in 1911 as the upmarket Grand Hotel Novak. Ideally located in the historic center, the rooms are cozy and peaceful, and the staff friendly and helpful. There is a ground floor cafe, with several tables on the street out front where a hearty breakfast is served.

Kukuljevićeva 6. www.sitra-hotel.hr. ✆ **042/659-659.** 11 units. Double 113€. **Amenities:** Cafe; Wi-Fi (free).

Pansion Maltar ★★ This welcoming family-run B&B occupies two separate buildings, just a 2-minute walk from one another. The reception is in the main building in the cafe, which is also a popular meeting place for locals. The cafe has a small terrace with several outdoor tables and serves a hearty breakfast with fresh fruit, yogurts, and eggs and bacon cooked to order. Most of the rooms are spacious (some have sofa beds, making additional space for kids), but the rooms under the roof have sloping ceilings and can seem a little cramped. The interiors are rustic, with elaborate wood paneling as the main decorative detail.

Franca Preserna 1. www.maltar.hr. ✆ **042/311-100.** 24 units. Double 65€. **Amenities:** Cafe; Wi-Fi (free).

WHERE TO DINE

Verglec ★★ REGIONAL CROATIAN With a great location close to the castle and the tourist information office, this friendly eatery has outdoor tables on a patio with climbing roses. The menu features hearty local dishes, including the house specialties, *paprikaš od divljači* (spicy game stew served with polenta) and *teleći odrezak* (veal baked in a clay pot, with porcini mushrooms, onion, bacon, and sour cream). There are also very tasty and reasonably priced pizzas. The restaurant takes its name from the barrel organ, an example of which sits at the entrance. Occasional *tamburica* (folk music, played on a small stringed instrument) performances are hosted here.

Silvija Strahimira Kranjčevića 12. www.verglec.com. ✆ **042/211-131.** Entrees 40kn–80kn. Sun–Thurs 9am–11pm; Fri–Sat 9am–1am.

Čakovec & Međimurje

Međimurje is sometimes called the "flower garden of Croatia," not just because of its fertile land, but because of its cultural, historical, and economic contributions to the nation's heritage. The region lies northeast of Varaždin and makes up the extreme northern part of Croatia where it borders Slovenia and Hungary. Međimurje's western half is characterized by gently rolling hills, vineyards, and orchards; in the east, flat, fertile farmland contributes a large portion of the country's grain and vegetable production.

The town of **Čakovec** is just 92km (55 miles) from Zagreb and is Međimurje's largest population center. The town's baronial 17th-century castle, which houses a museum, has been largely eclipsed by a slickly updated town square, centering on a fountain and ringed by stores, restaurants, and bars.

ESSENTIALS

VISITOR INFORMATION The **Tourist Board of Međimurje County** (www.tzm. hr; ✆ **040/390-191**) in Čakovec at R. Boškovića 3 provides a well-done map tracing Međimurje's wine road and points of interest. The map also indicates wineries where you can stop to taste or buy local vintages. Much of the same information is available at the **Čakovec Tourist Office** (www.tourism-cakovec.hr; ✆ **040/313-319**) at Trg Kralja Tomislava 2.

GETTING THERE There is frequent bus and train service to Čakovec from Zagreb, but if you want to explore the wine road and areas in rural Međimurje it is best to have your own transportation. Alternatively, people in the tourism office can arrange wine road tours. *Warning:* Međimurje's wineries are all family operations, so it is best to make arrangements in advance to ensure that vintners will be around when you arrive. For bus information, see "Orientation," p. 50, earlier in this chapter.

GETTING AROUND Walking is the best way to tour Čakovec, but if you want to see any of rural Međimurje, you'll need a car and a good map.

WHAT TO SEE & DO

The Međimurje region is one of Croatia's most underrated treasures, virtually ignored by tourists and untouched by the 1991 war. In the northwestern corner of Međimurje County, you can meander around hilly, winding roads that end in family wineries of varying sizes. Međimurje vineyards are places where you can walk the land with its owner and taste the wine he made there. You can sit on the deck of a hilltop dining spot and see Slovenia, Hungary, and Austria beyond the restaurant's Croatian vineyard. Međimurje's **wine road** is a relatively new feature in the area, though many of the wineries on the map have been there for generations. The county has lately gotten more forward-thinking about promoting its assets to tourists. Stop at any of the wineries on the map and you'll be offered a glass of wine and the opportunity to buy a bottle or two. In some cases, the wine tasting is more formal, but generally this is more like Napa, California, before it became popular.

Muzej Međimurja Čakovec ★ On the edge of town, set amid carefully tended parkland, sits Zrinski Castle, the largest medieval fortification in the county. Today's structure is an elegant, white Baroque castle, rebuilt after an earthquake destroyed the previous castle in 1738. The original builders were the Zrinksis, a powerful noble family who played an important role in defending the region from the Ottoman Turks. The building was converted to a museum in 1954 and now exhibits local costumes, paintings, and sculpture.

Trg Republike 5, Čakovec. www.muzej-medjimurja.hr. ℂ **042/313-499.** Admission 20kn. Mon–Fri 8am–3pm; Sat–Sun 10am–1pm.

WHERE TO STAY

Staying the night in Čakovec isn't recommended. There's no nightlife to speak of, and both Varaždin and Čakovec are close enough to Zagreb to be done as day trips, with the morning spent in one and the afternoon in the other.

WHERE TO DINE

Dining in Međimurje is always a treat, especially when you can pair fresh-off-the-farm food with fresh-from-the-winery vintages. This is an ideal place to indulge in local specialties, as the odds are they come straight from the restaurant's backyard.

Katarina ★★ REGIONAL CROATIAN   In the center of town, below a shopping center, Katarina occupies a vaulted red-brick cellar, decorated with the coats of arms of local noble families. It is a little more formal here, tending toward the pretentious side of things. At lunchtime the restaurant attracts tour groups, which can slightly spoil the atmosphere, which is more romantic and locals-oriented at night. The kitchen turns out delicious regional specialties, such as venison in a date and cranberry sauce, or fresh carp from the River Mura, which are best accompanied by local wines. Look out for Lovrec Chardonnay, made by one of the region's top small-scale wine producers.

Matice Hrvatske 6, Čakovec. www.restoran-katarina.com. ℂ **040/311-990.** Entrees 45kn–110kn. Daily 10am–11pm.

Mala Hiža ★★★ REGIONAL CROATIAN   Widely regarded as one of Croatia's top restaurants, Mala Hiža occupies an 1887 building that once stood outside Zagreb but was dismantled and reconstructed here in 1996. The rustic, wood and stone interior is cozy and welcoming, and the service is friendly and professional. The menu celebrates local cooking, with an emphasis on meat. House specialties include *kopun u umaku od vrganja* (capon in a porcini mushroom sauce) and *Međimurska gibanica,* a delicious cake consisting of layers of cream cheese, walnuts, poppy seeds, and apple. The wine list is extremely impressive—you would do well to let the waiter recommend wines produced by Međimurje vintners. On the top floor, under the sloping roof, there are two guest rooms and one apartment, which might be worth considering if you plan on indulging in those local wines over dinner.

Balogovec 1, Mačkovec (4km/2½ miles outside Čakovic). www.mala-hiza.hr. ℂ **040/341-101.** Entrees 55kn–180kn. Mon and Thurs 10am–10pm; Fri–Sun 10am–11pm.

OSIJEK & INLAND CROATIA

F ew visitors to Croatia include the region east of Zagreb in their itineraries. While many of the towns between Zagreb and the country's eastern border on the Danube have not recovered fully from the 1991 war, a visit to this region will help you build a fuller picture of the real Croatia, far away from the hedonistic Dalmatian beaches, exotic islands, and romantic harbor towns.

Inland Croatia is home to vast flat plains and the country's most fertile arable land, along with historic towns, rural wetlands supporting rare bird species, and gastronomic delights capable of wowing even the most jaded traveler. Visitors can walk through **Čigoć,** a village in the **Lonjsko Polje Nature Park,** where whole families of storks nonchalantly regard you from mammoth nests built atop centuries-old timber cottages. You can visit solemn **Jasenovac** and its poignant monument to victims of World War II's ethnic violence and feel the sadness in the air. In **Osijek,** the biggest city in Slavonia, you can take a turn around the promenade along the mighty Drava, and walk the perimeter of the city along the top of what's left of the medieval walls surrounding the Old Town. Then, in **Ilok,** you can taste local wines in a vast, centuries-old wine cellar. It's almost a certainty that you'll cringe at the devastation still visible in **Vukovar,** and you'll shake your head at the unspeakable cruelty that the town's citizens suffered when you visit the touching memorial to victims of a 1991 hospital massacre there.

Inland Croatia's rewards are subtle. This infrequently traveled region is the sum of all the "ah-ha!" moments that happen as you imagine the horror of war while gazing across the Danube at Serbia from a bluff in Ilok. The payoff isn't a transient thrill, but the understanding that something important happened there, something that formed the soul of contemporary Croatia.

ORIENTATION
Visitor Information

All areas of inland Croatia are served by tourist information offices, though not all have local facilities. For general information about the country's interior, in the U.S. start with the **Croatian National Tourist Office** (www. croatia.hr; ✆ **212/279-8672**) at 350 Fifth Ave., Ste. 4003, New York, NY 10118. Travel agencies and tour operators also are good sources of information. Contact information for local tourist information offices is listed throughout this chapter.

Getting There

Except for the smallest and most remote villages, all the cities and towns of inland Croatia are served by bus and train routes linked to or originating in Zagreb. For bus schedules and ticket information, contact **Autobusni Kolodvor (Main Bus Station)** in Zagreb at Avenija M. Držića bb (www.akz.hr; ℰ **060/313-333**). For train information, contact the **Glavni Kolodvor (Main Train Station)** at Trg Kralja Tomislava 12 (www.hzpp.hr; ℰ **060/333-444**). For travelers with a car, the highway system that runs through inland Croatia is modern and efficient. Expect two-lane secondary roads to the smaller towns and some gravel roads in Lonjsko Polje Nature Park.

Getting Around

Even tiny **Čigoć** is reachable by public bus, although once there, walking is the only way to see the nature reserve. Larger cities such as Osijek have public bus or tram networks. They also have connections to the rest of Croatia's larger population centers. However, travel to the rural areas of inland Croatia can be tedious and inconvenient on public transport, so it's easier to tour the region by car, if possible.

SISAK & THE LONJSKO POLJE

The area between **Sisak** and **Jasenovac** is best known for the **Lonjsko Polje Nature Park's** endangered wildlife and 19th-century villages. While the marshland area is a favorite of bird watchers, it is tiny, rustic **Čigoć** that attracts the most traffic. Čigoć is a designated European Stork Village and a living tribute to 19th-century Croatia. On a more somber note, nearby Jasenovac is home to an impressive memorial site, dedicated to the tens of thousands who lost their lives at a brutal concentration camp here during World War II.

Essentials

VISITOR INFORMATION The **Sisak Tourist Office** (www.sisakturist.com; ℰ **044/522-655**) at Rimska bb can provide maps of the town, and information on reaching Čigoć and Lonjsko Polje. In Čigoć, the **Information and Educational Center** (ℰ **044/715-115**) occupies a traditional wooden house; it provides information about Lonjsko Polje Nature Park and can arrange guided tours. In Jasenovac, the **Jasenovac Tourist Office** (www.opcina-jasenovac.hr; ℰ **044/672-490**) is in the city library building. The **Lonjsko Polje Nature Park Administration Office** (www.pp-lonjsko-polje.hr; ℰ **044/672-080**), where you can get maps and information on the park, is at Krapje 30.

GETTING THERE From Sisak, there are seven daily buses to Čigoć, on the edge of Lonjsko Polje Nature Park, with slightly reduced service on weekends.

GETTING AROUND Sisak, Lonjsko Polje, Čigoć, and Jasenovac all are best explored on foot, though a car is handy to reach the Holocaust Museum from Jasenovac, and to thoroughly explore Lonjsko Polje, which covers a huge area between Sisak and Jasenovac.

What to See & Do

Fortresses, storks, and rural villages are the area's main attractions, and each is spectacular in its own way.

Čigoć ★★★ Lying 30km (19 miles) south of Sisak, the quaint village of Čigoć is made up of beautifully restored 200-year-old wooden cottages. It has been declared the

Inland Croatia

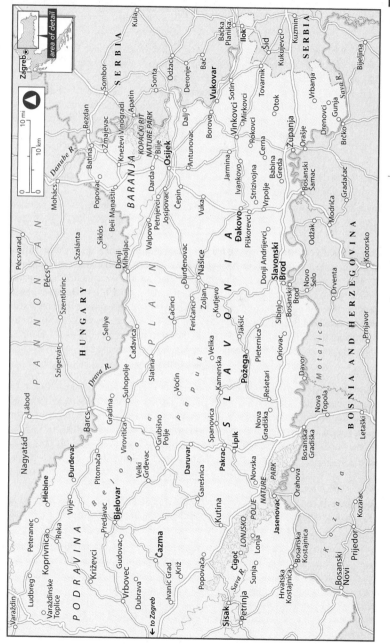

"European Village of Storks," in tribute to the dozens of big, white, docile storks that come to nest here on the steep-pitched rooftops each spring. Nearby, the villages of **Mužilovćica, Lonja,** and **Krapje** are also popular nesting spots.

Čigoć

Jasenovac ★★   The town of Jasenovac is known throughout Croatia for the **Jasenovac Memorial Site.** During World War II, Jasenovac was the biggest concentration camp in the Balkans, and tens of thousands of Serbs, Jews, and Roma (Gypsies) lost their lives here at the hands of the Croatian Ustaše, who were aligned with Hitler's Nazis. The site is marked by a gigantic reinforced-concrete Stone Flower, designed by architect Bogdan Bogdanović, and unveiled in 1966. From the flower, a footpath leads to the Jasenovac museum, passing several train carriages that were used to transport the prisoners to the camp. Inside the museum, you can see a moving multimedia presentation of the horrors these people endured. Darkness prevails, broken only by slideshows of photos from the camp, filmed interviews with survivors, and glass cases displaying abandoned possessions.

Braće Radić 147. www.jusp-jasenovac.hr. ℂ **044/672-319.** Free admission to the Jasenovac Memorial Museum. Mar–Oct Tues–Fri 9am–5pm, Sat–Sun 10am–4pm; Nov–Feb Mon–Fri 9am–4pm.

Lonjsko Polje Nature Park ★★   A favorite destination for bird watchers, **Lonjsko Polje** is Europe's largest wetland nature park, extending southeast from **Sisak** all the way to the Bosnian border. Some 250 bird species have been spotted in the park, and many choose to nest here, including several endangered species. The cormorants, stork, herons, and egrets are of particular interest to bird-watching enthusiasts. Visitors can also take boat rides through the park, and hire bicycles and canoes. The wetlands are flooded from November through April, then turn to rich pastures in the summer, when you can see the wild indigenous **Posavina horses** grazing here.

Lonjsko Polje Nature Park. www.pp-lonjsko-polje.hr. ℂ**044/672-080.** Entrance 40kn. Daily 9am–5pm.

Sisak ★ Sisak, lying 48km (30 miles) southeast of Zagreb, is not a very exciting town in itself, but it makes a good starting point for exploring **Lonjsko Polje.** It lies at the confluence of three rivers, the Sava, Odra, and Kupa, and is known to Croatians for the role it played in preventing the advancing towards Zagreb of the Ottoman Turks, who were defeated here in June, 1593.

Sisak.

Where to Stay

Lonjsko Polje can be done as a day trip from Zagreb, but there are several interesting accommodation options in traditional wooden houses in the old villages of Čigoć and Lonja, on the edge of the nature park.

Etno Village Stara Lonja ★   Accommodations here are in a traditional wooden house in a pastoral setting. The interiors are homey and rustic, with three double rooms and one spacious apartment (sleeping two), each with adjoining bathrooms and kitchenettes. The location is in the village of Lonja, in the heart of Lonjsko Polje Nature Park, 6km (4 miles) southeast of Čigoć. The owners have boats and bicycles to rent, and organize fishing trips, and canoe and photo safaris. Typical local dishes are served for lunch and dinner on request.

Lonja 50, Kratečko. www.etnoselo-staralonja.com. ℂ **044/710-619.** 4 units, 8 beds in total. Double room 44€, plus breakfast 6€ per person. **Amenities:** Bike and boat rental.

WHAT HAPPENED AT jasenovac?

According to United States Holocaust Memorial Museum records, Jasenovac was not just one big camp, but a cluster of five detention centers established by the Ustaša-supported government of the "Independent State of Croatia" during World War II. Collectively, the Jasenovac facility was huge—the third-largest detention camp in Europe—and it was infamous for its deplorable living conditions, unspeakable torture methods, and mass killings. Between 1941 and April, 1945, tens of thousands of Jews, Serbs, Roma (Gypsies), Croats, and miscellaneous political prisoners were brought to Jasenovac via trains from communities across Croatia. They were put to work if they had skills needed by the Axis regime, and savagely tortured and/or murdered if they didn't, according to museum research reports. Jasenovac was especially notorious for its brutal execution methods—strangulation, live burning, live burial, and murder by ax, ropes, and chains—as well as for the alleged participation of local Catholic clergy in those executions. Between the summer of 1942 and March, 1943, Croatian authorities reportedly emptied the camp of its remaining Croatian Jews (about 7,000 people) and sent them to Auschwitz-Birkenau, leaving only non-Jewish prisoners in the camp. The number of people who died here is still heavily debated—in April, 1945, the Ustaša guards deliberately destroyed the camp buildings and records when they realized Tito's partisan troops were closing in on them. Most estimates indicate those killed at Jasenovac's camps number more than 200,000.

EASTERN SLAVONIA

Venture across the fertile expanse that stretches east all the way to Ilok, above the River Drava and the border with Serbia, and you'll eventually see evidence of the violence that affected almost every town and village in the region. Skeletal remains of hothouses once filled with lush greenery and burned-out Borovo factories stand in silent witness to the conflict that left Vukovar and other eastern cities bullet-pocked and destitute. In theory, most areas have now been cleared of landmines, but you will still occasionally see the chilling skull and crossbones signs that indicate possible lingering explosive danger. Many more obvious, jagged scars from the violence provide constant reminders that inland Croatia is still suffering from the effects of the war.

OSIJEK

Osijek lies 283km (175 miles) east of Zagreb, and just 29km (18 miles) from the Hungarian border in the northeastern corner of Croatia. It is the largest city in Slavonia and the fourth largest in the country. During the war, all but 15,000 of Osijek's 80,000 citizens fled the city and sought shelter in other parts of Croatia or in foreign countries. Many have returned, a sign that the local economy is on the upswing and finally recouping some of its former vigor, some 20 years after the end of hostilities.

While the western skyline is a wall of socialist-era structures that belie the city's beauty, the city center is packed with parks, tree-lined streets, and mansions. The center is made up of three distinct areas: **Tvrđa, Upper Town,** and **Lower Town,** each of which has its own personality. The Tvrđa area is Osijek's biggest tourist draw, with its vestiges of Roman culture and Ottoman occupation, and many of the grand old buildings that line its cobbled streets are currently under restoration. It is also the site of Osijek's summer cultural program, which brings in big-name performers from afar.

The city's other highlight is its river walk, a paved path flanking both banks of the Drava that's used by joggers, cyclists, in-line skaters, and people fishing or exercising their dogs. The marina on the river houses hundreds of powerboats and sculls. A small bridge leads to **Copacabana,** the city's most popular beach.

Essentials

VISITOR INFORMATION   Osijek's **tourist office** (www.tzosijek.hr; ✆ 031/203-755) is located at Županijska 2. It can provide maps, brochures, and guidance on the city's sites and surrounding areas.

GETTING THERE   As the largest city in Slavonia, Osijek is served by regular bus and train services that link it to all parts of Croatia. The bus and train stations are adjacent to each other on Trg L. Ružička, at the south end of the town center. See "Getting There" on p. 64.

GETTING AROUND   Osijek has a fast and efficient tram system—the only one still working in Croatia outside the city of Zagreb. Once you're in the center of town, you can walk to all of Osijek's main attractions.

What to See & Do

Visitors can amble through Gornji Grad's 19th-century splendor in the city's northwestern quadrant, or go medieval in Tvrđa, the true center of town, where a fortress created by walls and former barracks is being transformed into a hip university center, with trendy restaurants and a vibrant nightlife.

Church of Sts. Peter and Paul ★★   Located on Osijek's main square, the Church of Sts. Peter and Paul is referred to by locals as the "katedrala" (cathedral), though in reality it is only a parish church. An imposing redbrick neo-Gothic edifice, it was designed by German architect Franz Langenberg and Austrian architect Richard Jordan in the 1890s. The interior is decorated with sacral paintings from the 1930s. The building's most striking feature is its bell tower, standing 82m (270 ft.) tall.

Trg Marina Držica, Gornji Grad. ✆ **031/369-626.** Access during Mass; also daily noon–3pm and 5–5:30pm.

Europska Avenue ★★   This leafy thoroughfare, running from Gornji Grad (Upper Town) to Tvrđa (the Fort), is lined by elegant Vienna Secessionist mansions, built between 1904 and 1905, as well as the delightful Urania Cinema from 1912.

Europska Avenue.

Museum of Slavonia ★   Housed in an imposing Baroque building on Holy Trinity Square, this museum displays local archaeological finds from the prehistoric period up to Roman times. The building was badly damaged during the recent war, but the exhibits survived unscathed.

Trg Svetog Trojstva 6, Tvrđa. www.mso.hr. ✆ **031/250-730.** Admission 15kn. Tues, Wed, and Fri 9am–7pm; Thurs 9am–8pm; Sat–Sun 10am–2pm.

Tvrđa ★★★   Osijek grew up around Tvrđa, a fortress built by the Austrians to accommodate their army in the 18th century (though there has been a settlement here since Roman times). Nowadays it is Osijek's main attraction, and its cobbled streets and proud Baroque buildings are home to several popular little cafes and art galleries. **Holy Trinity Square,** rimmed by carefully restored 18th-century Baroque buildings, is one of the most attractive town squares in Croatia. The main focus here is the plague column, erected in 1729 to ask God for mercy and for the protection of the people of Osijek from the plague.

Tvrđa.

Where to Stay

Osijek's hotel scene is improving, thanks to ambitious renovation projects that have restored or upgraded existing facilities.

Hotel Central ★   On the main square, a 15-minute walk from the train station, this reasonably priced hotel is friendly and welcoming. From the lobby, an impressive staircase with a wrought-iron balustrade leads to the upper floors. The hotel serves a decent continental breakfast with eggs cooked to order, and bicycles are available for use free of charge.

Trg Ante Starčevića 2. www.hotel-central-os.hr. ☎ **031/283-399.** 32 units. 71€ double. Free parking. **Amenities:** Cafe; loaned bikes; Wi-Fi (free).

Hotel Waldinger ★★   In the center of town, this smart 4-star hotel occupies a Vienna Secession building with high ceilings and elegant old-fashioned furniture. The 16 rooms are spacious and comfortable and each has a massage bathtub. The highly regarded Waldinger Restaurant Club serves contemporary cuisine—the house specialty is steak—while the Gradski Podrum in the basement specializes in traditional local dishes. In the courtyard, the adjoining Pension Waldinger offers seven additional rooms at slightly lower prices.

Županijska 8, 31000 Osijek. www.waldinger.hr. ☎ **031/250-450.** 23 units. 85€ double. Free parking. **Amenities:** 2 restaurants; cafe; fitness center; sauna; meeting rooms; Wi-Fi (free).

Where to Dine

Osijek is a mecca for Slavonian cuisine and no matter where you dine, you won't leave hungry. Many restaurants in this part of Croatia are family style, so don't be surprised when huge platters of food arrive for all to share.

Slavonska Kuća ★★★ SLAVONIAN   In Tvrđa, this rustic eatery, furnished with antiques and knickknacks, is popular with locals. There is no English-language menu, but the staff is friendly and will help you choose your meal from a selection of typical Slavonian dishes, such as *fiš paprikaš* (a spicy fish stew) and *čobanac* (goulash, served with gnocchi). As befits a local favorite, the place is cozy and inexpensive.

Kamila Firingera 26. www.slavonskakuca.com. ☎ **031/369-955.** Entrees 45kn–65kn. Mon–Sat 9am–11pm.

Waldinger Restaurant Club ★★ MODERN SLAVONIAN   In the Hotel Waldinger (see above), this rather formal restaurant serves creative contemporary cuisine, including dishes like honey-glazed duck breast with green pepper and orange sauce, or pork tenderloin served with squash seasoned with dill. The menu also has a section dedicated to classic Croatian barbecued meat, and there's an excellent wine list as well. Reservations are recommended.

Županuska 8. ☎ **031/214-671.** Entrees 40kn–150kn. Mon–Sat 11am–11pm; closed in Aug.

BARANJA

The region of Baranja extends beyond Croatia into Serbia and Hungary. On the Croatian side, the land northeast of Osijek and up to Croatia's eastern border is mostly farm and vineyard country, along with the **Kopački Rit** wetlands. Until recently, tourists avoided Baranja because of landmine threats, but most hazards have now been cleared, and Baranja is coming into its own as a center for farm stays, wine tours, and sustainable tourism.

Baranja Wine Road (Općina Kneževi Vinogradi) ★★★   The rural Baranja region is known for its excellent white wines, and this wine route takes you through a landscape of neatly cultivated vineyards to some 20 wineries, where you can taste the local vintages. Some wineries offer food and overnight accommodation as well. As most of these are small, family-run businesses, it is worth calling in advance before you visit, just to confirm there will be someone to receive you.

Hrvatske Republike 3, Kneževi Vinogradi. www.knezevi-vinogradi.hr. ✆ **031/730-938.**

Kopački Rit Nature Park ★★★   Lying 12km (8 miles) northeast of Osijek, Kopački Rit is a vast expanse of marshland lying at the confluence of the River Drava and the River Danube, including two lakes. This is a popular destination for bird watchers, as the wetlands attract some 285 bird species, including eagles, cormorants, and storks. It is possible to tour the park by boat from March through November. The park also offers one-day fishing permits and bicycles for hire.

Titov Dvorac 1, Lug. www.kopacki-rit.com. ✆ **031/752-320.** 20kn adults. Guided boat trip 70kn; guided bird-watching tour 100kn/hr. Daily 9am–5pm.

Where to Stay

The Baranja wine roads can be done comfortably as a day trip from Osijek or Vukovar. An increasing attention to agritourism is providing more options for overnights.

Ivica i Marica Agroturizam ★★   In the heart of the wine region, this agritourism center offers four rooms and five apartments, all beautifully designed, with wooden floors, handmade oak furniture, and some exposed brickwork. The family who runs the center will prepare meals on request, with the option of traditional live music accompaniment. They also keep horses and can arrange carriage rides. ("Ivica i Marica" translates to "Hansel and Gretel" in English, from Grimms' fairy tales). The location is 20km (13 miles) north of Osijek.

Ive Lole Ribara 8A, Karanac. www.ivica-marica.com. ✆ **091/137-37-93.** 9 units. 225kn per person. **Amenities:** Common space; kitchen; excursions.

Where to Dine

Baranjska Kuča ★★ SLAVONIAN   This rustic eatery occupies a former granary located 15km (9 miles) northwest of Kopački Rit. The house specialty is river fish, either carp or pike, which are served along with salad from the garden, locally made cheese, and freshly baked bread. The portions are generous, the prices acceptable, and on Friday and Saturday evenings diners are treated to live Gypsy folk music.

Kolodvorska 99, Karanac. www.baranjska-kuca.com. ✆ **031/720-180.** Entrees 40kn–120kn. Mon–Thurs 11am–10pm; Fri–Sat 11am–1am; Sun 11am–5pm.

VUKOVAR & ILOK

From a historical point of view, **Vukovar** is an important stop on any tour of Croatia, but until recently there wasn't much for tourists to see except ravaged structures languishing after the War of Independence. That's changed dramatically thanks to an infusion of grant money from the Croatian government, in recognition of the area's historical and archaeological significance. Today Vukovar is teeming with archaeologists working to uncover significant vestiges of long-gone civilizations, including Bronze Age settlements on the Danube. Vukovar once was known for its elegance and culture, and until 2006 it served as a powerful, living antiwar advertisement because of the rubble left over from the almost total devastation it suffered during the war that swept through Slavonia in 1991. Some say the city was offered to the Serbs and the Yugoslav People's Army (JNA) as a sacrificial lamb and left a shambles for years as a reminder of that event.

Before the war, Vukovar was a center of industry and manufacturing in Croatia, anchored by the Borovo tire factory. The city also enjoyed a modest tourism trade thanks to its Baroque center, its lovely riverfront location, and its vibrant society. However, Vukovar's large Serbian population (37 percent), and its position just across the river from Serbia, made it a prime target during the war. The result was a three-month-long siege in 1991 that all but leveled the city and emptied it of people.

Vukovar was finally returned to Croatia in 1998, but not all its citizens have come back, perhaps because there isn't much to return to. Many local businesses and homes lie in ruins, jobs are scarce, and some say the government has been slow to rebuild Vukovar because it wants the ravaged city to remain a physical symbol of the brutal siege.

About 39km (24 miles) east of Vukovar, **Ilok** is the easternmost city in Croatia, home to a 13th-century fortress and palace currently under excavation. Ilok also boasts an 18th-century Franciscan monastery that was built inside the walls where St. Ivan Kapestran (St. John Capistrano), a Franciscan warrior monk, successfully defended the banks of the Danube against invading Turks. St. Ivan died at the monastery after a battle in 1456. In 1526, another wave of Turks attacked and eventually prevailed. They held Ilok until 1697, when Austria took over. Subsequently, the Hapsburgs gave the entire town—perhaps as a reward—to Livio Odescalchi, an Italian military officer who helped defeat the Ottoman forces.

Ilock's **Fruška Gora** area has been known since Roman times for its microclimate, which supports lush vineyards and robust wine production. Ilok was taken by the Serbs during the War of Independence, but it was not as badly damaged as Vukovar because almost all its citizens were given the opportunity to flee before the attack. Today, several high-powered investors have become interested in Ilok and have been acquiring its vineyards and wineries. Ilok's wine industry is finally approaching prewar production levels.

THE VUČEDOL dove

The Vučedol Dove, a little pot made around 2500 B.C., is the most famous and popular artifact of Vučedol culture in southeastern Europe. (The culture flourished in this region from 3000 to 2300 B.C., based on a hunter-gatherer lifestyle, with an arts tradition that produced ceramics and possibly worked with copper as well.) The Vučedol Dove is a three-legged bird made of clay, probably originally intended as a fertility symbol. It was uncovered in the early 20th century about 5km (3 miles) south of Vukovar on the Danube. It has been reproduced and kept in almost every home in Croatia since the 1991 war. Regarded as the symbol of Vukovar, after Vukovar's destruction it was adopted by Croatians (at least the nationalists) as a symbol of their suffering. The original is displayed at the Archaeological Museum in Zagreb (see p. 41).

Essentials

VISITOR INFORMATION Vukovar's **tourism office** (www.turizamvukovar.hr; ✆ **032/442-889**) at J. J. Strossmayera 15 is on the way to the Eltz Palace. The Ilok **tourism office** (www.turizamilok.hr; ✆ **032/590-020**) at Trg Nikole Iločkog 2 is in the town center.

GETTING THERE Buses run through the flat farmland and vineyards between Osijek and Vukovar with convenient frequency; they also run between Vukovar and Ilok.

GETTING AROUND Both Vukovar and Ilok are best explored on foot, though Vukovar covers a much larger area. If you want to visit Ilok's wineries, you'll need your own transportation.

What to See & Do

Parts of Vukovar have been restored, but except for the remnants of war, there is little to see here besides the **City Museum** in the restored **Eltz Palace** and the **waterfront war monument.** Ilok and its vineyards suffered less damage in the war, so that city appears more welcoming to tourists.

City Museum ★★ This museum is housed in the 18th-century Baroque Eltz Palace, which once belonged to the powerful Eltz family (Roman Catholic nobility). It was badly damaged during the recent war, but following lengthy restoration, by 2011 it looked as it did before the conflict. The museum traces the history of the city, and also stages temporary art exhibitions and cultural events.

Županijska 2, Vukovar. ✆ **032/441-270.** 25kn. Tues–Fri 10am–6pm; Sat–Sun 10am–1pm.

Iločki Podrumi Winery ★★★ Ilok is home to the Iločki Podrumi, one of the largest wineries in Croatia. It produces predominantly white wines, including Traminac, Graševina, Chardonnay, and Riesling. It is open to the public for tours of the cellars and the vineyards, and for tasting. The setting is peaceful and romantic; besides the cellars, there is also a tasting room, a restaurant, and a souvenir shop. Production was halted during the recent war, but resumed again in 1999. Reputedly Queen Elizabeth II is very fond of the Iločki Podrumi Traminac white wine, and occasionally has a few bottles sent over to London.

Dr. Franje Tudmana 72, Ilok. www.ilocki-podrumi.hr. ✆ **032/590-003.** Guided tour of cellars 30kn; guided tour of cellars and vineyard with wine tasting 70kn. Daily 7am–11pm.

Ovčara Memorial Center ★★★ Lying 5km (3 miles) south of Vukovar, this harrowing memorial records the mass execution of 263 Croat men (and 1 woman), including hospital patients, in November, 1991. Inside, the dark interior shows photos of those who died. A circular space dedicated to a flickering memorial flame is scattered with the bullets that were used.

3km (1¾ miles) southeast of Vukovar on the Ovčara-Brabovo road. ✆ **032/512-345.** Free admission. Daily 10am–5pm.

Where to Stay

Neither Vukovar nor Ilok merits an overnight stay unless you have business in the area. Until recently there has been a dearth of acceptable accommodations in both cities, but that is changing. Both towns are now regular stops for Danube cruise ships, which drop their passengers at the dock in Vukovar to see the town's monument to fallen soldiers. Hotels in both towns are trying hard to respond.

Hotel Lav ★★   The original Hotel Lav dated to 1840, but having been destroyed no less than three times in various wars, the hotel as it appears today opened in 2005. Lying a 5-minute walk from the town center, the rooms are modern and comfortable, and afford views of either the river or the town. The staff is friendly and helpful, and the restaurant serves surprisingly good food, with outdoor tables on the terrace on sunny days.

J. J. Strossmayera 18, Vukovar. www.hotel-lav.hr. ℰ **032/445-100.** 42 units. 127€ double. **Amenities:** Restaurant; bar; cafe; Wi-Fi (free).

Where to Dine

Dining options in Vukovar and Ilok may be improving, but they're almost as thin as hotel options. Casual places serve pizza and simple grilled meat and fish dishes. On the plus side, there's been a surge in agritourism, with home-cooked meals served in very small rural wineries and inns. The area's Graševina white wine is excellent.

Dunavska Golubica ★★ SLAVONIAN   With a lovely terrace overlooking the River Danube, this waterside restaurant is much loved by locals and is a popular venue for wedding celebrations (watch out for Saturdays, which can get a little rowdy). The house specialty is *Mesna Plata Golubica,* a meat platter consisting of pork fillet, chicken breast, bacon, and sausages, served with oven-roasted peppers and potatoes. The house also does a generous fish platter, which combines fried carp, catfish, and grilled trout, and comes with Swiss chard and potatoes. The results are tasty and authentic.

Dunaska Šetnica 1. www.dunavksagolubica.com. ℰ **032/445-434.** Entrees 35kn–70kn. Mon–Thurs 7am–11pm; Fri–Sat 7am–midnight.

ISTRIA

stria is bucolic bliss in primary colors: Dark red earth, glistening blue sea, and rolling hills that tumble into valleys cloaked in shades of green and gold. Its sensory stimulation is packed into a triangular peninsula at the northwestern end of Croatia, dipping into the Adriatic just far enough to catch the seductive Mediterranean climate. Most of Istria's pine- and rosemary-scented coastal landscape is lined with pebble beaches and marinas framed by Venetian-style harbor towns.

Many nations have occupied Istria over the centuries, and it is remarkable that the peninsula has not become a cultural hodgepodge. Instead, the region has embraced the best of every country that contributed to its development through the ages, a philosophy that still informs Istrians' easygoing attitude, tolerance for diversity, love of fine food and wine, and above all, their passion for the land and sea.

Even the most transient tourist will recognize that Istrians have acquired Italian sensibilities without losing their Croatian souls. Istria was part of Italy until World War II, and many residents still communicate with each other in a local dialect that is a lilting blend of Italian and Croatian. Most towns are known by both their Italian and Croatian names and sometimes fool visitors into wondering if they've made an inadvertent border crossing.

Many of the region's coastal towns are dead ringers for Italian fishing villages, and much of the inland landscape's silvery olive groves and deep green vineyards could double as Tuscan. But when you get the bill for a meal or a hotel room, you'll know you're in Croatia and not Italy. The cost of a week in Istria is well below the cost of the same week just across the Adriatic—for now, at least. Istria is fast becoming a desirable destination, and hotels and restaurants in fashionable places like **Rovinj** are upgrading accordingly.

All this and a well-developed tourist infrastructure make Istria ideal for anyone looking for a vacation drenched in nature, history, and sybaritic pursuits. Croatia's tourist bureau color-codes Istria into Blue (coastal) and Green (inland) sectors. Most travelers gravitate to Blue Istria, which contributes big numbers to the region's more than 2.5 million annual visitors (mostly Europeans), the largest single block of tourism in Croatia.

Istria's past is also rich with heroes, conquerors, myths, statesmen and stateswomen, and long agricultural and commercial traditions. This mélange gives every town an intriguing sense of drama, smoothed by Mediterranean joie de vivre.

Those who believe in legends say the Greek hero Jason, his Argonauts, and their sailing ship *Argo* took shelter in the **Bay of Pula** during their quest for the Golden Fleece. Those who believe in miracles say St. Euphemia and her stone sarcophagus somehow washed up on the shores of

Istria

Rovinj shortly after disappearing from Constantinople in A.D. 800. Historians say Bronze Age tribes built primitive settlements in Istria's verdant hills and that an Illyrian tribe known as Histri gave its name to the land. There is no question that ancient Rome prospered from the trade that flowed through Istria's ports, which were lucrative profit centers coveted at one time or another by Venice, Austria-Hungary, and Italy, all of whom vied for control until Marshal Tito declared "game over" and made offshore **Brijuni** his vacation home.

Istria has been through centuries of unrest, and its turbulent past could have resulted in a legacy of despair. Instead, hard times gave birth to tolerance and acceptance in an enchanting region that is geographically rich, historically significant, and a feast for the senses.

ORIENTATION

Visitor Information

Tourism is a multi-million-euro industry in Istria, accounting for more than 40 percent of all tourist overnight stays in Croatia. It's no wonder that Istria County has its own efficient tourist association, with information offices in almost every town from **Pula** on the coast to **Grožnjan** in the interior highlands. The Istria Tourist Board maintains an exceptionally helpful and complete website (www.istra.hr), where you can find information ranging from maps of the region's olive oil roads to an up-to-date schedule of festivals and events in cities throughout Istria. The board also publishes a huge number of brochures, maps, CDs, and guides, some for special-interest travelers such as wine aficionados and spelunkers. Local tourist offices in most Istrian towns are staffed with knowledgeable people who will give you maps, brochures, and even advice on where to go to dinner.

Getting There

BY PLANE Istria's only major airport is at Pula, about 5km (3 miles) northwest of the center of town. It is served by Croatia Airlines (www.croatiaairlines.hr) as well as various European budget airlines in summer. Shuttle buses (30kn) and taxis run between Pula's airport and the town center, where you can connect to other major Istrian towns via bus.

BY BOAT In summer, **Venezia Lines** (www.venezialines.com; ✆ **052/422-8960**) runs regular catamarans from Venice to Poreč, Rovinj, and Pula.

BY BUS **Autotrans** (www.autotrans.hr) runs four daily buses from both Rijeka and Zagreb to Pula, and has other lines to major cities such as Umag and Rovinj on the coast. Most interior towns are connected to the coastal cities by at least one bus per day, but travel by bus to inland Istria can be inconvenient and time-consuming.

BY TRAIN There are train connections between Zagreb and Pula, but these are very slow (7 hr. on average) and may involve several changes. Locals agree that the easiest and most comfortable way to arrive in Istria is either by bus or car. See p. 220 for details on **Croatian Railways** (www.hzpp.hr; ✆ **060/333-444**).

BY CAR Auto travel is by far the most flexible way to see Istria, and the only sensible way to see the interior. There are car-rental agencies in most of the major population centers (see p. 219 for contact information).

Getting Around

BY CAR Parking limitations in Istria's pedestrian-only old towns notwithstanding, access to your own car is the only way to explore the peninsula's side roads that lead to tiny wineries, picturesque villages, and hidden treasures.

BY BUS Regular and frequent bus service links Istria's coastal cities, but service to inland villages is much less convenient for travelers who want to see a lot in a limited amount of time, or who are reluctant to walk a mile or more from a bus stop to get to a site. For information on bus travel in Istria, the best bus company is **Autotrans** (www.autotrans.hr).

BY TRAIN **Croatian Railways** (www.hzpp.hr; ✆ **060/333-444**) has a scanty network of trains in Istria. There is no time-efficient way to explore the interior—or even the coast—by train because schedules are not geared to touring.

PULA (POLA)

This bustling city of 57,200 at the southern tip of Istria is a working port as well as a repository of some of the best Roman ruins in Europe, including a well-preserved **amphitheater** from the 1st century A.D. that is Pula's biggest draw. Pula has other vestiges of Roman occupation (the **Temple of Augustus, Forum,** and **Arch of the Sergi**) that are worth seeing, too. Note that Pula's **Archaeological Museum** is currently closed for renovation and will not reopen before 2016, or maybe even later. Besides its cache of Roman artifacts, Pula's old town is also home to some elegant buildings dating from its centuries spent under Venetian and Austro-Hungarian rule.

Essentials

VISITOR INFORMATION   The **Tourist Information Office** (www.pulainfo.hr; ⓒ **052/219-197**) is off Forum Square at Forum 3, opposite the Temple of Augustus.

GETTING THERE   Pula's busy harbor enjoys healthy shipping and transportation traffic. In summer, several ferry and catamaran routes run to nearby Croatian islands, and even to Venice from here. For more detailed information, see "Getting There" in "Orientation," above.

GETTING AROUND   Pula is a very walkable city even outside its center, and its bus system can get you almost anywhere you need to go in town. Beyond that, a large number of bus routes run from Pula to Rijeka to Zagreb, to the Istrian coastal towns of Rovinj and Poreč, and to Trieste in Italy. If you want to explore the hills and valleys of the Istrian interior, you'll need a car.

What to See & Do

Pula's most interesting sites are its Roman ruins. Of these, the 1st-century amphitheater ("the Arena") is the most impressive.

Aquarium ★★   On Verudela peninsula, 4km (2½ miles) south of the city center, the town aquarium is housed in Fort Verudela, built by the Austrians in 1881. Appealing to children and adults alike, the fort's cool stone chambers hold huge tanks containing various species of fish, complete with rocks, algae, and seaweed. Separate small tanks accommodate other sea creatures such as octopuses and sea horses. The entire exhibition is well laid out, with informative explanations in Croatian and English. There's also a Marine Turtle Rescue Center—injured turtles are released back into the sea as soon as they're healed. The easiest way to reach the aquarium is to take bus no. 2a from Pula's main bus station.

Verudela bb. www.aquarium.hr. ⓒ **052/381-402.** Admission 60kn. Daily Jul–Aug 9am–10pm; Apr–May and Sept 10am–6pm; Oct–Mar 10am–4pm.

Arch of the Sergi ★★★   This arch was built at the end of the 1st century B.C. to honor three male members of the Sergi family, who had fought in the Battle of Actium in 31 B.C. Next to the arch, note the house where Irish author James Joyce once resided—there's a bronze statue of Joyce in front of the building, so you can easily spot it. The arch is near the beginning of the busy car-free shopping street of Sergijevaca.

Ulica Sergijevaca bb.

Arena ★★★   Pula's magnificent Roman amphitheater, known by locals as the Arena, was built between 2 B.C. and A.D. 14. One of the largest remaining buildings of its type in the world (the best known being the far bigger Coliseum in Rome), it has passed through the centuries remarkably well preserved. The outer wall remains intact,

For almost a year (October, 1904 to March, 1905), when he was a young man of 22, Irish author James Joyce lived in Pula, where he taught English to Austro-Hungarian naval officers through the Berlitz School. Today, Joyce is immortalized as a bronze statue, sitting at a table outside the coffee bar Uliks (Ulysses, see p. 80 below), just steps from the building where he taught.

though stone seats from the interior were carried away in medieval times for use on other buildings, including the town cathedral. The Arena was designed to seat 20,000 people (highlighting the importance of Pula during the Roman period), and would have hosted gladiatorial contests. Nowadays, it stages the 2-week Pula Film Festival each July, attracting international names from the world of cinema, in addition to hosting open-air summer concerts (Joss Stone and Status Quo played here in 2014).

Flavijevska bb. www.ami-pula.hr. ⓒ **052/351-300.** Admission 40kn. Daily Jul–Aug 8am–midnight; Apr 8am–8pm; May 8am–9pm; Jun and Sept 8am–9:30pm; Oct 9am–7pm; Nov–Mar 9am–5pm.

Cathedral of the Assumption ★   Built on the site of a former Roman temple, Pula's cathedral started out as a Christian basilica in the 5th century. Visitors can still see ancient mosaic fragments in the interior. The facade and bell tower were added in the 17th century, using in part stone from the Arena.

Kandlerova bb. Jun–Sept daily 9am–noon and 6–9pm; Oct–May open for mass only, Mon–Fri 7:30am and 6pm, Sun 9am and 10:30am.

Temple of Augustus ★★★   Standing on the city's car-free main square, which was once the Roman Forum, the Temple of Augustus was built between 2 B.C. and A.D. 14. The elegant facade comprises an open portico supported by six towering columns. The temple was dedicated to Octavianus Augustus, the first emperor of Rome. With the spread of Christianity, the temple was later converted into a church, but it no longer serves that function. Also on the Forum square you'll find the Pula Tourist Office.

Forum 3. www.ami-pula.hr. Admission 10kn. Jul–Aug Mon–Fri 9am–10pm, Sat–Sun 9am–3pm; mid-May and Jun Mon–Fri 9am–9pm, Sat–Sun 9am–3pm; Sept Mon–Fri 9am–8pm, Sat–Sun 9am–3pm; Oct Mon–Fri 9am–7pm, Sat–Sun 9am–3pm; Nov–Apr closed.

Where to Stay

There is a limited choice of small hotels in the center of Pula, plus plenty of private accommodations (the tourist office in Forum Square can help you with this). You'll find big, modern, waterside hotels south of the center on **Verudela Peninsula,** which can be easily reached by bus no. 2a from the main bus station.

EXPENSIVE

Park Plaza Histria ★★★   This waterside resort hotel lies on Verudela Peninsula, 4km (6½ miles) south of Pula's old town. Fully renovated in 2012, the light and airy guest rooms have a smart, minimalist look, with whitewashed walls and olive green details. The sea-view balconies are a nice additional touch. A fine choice for families, facilities here include a kids' club, in addition to an outdoor pool, a wellness center with sauna, massage, and a large indoor seawater pool, and a coastline dotted with pebble and rock beaches complete with sunbeds. Dining options include a surprisingly good buffet restaurant, plus a rustic tavern serving local seafood specialties overlooking the bay.

Verudela 17. www.parkplaza.com. ℗ **052/590-000.** 368 units. Double Aug from 279€. **Amenities:** 3 restaurants; 4 bars; beach; 2 pools; kids' club; wellness center; Wi-Fi (free).

MODERATE

Amfiteatar ★★   Standing just a 5-minute walk from the ancient Arena and the seafront, this small modern hotel makes an ideal base for sightseeing. Friendly and reasonably priced, it has 18 guest rooms which vary in size, layout, and aspect, but are all peaceful and comfortable. There's a ground floor restaurant serving Mediterranean cuisine, with outdoor tables through summer.

Amfiteatarska 6. www.hotelamfiteatar.com. ℗ **052/375-600.** 18 units. Double Aug from 99€. **Amenities:** Restaurant; Wi-Fi (free).

Scaletta ★★   This welcoming family-run hotel is conveniently located close to the ancient Arena and the seafront. There are just 12 rooms, which are rather small but perfectly adequate for a short stay. Scaletta puts on a tasty continental breakfast, plus eggs cooked to order, in the ground floor restaurant.

Flavijevska 26. www.hotel-scaletta.com. ℗ **052/541-025.** 12 units. Double Aug 98€. **Amenities:** Restaurant; Wi-Fi (free).

Vela Nera ★★★   In the village of Šišan, 5km (3 miles) east of Pula, this stylish hotel-restaurant occupies a converted farmhouse. The owner, Dušan Černjul, is a well-known Istrian chef, and many people come here specifically to eat in his award-winning ground floor restaurant (see below). Upstairs there are 13 spacious rooms and suites, decorated with ultra-minimalist design. The emphasis is on white, with occasional splashes of green, blue, or purple as accents. The hotel opened in 2011 and is set in a lovely Mediterranean garden with a pool. It stays open all year.

Franja Mošnje, Šišan. www.velanera.hr. ℗ **052/300-621.** 13 units. Double Jul–Aug 132€. **Amenities:** Restaurant; bar; pool; Wi-Fi (free).

INEXPENSIVE

Hostel Riva ★   On the seafront, close to the Forum (Pula's main square), this friendly hostel has seven dormitories with parquet floors and high ceilings, sleeping four, six, or eight, plus two private double rooms. There's a guests-only bar serving drinks at outdoor tables in a spacious courtyard, and a fully equipped kitchen where lodgers can prepare their own meals.

Riva 2a. www.rivahostel.com. ℗ **095/827-02-43.** 9 units. Dorm bed Aug 22€. **Amenities:** Bar; kitchen; Wi-Fi (free).

Where to Dine

There are some decent eateries in central Pula, but most of the better seafood restaurants are in the suburbs south of the center.

EXPENSIVE

Vela Nera ★★★ SEAFOOD   Lying 5km (3 miles) east of Pula, in the village of Šišan, this restaurant is well worth the drive or taxi ride. Owner-chef Dušan Černjul is known throughout Croatia for his innovative Mediterranean cuisine, prepared from fresh local ingredients, with an emphasis on seafood. The menu changes frequently, but might include shrimp risotto with champagne and peaches, or sea bream on a bed of spinach and pine nuts. In summer, guests dine on the poolside terrace, while in winter the rustic-chic dining room, complete with an open fireplace, comes into use. The restaurant is part of a stylish 13-room boutique hotel (see above). Reservations are recommended.

Franja Mošnje, Šišan. www.velanera.hr. ℗ **052/300-621.** Entrees 90kn–180kn. Daily 8am–midnight.

MODERATE

Batelina ★★★ SEAFOOD   This small restaurant, owned by a family of fisher-men, seats just 24 inside (in winter) or 50 on the waterside terrace (in summer). The menu is limited to seafood, always fresh that day. Everything is homemade and made with an innovative twist, so you might order crab salad, followed by *brudet* (fish stew served with polenta), and each dish will be unique in its own way. Batelina tends to use types of "poor" fish (and parts of fish) that many other chefs would discard, so you get dishes like monkfish liver with figs in wine, or pâté made from shark liver. Thanks to the sound knowledge of local seafood, the kitchen here can be more experimental than a classically trained chef might be. The wine list focuses on small Istrian produc-ers, and prices are acceptable. Batelina was featured on a 2012 episode of Anthony Bourdain's "No Reservations" and has since drawn foreign diners in addition to loyal locals. Reservations are therefore essential, preferably a few weeks in advance (and note that they don't take credit cards). The location in Banjole is 6km (4 miles) south of Pula, served by bus no. 28.

Čimulje 25, Banjole. ⓒ **052/573-767.** Entrees 90kn–120kn, more for fresh fish by the kilo. Open Sept–Jul, Mon–Sat 5–11pm; closed Aug.

Gina ★★ ISTRIAN   This family-run restaurant dates all the way back to 1969 and is still serving up homemade dishes based on mom's recipes (the namesake Gina). The menu includes delights such as crab ravioli, beef stewed in red wine, and exquisite homemade lavender ice cream with hot fig sauce. There's a cozy dining room with an open fireplace and romantic sunset views over Stoja Bay, 3km (2 miles) southwest of Pula's center.

Stoja 23. www.ginapula.com. ⓒ **052/387-943.** Entrees 65n–150kn. Daily noon–11pm.

INEXPENSIVE

Jupiter ★★ PIZZA   Recommended by locals for the best pizza in town, family-run Jupiter offers a vast choice of pizzas. The house special is topped with tomato, cheese, mushrooms, prosciutto, artichokes, and egg. In summer, tables are arrayed on a sunny terrace with white awnings. Note that it's cash-only here.

Castropola 42. www.pizzeriajupiter.com. ⓒ **052/214-333.** Small pizzas 26kn–45kn. Mon–Fri 10am–midnight; Sat noon–midnight; Sun 1pm–midnight.

Pula After Dark
BARS

Caffe Uliks ★★   Located next to the Arch of the Sergi, this cozy bar celebrates the fact that Irish author James Joyce once lived nearby ("Uliks" is Croatian for "Ulysses"). The bar is open daily till late for coffee and drinks.

Sergijevaca bb. ⓒ **052/219-158.** Mon–Fri 6am–2am; Sat 7am–2am; Sun 9am–2am.

BRIJUNI ARCHIPELAGO (BRIONI)

The 14 islands and islets of the Brijuni Archipelago, northwest of Pula, were mostly used as quarries until Austrian steel magnate Paul Kupelweiser bought the entire area in the late 19th century and cleaned it up in order to build a luxury health resort. After World War II, Marshal Tito chose the islands as the site for his private residence and official retreat. For 3 decades, Tito spent 6 months of the year receiving world leaders and celebrities amid Brijuni's natural wonders. Today, Brijuni is a national park and an official state residence and consequently only two of the islands—**Veliki Brijuni** and **Mali Brijuni**—are open to visitors, who must arrive via organized tours unless they're staying at one of Brijuni's hotels.

Essentials

VISITOR INFORMATION   The **Brijuni National Park Tourist Office** (www. brijuni.hr; ℂ 052/525-888) is at Brijunska 10 in Fažana, on the mainland, 7km (4 miles) northwest of Pula. National park boats depart from Fažana for a standard tour of Brijuni; reservations are essential. Tickets are sold at Fažana (Jul–Aug 210kn; Jun and Sep 200kn; Apr–May and Oct 170kn; Nov–Mar 125kn). In addition, many tourist agencies on Istria's west coast offer day trips to Brijuni. How much you will be able to see will depend on the excursion program of the agency concerned. Make sure that the tour you book allows you to disembark on the islands—some tours merely cruise around Brijuni without docking.

GETTING THERE & GETTING AROUND   You don't need more than a day to see the accessible parts of Brijuni, and it is easy to book an excursion. Tours leave from the dock at **Fažana** (a 30-min. drive from Pula, also accessible by the no. 21 Pula bus) several times per day, depending on the season. The boat ride to Brijuni from Fažana takes about 15 minutes and the guided land tour takes about 4 hours, including breaks and waits for the boat back to shore.

Once you land on **Veliki Brijuni,** you'll be escorted by an English-speaking guide through the park both on foot and on an environmentally friendly tram. The guided tour takes about 4 hours and hits the island's **safari park** (housing exotic animals given to Tito by various world leaders, today including an elephant, zebras, holy cows, and ostriches), a 1st-century **Roman villa complex** at **Verige Bay,** the ruins of a **Byzantine fortress,** and the outskirts of Tito's **White Villa.** Other points of interest are the **"Old Lady,"** a 1,600-year-old olive tree in the running for oldest tree in Croatia; a small archaeological museum, **Church of St. Germaine,** with copies of the **Baška Tablet** and **Dance of the Dead Fresco** from Beram; and the **Josip Broz Tito Memorial Museum,** a natural history museum with a collection of taxidermic animals on the ground floor, and a photo exhibit titled "Tito on Brijuni" on the second floor. The photos document Tito's activities on the island, providing context on his style of leadership. Each image shows Tito shaking hands or dining with a different head of state or celebrity, proof of his ability to use his strong personality to advantage for his country.

VODNJAN (DIGNANO)

Vodnjan, as with other Istrian towns, shows evidence of prehistoric settlements and of cultures from the Illyrians through the Italians, who ruled there before the Croatians took over. Vodnjan eventually developed into the most important center of commerce in southern Istria and remained so until 1856, when Pula became Istria's chief port. Today Vodnjan is a sleepy collection of villages known primarily for a large Italian-speaking population and the **Vodnjan mummies,** a collection of remarkably preserved bodies of holy people that lie in state at **St. Blaise Church** on the main square. Vodnjan is 11km (7 miles) north of Pula.

Essentials

VISITOR INFORMATION   **Vodnjan tourist office** (www.vodnjandignano.com; ℂ 052/511-700) is on the main square, at Narodni Trg 3.

Folk Architecture

The fields of southwest Istria are dotted with small dry-stone huts that look like giant gray beehives. Travelers often wonder what they are. Usually, the huts were built in the corners of fields to serve as shelters for shepherds and storage units for tools. Inside, small stone blocks often provided seating around an open hearth. The door and windows (if any) tend to face away from the prevailing winds and are the only openings in the structure. About 3,000 of these mostly intact folk buildings are in the vicinity of Vodnjan, and many still are in use. Many *kažuni* have been restored and some are even used as summer cottages.

GETTING THERE   See "Getting There," in "Orientation," earlier in this chapter.

GETTING AROUND   Tiny Vodnjan is best explored on foot.

What to See & Do

When you walk through the center of Vodnjan, you'll find that the main street is cobblestoned and uncharacteristically wide. As you get farther in, you'll notice that the town has a distinct medieval appearance with arched doorways; Gothic, Renaissance, and Baroque architecture; offshoot streets the size of alleys; and a main square where **St. Blaise and its campanile**—the tallest in Istria—stand. Vodnjan is only 6km (4 miles) from the sea and 11km (7 miles) from Pula. Today, it is not only a tourist stop between Pula and Rovinj, but also a town caught between Istria's agricultural and commercial traditions. Most visitors don't explore Vodnjan in depth, but instead go straight to St. Blaise Church and its mummies and then head out again.

Church of St. Blaise ★★   You'll find the 18th-century St. Blaise Church in the heart of Vodnjan's old town, on the main square. It is the largest church in Istria and its bell tower is said to be the tallest. Entrance to the church itself is free, but there is a charge to see its main attractions, the treasury of sacral art and the mummies. The treasury lies in the sacristy, and will undoubtedly appeal to those who like things morbid. It contains an astounding collection of some 370 relics (the body parts of saints), mainly bones, though one glass reliquary is said to contain the tongue of St. Mary of Egypt. The treasury also exhibits other religious paraphernalia, most notably a 14th-century polyptych of Blessed Leon Bembo, painted by Paolo Veneziano in 1321. Bembo is said to have had the ability to bring the dead back to life, and his mummified body is on display next door. Behind the altar, hidden by thick velvet curtains, you'll find the infamous Vodnjan mummies. There are six in all, saints dressed in period clothing and displayed in dimly lit glass-fronted cases. Expect to queue if you visit in high season. You'll then have approximately 10 minutes to view the mummies, accompanied by a recorded explanation (in English) about what you are looking at, with some historical background and details about the lives and deaths of the deceased. Note that when visiting churches in Croatia, you should be appropriately dressed—no bare shoulders or bare legs, for men or women, and no hats, either.

Trg Sveti Blaža. ⓒ **052/511-420.** 35kn to view the sacral art and mummies. Daily Jul–Aug Mon–Sat 9am–7pm, Sun 2–7pm.

ROVINJ (ROVIGNO)

Rovinj is one of the most photographed cities in Croatia, especially known for its amazing sunsets. From the air, its location on a promontory makes it look like a fairy-tale village suspended on a pillow of bright blue sea; at ground level, it looks like the quintessential Italian fishing village. Central Rovinj once was an islet, and it wasn't until 1763 that the channel separating it from the mainland was filled in. Today, Rovinj's Old Town is a protected monument and one of Istria's most visited sites. Rovinj has preserved the best of its architectural and cultural legacy by allowing development but keeping industry on the mainland, where the Rovinj tobacco factory and cannery still play major roles in the town's economy. The historic center is a tangle of steep pedestrian streets that are paved with sea-salt-polished cobblestones and marked with signs in Italian and Croatian. These narrow, winding streets are lined with galleries, quaint shops, and excellent restaurants, but it is becoming very touristy and can get extremely crowded. Most streets lead to the town's highest point, where **St. Euphemia Church** and its campanile dominate the skyline. Add to that Rovinj's strong Italian personality, which includes a thriving fleet of small fishing boats, a smattering of Venetian-style piazzas, numerous restaurants, cafes, and atmospheric rock walls set next to pounding waves, and you have a town that's both vibrant and historical.

Essentials

VISITOR INFORMATION The Rovinj **Tourist Information Office** (www.tzgrovinj.hr; ✆ **052/811-566**) is on the seafront at Pino Budicin 12.

GETTING THERE Rovinj is just 16km (25 miles) or a half hour by car north of Pula and linked by well-marked roads. There is frequent bus service to and from Pula; service to and from Croatian cities that range from Zagreb to Dubrovnik; and international service to select cities in Italy, Germany, and Slovenia. The main bus station (www.akz.hr; ✆ **060/333-111**) is at Trg Na Lokvi 6.

GETTING AROUND Rovinj is a wonderful walking city. To visit the Old Town, you'll have to leave your car in the city lot at the north end of town. You can rent a bike at the lot's exit if you don't want to rely on walking, or if you want to try Rovinj's picturesque bike trail. Local buses serve areas outside the Old Town area, as do taxis.

What to See & Do

Rovinj is a browser's paradise, with a labyrinth of streets and cubbyholes to explore. Most of the important sites are in the Old Town, but there are a few places of note outside the center. **Zlatni Rt-Punta Corrente Nature Park** is a fine reason to venture out: It's a densely forested park on a small peninsula southeast of the Old Town and the ACI sailing marina, rimmed with rocky beaches and crisscrossed by hiking paths. The **Lim Fjord** is a flooded karstic canyon less than 16km (10 miles) north of Rovinj. It looks like a ribbon of clear blue-green water framed with forested walls on two sides. Local legend says that pirates used the inlet as a base for ambushing merchant ships. Mussels and oysters are farmed here and you can sample them at any of the restaurants along the road that skirts the area. Excursions to the Lim Fjord leave from Rovinj and Poreč daily, and can be booked directly on the harbor or at local travel agencies.

Balbi Arch ★ From the main square, down by the seafront, you pass through the Balbi Arch to enter Rovinj's picturesque car-free old town. In medieval times, the town was fortified and had seven gates—the Balbi Arch was built in the 17th century on the site of one of those gates. From here, the narrow, winding, cobbled street of Grisia leads up to the Church of St. Euphemia. This used to be Rovinj's most interesting street, renowned for its quirky art galleries, but sadly it has been taken over by commercial souvenir shops selling tourist junk.

At the main square.

Batana House ★★   Rovinj's economy was founded on fishing, and the historic fishing boat of choice was the wooden *batana*. This exhibition uses a contemporary multimedia presentation to illustrate the importance of the batana and local fishing traditions, complete with video, music, and interactive displays. In summer, it is possible to take a nighttime sailing trip around Rovinj peninsula in a batana, which you can arrange through this petite museum.

Obala P. Budičina 2. www.batana.org. ℂ **052/812-593.** Admission 10kn. Jun–Sept daily 10am–2pm and 7–11pm; Mar–May and Oct–Dec Tues–Sun 10am–1pm and 4–6pm. Closed Jan–Feb.

Rovinj Heritage Museum ★   Close to Balbi Arch, in a Baroque palace which once belonged to a family of Italian aristocrats, this museum opened in 1954 as a place to display local works of art. Inside you can see a curious mixture of archaeological finds, Old Master paintings, and works by contemporary artists.

Trg Maršala Tita 11. www.muzej-rovinj.com. ℂ **052/816-720.** Admission 15kn. Mid-Jun to mid-Sept, Tues–Sun 9am–2pm and 7–10pm, closed Mon; mid-Sep to mid-Jun, Tues–Sat 10am–1pm, closed Sun–Mon.

St. Euphemia Church ★★   This hilltop church, built in the Baroque style between 1725 and 1736, is dedicated to Rovinj's co-patron saint, Euphemia (the other patron saint being St. George). Local legend has it that a marble sarcophagus containing Euphemia's body miraculously washed up from the sea in Rovinj in A.D. 800, having disappeared from Constantinople, where she had been honored as a saint following her martyrdom in A.D. 304. The sarcophagus is now on display inside the church, which was built specially to house it. The 61m (200 ft.) bell tower, a copy of St. Mark's in Venice, is one of the tallest campaniles in Istria—you can climb to the top for amazing views over the sea and hinterland.

Petro Stankovića. ℂ **052/815-615.** Admission to bell tower 20kn. May–Oct daily 10am–6pm; only during Mass other times.

Where to Stay

Rovinj is Istria's top destination in terms of range and quality of places to stay. The Maistra group is currently renovating and upgrading Yugoslav-era hotels along the coast, while locals are refurbishing old townhouses to make small boutique hotels. Visitors can therefore choose from 5-star waterside hotels with contemporary design, or quaint rooms furnished with antiques in the narrow cobbled alleys of old Rovinj.

VERY EXPENSIVE

Hotel Lone ★★★   In Zlatni Rt Park, overlooking the sea, Hotel Lone is Croatia's first and only member of the "Design Hotels" network. Designed by Zagreb-based architects 3LHD, it opened in 2011, complete with contemporary furniture and funky artwork and installations by local designers. Room interiors feature clean lines and sophisticated palettes. The Jazz room category doesn't have sea views, but makes up for it with balconies enhanced with infinity pools and private massaging bathtubs. The property has a vast and luxurious spa with an indoor seawater pool (ideal for winter visits) and an outdoor pool set amid lush landscaping with lots of trees for natural

THE LEGEND OF st. euphemia

St. Euphemia was probably just a teenager living in 4th-century Chalcedon near Constantinople when she fell victim to Diocletian's campaign to purge the Roman Empire of Christianity. The daughter of a prominent Chalcedon citizen, she was imprisoned with 49 other Christians when they refused to worship the town idol and deny their faith. Because of her refusal to deny Christ, the young Euphemia was tortured with fire and snakes and then had her bones broken on a wheel before being thrown to the lions, which miraculously didn't devour her body after they killed her. Christians recovered Euphemia's body and buried it in Chalcedon, but in the 7th century they moved it to Constantinople because they feared the body would be defiled by Persian invaders. In Constantinople, the Christian emperor Constantine ordered that a church be built in Euphemia's honor. Her sarcophagus remained there until A.D. 800, when the faithful again relocated it because they feared that the Emperor Nicephorus I might remove it to parts unknown.

No one knows for sure how the coffin and its contents got to Rovinj, but one legend says that Christian fishermen probably put it on their boats in an attempt to get it to a safe place, and then somehow lost it at sea. The legend goes on to attribute Euphemia's arrival on the shores of Rovinj to a miracle. One local legend further states that villagers who found the coffin couldn't budge the heavy stone container from the surf no matter how hard they tried. In the end it was a young boy with a pair of calves who was able to get the coffin out of the water after St. Euphemia appeared to him in a dream and told him what to do. The coffin is now a symbol of Rovinj and rests behind the altar in the right aisle of the church that carries the saint's name at the top of Rovinj's highest hill. Worshippers come to pray at the site daily, especially on September 16, the day that St. Euphemia died in A.D. 304.

shade. In summer 2014, the hotel saw the opening of Mulini Beach, with sunbeds and a seafront lounge-bar. The hotel appeals primarily to 30-somethings, traveling either as couples or young families with kids. It's located about a 15-minute walk from Rovinj's Old Town.

Luje Adamovića 31. www.lonehotel.com. ℂ **052/632-000.** 248 units. Double Jul–Aug 351€. **Amenities:** 3 restaurants; 3 bars; beach; 2 pools; spa; Wi-Fi (free).

Hotel Monte Mulini ★★★   Next to Hotel Lone, but hidden from it by trees, Monte Mulini overlooks the deep blue Adriatic. The main building, opened in 2009, has rooms which all feature large balconies. Spacious suites can be found in a separate building surrounded by gardens planted with fragrant herbs. For foodies, the highlight of a stay here is the a la carte restaurant Corsican Wine Vault, which serves beautifully presented creative Mediterranean cuisine and fine wines under the auspices of chef Tomislav Gretić. In the Art Wellness spa center, be sure to try the "floating room," where a tub is filled with water with such a high concentration of salt that it creates the Dead Sea effect, inducing a sensation of weightlessness. There's also a freeform outdoor pool and bathing area, and, as of summer 2014, the hotel shares the new Mulini Beach with Hotel Lone. Note that Monte Mulini attracts a slightly older clientele, generally 50-somethings and upwards.

A Smareglia 3. www.montemulinihotel.com. ℂ **052/636-000.** 113 units. Double room Aug 408€. **Amenities:** 2 restaurants; 2 bars; 4 outdoor pools; spa; Wi-Fi (free).

EXPENSIVE

Villa Valdibora ★★ In the heart of the car-free Old Town in a cluster of 17th-century buildings, Villa Valdibora holds five spacious apartments and three studios. More an upmarket B&B than a hotel, the property is welcoming and romantic, with rooms combining antique furniture and modern conveniences like coffee machines, icemakers, and hydro-massage showers. There's a small spa and gym in the basement, and a breakfast room, although no restaurant. Service is personalized—on arrival, staff will collect you in an electric golf cart and help with your luggage. Bikes are available for rent.

Silvana Chiurca 8. www.valdibora.com. ℂ 052/845-040. 8 units. Double Aug 229€. **Amenities:** Fitness room; spa; bike rental; Wi-Fi (free).

MODERATE

Casa Garzotto ★★ This small boutique hotel in the Old Town has four studios, six rooms, and two suites, spread across four separate Venetian-era buildings. Most units have wooden floors, and all are furnished with period antiques—two of the studios even have open fireplaces, making them ideal for winter visits. There is also a lounge-bar that serves a good breakfast, with everything locally sourced and home-made. Bicycles are available for guests' use.

Via Garzotto 8. www.casa-garzotto.com. ℂ 052/811-8440. 12 units. Double Jul–Aug 120€. **Amenities:** Bicycles; sauna; Wi-Fi (free).

Hotel Adriatic ★★ In a splendid location in the Old Town overlooking the fishing harbor, the Adriatic is Rovinj's oldest hotel, dating back to 1912. An Austro-Hungarian–style building, it closed for renovation in October 2014, with a scheduled reopening in summer 2015, complete with an upgrade to 4-star status. The rooms have lovely sea views and the ground floor bar-restaurant has a waterside terrace.

Trg Maršala Tita 5. www.maistra.hr. ℂ 052/800-250. 27 units. Double Aug 154€. **Amenities:** Restaurant; cafe; Wi-Fi (free).

La Grisa ★★ In the medieval hill town of Bale, 12 km (8 miles) inland from Rovinj, this family-run boutique hotel occupies a carefully renovated old building. Opened in 2011, the rooms combine existing elements like wooden floors and exposed stonework with contemporary furnishings. A generous breakfast is served in the hotel restaurant, with outdoor tables on a lovely terrace in summer. Reasonably priced Istrian meat and seafood specialties are served later in the day.

Grisa 23, Bale. www.la-grisa.com. ℂ 052/824-501. 22 units. Double Jul–Aug 96€. **Amenities:** Restaurant; Wi-Fi (free).

INEXPENSIVE

Pansion Baron Gautsch ★★ A 10-minute walk to Rovinj's Old Town, this welcoming and peaceful B&B has 16 basic but comfortable rooms, most with balconies. A nice breakfast is served, and up top there's a communal roof terrace affording amazing views of the Church of St. Euphemia rising above town. The perch is especially enchanting at night.

I.M. Ronjgova 7. www.baron-gautsch.com. ℂ 091/914-96-11. 16 units. Double Aug 78€. **Amenities:** Wi-Fi (free).

Where to Dine

The restaurants that line the waterfront are touristy and predictable, and their prices are inflated. However, all serve respectable seafood and excellent pizza and pasta. Venture uphill into the warren of streets or across the bay for menus that go beyond the expected.

EXPENSIVE

Monte ★★★ MODERN CROATIAN Set in a romantic garden close to Rovinj's hilltop church, dinner at upmarket Monte is a multisensory experience, stimulating sight, taste, and scent. The menu features exquisitely presented nouvelle cuisine, with an emphasis on Istrian produce and Adriatic seafood. Owner-chef Danijel Dado Dekić experiments with unusual combinations of flavors and textures, so while your waiter or waitress will explain each dish to you in detail, it's still challenging to try to identify the different elements. You might begin with octopus and artichoke with lentil salad, followed by monkfish served with squid croquettes and a purée of Swiss chard and scallops. The presentation of the food is likewise surprising and sophisticated. There's an excellent sommelier, and the setting is divine, in a walled garden draped with bougainvillea on a terrace shaded by awnings and lit by chandeliers. To try a selection of dishes, opt for the seven-course degustation menu, with optional wine pairings. There are also vegetarian options and (surprisingly) a children's menu. Reservations are recommended.

Montalbano 75. www.monte.hr. ☎ **052/830-203.** Entrees 220kn–280kn, 7-course degustation menu 549kn. Jun–Sept daily noon–2:30pm and 6:30–10pm; Oct–May Mon–Fri 6:30–10pm, Sat–Sun noon–2:30pm and 6:30–10pm.

MODERATE

Giannino ★★★ SEAFOOD This cozy family-run restaurant, dating from 1982, has outdoor tables on a small square and offers respite from the more touristy restaurants on the seafront. House specialties include Istrian pasta dishes, *list sa tartufima* (sole with truffles), and *brancin* (sea bass) baked in an oven with cherry tomatoes, zucchini, and potatoes. Order a carafe of the house white, Malvazija, to accompany your meal.

A. Ferri 38. ☎ **052/813-402.** Entrees 80kn–140kn. Apr–Dec Tues–Sun 10am–3pm and 6–11pm. Closed Jan–Mar.

La Puntulina ★★★ ISTRIAN This romantic family-run restaurant serves authentic local seafood dishes and fine wine on a stone terrace that affords magnificent sea views. It does get busy here, so you may have to wait for a table. On a lower level, down by the water, wine and cocktails are served, making an ideal venue for a sunset aperitif.

Sv. Križa 38. ☎ **052/813-186.** Entrees 80kn–150kn, more for fish by the kilo. Apr–Oct daily noon–midnight.

Masera ★★ ISTRIAN A 15-minute drive east of the Old Town, within the grounds of the tennis center, Masera offers fine dining at affordable prices. The chef prepares gourmet cuisine from traditional Istrian ingredients: Expect beautifully presented dishes such as sea bass carpaccio, fettuccine with truffles, and fresh fish grilled whole and filleted at the table by your waiter (service is impeccable). The dining room combines traditional exposed stonework and wooden beams with modern furniture.

Polari 14. www.masera.hr. ☎ **052/434-391.** Entrees 65kn–120kn, more for fish by the kilo. Apr–Sept daily 2pm–midnight; Oct–Dec and Feb–Mar daily 3–11pm; closed Jan.

INEXPENSIVE

Da Sergio ★ PIZZA In a quaint building with ochre-colored walls and a woodbeamed ceiling, this pizzeria stands on Grisia, a cobbled alley that leads up to Rovinj's hilltop church. The dining room is packed with long wooden tables and benches, and can feel cramped when busy. Unfortunately there is no outdoor seating. Come here for Italian-style thin-crust pizzas: Try the Istriana, topped with *pršut* (prosciutto) and sheep's cheese.

Grisia 11. ☎ **052/816-949.** Pizza 40kn–85kn. Apr–Oct daily noon–3pm and 6–11pm.

Kantinon ★★★ SEAFOOD   Kantinon occupies an old stone warehouse which was transformed into a chic but unpretentious eatery in spring 2013. The interior is simply decorated, with a flagstone floor, bare wooden tables and benches, and big black-and-white photos of Rovinj as it once was. The menu is written like a newspaper; everything it offers is made exclusively from fresh seafood and local seasonal ingredients. The venue overlooks the harbor in Rovinj's Old Town.

Obala A. Rismondo bb. ✆ **052/816-075.** Entrees 55kn–110kn. Open Wed–Sun noon–10pm; closed Mon–Tues.

Rovinj After Dark

Valentino's ★★ COCKTAILS   Close to Puntulina restaurant, this chic little bar serves champagne and cocktails down by the water's edge, where guests sit on cushions strewn on the rocks. It is incredibly romantic, although a little pricey. You'll find it down a steep staircase leading off Križa Street—you can spot it from the underwater lights, which give the sea a marvelous turquoise glow.

Sv. Križa 28. www.valentino-rovinj.com. ✆**052/830-683.** Apr–May daily noon–midnight; Jun–Sept daily 6pm–1am.

POREČ (PARENZO)

"Something for everyone" could be Poreč's motto—the seaside resort offers a wide variety of attractions, from a UNESCO-listed Byzantine basilica complex to endless shopping opportunities to slick resort hotels so crammed with activities and services that you'd think you were in Disney World. Poreč courts tourism, supports tourism, and profits from tourism, but the town and surrounding area still manage to intrigue, perhaps because they are a seamless blend of medieval heritage, a well-oiled service industry, idyllic vineyards and olive groves, and blatant commercialism. Old Town is the epicenter of this tourist mecca, with immaculate cobblestone streets, precisely clipped plantings, multilingual signs explaining all points of interest, and enough jewelry stores and *gelaterias* (Italian ice cream shop) for every tourist in Croatia.

Essentials

VISITOR INFORMATION   The Poreč Tourist Information Office (www.to-porec.com; ✆ 052/451-293) is at Zagrebačka 9.

GETTING THERE   See "Getting There" in "Orientation," earlier in this chapter.

GETTING AROUND   Poreč's Old Town is easy to navigate on foot, though its end-to-end shopping opportunities might slow you down. Buses serve the Lanterna complex south of town (the bus station is .5km/¼ mile from the town center) as well as nearby towns, but a car is necessary if you want to stay outside of the population center, or if you want to explore the surrounding area.

What to See & Do

Poreč's Old Town is small, but it is packed with treasures, chief of which is the **Euphrasius Basilica** and its stunning mosaics. The rest of Old Town's attractions pale in comparison, although they're interesting enough to warrant a walk-through. *Note:* The Poreč **Regional Museum** (www.muzejporec.hr) is closed for renovation and will not reopen before 2017.

Baredine Cave ★★★   Lying 7km (4 miles) northeast of Poreč, on the road to Višjan, these limestone caves are filled with stalactites and stalagmites, and make an

THE LEGEND OF baredine cave

Baredine's love story is a sad one that originated in the 13th century. According to the legend, a highborn young man named Gabriel fell in love with a beautiful shepherdess named Milka from Nova Vas. Gabriel's mother didn't approve of her son consorting with a mere farm girl and when she couldn't dissuade him from the romance, she hired bandits to kill the girl. Instead of killing her, the robbers took the mother's three pieces of gold and threw Milka into Baredine Cave. When Gabriel discovered the treachery, he supposedly tried to rescue his beloved and disappeared. (Gabriel's horse was found wandering near the cave, so it was presumed he had gone in to find Milka, but neither was heard from again.) The legend goes on to say that Milka's body eventually turned to stone in the cave and is slowly sinking to another chamber where Gabriel has been waiting for her for centuries.

interesting and unusual day trip out of town. The admission ticket includes the services of a guide, who will give you a 40-minute tour of the underground chambers and tell you of a tragic love story related to the caves (see box).

Nova Vas. www.baredine.com. ✆ **052/421-333.** Admission 60kn. Daily July–Aug 9:30am–6pm; May–June and Sept 10am–5pm; Apr and Oct 10am–4pm; Nov–Mar closed.

Euphrasius Basilica ★★★   In the heart of the old town, this 6th-century basilica is best known for the stunning golden Byzantine mosaics above the main apse, which have earned it the status of a UNESCO world heritage site. The complex also includes an atrium, an octagonal baptistery, a 16th-century bell tower, and the bishop's palace, which houses a small museum of religious art.

Eufrazijeva Ulica 22. Admission 40kn. Jun–Sep daily 8:30am–8pm; Oct–May 9am–6pm.

St. Nicholas Island ★★   You'll find some of Poreč's better bathing spots—concrete platforms lined with sunbeds, offering easy access into the sea—on this tiny island, a 5-minute taxi-boat ride from the harbor. The sea here has a Blue Flag certification for cleanliness and high environmental standards.

In summer, taxi boats leave the dock every ½ hr.

Trg Marafor ★   At the tip of the Old Town peninsula is the square Trg Marafor, where you'll find the remains of Poreč's Roman Forum and the crumbling ruins of two Roman temples dedicated to Mars and Neptune. Today the square is the site of several lively cafes and cocktail bars.

Trg Marafor.

Where to Stay

Poreč is the most visited destination in Istria, and as such it has a wide inventory of accommodations. The area offers everything from luxurious all-inclusive hotels with sophisticated entertainment to rooms in rural homes surrounded by olive groves and vineyards. Most hotels in Poreč are managed by a large Croatian chain, but there is a lot of variety available, especially if you opt for a small hotel outside the center. Nothing within a couple of miles of the center can be classified as inexpensive. No matter which option you choose, you'll have to book well in advance if you plan to stay any time during the "season," which runs through July and August.

EXPENSIVE

Grand Hotel Palazzo ★★   Dating back to 1910, when it opened as Poreč's first hotel (originally called the Riviera), this building reopened as the Palazzo in 2009 following a total renovation. Overlooking the Adriatic, on the Old Town peninsula, most of the property's 70 rooms and all four of its vast suites have sublime sea views. Interiors are light, with earth tone accents and attractive wooden furniture. The majority of en suite bathrooms come with separate showers and tubs. Note that the hotel's ground floor Café del Mar has a waterside terrace which stays open into the early hours—rooms above it tend to suffer from the late-night noise. The hotel also has a plush spa and a heated outdoor pool.

Obala Maršala Tita 24. www.hotel-palazzo.hr. © **052/858-800.** 74 units. Double Aug from 181€. **Amenities:** Restaurant; cafe; bar; outdoor pool; spa; Wi-Fi (free).

Hotel San Rocco ★★★   A 15-minute drive from Poreč, this heritage boutique hotel occupies a carefully renovated old stone farmhouse in the peaceful village of Brtonigla. The 14 guest rooms feature wooden beamed ceilings and slick, spacious bathrooms with either tubs or hydro-massage showers. The property's gourmet restaurant serves local specialties prepared from fresh seasonal produce with creative flair—the degustation menu is recommended. There's a pool in the garden, plus a small wellness center with an indoor pool and sauna.

Srednja Ulica 2, Brtonigla. www.san-rocco.hr. © 052/725-000. 14 units. Double B&B Jul–Aug from 189€. **Amenities:** Restaurant; bar; pool; sauna; wine cellar; access for those w/limited mobility; Wi-Fi (free).

Valamar Riviera Poreč ★★   In a prime position on the palm-lined seafront promenade, the Riviera reopened after renovation in 2010. The rooms and suites have wooden floors, pine furniture, and blue fabrics that discreetly suggest a nautical theme, which runs throughout the hotel. There's a ground floor restaurant and cafe with tables on a waterside terrace, complete with big white parasols and potted olive trees. The Riviera receives many return visitors, the majority in their 50s and older, most agreeing that it's worth paying a little extra for a sea view and balcony.

Maršala Tita 15, Poreč. www.valamar.hr. © 052/400-800. 105 units. Double Jul from 145€. **Amenities:** Restaurant; cafe; wine bar; Wi-Fi (free).

MODERATE

Kaštel Pension and Restaurant ★★   In the village of Kaštelir, 7km (4 miles) northwest of Poreč, this 18th-century house, complete with exposed stone walls and wooden beams, has been carefully renovated to make a small pension. There are four cozy rooms and apartments, each individually furnished with rustic antiques. The excellent restaurant serves a delicious breakfast, with fresh fruit, homemade croissants and pancakes, and eggs cooked to order. The restaurant is also open for lunch and dinner, the menu highlighting Istrian specialties made from the pension's own farm produce.

Kaštelir 28, Kaštelir. www.kastel-kastelir.hr. © **052/455-310.** 4 units. Double Aug 96€. **Amenities:** Restaurant; Wi-Fi (free).

INEXPENSIVE

Hostel Papalinna ★★   Opened in May 2014, this hostel stands out in the Old Town, one block back from the seafront and just a 5-minute walk from the bus station. The property is large and modern and extends over two floors, with dormitories holding either four or eight bunk beds. Each bed has a privacy curtain, a shelf, a reading light, and two power sources. The staff is friendly and helpful, too.

Vladimira Nazora 9. www.hostelpapalinna.com. ℰ **052/400-900.** 22 units. Dorm bed from 25€ Jul–Aug. **Amenities:** Bar in courtyard; Wi-Fi (free).

Where to Dine

Dining in Old Town Poreč tends to be a one-note experience with only a couple of exceptions. Almost all the restaurants here rely on pizza, pasta, and grilled seafood for menu mainstays. If you want to taste authentic grilled lamb or more unusual Istrian preparations, your best bet is to get out of town.

EXPENSIVE

Divino ★★★ MODERN ISTRIAN Divino's location is superb, with a front terrace overlooking the yachts moored up along the seafront in Poreč's Old Town. The menu includes upmarket dishes such as tuna carpaccio and Boškarin steak (Boškarin being a breed of cow native to Istria). It's pricey, but worth it, with professional service, and a crowd centered on wealthy summer visitors. In winter, a fixed-price menu is added to attract locals.

Obala Maršala Tita 20. www.divino.hr. ℰ **052/453-030.** Entrees 120kn–160kn, more for seafood sold by the kilo. Daily 11am–midnight.

Sveti Nikola ★★★ MODERN ISTRIAN On the seafront in the Old Town, overlooking the sailing boats that moor up along the quay, Sveti Nikola is chic and rather formal. The interior has Persian rugs and white tablecloths, while the sidewalk seating offers good people-watching opportunities. Try the cream of scampi soup, followed by the red mullet stuffed with black truffles—everything comes to the table beautifully presented, although expect a slightly hefty bill at the end of your meal.

Obala Maršala Tita 23. www.svnikola.com. ℰ **052/423-018.** Entrees 110kn–160kn, more for seafood sold by the kilo. Daily 11am–1am.

MODERATE

Restoran Hrast ★ SEAFOOD Hrast may be unassuming from the outside, but it has a lovely waterfront terrace affording spectacular views back to Poreč across the bay. Founded in 1979, the restaurant has a firm local following and is noted for fresh seafood, with favorites like fried calamari and black gnocchi with prawns and arugula. The house white, an Istrian Malvazija, is quite palatable as well. The restaurant is on the coast, a 5-minute walk north of the Old Town.

Nikole Tesle 13. ℰ **052/433-797.** Entrees 40kn–95kn, more for fish by the kilo. Mon–Sat 11am–11pm; closed Sun.

INEXPENSIVE

Pizzeria Nono ★ PIZZA Poreč has a limited choice of reliable inexpensive eateries. Nono, located opposite the tourist office, is a welcome exception, with a warm atmosphere and delicious food, which is much loved by locals, keeping it busy all through the year. Most people come here for the pizzas, which are excellent, but the menu also includes pastas, salads, and barbecued meats, plus a succulent steak in green pepper sauce. In nice weather, the outdoor seating is very pleasant. Cash only.

Zagrebačka 4. ℰ **052/453-088.** Pizzas 45kn–80kn. Daily noon–11pm.

Poreč After Dark

BARS & CLUBS

Byblos ★★   The biggest nightclub in the region, Byblos is popular with locals and visitors alike. It hosts international guest DJs and live concerts—Fat Boy Slim played here in July 2014, and Goran Bregović in August 2014. You'll find the club within the Zelena Laguna resort complex, on the coast, south of the Old Town.

Zelena Laguna. www.byblos.hr. ✆ **091/292-56-78.** Jun–Aug daily 11pm–6am.

Epoca ★★   Epoca is busy all the day through, serving coffee, cocktails, and local wines by the glass. It stands between the Hotel Palazzo and the Sveti Nikola restaurant, with an open-air terrace on the seafront promenade.

Obala Maršala Tita 24. www.epoca.hr. ✆ **098/367-942.** Daily 8am–2am.

UMAG (UMAGO) & SAVUDRIJA (SALVORE)

Umag hits visitors in the face with its huge modern hotels, concrete beach, and banners everywhere advertising the city's festivals, concerts, restaurants, and annual international ATP Croatia Open tennis tournament. The crowded waterfront shops look more like bus station concessions than resort boutiques, and the atmosphere shouts "vacation package deal." **Savudrija,** on the other hand, is a hard-to-find, lazy, rural village on the sea with nothing but vineyards and farmland at its back. The area's main boost was the opening of the ultra-luxurious Kempinski Hotel Adriatic on the edge of town in August, 2009: a sprawling resort with a plush spa and the 18-hole Golf Club Adriatic.

Essentials

VISITOR INFORMATION   Umag's **tourist information office** (www.colours ofistria.com; ✆ **052/741-363**) is at Trgovăka 6.

GETTING THERE   See "Getting There" in "Orientation," earlier in this chapter.

GETTING AROUND   Most of Umag's tourist activity is at the waterfront or in Old Town, where everything is within walking distance. Airport transfers to the Kempinski Hotel Adriatic can be made via land, sea, or air—the hotel has its own heliport. Access roads traverse vineyards from the main road to the hotel and while there is no marina as yet, it is possible for boats to dock nearby.

What to See & Do

Umag's beaches are more like concrete slabs in the water and not very appealing, but most of the big hotels have a full slate of activities and sports available, as well as programs for children. Savudrija in far northwest Istria is the newest darling among the region's many vacation towns, due to its proximity to the Slovene border and Italy (2 hr. by catamaran from Venice), coupled with the opening of the aforementioned Kempinski.

Golf Club Adriatic ★★★   Part of the Kempinski Hotel Adriatic complex, this 18-hole golf course was designed by Austrian landscape architect Diethard Fahrenleitner. Overlooking the sea, and set against a backdrop of vineyards and woodland, it is an impressive 7km (4 miles) in length. Facilities include a clubhouse, restaurant, and bar. The course golf school offers sets of 10 lessons in small groups with PGA professional Dean Dužaić. Hotel guests can sign up for a single round of play or more.

Alberi 300A, Savudrija. www.golf-adriatic.com. ✆ **052/707-100.** Greens fees for guests are 60€/round Mon–Thurs and 70€/round Sat–Sun. Cart rentals 35€/day.

Where to Stay

Accommodations in Umag range from several large chain hotels to a huge inventory of private accommodations to a string of camping facilities that cater to a wide range of tastes. Savudrija has an apartment village on the sea, private accommodations, and the plush Kempinski Hotel Adriatic.

VERY EXPENSIVE

Kempinski Hotel Adriatic ★★★   Opened in 2009, the luxurious Kempinski Adriatic is set amid lush landscaping, with olive trees and fragrant herbs. Inside, marble and glass predominate, the spacious guestrooms outfitted with elegant contemporary furnishings and pastel fabrics. Bathrooms have separate tubs and showers and rooms have balconies—although you pay a little extra for a sea view, it's worth it. The Carolea Spa offers a wealth of hedonistic treatments and sensual experiences. There's a hotel beach with sunbeds and umbrellas, and the hotel's Golf Club Adriatic is a beautifully tended 18-hole course with blissful sea views (see above).

Alberi 300A, Savudrija. www.kempinski.com. 𝒞 **052/707-000.** 186 units. Double Aug from 290€. **Amenities:** 2 restaurants; 3 bars; 18-hole golf course; kids' club; 3 pools; spa; 4 tennis courts; heliport; Wi-Fi (free).

MODERATE

Hotel Villa Rosetta ★★   On the coast between Savudrija and Umag, this small modern hotel opened in 2007. Though the exterior is somewhat sterile, inside you'll find comfortable guestrooms with walnut parquet floors and balconies (the best ones have amazing sea views, too). The house restaurant serves creative Mediterranean cuisine and a spa offers indulgent beauty treatments. Out front there's a rock and pebble beach complete with wooden sunbeds, umbrellas, and a small beach bar.

Crvena Uvala 31, Zambratija. www.villarosetta.hr. 𝒞 **052/725-710.** 24 units. Double Aug from 160€. **Amenities:** Restaurant; bar; spa; Wi-Fi (free).

Where to Dine

As you might expect, Umag is full of pizzerias, spaghetterias, and other family-friendly dining spots. Most people who stay in the resort hotels take half-board and their meals there, but there are a few upscale options for those who want to go a la carte. Savudrija has the Adriatic's **Dijana** and **Kanova,** and **Slice,** the golf club's restaurant.

Konoba Nono ★★ ISTRIAN   This reasonably priced eatery has a dining room with a terracotta tile floor and outdoor tables in summer. House specialties include homemade pasta with asparagus and truffles and Boškarin (Istrian ox) steaks. Seasonal dishes are also served throughout the year. The tavern is in Petrovija, 3 km (2 miles) inland from Umag on the road to Buje. Guests are welcome to visit the adjoining farm, with animals that will appeal to kids.

Umaška 35, Petrovija, Umag. www.konoba-nono.com. 𝒞 **052/740-160.** Entrees 65kn–120kn. Open daily 11am–11pm.

INLAND ISTRIA

It isn't easy being green in a country where blue is the dominant color. The Istrian interior's countless hues of vegetation hint at the unspoiled nature and unique experiences that await those who venture into this often overlooked part of Croatia. It first hits you as you exit the deep blackness of **Učka Tunnel** in the east, or as you drive away from the golden brightness of the **Istrian Coast** in the west: This is territory that feeds the senses—all of them. In **Green Istria** you can take time to breathe the perfumed air, listen to the birds chatter, touch the rough stone of a medieval castle, or savor the taste of local wines.

In this land of discovery, you can climb a hill to listen to cool jazz at **Grožnjan,** travel the wine road through **Momjan,** or watch films under a night sky in **Motovun.** Inland Istria is also where you can marvel at still-vibrant 15th-century frescoes in a woodland church near tiny **Beram,** or tramp through the woods outside **Buzet** while following a couple of dogs hunting truffles. While you're here, you can feast on an elaborate dinner in an award-winning restaurant in **Livade** and wake up the next morning to a breakfast of home-smoked ham, homegrown fruit, and homemade cheese in the kitchen of the rural farmhouse where you spent the night. You can also nose around Glagolitic artifacts in tiny **Hum,** or explore the historic walled city of **Roč.**

Inland Istria is waiting to immerse you in the land.

Essentials

VISITOR INFORMATION   Every town in Green Istria has its own tourist information center, though some offices in smaller towns have limited hours and are difficult to find. To help visitors get the most out of their trip, the **Istria Tourist Board** (www.istra.hr; ✆ **052/452-797**) has produced some exceptional materials. These include attractive publications on farmhouse stays, cultural itineraries, wine roads, olive oil roads, and truffle-hunting opportunities. Many other topics are also covered by the association, whose main office is in Poreč at Pionirska 1.

GETTING THERE   No matter how you get to Istria—by plane to Pula, by boat to one of the coastal cities, or by bus to Pazin—you will need a car to thoroughly explore the inland area unless you are on a guided excursion.

GETTING AROUND   Most towns in Inland Istria are small; one of them, Hum, is known as the smallest town in the world. The main attractions in all of Istria's inland towns can be accessed on foot, although note that many sites are extremely hilly and must be approached by walking over irregular cobblestone streets. To get to Motovun, for example, you have to leave your car at the bottom of a steep street and walk more than a quarter of a mile uphill. Some of the smaller towns are quite remote, so driving your own car is the only practical way to cover the territory between them.

Pazin (Pisino)

Sleepy Pazin in the center of Istria is the antithesis of the touristy coast. While it doesn't have glitzy resorts or hordes of tourists, it does have historic sites worth visiting. Pazin is not a huge transportation hub, but regular bus service connects it to other parts of the country; buses from the west coast pass through on their way to Rijeka and Zagreb. Pazin's main attractions are a medieval castle with a deep chasm that inspired author Jules Verne while he was writing "Mathias Sandorf," and the amazing frescoes at St. Mary of the Rock in the nearby village of **Beram.** Pazin's personality is actually similar to that of any small town in America: It's in the middle of nowhere, with a strong agricultural base, a little industry, and a neutral location that was a factor in its choice as a regional seat of government. It makes a fine day trip, but it's not somewhere you'd choose to linger much longer.

ESSENTIALS
VISITOR INFORMATION   The Pazin **tourist office** (www.tzpazin.hr; ✆ **052/622-460**) is at Franine I Jurine 14.

GETTING THERE   Trains and buses serve Pazin from Zagreb, Rijeka, and cities in Istria. See "Getting There" in "Orientation," earlier in this chapter.

GETTING AROUND   Pazin is a small town, so its main attractions are best reached on foot.

WHAT TO SEE & DO

It takes half a day to see Pazin. While there, be sure to check out the stunning medieval frescoes in the tiny Church of St. Mary of the Rock, close to the village of Beram, which can be reached from Pazin by following a marked footpath, or by local bus.

Frescoes at the Church of St. Mary of the Rock ★★★   Tiny Beram is a little more than 5.6km (3½ miles) west of Pazin. It's a one-street town with a nice church, but that isn't the church you're looking for. You need to find "the keymaster," who has the key to St. Mary's, where the famous frescoes reside. As of summer, 2014, the holder was Mrs. Sonja Šestan (Beram 38; ℰ **052/622-903**), but the townspeople will help you locate whomever it is. The tiny Gothic-style St. Mary's is hidden away in the woods, 1.2km (¾ mile) northeast of the village, about a 10-minute walk. Inside, the walls are covered with frescoes, stunning in their brightness and detail, depicting scenes from the New Testament created by Croatian artist Vincent de Kastav in the 15th century. The main attraction is the bizarre "Dance of the Dead," showing a succession of skeletons carrying scythes as they lead the newly deceased into the netherworld. You will find explanations printed in English, though your guide will probably only speak Croatian. There is no entry charge to the church, but it is customary to offer the keymaster a gratuity for her time (you may also have to offer her a lift to the church and back).

1.2km (¾ mile) northeast of Beram.

Pazin Castle and the Istrian Ethnographic Museum ★★★   Housed in Pazin's well-preserved medieval castle (known to locals as Kaštel), this museum displays traditional Istrian folk costumes, farming implements, and a model of an old-fashioned Istrian kitchen. On the ground floor, a collection of church bells, dating from between the 15th and 20th centuries, were removed from local village churches to stop the fascists from using them to make bullets during World War II. They are said to be the only bells in the region that survived the war.

Trg Istarskog Razvoda 1275, br 1. www.emi.hr. ℰ **052/622-220.** Admission 25kn. Daily 10am–6pm.

Pazin Chasm ★★★   Next to the castle, this dramatic 91m-deep (300-ft.) gorge is said to have inspired science fiction author Jules Verne to write "Mathias Sandorf" (1885) and "Journey to the Center of the Earth" (1864). As a tribute, every June Pazin stages Jules Verne Days (www.julesvernedays.com). The 2014 event included theatrical performances for children, a fair with traditional toys, an adventure race called "Around Pazin in 80 Minutes," a zip-line across the gorge, and evening concerts.

Next to Pazin Castle.

St. Nicholas Church ★   Standing opposite the tourist office, this church dates back to 1266, though its appearance has been altered several times through the centuries. It's worth taking a look inside to see the 14th-century frescoes above the altar, depicting the Way of the Cross and scenes from the Old Testament.

Eufrazijeva Ulica 22, opposite the tourist office. Mon–Sat 9am–12:30pm, Sun 9:30am–noon and 6–8pm.

WHERE TO DINE

Pazin is not really a place you would plan to stay overnight, but it makes a fine day trip. There are several good traditional eateries in the area. The area is particularly notable for agritourism centers, which are in the surrounding villages and countryside, rather than in the town of Pazin itself. If you are visiting the frescoed church, you might have lunch in Beram.

Agroturizam Ograde ★★ ISTRIAN   This agritourism destination features a dining room with an open fireplace, exposed stone walls, and rustic wooden tables and chairs. Guests here feast on homemade cheeses and cured meats, *štruclji* (a type of Istrian pasta) served with a rich chicken sauce, and seasonal specialties such as asparagus (in spring) or mushrooms (in autumn). The owners also bake their own bread in a brick oven, and serve their own Teran-grape red wine by the carafe. Note that you need a car to get here.

Lindarski Katun 60, 10km (6 miles) south of Pazin. www.agroturizam-ograde.hr. © **052/693-035.** Entrees 65kn–110kn. Opening hours are variable, so it's best to telephone in advance to make sure that they are working.

Konoba Vela Vrata ★★★ ISTRIAN   In an old stone building in Beram, with fantastic views down onto the valley, this small and unpretentious eatery serves up delicious Istrian fare at reasonable prices. The menu includes standouts like homemade pasta with truffles, steak with truffles, and a delicious ricotta, almond, and honey cake. The staff is friendly, attentive, and very professional, and it's a place you'll want to come back to. The tavern is ideal for lunch after visiting the Church of St. Mary of the Rock.

Beram 41, Beram. © **052/622-801.** Entrees 60kn–90kn. Tues–Sat noon–11pm; closed Mon.

Grožnjan, Buje & Momjan

The roads that link **Buje** (Buie), **Momjan** (Momiano), and **Grožnjan** (Grisignana) are narrow, steep, and winding, but they snake through some of the most scenic real estate in Istria. **Buje** is a short hop from Umag on the coast, and the town itself is fairly uninteresting, except for an 18th-century church (Sv. Servula Mučenika) and a monument and plaque commemorating Tito's 1954 visit to the town. At that time, Tito became an honorary citizen of Buje and dedicated a World War II monument to the freedom fighters from the area. The road out of Buje northeast toward **Momjan** is a jumping-off point for both the wine and olive oil roads of the region, meandering past tavern **Konoba Marino** and the ruins of **Momjan Castle.** The Momjan area is a good place to try the region's outstanding wines, especially those from the **Kozlović Winery,** which has a beautiful tasting room built into its original 100-year-old winery building.

South of Momjan, the tiny hilltop village of **Grožnjan** is one of the prettiest hill towns anywhere in Croatia. **Grožnjan** was almost deserted 45 years ago, after most of its Italian population left for economic opportunity. In 1965, the town saw an influx of artists, who took over the town and saved it from extinction by renovating its old town core. Since then, Grožnjan has blossomed into a full-fledged artist's colony, replete with galleries, shops, restaurants, and a jazz festival in July and August that attracts big-name talent and plenty of fans. If you can't get there for a performance, you can stop at one of the village's pleasant restaurants for a bite while listening to the mellow sounds emanating from all corners of the village during daytime practice sessions. It's also fun to poke around the loggia, gates, walls, and maze of small cobbled streets. In keeping with Grožnjan's reputation as a "town of artists," numerous shops and ateliers in town sell original paintings, pottery, and jewelry made by local craftspeople.

ON THE wine & olive oil ROAD

The best way to explore Istria's wine and olive oil roads is to pick up a map produced by the Istria Tourist Board (www.istra.hr) that lists about six dozen winemakers and two dozen olive oil producers in the region. Most of Istria's wineries are in the country's north-central region, and you will need a car to get from one venue to the next. Roads do have directional signs for the wine and oil routes, and producers have marked the paths to their doors in some cases. Don't miss the cellars of **Kozlović** and **Kabola,** both full-fledged wineries that have expanded their production into microclimate vintages. Kozlović is not set up for unannounced tasters, so call ahead; Kabola welcomes drop-ins.

Kozlović Winery (www.kozlovic.hr; ⓒ **052/779-177**) is at Vale 78 in Momjan, open from 10am to 7pm Monday through Saturday. It produces an impressive 100,000 bottles a year. Look for their red Teran, white Malvazija, and *muśkat* dessert wine.

Kabola Winery (www.kabola.hr; ⓒ **052/779-208**) is at Kanedolo 90 between Buje and Momjan. It includes a small winemaking museum and a knockout eatery, **Konoba Marino** (see listing). The winery is open for tasting from 10am to 8pm Monday through Saturday. Kabola is known for the classics, Istrian red Teran and white Malvazija, plus a white sparkling wine called Re (brut).

Tip: You can stop in at any of the olive oil producers on the map to purchase products, but if you want to see a pressing in action or pick a few olives, reservations are required. Consult Istria's Olive Oil Road Map for details and contact information.

ESSENTIALS

VISITOR INFORMATION   Facts about this cluster of towns are available at the Istria Tourist Board office in Poreč (see above). Grožnjan's **tourist office** (www.tz-groznjan.hr; ⓒ **052/776-131**) is at Gorjan 3.

GETTING THERE   See "Getting There" in "Orientation," earlier in this chapter.

GETTING AROUND   The important sites in all of these towns can be easily explored on foot, but if you intend to visit wineries or sites in between, a car is a must.

WHAT TO SEE & DO

All of the towns in this group are worth a few hours of wandering at any time. Besides the old buildings and beautiful views, each town also has at least one marquee event during the year. Of the group, Grožnjan is the most accessible because of its large number of venues and restaurants concentrated in a central location.

Grožnjan Musical Summer and Jazz Festival ★★★   In summer, Grožnjan's car-free cobbled alleys resound with musical instruments of all kinds. A local young musicians' summer school (www.hgm.hr) stages daytime lessons, so you'll hear instruments being tuned in the practice rooms. Regular concerts are arranged on balmy evenings through July and August. Simultaneously, the 3-week Jazz is Back (www.jazzisbackbp.com) festival attracts highly acclaimed international musicians—American jazz trombonist Luis Bonilla played here in July 2014.

Grožnjan.

Momjan Wine Festival ★★   Set amid rolling vineyards, Momjan is an important center of wine making, with many highly regarded producers in the immediate vicinity. Every autumn from November 9 through 11, the town celebrates the new vintage and the Day of St. Martin (the patron saint of winemakers) with enthusiastic festivities, including copious amounts of wine, food, and music. Go to www.colours ofistria.com for more information.

Momjan.

WHERE TO DINE

Konoba Marino ★★★ ISTRIAN   Located 3km (2 miles) northeast of Buje on the road to Momjan, this highly regarded rural eatery boasts an elegant dining room with an open fireplace and a covered summer terrace lined with geraniums. It makes a fine choice for savoring local seasonal specialties, notably dishes prepared from mushrooms, truffles, and game. Excellent Kabola wines, produced by the same family, make a perfect accompaniment. The tavern also has several rooms to rent, should you choose to make it a late night.

Kremenje 96B, Momjan. www.konoba-marino-kremenje.hr. ✆ **052/779-047.** Entrees 50kn–120kn. Daily noon–10pm.

Konoba Morgan ★★★ ISTRIAN   Located on a hillside approached up a private road 5km (3 miles) from Buje, this family-run eatery more than warrants the journey. There's an elegant dining room with an open fireplace, and a summer terrace with lovely views. The food is authentic and really special, with an emphasis on hearty meat dishes—try the gnocchi with venison goulash, homemade sausages, or wild boar, well accompanied by quality local wines.

Bracanija 1, Brtonigla. www.konoba-morgan.eu ✆ **052/774-520.** Entrees 60kn–110kn. Wed–Mon noon–10pm; closed Tues.

Restoran Bastia ★★ ISTRIAN   Bastia is one of the few local eateries that stays open all year. Warm weather sees outdoor tables on the main square of Grožnjan's car-free old town, and in winter the cozy dining room comes into use, with a wood-burning fireplace. The menu includes homey local dishes such as arugula and shrimp salad, mushroom risotto, Wiener schnitzel, and a delicious tiramisu.

Svibnia 1, Grožnjan. ✆ **052/776-370.** Entrees 50kn–140kn. Daily 8am–11pm.

Zigante Enoteka ★ WINE BAR   One of several Zigante franchises in Istria (see p. 99 and p. 100), this small deli sells brand-name truffle products (including cheeses and olive oils) and local wines. In addition to shopping here, you can sit down and have a glass of wine with some savory nibbles.

Gorjan 5, Grožnjan. www.zigantetartufi.com. ✆ **052/776-099.** May–Oct daily 10am–11pm.

Motovun, Livade & Oprtalj

Motovun (Montona) is one of Istria's better-known interior towns, perhaps because it hosts events like the Motovun Film Festival, hot-air balloon competitions, and a festival celebrating truffles and wine. It doesn't hurt that this hilltop town is just 14km (9 miles) north of Pazin and that it is home to the delightful **Kaštel Hotel.**

A short distance north of Motovun is the village of **Livade** (Levade), fast becoming a center for gastronomic delights, including the locally venerated truffle. In the countryside around Livade, you'll see huge tracts of vineyards and olive trees, with workers toiling in the fields no matter what the season. There are new vineyards as well as old, along with lots of hand-painted signs on side roads advertising homemade wine, olive oil, and grappa (Italian brandy) for sale.

If you continue on the same road a little farther, you'll reach **Oprtalj** (Portole), a charming town on a hill high above the Mirna river valley. It is home to the

15th-century **St. Mary's Church** and the 16th-century **Church of St. Rock,** both of which have a few lovely but minor frescoes. However, you'll probably have to be content with looking at these through the church windows, as they are rarely open.

Despite their remoteness and lack of efficient public transportation, all these tiny towns are quickly becoming centers of activity for lovers of film, music, fine dining, and other activities that feed the senses.

ESSENTIALS

VISITOR INFORMATION   Information on all three towns and their festivals is available at the Istria Tourist Board in Poreč (see above). Motovun's **tourist office** (www.tz-motovun.hr; © 052/681-726) is at Trg Andrea Antico 1.

GETTING THERE   See "Getting There" in "Orientation," earlier in this chapter.

GETTING AROUND   The important sites in each of these towns can easily be explored on foot.

WHAT TO SEE & DO

These Istrian towns are ideal places to wander about in search of medieval treasures. They also have excellent restaurants, fine wines, and, of course, truffles in abundance. The Motovun Film Festival in July and ballooning events in October are also big draws.

Motovun Film Festival ★★   Founded in 1999, the Motovun Film Festival quickly established a firm following. Movie buffs flock here for five days each summer to view European art-house films. It's a small and informal affair, with no barriers between the artists and the public, and plenty of partying. Former guests include British director Michael Winterbottom and Hungarian director Béla Tarr. The festival's well-organized eco-camp makes a good alternative to more conventional accommodation.

Motovun Film Festival. www.motovunfilmfestival.com. © 01/374-07-08. Late Jul, dates are variable.

Zigante Tartufi ★   Zigante dominates Livade, and there's little else of interest in this town aside from the Zigante store, selling truffle products and wine, and the Zigante Restaurant (see below), serving up exquisite (and pricey) truffle dishes. Offerings at the store run from fresh truffles to cheese with truffles to olive oil infused with truffles to recipe books dedicated to cooking with truffles. The store also has a model of the giant truffle that put Zigante in the "Guinness Book of World Records"—a normal truffle is the size of an egg, whereas this one is closer to a small cantaloupe.

Livade 7, Livade. www.zigantetartufi.hr. © **052/664-030.** Daily Jun–Sept 9am–9pm; Oct–May 10am–6pm.

WHERE TO STAY & DINE

Besides the Kaštel Hotel in Motovun, the only accommodations in these villages are in private establishments, making this an ideal opportunity to try a farmhouse stay after savoring the flavors of Istria at one of the area's fine-dining establishments.

Hotel Kaštel ★★   Set in a lovely garden next to the old town walls, this romantic hotel occupies an aristocratic 17th-century palazzo. The rooms and suites vary in size and configuration, but are generally spacious and come with modern bathrooms. Furnishings are stylish, with color schemes ranging from subdued beiges to dramatic tomato-red ceilings. To sleep amid 17th-century stucco work, request the Castellum Room, which has retained its original period detail. The ground floor Restoran Palladio (see below) is popular with hotel guests and other travelers alike, serving local specialties and wines. There's a small spa offering sauna, massage, and beauty treatments, plus an indoor pool affording fine views down onto the Mirna Valley. The hotel can arrange wellness and gourmet packages. If you call ahead, they'll also collect you at the bottom of the road leading up to Motovun, so you don't have to carry suitcases uphill.

Trg Andrea Antico 7, Motovun. www.hotel-kastel-motovun.hr. ✆ **052/681-607.** 33 units. Double Jul–Aug 110€. **Amenities:** Restaurant; excursions; spa; Wi-Fi (free).

Konoba Mondo ★★★ ISTRIAN   This tiny eatery, hidden away just outside Motovun's medieval walls, was featured on Anthony Bourdain's "No Reservations" in 2012. Consequently, it now attracts a lot of American visitors. The tavern is family-run and specializes in traditional Istrian cuisine, with an emphasis on truffle dishes— you might start with a delightful beef carpaccio with truffles and arugula, followed by homemade ravioli in a creamy truffle sauce. On a sunny day you can eat on the informal terrace, lined with potted geraniums, out front.

Barbacan 1, Motovun. ✆ **052/681-791.** Entrees 85kn–150kn. Wed–Sun 12:30–3:30pm and 6:30– 10:30pm; Mon–Tues lunch only.

Restoran Palladio ★★ ISTRIAN   On the ground floor of Hotel Kaštel, with additional outdoor tables out front and amazing views down onto the valley, Restoran Palladio serves up refined Istrian cuisine, with quality local wines to match. Favorites include cream of truffle soup with saffron, *frkanci* (a homemade Istrian pasta that's kind of a cross between gnocchi and noodles) with prosciutto and asparagus, and Boškarin (Istrian ox) beef. The restaurant has a degustation menu for those who want to sample a variety of dishes.

Trg Andrea Antico 7, Motovun. www.hotel-kastel-motovun.hr. ✆ **052/681-607.** Entrees 60kn– 125kn. Daily 8am–10pm.

Zigante Restaurant ★★ GOURMET ISTRIAN   The menu here focuses on truffles, changing with the seasons. To experience the range of chef Damir Modrušan's creative cuisine, opt for a degustation menu. There are two: The four-course Diamond menu (670kn) and the six-course Prestige menu (990kn), which include delights such as duck breast with glazed beetroot and white truffle and fallow deer steak in a hazelnut crust with a black current and port sauce, accompanied by celery purée and white truffle. Ask the sommelier to advise you on the wines. The restaurant interior is rustic, with stone walls, tan tablecloths, and wrought-iron fixtures. Reservations are required. There are overnight accommodations here as well: Three double rooms which go for 160€ per night in August and include a truffle-based breakfast.

Livade 7, Livade. www.restaurantzigante.com. ✆ **052/664-302.** Entrees 165kn–295kn. Mid-Mar to mid-Jan daily noon–11pm.

Buzet, Hum & Roč

The stretch of road that connects **Roč** (Rozzo), **Buzet** (Pinguente), and **Hum** (Colmo) is as rural as they come. The strip linking Roč and Hum is just 6.4km (4 miles) long, but it's considered a historic corridor because of its commemorative Glagolitic sculptures. The string of 10 outdoor sculptures dotting the road were erected between 1977 and 1981 to celebrate and preserve Glagolitic script. One of the sculptures, **Razvoda,** is an arrangement that looks like a Stonehenge garden. Today, Roč is known as a center of Glagolitic literature.

Dubbed the "City of Truffles," **Buzet** stands atop a 137m (450-ft.) hill, amid prime truffle-hunting territory.

Hum's biggest claim to fame is its nominal status as the world's smallest town. However, from the looks of the state of tourism in the present-day village, that could be changing. Tiny Hum has spiffed itself up recently and is quite appealing.

ESSENTIALS

VISITOR INFORMATION   The **Tourist Information Office** (www.tz-buzet.hr; ✆ **052/662-343**) in Buzet also serves Roč and Hum. It is at Šetalište Vladimira Gortana 9 in Buzet.

GETTING THERE   See "Getting There" in "Orientation," earlier in this chapter.

GETTING AROUND   Small towns in central Istria are best seen on foot, but travel between them requires a vehicle. Buses do serve the area, but not all routes are covered every day; in some cases there is only one bus per day. Even then, you'll sometimes have to walk a mile or more from the bus stop to the center of town.

WHAT TO SEE & DO

Buzet, the "City of Truffles," is worthy of a visit, especially during **Truffle Day** (usually the second Saturday in September). During this celebration of the earthy delicacy, the whole town throws a block party with music, food, and, of course, truffles. Cars are allowed up the narrow, twisting street into town, but don't try driving up there unless you're sure your brakes are good.

In contrast, 8km (5 miles) southeast of Buzet, Roč is ringed by an unusually low medieval wall surrounding a fortified town. The medieval walls, town gates, and a tower are nice to see; interesting Roman tombstones are displayed just inside the main gate arch. **Roč** is primarily known as a center of Glagolitic literature. Every year the town puts on the **Small Glagolitic Academy** so that Croatia's kids can keep the traditional writing alive. Private rooms are available in Roč (there are signs on the road), and there is a decent *konoba*.

Only about 20 people live within Hum's well-preserved walls, which enclose two small streets and two churches, one of which dates from the 12th century. A recent spruce-up has made the town an inviting destination.

Karlić Truffle Hunting Excursions ★★★   You can try truffle-hunting yourself with the Karlić family in Paladini, 13km (8 miles) between Buzet and Livade. From April through November, the family arranges tours with their 12 trained dogs in the oak woods surrounding their home. Tours take 2 to 3 hours and begin with truffle tasting. Note that black truffles can be harvested for most of the year, but white truffle season runs exclusively from September through November.

Paladini 14, Buzet. www.karlictartufi.hr. ✆ **052/667-304.** 2 persons for 130€ total; groups of 3 for 55€/person; groups of 4 for 45€/person; groups of 15 or more, 30€/person.

BLACK (& WHITE) gold

Istria is fast becoming as famous as France and Italy for its truffles—pungent, underground tuberous fungi used in many traditional Istrian dishes and sauces. In Istria, specially trained dogs (Istrian Hunters) are used to sniff out the malodorous treasures that grow a foot beneath the floor of the forests around Buzet. (France and Italy traditionally use pigs, although dogs are becoming common there, too.) True truffle madness takes over the area during Truffle Days, which occur at the start of the season in the area's villages. The most famous of these celebrations is the second Saturday in September in Buzet, where an omelet the size of the local mythic giant Veli Jože is cooked up with truffles and shared among all the merrymakers in town. Truffles' strong, distinctive flavor makes them an acquired taste, and their rarity and astronomical price make them a delicacy. Truffles are less expensive in Croatia than they are in other countries and thus are used more liberally in the cuisine.

Most accommodations in these small towns are in private apartments, rooms, or farmhouses, which makes this area a center of agritourism. Information on private accommodations is available at the tourist office in Buzet. Opportunities to sample authentic Istrian specialties abound in this rural area, which has a nice selection of excellent *konobas*.

Hotel Fontana ★★ Although this hotel dates to 1981, its building was refurbished in 2013. The lobby gleams, with a high-tech feel, and the spacious guestrooms have attractive contemporary furnishings. The staff is welcoming and helpful, and can arrange bicycles for hire on request. There's an a la carte restaurant specializing in local truffle dishes and regional wines, with outdoor tables through summer. The property's small vitality zone offers massage and beauty treatments.

Trg Fontana 1, Buzet. www.hotelfontanabuzet.com. ℂ **052/662-615.** 57 units. Double Jul–Sept from 68€. **Amenities:** Restaurant; wellness center; bicycles for hire; Wi-Fi (free).

Humska Konoba ★★ ISTRIAN In an old stone building in the so-called smallest town in the world, this tiny eatery attracts the crowds through summer (additional tables are set up outdoors on a terrace that affords fine views over the surrounding countryside). Local dishes on offer include appetizers such as prosciutto and sheep's cheese, followed by mushroom omelets or venison goulash served with gnocchi. Istrian wines—red Teran and white Malvazija—are served by the carafe, and the house also serves *biska* (a potent liquor made from mistletoe) as an aperitif. The tavern is cash-only.

Hum 2, Hum. ℂ **052/660-005.** Entrees 50kn–85kn. Mid-May to mid-Oct daily 11am–10pm; mid-Oct to mid-May Sat–Sun 11am–10pm.

Konoba Valter Kolinasi ★★ ISTRIAN Located just 1km (½ mile) outside Roč, on the road to Buzet, this old-fashioned *konoba* serves delicious, authentic, local dishes at very reasonable prices. Try the house-cured prosciutto and sheep's cheese, followed by a generous portion of tagliatelle with truffles. Wash it all down with a carafe of red wine. The setting is timeless—a traditional farm building with exposed stone walls and a wood-beamed ceiling. (Credit cards are not accepted.)

Kolinasi bb, Roč. www.konoba-kolinasi.com ℂ **052/666-624.** Entrees 50kn–110kn. Daily noon–10pm.

Restoran Vrh ★★ ISTRIAN On the road to Ponte Porton and Buzet, this welcoming eatery serves up tasty local dishes, with the typical local emphasis on meat, truffles, and pasta. Opt for either the homemade *fuži* pasta (kind of a rolled tube) with truffles, or a fillet steak (also with truffles, of course). You can also try a *peka* dish here (see below). Round off with a slice of rich, dark chocolate cake. Note that credit cards are not accepted here, and the restaurant is open weekends only in the early months of the year.

Vrh 1. Buzet. ℂ **052/667-123.** Entrees 60kn–140kn, more for *peka* sold by the kilo. May–Dec daily 1–10pm; Jan–Apr Sat–Sun 1–10pm.

ORDERING A "peka" DISH

Food cooked under a *peka*, or cooking bell, is usually ordered 24 hours ahead of time. The peka is covered with hot ashes while underneath it the meat (normally lamb, or sometimes octopus) bakes with potatoes and vegetables. Complete cooking usually takes several hours. The results are tender and lovely. Some of the best places to try peka cuisine are **Lambik** in Milna on Hvar, **Panorama** above Orebić on Pelješac, **Konoba Mate** in Pupnat on Korčula, and **Konavoski Dvori** near Cavtat in the Dubrovnik area.

RIJEKA & THE KVARNER GULF

C entering on the industrial port town of Rijeka, the Kvarner region is backed by mountains and overlooks the deep blue waters of the Kvarner Gulf. The region's best known and oldest tourist destination is Opatija, with its 19th-century villas, lush gardens filled with palm trees, and upmarket waterside seafood restaurants.

From the port of Rijeka, travelers can catch ferries and catamarans to the islands (most—but not all—leave from Rijeka). To visit the island of **Krk,** with its lovely long pebble beach in Baška, you don't even need to board a boat—it's joined to the mainland by a bridge, so a bus journey will suffice.

The island of Lošinj does requires a boat journey. Its main town, pretty **Mali Lošinj,** is one of the region's top destinations. Ecologically savvy tourists can explore the rocky hills of **Cres Island,** joined to Lošinj by a bridge, where rugged paths monitored by grazing sheep run a dizzying course to deserted azure coves.

Kvarner's southernmost island, Rab, is connected by regular boat service to both Rijeka and the island of Krk, so with a bit of planning you can island-hop around the region and see several places in one go.

Visitors to the mainland can expect a broad range of accommodations and services, while island hoppers will find large package hotels along with modest family-run hotels, rooms to rent, and campsites.

RIJEKA

No matter which part of the Kvarner Gulf region you explore, you'll probably go through Rijeka, which is connected to Zagreb by *autocesta* (highway). A once grand industrial port, Rijeka's 19th-century Austro-Hungarian buildings have fallen into slight disrepair, and are now in the process of being gradually restored. Most people breeze straight through on their way to a more restful destination, either on the mainland coast or one of the nearby islands.

Getting There

BY CAR Almost all roads in Croatia eventually lead to Rijeka, but the Zagreb-Rijeka *autocesta* (A-6) from the north gets travelers there in less than 2 hours. The A-6 also connects to the A-1 autocesta from Split in the south. From Ljubljana in Slovenia, take E-70 via Postojna and connect with local Route 6 at Illirska Bistrica. You will encounter a border crossing at Rupa and occasionally there is some hassle there, so be sure your documents are in order. Across the border, follow E-63/E-61 to Rijeka. Ferries from several nearby islands stop at Rijeka and dock near the *Riva* (boardwalk) south of the center. A schedule and prices can be obtained from www. jadrolinija.hr (© **051/211-444**).

BY TRAIN   Rijeka is connected to Zagreb by train. There are two daily, with a journey time of approximately 4 hours (www.hzpp.hr; © **060/333-444**).

BY BUS   Buses to and from Rijeka connect with other parts of Croatia, as well as with other cities in Europe. The main bus hub is at Trg Žabica 1 (© **060/302-010** for reservations and information).

BY PLANE   Rijeka is accessible by air, though the airport is actually near **Omišlj** on **Krk Island,** 24km (15 miles) south of the city. The airport is served by an airport bus, which takes you to Rijeka bus station. You can also grab a taxi outside the airport, but it will be much more expensive. Call **Rijeka Airport** (www.rijeka-airport.hr; © **054/841-222**) for flight info (© **051/842-040**).

Getting Around

Walking is the most convenient way to explore Rijeka, and maps and information about restaurants, shows, and monuments can be obtained at the **tourist information center** (www.visitrijeka.hr; © **051/335-882**) at Korzo 14.

Taxis are plentiful and you can hail one off the street that will take you anywhere within the city limits. Buses make regular runs from 5am to 11:30pm daily.

Where to Stay

Despite its position as the third-largest metropolis in Croatia, Rijeka has few standout hotel and restaurant options; fortunately, you won't go wrong with the selections below.

Best Western Hotel Jadran   Close to the town center, just a 10-minute walk east of the port, this hotel has amazing views over the Adriatic. It's worth paying a little extra for a superior room with a sea view and balcony. From the upper floors, an elevator takes you down to a private beach area—a concrete bathing platform lined with sunbeds and affording easy access to the water. The hotel puts on a hearty buffet breakfast, with the best tables on a small terrace overlooking the sea.

Šetalište XIII Divizije 46. www.bestwestern-ce.com. © **052/494-000.** 69 units. Doubles Aug from 97€. **Amenities:** Restaurant; cafe; bar; beach; car rental; Wi-Fi (free).

Botel Marina   This is a great idea: A ship, built in 1935, turned into a hostel, which opened in the fall of 2013. Docked on the seafront in the center of Rijeka, the ship's 35 cabins are now single, double, triple, and quadruple rooms, joined by several dorms. The berths are quite small, with low ceilings, but they have good air-conditioning and en suite showers, plus portholes for windows. The staff is friendly and welcoming, and there's a bar on the top deck.

Adamiće gat. www.botel-marina.com. © **051/410-162.** 112 beds, 35 rooms. 15€ per dorm bed in Aug. **Amenities:** Bar; breakfast room; TV room; Wi-Fi (free).

Grand Hotel Bonavia ★   The oldest part of this building dates back to 1876, while a modern extension has increased its height to seven floors. In the Old Town, just a 2-minute stroll from the Korzo, it makes a fine choice for tourists and business travelers alike. The best rooms are up on the top floor, with balconies that boast amazing views over the bay. Kirk Douglas and Tina Turner have stayed here.

Dolac 4. www.bonavia.hr. © **052/357-100.** 121 units. Double Jul–Aug from 100€. **Amenities:** 3 restaurants; 2 bars; spa; fitness center; pets allowed; Wi-Fi (free).

Kvarner Gulf

Where to Dine

Bracera   PIZZA   Under the same management as the more upmarket Zlatna Školjka next door, Bracera serves delicious pizzas in a colorful dining room with exposed stone walls, wooden beams, long wooden tables and benches, and colorful naïve paintings by local artist Vojo Radoičić. A wood-fired grill also turns out Pag specialties like lamb on a spit and lamb roasted under a *peka*.

Kružna 12a. www.pizzeria-bracera.com.hr. ℰ **051/213-782.** Pizza 35kn–80kn. Daily 11am–11pm.

Konoba Feral   SEAFOOD   In a cellar dating from 1789, with exposed stone and brickwork, Feral is much loved by locals and does get busy. It's renowned for traditional Adriatic fresh fish and seafood dishes. Try the *crni rižot* (black risotto made from cuttlefish ink) or the *brodet* (fish stew), along with a carafe of the house white wine, a light Malvazija.

Matije Gupca 5b. www.konoba-feral.com. ℰ **051/212-274.** Entrees 45kn–90kn, more for fish priced by the kilo. Mon–Sat 8am–midnight; Sun noon–6pm.

Zlatna Skoljka   SEAFOOD   Founded in 1885, the "Golden Shell" claims to be the oldest restaurant in town. The menu features seafood specialties such as *špageti* *sa dagnjama* (spaghetti with mussels) and *file grdobine u pršutu, tikvici i patlidžanu na kremi od škampi* (monkfish with prosciutto, zucchini, and eggplant in a scampi crème sauce). You'll find it in a side alley, close to the Korzo.

Kružna 12. www.zlatna-skoljka. ✆ **051/213-782.** Entrees 70kn–110kn, more for fish priced by the kilo. Mon–Sat 11am–11pm.

Exploring Rijeka

The wide pedestrian street called **Korzo** originally was constructed along the path of the town walls. It was rebuilt in 1750, after the earthquake that just about leveled the city. Today the Korzo is lined with stores, cafes, restaurants, and even an enclosed shopping mall, which makes it a center of commerce and a great meeting place in the city. Note that most stores on the Korzo close at 1pm on Saturday and don't reopen until Monday morning, making the area pretty dead on weekends.

Also noteworthy in Rijeka is **Gradski Toranj (City Tower).** Baroque and bright, this yellow tower above the preserved city gate once was Rijeka's main entry point. It is one of the few structures to have survived the 1750 quake, although it was renovated and tinkered with for over a century, further altering its appearance. The clock was added in 1873 and the dome at the top in 1890. Today, fashionable retail outlets flank the tower, which is a popular meeting place.

Walk through the portal below the City Tower from the Korzo to **Trg Ivana Koblera** and you will run into the **Stara Vrata (Roman Gate),** Rijeka's oldest surviving structure. The Roman Gate once served as the portal to the Roman Praetorium, which was Rijeka's military command center. The gate looks like a loose arrangement of cemented rocks growing out of a strange mixture of buildings, including a Hapsburg residence, a church, and a building left over from the socialist era. Once you pass through the gate, you will see more Roman excavations.

Much of Rijeka's Old Town (**Stari Grad**) was demolished to make way for modern infrastructure, but vestiges still remain. Remnants of the ancient city of **Tarsatica,** which once stood in what is now the middle of town, are visible in the vicinity of **St. Vitus Cathedral.**

What to See

Rijeka Market   Known to locals as "Placa," the city market consists of three neighboring pavilions—one from 1880 selling fresh and cured meats; another from 1880 selling dairy products, including local cheeses; and the most elegant of all, built in Vienna Secession style in 1916, which sells fresh fish displayed on mounds of crushed ice. You'll find the market close to the port, in the center of town, working only in the earlier hours of the day.

Ulica Vatroslava Lisinskog. Mon–Sat 7am–2pm; Sun 7am–noon.

St. Vitus Cathedral ★   Legend has it that when a disgruntled 13th-century gambler threw a rock at the crucifix that now resides on St. Vitus's main altar, the rendering of Christ's body on the cross began to bleed and the gambler was swallowed up by the earth whole (except for his hand). How the church got the crucifix is a mystery, but it is known that the Jesuits built the current cathedral in 1638 in honor of St. Vitus, Rijeka's patron saint. The structure has an unusual rotunda, containing Baroque and Gothic touches, with a separate bell tower.

Trg Grivica 11. ✆ **051/330-879.** Free admission. Daily 6:30am–noon and 5–6:30pm.

Trsat

Trsat is an attractive suburb in the hills above Rijeka, with terraced gardens, villas, and tree-lined streets that skirt a cute center and a beautiful castle. To reach Trsat from Rijeka city center, you can either climb the 561 steps that make up the **Petar Kružić Stairway,** built in 1531, or catch bus no. 2.

Our Lady of Trsat Church ★   According to local legend, the Trsat Shrine was founded in 1291, when angels carrying the Holy House (where the Archangel Gabriel visited the Virgin Mary) from Nazareth dropped it here. Franciscan monks built a church on the site, and since then both the church and the adjoining 17th-century Franciscan monastery have been places of pilgrimage. The main attraction is the Chapel of Votive Gifts, filled with valuable tokens, including gold, silver, and jewels, donated by the faithful as a way of giving thanks.

Frankopanski trg 12, Trsat. www.trsat-svetiste.com. ✆ **051/452-900.** Church open daily 6:30am–7:30pm.

Trsat Castle ★★★   Although there has been a castle here since the 13th century, what you see today dates from the 19th century, when an eccentric count purchased the ruined medieval fortress and rebuilt it in whimsical neo-Gothic style. Affording fantastic views down onto Rijeka and out across the Kvarner Gulf, in summer it hosts an open-air cafe as well as cultural events.

Petra Zrinskog bb. ✆ **051/217-714.**

THE OPATIJA RIVIERA

Opatija

Opatija started as a tiny fishing village with a church. In the mid-19th century, the mild climate and spectacular seashore caught the fancy of Iginio Scarpa, a wealthy Italian businessman who built the lavish **Villa Angiolina** (named after his late wife), surrounded it with a jungle of exotic flora from around the world, and invited his aristocratic friends for a visit. Privileged Europeans were so taken with Villa Angiolina and Opatija that they erected villas of their own, each bigger and more ornate than the next, thus cementing Opatija's reputation as a winter playground for the wealthy.

In 1873, the opening of the railway from Opatija to Ljubljana and beyond made the coast more accessible to Central Europeans. Opatija soon became known as a mild and clement health resort for Austrian snowbirds; its season ran from October to May. Regal hotels such as the **Kvarner** (Opatija's first hotel), the **Imperial** (formerly Kronprinzessin Stephanie), and **Palace-Bellevue** were built to accommodate the fancy new tourists.

From the mid-1880s to the start of World War I, Opatija was the retreat of choice for such notables as Isadora Duncan, Anton Chekhov, and a horde of Hapsburg aristocrats. World War I put a crimp on European vacations, and Opatija was not immune to the downturn, but tourists never really abandoned it, either. After two subsequent wars, modern Opatija remains popular with European tourists, who flock to the resort all year long, especially from mid-July to mid-August.

Getting There & Getting Around

BY CAR   If you've driven to Rijeka, it's only another 20 minutes to Opatija via the coastal highway.

BY BUS   Local bus no. 32 (www.autotrolej.hr) stops in front of the Rijeka train station and travels the length of the riviera to Lovran every 20 minutes.

Visitor Information

OPATIJA TOURIST INFORMATION OFFICE   The **tourist office** (www.opatija-tourism.hr; ✆ **051/271-310**) provides maps and local information. It is located at M. Tita 128, on the main thoroughfare through the center of town.

What to See

Šetalište Franza Josefa (aka Lungomare)   This lovely waterside promenade runs 12km (8 miles), all the way from **Volosko** to **Lovran**, passing through Opatija en-route. There are plenty of open-air cafes and restaurants along the way, as well as places where you can sunbathe or take a quick swim off the rocks. It was built in the late 19th century, when Opatija first began developing into a tourist resort.

Between Volosko and Lovran.

Villa Angiolina   On the edge of the lush Park Angiolina, this neo-classical villa, complete with mosaics and frescoes, dates from 1844, when it was the first of the Opatija mansions (see introduction above). Carefully restored in 2000, it now houses a small Museum of Croatian Tourism, and is also used to host local cultural events and wedding celebrations.

Park Angiolina 1. www.hrmt.hr. ✆ **051/603-636.** 10kn. Daily 10am–8pm.

Volosko   A 20-minute stroll north of Opatija, following the seaside promenade, this pretty fishing village has retained its old-fashioned charm, with a harbor filled with wooden boats and fishing nets hanging out to dry. Besides being quaint and peaceful, it's also a must-do destination for foodies, with a handful of gourmet eateries serving outstanding contemporary cuisine, including **Plavi Podrum** and **Le Mandrać.**

Volosko.

Where to Stay
VERY EXPENSIVE

Bevanda   Opened in 2013, this slick, ultra-modern, five-star hotel and gourmet restaurant is built on a tiny peninsula. The location is the site of the original Bevanda Restaurant, which dates to 1971 and has long been recognized as one of Croatia's top seafood eateries. There are just ten rooms and suites in the hotel, all with floor-to-ceiling windows opening onto private balconies, so you wake to amazing views over the Kvarner Gulf at your feet. Bathrooms, partitioned from bedrooms by glass walls, have Jacuzzis and are stocked with Lanvin toiletries. Each room is named after a famous person who has visited Opatija, such as Vladimir Nabokov, James Joyce, and Albert Einstein. Some rooms are interconnected, making them suitable for families. Bevanda is expensive, but it's also very special, and needless to say you will eat extremely well here. It sits a 5-minute walk from the center of Opatija.

Zert 8. www.bevanda. ✆ **051/493-888.** 10 units. Double Jul–Aug 350€. **Amenities:** Restaurant; bar; garden; Wi-Fi (free).

EXPENSIVE

Mozart   In an impressive pink Art Nouveau building from 1894, this elegant boutique hotel has spacious rooms, high ceilings, wooden floors, canopied beds, and period antiques. Standard rooms look onto the park, while deluxe rooms cost a little more but come with glorious sea views and balconies. Guests enjoy an ample and tasty breakfast on the garden terrace, where dinner is served later in the day. The Mozart was fully renovated in 2007, when the luxurious spa was added. The location is excellent, close to the sea in the center of Opatija.

Maršala Tita 138. www.hotel-mozart.hr. ✆ **051/718-260.** 29 units. Double Jul–Aug from 187€. **Amenities:** Restaurant; cafe/piano bar; spa; Wi-Fi (free).

Remisens Premium Hotel Ambassador ★★★ Built in 1966, this 10-floor modern block stands on Opatija's seafront promenade. The 200 rooms and suites here are decorated in earthy tones of beige and brown, and all have balconies—those on the top floor were renovated in 2013 and afford the most stunning views. Facilities include the Five Elements Wellness & Spa, which was added in 2007, and extends over two whole floors; an outdoor pool filled with heated seawater; and a bathing area lined with sunbeds and big white parasols that affords easy access into the sea. The staff is friendly and professional, and full of local advice and recommendations.

F. Peršića 5. www.remisens.com. ✆ **051/710-444.** 200 units. Double Jul–Aug 180€. **Amenities:** 3 restaurants; cafe; bar; outdoor and indoor pool; spa; 3 rooms for those w/limited mobility; Wi-Fi (free).

MODERATE

Villa Ariston ★★ Set in a terraced garden overlooking the sea, a 15-minute walk along the coastal path from the center of Opatija, this villa dates from 1924. Guest rooms are furnished with antiques and have wooden parquet floors. The highly regarded a la carte restaurant has tables on a lovely waterside terrace, and there's a bathing area out front with a ladder for easy access to the sea.

Maršala Tita 179. www.villa-ariston.hr. ✆ **051/271-379.** 10 units. Double Aug 113€. **Amenities:** Restaurant; wine cellar; garden; Wi-Fi (free).

Villa Hotel Kapitanović ★★ On a steep hillside above Opatija (served by a free hotel shuttle bus), this property makes for a peaceful hideaway, ideal for travelers whose top priority isn't being by the sea. The hotel restaurant, Laurus, serves meals on a terrace affording fantastic views down over the bay. Freshly baked croissants and omelets cooked-to-order are on the breakfast menu, followed by a Mediterranean array at dinner, including lobsters fresh from a tank. There's an outdoor pool rimmed with sunbeds, and a small spa with a sauna and Jacuzzi. The 24 rooms and 3 spacious suites all have wooden floors and basic but comfortable furnishing—it's worth paying extra for a superior room with a balcony and sea views.

Nova cest 12a. www.villa-kapetanovic. ✆ **051/741-355.** 27 units. Double Aug 140€. **Amenities:** Restaurant; bar; pool; sauna; Wi-Fi (free).

INEXPENSIVE

Stancija Kovačići ★ In the peaceful little village of Matulji, 5km (3 miles) north of Opatija, this welcoming B&B is run by a young couple, with the husband serving as chef. There are five spacious rooms, all tastefully decorated, with en suite bathrooms and hydro-massage tubs (but no shower). The highlight is the restaurant, popular with residents and non-residents alike, which serves creative Mediterranean cuisine prepared from local ingredients such as cheeses, seasonal tomatoes and figs, and Istrian truffles. A rich breakfast is served at outdoor tables on a patio in the garden.

Rukavac 51, Matulji. www.stancija-kovacici.hr. ✆ **051/272-106.** 5 units. Double Aug 88€. **Amenities:** Restaurant; Wi-Fi (free).

Where to Dine

EXPENSIVE

Bevanda　★★★　SEAFOOD　A romantic venue for a special celebration, this gourmet restaurant has outdoor tables on a small peninsula overlooking the sea and Opatija's waterside promenade. Founded in 1971, it has won many awards. In summer 2013, it reopened as an ultra-modern restaurant and small luxury hotel on the site of the original eatery. Dishes include delights such as risotto with shrimp and wild asparagus, and lobster with tagliatelle, which you should follow with fresh fish, the options depending on the previous night's catch. To try a bit of everything, opt for the six-course degustation menu. It is very expensive, but most people agree that it's worth it. Reservations are recommended.

Zert 8. www.bevanda.hr. ✆ **051/493-888.** Entrees 130kn–320kn, more for fish priced by the kilo. Tasting menus 350kn–650kn. Daily 10am–2am.

Plavi Podrum　★★★　SEAFOOD　With outdoor tables shaded by blue canvas awnings overlooking the harbor, this upmarket restaurant dates back to the early 1900s, making it one of the oldest in the region. The kitchen turns out creative seafood dishes prepared from local ingredients. The signature menu, the "homage to scampis from Kvarner," features four scampi dishes, of which the highlight is pasta with scampi and truffles. For something simpler, opt for the seafood platter for two, a good bottle of crisp white wine, and chocolate dessert. Also be sure take a look inside, where the walls are hung with the hospitality awards the restaurant has won.

Obala F. Supila 4, Volosko. www.plavipodrum.com. ✆ **051/701-223.** Tasting menus 330kn–440kn. Daily noon–midnight.

MODERATE

Konoba Ribarnice Volosko　★　SEAFOOD　Owned by a local fisherman, this down-to-earth eatery serves the previous night's catch, straight off the boat. Besides the more expensive fish, such as sea bass and gilthead bream, the restaurant also offers the cheaper "blue" varieties, like sardines, anchovies, and mackerel. They're cooked with garlic and lots of olive oil and served with the classic side dish, Swiss chard and potato. The place is small and popular with locals, so it can get crowded, and you might be expected to share a table with other guests. Also down-to-earth is the no-credit-card policy.

Andrija Stangera 5, Volosko. ✆ **051/701-483.** Entrees 40kn–70kn. Mon–Sat 9am–10pm; Sun 10am–3pm.

INEXPENSIVE

Pizzeria Moho　★★　PIZZA　In Volosko, next door to Le Mandrać, this chic eatery serves delicious pizzas from a brick oven, plus a modest selection of pasta dishes and colorful salads. The portions are generous and the prices reasonable. There are outdoor tables on a terrace looking onto the harbor, and a subtly lit dining room with a lovely vintage photomural of a waterfront scene.

Obala Frane Supila 8, Volovska. ✆ **099/256-22-89.** Pizzas 50kn–80kn. Daily noon–11pm.

Lovran & Environs

Slower-paced and more casual than Opatija, the picturesque town of Lovran, 6km (4 miles) to the north, is the choice of tourists who want the Riviera's beaches and recreation opportunities but not the upscale lifestyle. Lovran is where Opatija's Lungomare ends—or begins—depending on your point of view.

Excitement in Lovran (named for its numerous laurel trees) is not limited to toasting on the beach. For three weekends every October, the chestnut is king, and you can feast on the celebrated nut in many forms at the annual **Chestnut Festival (Marunada).** There is also a **Wild Asparagus Festival** in April and **Cherry Days** in June. There are reasons other than produce to consider a stay in Lovran, including stunning villas on the town's periphery; a quaint old town complete with a 12th-century church **(St. George's)** with lovely frescoes and Glagolitic inscriptions; and two municipal beaches.

GETTING AROUND
Buses to and from Rijeka breeze through Lovran every 20 minutes or so. If you have your own car, you can get to Lovran from Opatija in about 10 minutes. You can even get here on foot, following the Lungomare from Opatija or any point north of town along the 12km (7½-mile) promenade.

VISITOR INFORMATION
The **Lovran Tourist Information Office** (www.tz-lovran.hr; ℂ **051/291-740**) at Trg Slobode 1 near the harbor provides maps and other helpful information.

WHERE TO STAY
Draga di Lovrana ★★★   Dating from 1909, Draga di Lovrana is located up a steep, narrow, winding road above the coast. You can reach it by bus from Lovran: The stop is in front of the hotel and the owner provides bus schedules. There are six reasonably priced rooms, plus a luxurious suite with an open fireplace, sauna, and Jacuzzi. Most guests come here specifically to eat at the gourmet restaurant, which serves local specialties on a terrace with spectacular views. Breakfast, like dinner, is truly delicious, with freshly squeezed orange juice and omelets cooked to order.

Lovranska Draga 1, Lovran. www.dragadilovrana. ℂ **051/294-166.** 7 units. Double 89€ year-round. **Amenities:** Restaurant; Wi-Fi (free).

Hotel Villa Vera ★   In the center of Lovran, this villa is set in a lovely lush garden, which runs all the way down to the seaside promenade. The decor is a little old-fashioned—guestrooms have carpets and heavy brocade curtains and bed covers—but the overall atmosphere is romantic and intimate. The hotel serves a delicious breakfast on the restaurant terrace, in the garden, followed by creative Mediterranean cuisine later in the day. There's a wellness center, with lots of natural light, housing an indoor pool and Jacuzzi.

Maršala Tita 5, Lovran. www.hotel-villavera.hr. ℂ **051/294-120.** 17 units. Double Jul–Aug 160€. **Amenities:** Restaurant; garden; fitness center; spa; Wi-Fi (free).

WHERE TO DINE & DRINK
Wine Bar Loza ★★   TAPAS   On the square in the old town, this romantic little wine bar has a rustic candlelit interior, with whitewashed walls, wooden beamed ceilings, and red and white checked tablecloths. There are also tables outside, under a walnut tree. The food is simple, fresh, and local: Think a basket of freshly baked bread and a wooden platter of cheese, prosciutto, and salami, intended to complement quality local wines, which your waiter will tell you about.

Stari Grad 5, Lovran. www.winebar.hr. ℂ **051/294-444.** Entrees 50kn–85kn. Tues–Sun 5pm–1am.

KRK ISLAND

Croatia's largest island (pronounced "kirk," with a strong Scottish burr) is also the country's most developed, especially in the north where the island is connected to the mainland via a mile-long toll bridge. Add Rijeka's airport, an oil storage facility, and an oil pipeline to the mix, and you have the ingredients for an industrial region.

Tourism destinations on "The Golden Island" (Krk's official nickname) are mostly on the island's coasts, and they run the gamut from partially walled historic **Krk Town** on the west coast, to the long curving beach with promenade that is **Baška** in the south, to the rather less appealing package resorts in **Omišalj, Njivice,** and **Malinska** on the northwest coast.

Krk Town's settlement followed the familiar Illyrian-Roman-Byzantium-Venetian-Hungarian chain of control that is characteristic of many Croatian coastal cities. In the 11th century the city became an important center for the country's Glagolitic script, which was used until the beginning of the 19th century. At that time, Austria-Hungary took Krk from the Frankopans (the dukes of Krk, a powerful feudal family), who had held it since the 12th century.

As with most of Croatia's islands, tourism is an economic mainstay for Krk, though there is some agriculture, and the island is particularly noted for its Vrbnička Žlahtina, a crisp white wine produced in the village of Vrbnik on the east coast.

Getting There & Getting Around

BY CAR   The Krk Bridge connects the mainland with the island. Ferries leave from **Valbiska** on the west side of the island for **Cres** and **Lošinj,** while another ferry line makes regular runs between **Lopar** on **Rab** and **Baška** on Krk's southern end during the summer months. There are several ferries each day from June through September, but schedules are limited the rest of the year. Check the **Jadrolinija Lines** website (www.jadrolinija.hr) for schedule and price details.

BY BUS   Krk Town is well served by buses from Rijeka, most of which continue to the beach resort of Baška in the extreme southern part of the island. Even if you don't have your own car, you can see all of Krk's main sites. Buses run regular routes between major towns and connect with less frequent local lines.

Visitor Information

The **Krk Town Tourist Office** (www.tz-krk.hr; ✆ **051/221-414**) at Vela Placa 1 provides maps and local information. **Baška Tourist Office** (www.tz-baska.hr; ✆ **051/856-817**) at Zvonimirova 114 gives out maps, brochures, and directions.

What to See & Do
KRK TOWN

Krk Town, located halfway down Krk's west coast, is the island's chief settlement. It has an enchanting car-free historic center, which is still partly fortified, and a busy little waterfront promenade lined by restaurants, cafes, shops, and bars. It is a popular weekend resort because it is so accessible to the mainland. If you're there just to see the important and interesting sites, you don't need to stay more than a couple of hours.

The town's main attraction is the impressive **Katedrala Uznesenja (Cathedral of the Assumption)** on the main square, Trg Vela Placa. Built on the site of Roman baths, which later became a 5th-century basilica and a 9th-century monastery, the cathedral as seen today dates largely from the 13th century. Through the years, Roman columns, ancient mosaics, and medieval stone carvings have been integrated into the cathedral; the bell tower was added much later, in the 18th century.

Next to the Cathedral is the 11th-century Romanesque church of **Sveti Kivrin (St. Quirinus),** dedicated to Krk's patron saint. It has a small treasury displaying sacral art.

BAŠKA

Baška lies 19km (12 miles) southeast of Krk Town. The main attraction here is **Baška beach,** a 2km (1¼-mile) stretch of fine pebble, which gently curves around a southeast-facing bay, making this former fishing village a sun worshipper's paradise. Today Baška retains some of its former charm, but it is undeniably aimed at tourists, with lots of modern hotels and restaurants offering fixed menus in countless languages.

For Croatians, Baška is also synonymous with the 900-year-old **Baška Tablet,** which was discovered in 1851 in the tiny Romanesque **Church of St. Lucy** in the hamlet of Jurandvor, less than a mile north of Baška. One of the nation's most important archaeological discoveries, this large, flat stone slab was set in the church floor. It's engraved in Glagolitic script, the oldest Slavic alphabet, which dates back to the 9th century. Besides its value as a cultural artifact, the Baška Tablet is also the first record of a Croatian king—it commemorates a gift from the first Croat King, Zvonimir, to the church. What you see here in Jurandvor today is a copy; the original was moved to Zagreb's Academy of Arts and Sciences in 1934.

Where to Stay

If your agenda is making day trips and doing some cultural sightseeing, base yourself in Krk Town. If you simply want to enjoy the sea and sunshine and relax, then stay in Baška by the beach.

EXPENSIVE

Atrium Residence Baška   Baška's most luxurious hotel, the purpose-built Atrium, opened in 2008. Overlooking the beach, it lies just a 5-minute walk from the old town, and has 18 rooms and 46 luxurious apartments, all with balconies. The apartments have fully equipped kitchenettes, and the best ones have outdoor hydro-massage tubs on the balconies. You'll pay a little more for a sea view, but it's worth it. Guests have the use of the wellness center and pools at sister hotel Corinthia next door.

Emila Geistlicher 39, Baška. www.hotelibaska.hr. ℰ **051/656-890.** 64 units. Double Jul–Aug from 166€. **Amenities:** Restaurant; cafe; bar; Wi-Fi (free).

Marina   Ideally located on the seafront in Krk Town, close to the cathedral, this hotel dates back to 1925. Renovated in 2008, it is now stylish and modern, with seven rooms and three suites. Bathrooms are slick and spacious, combining both a large bathtub and a shower. All units have lovely sea views over the harbor, and most come with private, furnished balconies, so you can sit and watch the yachts sail in and out of the marina. The hotel restaurant has a blissful waterside terrace where you can enjoy a plentiful breakfast.

Obala Hrvatske Mornarice 8. www.hotelmarina.hr. ℰ **051/221-128.** 10 units. Double July–Aug 180€. **Amenities:** Restaurant; bar; Wi-Fi (free).

MODERATE

Hotel Placa ★   In the heart of Krk Town's car-free historic center, just off the main square, this boutique hotel occupies an old stone building. There are just five guest rooms, all with wooden floors, whitewashed walls, mismatched wooden furniture, chiffon drapes above the beds, and mosaic-tile bathrooms with showers. The price includes a champagne welcome, plus an excellent cooked-to-order breakfast, served at the restaurant across the street.

Ribarska 5, Krk Town. www.hotel-placa.com. ℭ **051/587-429.** 5 units. Double Aug from 130€. Wi-Fi (free).

Hotel Tamaris ⭐⭐ Overlooking Baška's lovely pebble beach, this friendly family-run hotel provides everything you need for a no-frills seaside vacation. There are 15 rooms and 15 apartments, all basic but comfortable, with blue carpets and slightly dated modern furniture. Ground floor apartments have 2 rooms—a bedroom with a double bed, and a living room with a kitchenette and sofa-bed (sleeping two)—plus a private terrace with sunbeds, making them the perfect option for families with kids. The house restaurant has a pleasant sea-view terrace.

Emila Geistlicha bb, Baška. www.baska-tamaris.com. ℭ **051/864-200.** 30 units. Double Aug 126€. **Amenities:** Restaurant; Wi-Fi (free).

INEXPENSIVE

Villa Ana ⭐ In Krk Town, just outside the historic center and just a 5-minute walk from the beach, Villa Ana is a peaceful and welcoming B&B. There are six basic but comfortable rooms, plus two apartments complete with cooking facilities, sofa beds affording extra space for kids, and furnished patios for open-air dining. The owner puts on a hearty buffet breakfast, with fresh bread, cheese, ham, yogurt, and coffee.

Slavka Nikolića 30, Krk Town. www.juresic-krk.com. ℭ **051/222-220.** 8 units. Double Jul–Aug 65€. **Amenities:** Parking; Wi-Fi (free).

Where to Dine

Bistro Francesca ⭐⭐ SEAFOOD Hidden in the old part of Baška, away from the typical tourist restaurants along the seafront, this welcoming eatery offers very reasonably priced Mediterranean dishes, prepared from local ingredients. Look out for the octopus salad with orange, and the barbecued tuna steak served with green sauce and polenta. In the spring of 2014, the bistro relocated and now has a dining room and outdoor tables in a small internal courtyard draped with vines. Run by a young team, it offers friendly and professional service, and a romantic atmosphere, with mellow background jazz. Reservations are recommended.

Zvonimirova 56, Baška. www.bistrofrancesca.com. ℭ **099/654-75-38.** Entrees 60kn–120kn. May–Sept daily noon–midnight.

Konoba Šime ⭐⭐ SEAFOOD With outdoor tables overlooking the seafront in Krk Town, this informal eatery is a sound choice. The menu includes local seafood specialties, such as scampi risotto and grilled calamari served with boiled Swiss chard and potato, as well as some tasty meat dishes, including a tender, delicious fillet steak in green pepper sauce. Note that it's cash-only here.

Antuna Mahnica 1. ℭ **051/220-042.** Entrees 40kn–150kn. Daily 10am–11pm.

Restaurant Cicibela ⭐ SEAFOOD & PIZZA On Baška's seafront promenade, this restaurant is obviously aimed at tourists and passing visitors. However, it offers a lovely view over the bay, and good fresh fish—a waiter will bring a platter to show you what fish they have, which will then be cooked, brought to your table, filleted, and served. For a cheaper meal, they also do very acceptable pizza and pasta dishes.

Emila Geistlicha 22a, Baška. www.cicibela.hr. ℭ **051/856-013.** Entrees 40kn–150kn, more for fish priced by the kilo. Apr–Oct daily 10am–midnight.

Restaurant Nada ★★★ MEDITERRANEAN For an unforgettable meal (reservations are recommended), drive up to this award-winning eatery in the tiny hilltop village of Vrbnik, looking down onto the sea, 11km (7 miles) northeast of Krk Town. Nada dates to 1974, and is known for its good, fresh seafood, but many people come here specifically to drink the local Žlahtina white wine, accompanied by platters of sheep's cheese and *pršut* (prosciutto). With a prior booking, you can also tour Nada's wine cellar.

Glavača 22, Vrbnik. www.nada-vrbnik.com. 🕜 **051/857-065.** Entrees 55kn–260kn. Mar 15–Nov 1 daily noon–11pm.

RAB ISLAND

Like an actor who insists on being photographed from his "better side," Rab's terrain has two halves that are quite different from each other. If seen from the mainland, Rab resembles a strip-mined mountainside devoid of vegetation and inhospitable to intelligent life. The southwestern side of the island, however, is a very different story. Tranquil beaches and coves, green spaces, and a beautifully kept medieval old town belie travelers' first impressions. Rab has been a haven for tourists since the 19th century, but its history goes back even further.

Like Pag to the south, Rab was settled by Illyrians, who were succeeded by a series of conquerors: Romans, Byzantines, Croat-Hungarians, and finally the Venetians, who plundered the timber on Rab and other offshore Kvarner islands to build their ships. This wholesale environmental piracy left a vast swathe of ruined terrain. It wasn't until the late 19th century that tourism began to cross Rab's forlorn-looking east side to get to the island's verdant southwest side, where hotels began to sprout for aristocrats intent on frolicking in the surf.

Today the island's main tourist destinations are **Rab Town,** with its medieval center and series of Venetian campaniles (bell towers), and **Lopar Peninsula** at the island's northern tip, with its sandy beach and shallow water. Rab is also becoming a popular overnight stop for luxury yachts, which become tourist attractions themselves when they tie up in Rab Town's horseshoe-shaped harbor.

Getting There

BY CAR AND/OR BOAT You can reach the island of Rab from either the mainland or from several nearby islands, either by ferry or catamaran. Various companies cover different routes, so you need to give some attention to planning your route.

Jadrolinija (www.jadrolinija.hr) runs a regular car ferry from Prizna (on the mainland) to Žigljen on Rab, as well as a fast catamaran (foot passengers only) from Rijeka to Novalja on Pag, stopping at Rab Town en-route.

Linijska Nacionalna Plovidba (www.lnp.hr) operates ferries from Valbiska (Krk) to Lopar (Rab).

Rapska Plovidba (www.rapska-plovidba.hr) runs ferries from Jablanac (on the mainland) to Mišnjak (on Rab), and between Rab Town (Rab) and Lun (on Pag).

Service is more frequent in summer (Jun–Sept), and slightly reduced during the rest of the year (Oct–May).

BY BUS There are daily buses from Rijeka to Rab via the Jablanac ferry connection, and from Zadar to Rab, also via Jablanac.

Getting Around

Moving around the island is no problem as there is frequent bus service between Lopar and Rab Town. From Rab Town, water taxis also serve the island's main beaches.

Visitor Information

Rab Town Tourist Office (www.tzg-rab.hr; © **051/724-064**) at Trg Municipium Arba 8 gives out maps and local information.

Rab Town

Rab Town is a medieval wonder, rich with ancient churches and narrow, cobbled streets that seem to be vertical at points. There also is a wealth of stone buildings with red-tiled roofs, and four Venetian-inspired campaniles standing sentry at the harbor.

Orientation

The old town is immediately behind the *Riva* (boardwalk) and the marina. You have a choice of three narrow uphill paths, **Donja, Srednja,** or **Gornja** (lower, middle, and upper) to get there. The bus station is a 5-minute walk north of the old town, and to the west are **Komrčar Park** and the **Franciscan Monastery and Cemetery.** The town's beaches are on its south end.

What to See & Do
CHURCHES & BELL TOWERS

Rab Town is a city of churches (note that church opening hours are somewhat unreliable, so you'd do well to inquire at the tourist office to be sure of the exact hours during your visit). Most of these are along the Gornja spur (upper road) that parallels the *riva.* Some of the churches are open only for Mass, but most leave vestibule doors open all day so you can peek through a window or iron grate and get a glimpse of the inside. If you are heading uphill from the harbor, be sure to take a look at the fountain in **Trg Svetog Kristofora** (St. Christopher's Square), adorned with sculptures of the mythical star-crossed lovers Kalifront and Draga. Between the fountain and the churches are a few 15th-century palaces built by highborn families. **Dominus Palace** and **Nimira Palace** are the most impressive, but both are closed to the public.

If you are coming from the Nimira Palace and continue on to the top of the hill, you'll run right into **St. Christopher's,** which was once part of the city's highest tower. A small lapidarium next door holds ancient tombstones and other artifacts. Turn down Gornja Ulica, and you'll come to **St. John the Evangelist Church (Sveti Ivan Evandelista),** which dates to the 6th or 7th century and is little more than a ruin. The church served as a monastery for various religious orders as well as a bishop's residence, but it was closed in the first third of the 19th century and many of its bricks were used to repair other churches in the city. The 13th-century bell tower next door can be climbed.

Next is **Holy Cross Church (Sveti Križ),** which, according to legend, has a crucifix with a Christ figure that wept because of the townspeople's immoral conduct. **St. Justine Church (Sveti Justina)** follows, with its 16th-century bell tower and collection of sacral items, including a reliquary that supposedly holds the skull of St. Christopher. Continue on past **Trg Slobode** and you'll come to a third bell tower at **St. Andrew Church (Sveti Andrije),** which dates from the 12th century.

Just beyond that is the Romanesque **Church of St. Mary the Great (Sveta Marija Velika),** which is not only on the highest hill in town, but also has the biggest bell

Croatia was the first country in the world to offer nudist vacations. It's common to find naked people on designated naturist beaches along the coast, not just in nudist camps. Each year, an estimated one million vacationers from around the world choose Croatia for their vacation specifically so they can enjoy naked bathing. Some of Croatia's best nudist beaches include **Nugal** near Makarska, **Paklina** in Bol on Brač, and **Jerolim** on the Pakleni Islands opposite Hvar (all in Dalmatia). The Croatians say the British royals started the whole thing off when King Edward VIII and his mistress, Wallis Simpson, vacationed on Rab in 1936 and took a nude swim in the Bay of Kandarola off Frkanj peninsula.

tower. Both the church and tower were built in the 12th century. The Pietà above the church door dates to the early 16th century. The church itself is packed with history, including an 11th-century altar canopy, 15th-century choir stalls, and interior additions made during the 16th century. But it is the bell tower that draws the most attention. Situated on Roman ruins, the 23m-tall (75-ft.) tower has four floors and includes a balustraded pyramid on top, which you can climb up to. If you look at the four bell towers from the sea, they clearly slope from tallest to shortest.

The last church on the route is Baroque **St. Anthony (Sveti Antun),** which has an impressively carved marble altar.

ACTIVITIES

Beyond looking at churches and bell towers, Rab offers a range of watersports.

DIVING   Scuba diving excursions can be arranged through **Mirko Diving Center** (www.mirkodivingcenter.com; © **051/721-154**) at Barbat 17 or through **Kron Diving Center** (www.kron-diving.com; © **051/776-620**) at 413a Kampor. One of the most spectacular dive sites in the area is off the tiny island of Mali Čutin, which lies west of Rab, close to the east coast of Cres. Here you can explore a dramatic seawall that drops 48m (157 ft.), home to red and yellow Gorgonians, schools of fish, and sponges.

Where to Stay

EXPENSIVE

Arbiana Hotel   Overlooking the harbor, in a splendid Art Nouveau building from 1924, this luxurious boutique hotel reopened in 2007 after a total renovation. Rooms vary in size and shape, but are generally spacious and sumptuously furnished, with sweeping curtains and upholstered furniture in deep colors, and slick en-suite bathrooms with tubs. A regal breakfast with eggs cooked to order is served on the restaurant terrace, lined with potted olive trees. The staff is friendly and professional, and the hotel is noted for its personalized service.

Obala Kralja Petra Krešimira IV 1a. www.arbianahotel.com. © **051/775-900.** 28 units. Double Jul–Aug 165€. **Amenities:** Restaurant; grill; 2 bars; babysitting (extra charge); room service; rooms for those w/limited mobility; Wi-Fi (free).

MODERATE

Pansion Tamaris ★   Overlooking a small marina in a peaceful bay, a pleasant 20-minute walk from Rab Town, this welcoming little hotel has just 14 rooms, the best of which offer sea views and balconies. There's a covered terrace restaurant serving tasty local seafood—many guests opt for half-board and eat dinner here.

Palit 285. www.tamaris-rab.com. © **051/724-925.** 14 units. Double Jul–Aug 90€. **Amenities:** Restaurant; terrace; Wi-Fi (free).

Residence Astoria ⭐ In a Venetian palazzo on Rab's main square overlooking the harbor, this building started out as the local Customs House, later becoming one of Rab's first hotels. It has just five self-catering apartments, sleeping two, four, or six persons. Some have exposed stonework and balconies with amazing views over the old town. The ground floor Mali Café, with tables on the main square, and Restaurant Astoria, on an upper-level terrace that affords lovely views down onto the square, both come under the same management and offer a discount for Astoria guests.

Trg Municipium Arba. www.astoria-rab.com. © **051/774-844.** 5 units. Apartment Jul–Aug 100€. **Amenities:** Restaurant; cafe; Wi-Fi (free).

Where to Eat

Rab is packed with eateries, aimed primarily at tourists. With a few exceptions, they all dish up roughly the same kind of fare, rooted in the fresh bounty of the sea.

Konoba Rab ⭐ SEAFOOD In a narrow side alley between Srednja Ulica and Gornja Ulica, this informal eatery stays open most of the year and is highly regarded by locals. With exposed stone walls and low ceilings, the atmosphere is warm and cozy. Start your meal with the Adriatic Platter (a selection of prosciutto, octopus salad, and sheep's milk cheese from Pag), followed by either barbecued fresh fish or a succulent steak.

Kneza Branimira 3. © **051/725-666.** Entrees 40kn–120kn. Feb–Nov daily 10am–midnight.

Labarint ★ SEAFOOD In the heart of Rab's old town, with a lovely upper-level terrace affording views over the terracotta rooftops, Labarint makes a fine choice for a romantic meal. The menu features delights such as *rezanci s pinjolima i gorgonzolom* (pasta with pine kernels and gorgonzola cheese), *brudet* (fish stew), and *Rapska torta* (Rab Cake, made with almonds). The waiters are friendly and polite, and wear traditional Dalmatian white shirts with big puffed sleeves.

Srednja ulica 9. © **051/771-145.** Entrees 50kn–100kn. Apr–Oct daily noon–3pm and 5:30–11pm.

Marco Polo ★ SEAFOOD With a spacious terrace by the sea in Banjol, this informal eatery serves inexpensive dishes prepared from fresh local seafood and vegetables from the owner's garden. Expect classics such as *skampi buzara* (scampi cooked in a thick garlic and tomato sauce) and barbecued sea bass served with Swiss chard and boiled potatoes.

Banjol 486, Banjol. www.marcopolo-rab.com. © **051/725-846.** Entrees 40kn–90kn. Daily 10am–11pm.

CRES & LOŠINJ ISLANDS

Cres and Lošinj are really a single island, separated only by a 48m-wide (30 ft.) manmade channel that has been bridged by a roadway. Despite their proximity and historical links, these destinations couldn't be more different. Cres stretches 60km (40 miles) from tip to tip and is twice as long as Lošinj. Both islands are covered with biking and hiking trails, but it is Cres that is a haven for nature lovers and outdoor enthusiasts. Lošinj, on the other hand, is the island of choice for the yachting set and tourists looking for waterside cafes and hotels with wellness centers. More than half of Cres is covered with rocks and scrub grass, a landscape interrupted only by intersecting rock fences and sheep shelters that create a crisscross pattern on the inhospitable terrain. Lošinj is blanketed with a thick tree cover, well-groomed pebble beaches, lots of shops and restaurants, and several large resort hotels.

Cres's main tourist destination is Cres Town, which could double as a fishing village in Italy. (Cres and Lošinj have been popular vacation destinations for Italian tourists for years, probably because of the islands' proximity to Venice, and because both were once under Venetian rule.) Near Cres Town, several minuscule, remote villages—**Beli, Lubenice,** and **Valun** among them—are worth a detour. Lošinj's main villages are **Mali Lošinj** and **Veli Lošinj.** Both attract a large number of tourists, but it is Mali Lošinj that is the more developed center, probably as a result of Lošinj's former status as a shipyard and winter vacation destination for wealthy Austrians. Today, both islands retain their own character, while reaping most of their revenue from tourism.

Cres and Lošinj have been inhabited since the Stone Age and followed the familiar settlement pattern of the rest of Croatia's offshore islands. The islands were home to the Illyrians (more than 3,000 years ago) until the Romans came along in the 1st century, followed by the Byzantines and the Slavs. The Venetians, the Croat-Hungarians, the Austro-Hungarians, and the Yugoslavs followed, until the islands finally came under Croatian control in 1991. Today, Lošinj in particular is a thriving tourist destination.

Getting There & Getting Around

BY CAR AND/OR BOAT Getting to Cres and Lošinj is easy if you are driving or taking the ferry; and a little more complicated if you are traveling some other way. The shortest ferry crossing is from **Brestova** on the mainland to **Porozina** at the northern end of Cres, though you may have a long wait before boarding in peak season. There is another crossing from **Valbiska** on Krk to **Merag** farther down on Cres. Contact **Jadrolinija** (www.jadrolinija.hr) or **Lošinjska Plovidba** (www.lnp.hr) for schedules and routes.

BY BUS There are several daily buses from Veli Lošinj to Cres Town, and all stop at Mali Lošinj on the way. Buses also run to each of the islands' main ferry ports—Merag, Porozina, and Valbiska—and to Rijeka. For details and schedules, contact any tourist office on the island or the main bus station in Rijeka (p. 104).

LOCAL BUSES Several daily buses run the 3km (2 mile) stretch between Mali Lošinj and Veli Lošinj, though this also makes a pleasant walk.

Visitor Information

Cres Tourist Office (www.tzg-cres.hr; ✆ **051/571-535**) at Cons 10 in Cres Town and **Mali Lošinj Tourist Office** (www.tz-malilosinj.hr; ✆ **051/231-884**) at Riva Lošinjskih Kapetana 29 are the two main offices.

What to See on Cres

CRES TOWN

During the day, Cres Town resembles a deserted coastal village somewhere in southern Italy, thanks to its complement of small fishing boats, Venetian-style architecture, and relentless sun. The sound of Cres's peculiar chatter is a mix of Croatian and Italian that makes you forget that you're in Croatia.

Cres's main square, **Trg F. Petrića,** extends to the harbor. It is home to a lovely 16th-century loggia where public announcements once were posted. It also has an impressive 16th-century clock. From Trg F. Petrića, go through the 16th-century gate to **Pod Urom,** another square where you will find the church of **St. Mary of the Snow.** This little church has a graceful 15th-century portal adorned with a relief of the Virgin and Child. It is open during services only, but it's worth trying to coordinate your visit with Mass so you can see the carved wooden Pietà inside.

BELI, VALUN & LUBENICE

North of Cres Town, the island becomes steep and the road becomes a twisting, narrow ribbon more like a roller coaster track than a thoroughfare. About 8km (5 miles) past Cres Town, the road forks into **Beli,** a captivatingly rustic hilltop village that is practically deserted, with a pleasant pebble beach down below. In the past there was a bird sanctuary in Beli, dedicated to protecting the region's endangered griffon vultures, but sadly it has now closed down.

Valun is just 14km (9 miles) southwest of Cres Town, and can only be accessed by private transportation. Even with a car, you have to walk down a long flight of stairs to the harbor. Like Beli, Valun is anything but crowded. There are a few restaurants for those who are attracted by Valun's beaches. For history buffs, Valun is home to the **Valun Tablet,** which is really an 11th-century Glagolitic-inscribed tombstone. The Valun Tablet (with Latin translation in case you can read *that* dead language) can be viewed in the town's parish church.

Lubenice is 4.8km (3 miles) southwest of Valun atop a windy ridge high above a beautiful clear-water cove. The view from this tiny hilltop village is breathtaking. There's just one small eatery, **Konoba Hibernica,** where you can taste local lamb. You can get to the water below by picking your way down the gravel slope, but invest in a bottle of water first. Don't forget that you have to climb back up, unless someone meets you with a boat in the bay.

Where to Stay on Cres

There is only one big modern hotel on Cres (Hotel Kimen, below), but plenty of low-key private accommodations can be found.

MODERATE

Hotel Kimen ★   On the edge of Cres Town, a pleasant 10-minute walk along the coast from the harbor, this is the only big hotel option on the entire island. Overlooking the sea and backed by woodland, it is made up of three separate buildings—the main hotel, a villa, and an additional dependence. The hotel was fully renovated in 2008, and all rooms now have smart modern bathrooms and A/C, as well as sea views and balconies. (Rooms in the other two buildings have not been renovated and remain without A/C). Facilities include a Mediterranean/Croatian restaurant, and a spa offering beauty treatments.

Melin I/16. www.hotel-kimen.com. © **051/573-305.** 221 units. Double Aug 124€. **Amenities:** Restaurant; bar; spa; parking; Wi-Fi (free).

INEXPENSIVE

MaMaLu   In the pretty seaside village of Valun, 14km (9 miles) southwest of Cres Town, this friendly, family-run B&B offers eight basic but comfortable rooms, all with sea views and most with balconies. Downstairs there's a waterside terrace restaurant (see below) with potted geraniums, where an extensive breakfast is served—many guests opt for half board and enjoy a home-cooked dinner, too. There are a couple of decent pebble beaches nearby, so you can have a swim while your meal is prepared.

Valun 13a, Valun. www.mamalu-valun.hr. © **051/525-035.** 8 units. Double Jul–Aug 65€. **Amenities:** Restaurant; Wi-Fi (free).

Pansion Tramontana ★   In the small village of Beli, this welcoming B&B offers seven double rooms, three triple rooms, and two family rooms. There's an informal ground floor eatery serving home-cooked food (because there is nowhere else to eat nearby, most guests opt for half board.) Some visitors may consider the accommodations a little spartan, but it makes a fine base for outdoor enthusiasts. The *pansion* is right on the edge of the Tramontana forest, which is crisscrossed by hiking paths, and it's just a 20-minute walk down a steep hill to the beach, where the owners also run a scuba diving center.

Beli. www.beli-tramontana.com. ⓒ **051/840-519.** 7 units. Double Jul–Aug 90€. **Amenities:** Restaurant; Wi-Fi (free).

Where to Dine on Cres

The harbor in Cres Town is ringed with pizza places and a few grills—most are pretty much the same and can be crowded on summer evenings. For more authentic local cooking (noted below), drive out to nearby villages for fresh fish or the island's specialty, roast lamb.

Bukaleta   ROAST MEAT   Widely regarded as the best restaurant on the island, cozy, rustic Bukaleta specializes in local lamb, either roasted or stewed. It's also known for its delicious sheep's cheese, served with freshly baked bread as an appetizer. The location is in the hill village of Loznati, with a terrace affording amazing views over the Kvarner Gulf, 5km (3 miles) southeast of Cres Town.

Loznati. ⓒ **051/571-606.** Entrees 40kn–90kn. Apr–Sept daily noon–midnight.

MaMaLu   SEAFOOD   The owner of this family-run eatery is a fisherman and his specialty is catching shrimp. Take a table on his lovely waterside terrace to enjoy generous portions of reasonably priced seafood, including a delicious *rižot od škampi* (scampi risotto) and fresh fish barbecued over charcoal. Everything is served with local olive oil and wine, and the eatery doubles as a B&B, with eight rooms upstairs (see above).

Valun 13a, Valun. www.mamalu-valun.hr. ⓒ **051/525-035.** Entrees 40kn–80kn. May–Sept daily noon–midnight.

Pizza Luna Rossa   PIZZA   In the center of Cres Town, with outdoor tables overlooking the main square and the harbor, this informal eatery serves a good selection of pizzas, pastas, and salads. Try the Cherso pizza, topped with tomato, cheese, ham, a splash of cream, and parmesan. It's all very reasonably priced (cash only), and popular with locals and visitors alike.

Palada 4. www.pizzeria-lunarossa.hr. ⓒ **051/572-207.** Pizzas 23kn–56kn. Apr–Oct daily noon–11pm.

Restoran Riva   SEAFOOD   This is a great spot for an indulgent seafood feast, with tables on a terrace overlooking the colored boats of Cres Town's pretty fishing harbor. Order the fish platter for two, including barbecued *brancin* (sea bass), *škampi* (scampi) and *lignje* (calamari), plus a carafe of chilled Malvazija white wine. This is one of Cres's more expensive restaurants, and attracts guests from the nearby sailing marina.

Riva Creskih Kapetana 13. ⓒ **051/571-107.** Entrees 40kn–90kn, more for fish priced by the kilo. Apr–Oct daily noon–11pm.

What to See on Lošinj

Mali Lošinj, the main settlement on the island of Lošinj, started building its reputation as a tourist destination at about the same time it stopped building ships for the Austro-Hungarian Empire. The town prospered despite the decline in industry because wealthy Austrians began to winter there, as they had in Opatija, albeit on a smaller scale.

Some of the villas built on Lošinj in that era still exist (the town peaked as a building center in 1868), as does the shipyard itself, which is still working. Despite its annual influx of foreign tourists from all around the globe, Mali Lošinj has retained its charm and character, mostly by keeping the big resort complexes outside of town on Čikat Bay, west of the center. On summer nights, the **Riva Lošinjskih Kapetana** (promenade) along the harbor can resemble New Orleans at Mardi Gras, and getting a table at a restaurant or a room in a hotel can be impossible. But Mali Lošinj manages to handle the chaos without blinking an eye.

Lošinj Museum ★   Mali Lošinj isn't flush with vintage buildings and monuments, but it does have a collection of Italian and Croatian masters accumulated by the Mihičić and Piperata families. The collection is housed in the Fritzy Palace behind the harbor.

Vladimira Gortana 35. www.muzej.losinj.hr. ✆ **051/233-892.** Admission 10kn. May–Sept Tues–Fri 10am–1pm and 6–8pm; Sat 10am–1pm.

Where to Stay on Lošinj
EXPENSIVE
Hotel Apoksiomen ★   Owned by an Austrian company, this four-star property occupies the former Hotel Istra on Mali Lošinj's palm-lined seafront promenade, with views onto the pretty fishing harbor. Renovated in 2005, its rooms are vibrant, with blue carpets, mustard-yellow bedspreads, and floral curtains. All feature en suite marble bathrooms. Note that the accomodations in the back can be a bit dark, so it's worth paying extra for a sea view. There's a sunny waterside terrace where you can enjoy the buffet breakfast, followed by an a la carte dinner in the evening.

Riva Lošinjskih Kapetana 1, Mali Lošinj. www.vi-hotels.com. ✆ **051/520-820.** 25 units. Double Jul–Aug 160€. **Amenities:** Restaurant; cafe; room for those w/limited mobility; Wi-Fi (free).

Vitality Hotel Punta   Set amid pinewoods overlooking the sea, on the edge of Veli Lošinj, this big modern hotel reopened in spring 2012 following a complete renovation. Due to its sheer size it obviously can't offer the personalized service of a smaller hotel, but its luxury spa and extensive sports facilities—including a rocky beach, a water-skiing school, and bikes for hire—make it an attractive option. Its season is limited, just March through October.

Šestavine bb, Veli Lošinj. www.vitality.losinj-hotels.com. ✆ **051/622-000.** 235 units. Double Aug 203€. **Amenities:** 3 restaurants; 4 bars; 2 pools; spa; 13 clay tennis courts; watersports; Wi-Fi (free).

MODERATE
Hotel Televrin   Overlooking the harbor in the small village of Nerezine, a 10-minute drive from Mali Lošinj, this family-run hotel occupies a 1910 port authority and town hall. Rooms look onto either the seafront or the market square, and all have balconies. The a la carte restaurant serves local seafood specialties, with outdoor tables on the terrace in summer.

Obala nerezinskih pomoraca, Nerezine. www.televrin.com. ✆ **051/237-121.** 15 units. Double Jul–Aug 120€. **Amenities:** Restaurant; bar; Wi-Fi (free).

Mare Mare Suites   This small hotel offers seven rooms and suites, all with sea views. There's a pleasant communal living room, a terrace with an outdoor Jacuzzi, and guests have complimentary use of bicycles and kayaks. You'll find it on the harbor in Mali Lošinj. There is no restaurant as such, but breakfast is served.

Riva Lošinjskih Kapetana 36, Mali Lošinj. www.mare-mare.com. ✆ **051/232-010.** 7 units. Double Jul–Aug from 112€. **Amenities:** Bar; Wi-Fi (free).

INEXPENSIVE

Pansion Ana ★   In the seaside village of Artatore, 8km (5 miles) from Mali Lošinj, this friendly B&B is just a quick walk from the beach. It has 17 rooms, all with wooden floors, A/C, satellite TV, fridges, bathrooms with showers, and a balcony. There's a dining room where a generous breakfast is served: orange juice, cereal, platters of cheese and ham, pastries, and coffee. It's possible to opt for half board and eat dinner here, too.

Artatore 75, Lošinj. www.pansion-ana.com. ✆ **051/232-975.** 17 units. Double Jul–Aug 86€. Closed Nov–Apr. **Amenities:** Restaurant; Wi-Fi (free).

Where to Dine on Lošinj

As a general rule, the restaurants that line the harbor in Mali Lošinj are a little higher priced and more orientated towards tourists. For more authentic dining options, head to Veli Lošinj or other smaller settlements on the island.

Artatore   SEAFOOD   Lying 8km (5 miles) north of Mali Lošinj in Artatore Bay, this restaurant is much loved by sailing types, who moor their boats right out front. Founded in 1972, Artatore has a good reputation throughout Croatia, where it's noted for its seafood dishes, such as creamy crab soup, lobster with spaghetti, and oven-baked fish with potatoes.

Artatore 132, Artatore. www.restaurant-artatore.hr. ✆ **051/232-932.** Entrees 50kn–130kn, more for fish priced by the kilo. Apr–Oct daily 10am–midnight.

Bora Bar   TRATTORIA   Bora overlooks the colored wooden fishing boats of a small harbor, just a 10-minute walk from Veli Lošinj. Italian chef Marco Sasso, who spent several years in the U.S., keeps the atmosphere relaxed and informal. The kitchen serves refined contemporary cuisine, with truffles being the house specialty. The day's menu is chalked up on a blackboard, but look out for those truffles and homemade ravioli, along with standout tuna carpaccio and scampi risotto. Round things off with a chocolate soufflé.

Rovenska 3, Veli Lošinj. ✆ **051/867-544.** Entrees 60kn–150kn. Apr–Oct daily 9–2am.

Mol   SEAFOOD   A couple of doors down from Bora Bar, with outdoor tables likewise overlooking the quaint fishing harbor, Mol specializes in seafood. The menu includes delights such as tuna tartar, grilled scampi, and fresh fish, cooked to perfection on a barbecue and served with fries.

Rovenska 1, Veli Lošinj. ✆ **051/236-008.** Entrees 40kn–110kn, more for fish priced by the kilo. Apr–Oct daily 10am–midnight.

Za Kantun   SEAFOOD   Locals recommend this restaurant, hidden on a Mali Lošinj side alley, away from the chaos of the seafront. Unassuming from the outside, the food here is superb—expect dishes such as risotto with artichoke hearts and prosciutto, calamari stuffed with zucchini, and veal medallions in a mushroom sauce. The atmosphere is pleasant, with a raised stone terrace shaded by white awnings.

V Gortana 24, Mali Lošinj. ✆ **051/213-840.** Entrees 50kn–110kn. Apr–Oct daily noon–11pm.

UPPER DALMATIA

9

The region known as Upper Dalmatia, lying between Kvarner and Lower Dalmatia, with Zadar as its main city, is a collection of contradictions: The cities and sites are among some of Croatia's most accessible and enchanting, but the region is also home to what is arguably some of the most forbidding and barren terrain in the world. Still, there is something for everyone in this gateway to Croatia's glorious coast, whether your interests tend toward climbing the rugged peaks of the challenging **Velebit** mountain range, sailing the deep blue Adriatic to explore the uninhabited rocky islets of the **Kornati,** or listening to classical music at the medieval **Church of St. Donat** in Zadar.

All roads to and from Upper Dalmatia seem to go through Zadar, the largest city on the region's coastal highway. In many ways, Zadar's mix of monuments and commerce, of ancient history and contemporary nightlife, make it one of Croatia's most cosmopolitan centers.

From Zadar, you can visit the arid rocky island of **Pag,** known for its delicious *Paški sir* (a sheep's milk cheese similar to Parmesan), and the all-night summer parties hosted on **Zrće** beach in Novalja.

South of Zadar, the coastal city of **Šibenik** is home to a splendid UNESCO-listed cathedral, and from here you can make day trips to the waterfalls of **Krka National Park** and the islands of **Kornati National Park.**

ORIENTATION
Exploring the Region

Transportation vagaries in Upper Dalmatia make logistics difficult for people who want to see a lot in a short time. Covering the maximum amount of territory during a trip to the coast north of Split can be accomplished with careful planning, however. Most visitors to Pag spend a weekend or more on the beach at **Novalja,** swimming and sunbathing by day and enjoying music and dancing by night, while visitors to Zadar might make that city a base for a week or more of excursions to the mountains of **Paklenica National Park** and the scattered islets of **Kornati National Park.**

Others might spend their entire stay in Zadar, investigating its imposing churches and ancient monuments before venturing out of the city for day trips on local ferries to see some of the area's numerous offshore islands, such as **Dugi Otok** and **Pašman** in the Zadar Archipelago. Those who head south will need at least a day to discover **Šibenik,** plus a day to see **Krka National Park.**

It's fairly simple to access all the major coastal sites in Upper Dalmatia by driving down from Rijeka (in the neighboring Kvarner region), but it's

Upper Dalmatia

much trickier to coordinate ferry connections from the mainland to and between the islands.

Essentials

VISITOR INFORMATION   Coastal Dalmatia is Croatia's most celebrated region, and tourism services are well organized and developed. For tourist office contact information in Upper Dalmatia, see "Visitor Information" for individual cities below, or contact the Croatia National Tourist Office (www.croatia.hr).

GETTING THERE   **Bus travel,** which is efficient and economical in this region, is the most popular mode of public transportation. Croatian buses are air-conditioned and can not only get you from one mainland destination to another, but they'll also provide transport to islands served by larger ferries. See the Zagreb bus station website (www. akz.hr) for times.

GETTING AROUND   **Private auto** is the most efficient and comfortable way to visit the Upper (or Lower) Dalmatian coast because you'll be able to set your own schedule, linger where you find something you like, and move on when you don't. But note that parking can be a problem (most old towns are pedestrian-only, so you have to leave your car outside the walls) and taking the car onto ferries adds huge expense to your journey. For those who don't have their own transportation, **buses** are the next best way to explore the mainland coast. Regular **ferries** link coastal towns with major Dalmatian islands. To discover the islands in the best way possible, if you have the means, you can rent a **yacht** and map out a sea tour with the help of a professional skipper. Split and Dubrovnik have major **airports,** and Zadar has a smaller (but increasingly busy) one. All are connected by air with Zagreb. Note that **rail travel** is not a convenient way to explore Upper Dalmatia, as very few towns have train stations (though it is the ideal way to travel direct from Zagreb to Split in Lower Dalmatia).

ZADAR

Zadar has had a traumatic history, but despite its frequent reconstruction, it remains a beautiful city brimming with more than 3,000 years of history and culture. Like most cities on the Dalmatian coast, Zadar evolved from a prehistoric settlement to an Illyrian village to a Roman municipality. It came under the control of Byzantium, was ransacked by the Crusades, spent several centuries under the Venetians, and then passed to the Austro-Hungarian Empire.

Zadar is first mentioned in 9th-century writings as the residence of Bishop Donat, the cleric who built the Church of the Holy Trinity in the former **Roman Forum,** remains of which lie next to the cathedral. Today that 9th-century church is known as **St. Donatus** to honor Bishop Donat, and it has become the city's symbol. After the construction of **St. Donatus,** many other churches were built in Zadar, making it a center of Roman Catholicism.

When Venice tried to capture every city on the Dalmatian coast starting in the late 10th century (it took Venice until the 15th century to finally succeed), Zadar fought back harder than any other municipality. From 1096 to 1346, Zadar was conquered and liberated an incredible seven times, and then taken over six more times until it was sold in 1409 to Venice by King Ladislav of Naples, who was Zadar's ruler du jour. Following the sale, Venice had authority over Zadar for almost four centuries, until 1797. During that time, the Venetians developed the city and its economy, but only to the extent that those efforts benefited Venice.

Eventually, the Venetians were driven out, and for 120 years or so after that Zadar was governed by Austria (with a short stint of French rule), a regime that ended with World War I, but did not end Zadar's occupation. From 1920 to 1944 Zadar was governed by Italy and forced to accept Italian acculturation, though many citizens left rather than submit to Italianization.

During World War II, Zadar was heavily bombarded by Allied forces, though it was mostly rebuilt during the postwar Yugoslavia era. Then, during the 1991 war, the city suffered isolation due to its position—Serb forces in the hinterland effectively cut the city off from the rest of the country. The road to Zagreb did not reopen until 1993. In 1995, during Operation Storm, the Croatian army reclaimed outlying rural areas, which had historically had a sizeable Serb population.

Today's Zadar is an exceptional combination of new and old architecture and a diverse mix of cultures. It is also fiercely nationalistic, a characteristic that took hold while the city was isolated from the rest of Croatia by the Serbs.

Essentials

VISITOR INFORMATION Zadar is a tourist-friendly town with well-marked streets and addresses and large illustrated explanatory posters installed in front of

CHERRIES in a glass

Before you leave Zadar, try the local drink that has become one of the city's specialties. Maraschino is made from a unique variety of *maraska* cherry grown in the region, and it can be had in both alcoholic and nonalcoholic forms. According to legend, alcoholic maraschino, usually a treacly sweet cherry liqueur, was first made by monks in the 16th century and was thought to improve the disposition. Today the liqueur is made in Zadar in a factory near the footbridge. The factory is not open to visitors or tour groups, but all the local general stores and liquor stores sell the liqueur, which makes a fine gift to bring home. The most obvious place to taste the stuff is at Maraschino Bar (see below).

almost every notable building. For more detailed information, maps, and brochures, you can check with the local **Tourist Information Center** (✆ 023/316-166) at Mihovila Klaića 1 or the **Zadar Tourism Board** (www.tzzadar.hr; ✆ 023/212-222) at Ilije Smiljanića 5. For information on Zadar and the surrounding region, contact the **Zadar County Tourist Board** (www.zadar.hr; ✆ 023/315-316) at Sv. Leopolda B. Mandića 1.

GETTING THERE

Almost every mode of transportation flows through Zadar, but some methods are better than others.

BY CAR Driving is one of the easiest ways to reach Zadar thanks to the A1 superhighway along the coast. The drive time between Zagreb and Zadar is about 3 hours.

BY BUS Bus service to Zadar from Zagreb is convenient and inexpensive, as is the service to Zadar from Split. Zadar's bus station lies a 15-minute walk (also served by bus nos. 2 and 4) northeast of the Old Town. For schedule and ticket information contact the **Zadar Coach Station** (www.liburnija-zadar.hr; ✆ 060/305-305) at Ante Starčevića 1.

BY BOAT **Jadrolinija** operates overnight ferry service between Ancona (Italy) and Zadar, as well as twice-weekly summer coastal service from Rijeka to Dubrovnik, including stops in Zadar, Split, Stari Grad (Hvar), and Korčula. From Zadar, you can also catch regular ferries and catamarans to the nearby islands of the Zadar archipelago. The Jadrolinija Zadar office (www.jadrolinija.hr; ✆ 023/250-555) is at Liburnska obala 7.

BY PLANE **Zadar Airport** (www.zadar-airport.hr; ✆ 023/205-800), about 8km (5 miles) south of the city, handles an average of 12 scheduled domestic and international flights per day (more on weekends), including Croatia Airlines shuttles and European budget airlines. Zadar Airport is located in the small municipality of Zemunik Donji.

BY TRAIN The train station stands next to the bus station, but unfortunately **train service** (www.hzpp.hr) from Zadar is minimal and not really useful for tourist destinations.

GETTING AROUND

Croatia Airlines provides shuttle service between the airport and Zadar bus station, scheduled to coincide with flights, for 25kn. Zadar's Old Town is a lovely place to explore on foot, as it is closed to vehicular traffic.

[FastFACTS] ZADAR

Airport Zadar Airport (www.zadar-airport.hr; ℂ **023/205-800**).

ATMs & Banks There are numerous ATMs (Bankomats) in Zadar where you can withdraw cash using American Express, Diners Club, Maestro/MasterCard, and Visa. Most banks are open Monday to Friday 8am to 7pm and Saturday 8am to noon.

Bus Station Zadar Bus Station, Ante Starčevića 1 (www.liburnija-zadar.hr; ℂ **060/305-305**).

Emergency For police dial ℂ **192;** for an ambulance, ℂ **194;** to report a fire, ℂ **193.**

Ferry Office Jadrolinija, Liburnska Obala 7 (www.jadrolinija.hr; ℂ **023/250-555**).

Hospital Hospital Zadar, Bože Peričića 5 near the Hotel Kolavare (ℂ **023/505-505**).

Internet Almost every hotel and hostel now offers free Internet access to guests, as do many cafes.

Pharmacy Ljekarna Donat at Braće Vranjanin bb (ℂ **023/251-480**) and

Ljekarna Zadar at Jurja Barakovićca 2 (ℂ **023/302-932**) take turns in working 24-hour shifts.

Police Police Station, Andrije Hebranga bb (www.mup.hr; ℂ **023/345-111**).

Post Office Central Post Office, Kralja S. Držislava 1 (ℂ **023/222-355**). Hours Monday to Friday 7am to 8pm, Saturday 7am to 7pm.

Taxi Call ℂ **023/251-400.**

What to See & Do

Zadar is a city of dichotomies that juxtapose modern construction with ancient architecture, live-and-let-live attitudes with fiercely patriotic conviction, and bustling entrepreneurship with laid-back Mediterranean style. You can visit the city's historic sites and countless churches, stop for gelato in Old Town, then go on to browse the glitzy shops that line the narrow streets, but it's much more interesting to seek out Zadar's less obvious charms.

Built compactly on a small peninsula, Zadar's pedestrian-only Old Town was fortified by the Venetians, and sections of the city walls and four of its gates (the most notable being the impressive **Land Gate** from 1543) still remain. The perimeter of the peninsula is rimmed by the *Riva* (seaside promenade), where you can watch ferries sail in and out of port while witnessing some of the world's most beautiful sunsets. For many people, locals and visitors alike, one of Zadar's most memorable features is the ingenious **Sea Organ,** a modern installation which plays eerie melodies powered by the sea, located at the end of the Riva close to the tip of the Old Town peninsula.

Archaeological Museum ★ Overlooking the Forum Square, this modernist concrete building, erected in the 1970s, houses a museum that traces the region's history from prehistoric times up to the 12th century. The main emphasis is on the Roman period, with exhibits including ancient marble statues, mosaics, and weaponry.

Trg Opatice Čike 1. www.amzd.hr. ℂ **023/250-516.** Admission 15kn. Jun–Sept daily 9am–9pm; Apr–May and Oct–Dec Mon–Sat 9am–3pm; Jan–Mar Mon–Sat 9am–2pm.

Church of St. Simeon ★★ This 17th-century church is best known as the home of the mummified body of St. Simeon, one of Zadar's patron saints. The relic is contained within an ornate silver casket, depicting scenes from the saint's life, crafted by Zadar silversmiths in 1381. Regarded as one of the finest examples of silverwork ever produced in Zadar, it takes pride of place on the main altar. Each year on October 8, the saint's feast day, the casket is opened and Simeon's body is put on public display.

Trg Šime Budinića. Open during Mass only.

Forum ★★ Dating back to the 1st century B.C., the Roman Forum would once have been the city's principle public meeting space, where people would trade and barter, discuss politics, and also worship at the temple. The site of the Forum as you see it today, with ancient paving stones and some crumbling ruins, was only discovered in the 1930s. Nowadays, it is overlooked by the Church of St. Donat, the cathedral, the Archaeological Museum, and several open-air cafes.

Zeleni trg (aka Forum).

The Gold and Silver of Zadar ★★★ Guarded since World War II by nuns from the neighboring Benedictine convent, this horde of gold and silver reliquaries and sacral art attests to Zadar's historical wealth. The reliquaries supposedly hold body parts of various saints, including arms and legs, which were encased in gold or silver and often elaborately decorated with jewels and filigree as a show of reverence and respect. Other exhibits at this convent museum include gold and silver church paraphernalia (mainly crosses) and religious paintings from the 15th and 16th centuries.

Trg Opatice Čike 1. © **023/211-545.** Admission 20kn. Mon–Sat 10am–1pm and 6–8pm; Sun 10am–noon.

Greeting to the Sun ★★★ Installed in 2008 on the Riva next to the Sea Organ (see below), which was also designed by local architect Nikola Bašić, the Greeting to the Sun features 300 glass plates set in a large circle within the stone paving. During the day, light-sensitive solar modules below the glass plates absorb energy from the sun, which is then used to put on a solar-powered multi-colored light display as the sun sets.

On the Riva at the south end of the Old Town.

Museum of Ancient Glass ★★ Opened in 2009, this impressive museum displays a collection of over 5,000 pieces of Roman glassware, including goblets, jars, and vials, retrieved from archaeological sites across Dalmatia. The artifacts date from the 1st century B.C. to the 5th century A.D. On the top floor, you can watch a craftsman working with glass, employing the same techniques that the ancients used. The excellent gift shop stocks replicas of ancient glassware, in subtle blues or greens, making tasteful and unusual gifts to bring home. You'll find the museum inside the 19th-century Cosmacendi Palace, on the eastern side of the Old Town peninsula, close to the sea channel.

Poljana Zemaljskog odbora 1. www.mas-zadar.hr. © **023/363-831.** Admission 30kn. Mon–Sat 9am–4pm.

St. Anastasia Cathedral and Bell Tower ★★ On the northern side of the Forum, Zadar's Romanesque cathedral dates back to the 12th century. The facade holds three doors and two central rose windows, while inside, a 9th-century stone casket is said to contain the remains of St. Anastasia, after whom the cathedral is named. You can climb some 180 steps to reach the top of the freestanding bell tower for amazing views over the city and out to sea.

Trg Sveti Stošije 1. © **023/251-708.** Admission 15kn. May–Oct Mon–Sat 8am–8pm.

St. Donatus ★★ On the Roman Forum, this monumental 9th-century Byzantine rotunda started out as the Church of the Holy Trinity, but was later renamed in tribute to Bishop Donatus. Circular in plan, with three apses, it is very bare inside, with no decoration and just a circular stairway leading to an upper level balcony where female members of the congregation would once have sat. It was deconsecrated over two centuries ago, but is now used for occasional classical music recitals thanks to its excellent acoustic qualities.

On Zeleni trg (aka Forum). Admission 20kn. Jun–Sept daily 9am–9pm; Apr–May and Oct daily 9am–5pm; Nov–Mar closed (opened on request).

Sea Organ ★★★   Midway along the south side of the Riva, the much-loved Sea Organ was designed by local architect Nikola Bašić and installed in 2005. Made up of 35 pipes with underwater whistles set inside smooth white-stone steps, it creates constantly changing sounds depending on the movement of the sea, which in turn is influenced by the waves, the tide, the wind, and passing ships. During any season and at practically any time of day, you are guaranteed to find people sitting on the steps, or on the benches nearby, listening to the haunting humming and moaning produced by the organ in union with the forces of nature.

On the Riva on the south side of the Old Town.

WATERSPORTS

Anyplace you can touch the water on the Dalmatian coast is a potential swimming hole, but diving opportunities are fewer and require planning. From Zadar you can access diving operations on offshore islands and up and down the coast.

Zlatna Luka Diving Center ★★   Half-day excursions with Zlatna Luka include two dives, full tanks, and weights. Weekend tours are offered to Kornati National Park and other Adriatic locations. The center is about 7km (4½ miles) south of Zadar, at Marina Dalmacija, Bibinje-Sukošan (www.diving-zlatnaluka.net; ✆ **091/252-80-21**).

Where to Stay

The nicest place to stay in Zadar, and the most convenient for sightseeing, is the Old Town, which now offers several fine accommodation options. Zadar's big modern resort hotels lie outside the center, along the coast.

VERY EXPENSIVE

Iadera Hotel & Spa ★★★   In the village of Petrčane, 12km (8 miles) from Zadar, this luxurious ultra-modern hotel is set amid landscaped grounds with an infinity pool. The Iadera has 160 spacious rooms and 50 suites, all with wooden floors, sensual open-plan bathrooms with both a tub and shower, and floor-to ceiling windows that open onto private balconies. The highlight of the property is the vast Aquapura Spa, probably the best in Croatia. The hotel is positioned on a mile-long stretch of meandering coast, dotted by secluded pebble beaches, and offers watersports like water skiing, with a private motorboat available for charter. This is an ideal choice for those in search of a self-indulgent seaside vacation, although because of its large size, the hotel does slightly lack in atmosphere (it opened in 2011). You could easily forget which part of the world you're in.

Punta Skala, Petrčane. www.falkensteiner.com. ✆ **023/555-601.** 210 units. Double Jul–Aug 408€. **Amenities:** 4 restaurants; 3 bars; spa; watersports; outdoor pool; Wi-Fi (free).

EXPENSIVE

Art Hotel Kalelarga ★★   On Kalelarga, the main thoroughfare through the heart of Zadar's car-free Old Town, this chic boutique hotel has just 10 spacious rooms, plus a top floor suite with an outdoor Jacuzzi on the balcony. Expect wooden floors; some exposed medieval stonework; fabrics in earthy shades of cream, beige and brown; and bathrooms with fantastic rain showers. The ground floor gourmet restaurant is popular with locals and serves an excellent a la carte breakfast.

Ulica Majke Margarite 3. www.arthotel-kalelarga.com. ✆ **023/233-000.** 11 units. Doubles Jul–Aug 219€. **Amenities:** Restaurant; Wi-Fi (free).

MODERATE

Central Royal Apartments ★★   Central Royal now includes 10 individually furnished apartments, all recently refurbished and equipped with slick kitchenettes, positioned at various locations in the Old Town. Upon arrival, the manager will meet you, take you to your apartment, and provide a local's advice on things to do and see, and places to eat and drink.

Široka ulica 22. www.centralroyalapartments.com. © **091/243-68-80.** 10 units. Apartment sleeping 2 Jul–Aug from 120 €. **Amenities:** Wi-Fi (free).

Hotel Niko ★★   Located by the sea in Puntamika, 3km (2 miles) from the Old Town, this peaceful, family-run hotel offers spacious rooms with thick red carpets and classical furnishing (the best ones have sea views and balconies, too). The main draw, however, is the ground floor restaurant Niko, which has been serving high-quality fresh fish on a waterside terrace since 1963—and also does a sumptuous breakfast for hotel guests.

Obala Kneza Domagoja 9, Puntamika. www.hotel-niko.hr. © **023/337-880.** 15 units. Double Jul–Aug from 140€. **Amenities:** Restaurant; bar; Wi-Fi (free).

INEXPENSIVE

Hostel Forum ★   In a great location in the Old Town, with windows looking onto the Forum and St. Donat's Church, this slick modern hostel offers (slightly cramped) four-bed dorms, where each bunk bed has a privacy curtain; two-bed rooms with privacy curtains; and "lux" doubles on the top floor, with amazing Old Town views, ideal for couples. Minimalist white predominates throughout the building, and there's a communal lounge with TV, breakfast-to-go served in cardboard boxes, and vending machines for snacks.

Široka ulica 20. www.hostelforumzadar.com. © **023/250-705.** 110 beds. Dorm bed Aug 27€. **Amenities:** Communal lounge.

Where to Dine

Zadar offers a wide range of dining choices, from hole-in-the-wall *konobas* ("taverns") to gourmet restaurants featuring inventive menus with blowout prices.

Dva Ribara ★★★ DALMATIAN   In the Old Town, a couple of blocks off Kalelarga, this restaurant has a modern minimalist interior, putting a contemporary twist on traditional Dalmatian seafood dishes. Try the monkfish wrapped in bacon, served with Swiss chard and potato, and round it off with a glass of the local tipple, maraschino, made from sour cherries. It's surprisingly reasonably priced, and for those seeking a quick, cheap meal, the restaurant also does the best pizzas in town.

Blaža Jurjeva 1. www.restorani-zadar.hr. © **023/213-445.** Entrees 45kn–130kn. Daily 8am–midnight.

Foša ★★ SEAFOOD   Overlooking the small harbor immediately outside the Old Town's eastern walls, this longstanding seafood restaurant combines the traditional with the contemporary both in terms of cooking and design. The waterfront terrace is elegant, trimmed in white, and the interior is just as inviting, pairing ancient walls with flattering contemporary lighting. Besides fixed menu lunches, Foša offers dishes like tuna carpaccio, scampi risotto, and grilled fresh fish served with a purée of potato and zucchini. For those who don't want seafood, there's a tasty steak in truffle sauce, and the kitchen even does a tofu and vegetable risotto for vegetarians. Reservations are recommended.

Kralja Dmitra Zvonimira 2. www.fosa.hr. © **023/314-421.** Entrees 40kn–230kn. Daily noon–11pm.

Kalelarga Gourmet ★★ MODERN CROATIAN   On the ground floor of Hotel Kalelarga in the Old Town, this light and airy eatery serves contemporary cuisine prepared from local ingredients. The menu changes frequently, depending on the season, but you can expect colorful creative dishes employing freshly caught seafood and vegetables from the open-air market. There's also a very good wine list—ask your waiter for a complementary recommendation.

Ulica Majke Margarite 3, Zadar. www.arthotel-kalelarga.com. ℂ **023/233-000.** Entrees 70kn–130kn. Daily 8am–midnight.

Konoba Stomorica ★ DALMATIAN What started out as a local wine bar serving lunchtime snacks has expanded into a full-blown restaurant, a fine spot for inexpensive local seafood in the Old Town. Stomorica has heavy wooden tables and benches both indoors and on the street out front, with extra tables in a small courtyard at the back. It's informal and fun, although it can get noisy accordingly. Bread is fresh, as is cuttlefish, served with chickpeas and potatoes. The house white wine goes down like a treat. Note that it's cash-only here.

Stomorica 12. ℂ **023/315-946.** Entrees 30kn–65kn. Daily 9am–midnight.

Na Po Ure ★★ DALMATIAN This informal budget eatery serves up generous portions of real home cooking. The menu changes daily, depending on what local produce the owner-cook finds at the morning market, but you can expect a range of hearty meat and fish dishes, served in substantial portions. It stays open all year and is much loved by locals.

Špire Brusine 8. ℂ **023/312-004.** Entrees 35kn–80kn. Mon–Sat 10am–11pm.

Zadar After Dark

Much of Zadar's nighttime action is outdoors on the Riva or at other seaside locations.

Café Gallery Đina ★ In the heart of the Old Town, Đina is popular with 30-somethings and even those a little older, who come here for morning coffee or a chat over a glass of wine in the evening (note that it's cash-only). The cafe also stages temporary exhibitions of paintings and photos by local artists.

Varoška 2. Daily 7am–1am.

The Garden ★★★ Nestled in the Venetian walls above the sea, close to the tip of the Old Town peninsula, this sophisticated open-air summer lounge/bar is laid out on a large stone terrace, with wooden decks and white furniture. Guests come here to see and be seen, while sipping on pricey cocktails to the strains of international guest DJs. Summer 2014 saw the installation of a funky new color-changing LED lighting system, adding to the romantic atmosphere.

Bedemi zadarski pobuna 13. www.watchthegardengrow.eu. ℂ **023/250-631.** Jun–Sept daily 10–1am.

Kult ★ With tables on a leafy terrace shaded by trees and big white parasols, Kult is a favorite spot with local students, who meet here for coffee during the day, or for cold beers after dark. You'll find it in the Old Town, where it stays open all year (cash only).

Stomorica 6. Daily 7:30am–1am.

Maraschino Bar ★★ This is the largest bar in Zadar, serving as a waterside cafe during the day, and a club with DJ music after 10pm through the summer. The large front terrace affords views of the Old Town across the sea channel. Along with a full bar, you can find the namesake maraschino in cocktails here (the interior is themed around the liqueur, with old bottles and tools on display). Much of the lighting is cherry-red and the music is predominantly house and R 'n' B.

Obala kneza Branimira 6a. www.maraschinobar.hr. ℂ **091/421-23-23.** Jun–Sept daily 7am–5am; Oct–May Sun–Thurs 7am–11pm, Fri–Sat 7am–5am.

DALMATIAN DISH decoder

Brujet/brudet/brodetto: Casserole made with a variety of fish pieces, onions, tomatoes, olive oil, and tomatoes.

Crni Rižot: Black risotto made with cuttlefish ink.

Dalmatian pršut: Dalmatian smoked ham. The ham is salted, smoked, and left to dry in the open air.

Janjetina s ražnja: Lamb barbecued on a spit over an open-wood fire.

Pašta-fažol na brujet: Bean stew with pasta, a local specialty on the island of Vis.

Pašticada: Sauce made from beef that has been marinated in vinegar and red wine, then cooked with vegetables. Usually served with gnocchi.

Rožata: Dalmatian crème caramel.

ZADAR ENVIRONS

Zadar is the point of departure for many other destinations in Upper Dalmatia. From the city, it's an easy drive to **Paklenica National Park,** a challenging environment for hikers, rock climbers, and spelunkers. You can also drive over to the nearby island of **Pag,** joined to the mainland by a bridge close to its southern tip, and travel up the island to the lively little resort of **Novalja** with its late-night bars lining **Zrće** beach.

Zadar is also a ferry port for the decidedly undeveloped northern Dalmatian islands of **Ugljan, Pašman, Dugi Otok,** and **Silba.** Sometimes known as the islands of the Zadar Archipelago (see p. 135), the first three are the most visited, but none are overrun by tourists. In addition, there are daily excursion boats from Zadar that depart for tours around **Kornati National Park,** which is really a portion of the southern islands of the Zadar Archipelago.

South of Zadar, on the way to Split in Lower Dalmatia, you'll pass **Šibenik,** a charming seaside town which is often overlooked by vacationers, but more than warrants a visit. It is accessible by bus or car.

Paklenica National Park

ESSENTIALS

VISITOR INFORMATION   Paklenica information can be had at the Starigrad Paklenica **tourism office** (www.rivijera-paklenica.hr; ℂ **023/369-255**) at Trg Tome Marašovića 1, which is open from June through September.

GETTING THERE   Paklenica is a little less than 3 hours from Zagreb on the Zagreb-Split highway. Exit at the sign for the park (before you get to Zadar) and continue on the old road that skirts the sea. You'll pass lots of SOBE signs before you get to Starigrad Paklenica; a sign pointing to the park turns into a one-lane road that appears to go through a residential area. This road leads to park reception, where you can leave your car, buy a ticket, and enter the park on foot. There is no direct public transportation to the park.

GETTING AROUND   Paklenica is all about walking and climbing. No motorized vehicles are allowed inside the park boundaries.

WHAT TO SEE & DO

Paklenica is the Velebit's best hiking territory and has many gorges, mountains, and caves to tempt adventurous explorers.

Paklenica National Park ★★★   Paklenica National Park, which encompasses a 20km (13 mile) stretch of the southeastern slopes of the Velebit mountains, is a haven for hikers and free-climbers. The entrance to the park, at Starigrad Paklenica, lies 44km (28 miles) north of Zadar. From here, with the help of maps (available at the park entrance), you can set out to explore over 40km (60 miles) of well-marked hiking trails. You might plan anything from a couple of hours of strolling to a full 2-day trek, and the farther you go, the more wild the mountainous landscape becomes, taking in limestone gorges, dense pine forests, and dramatic rocky peaks. You might even spot rare birds of prey such as falcons and eagles. Camping within the park is not allowed, but there are a couple of mountain huts offering basic accommodation (information is available at the park entrance) for hikers. Be sure to wear good hiking boots and carry a big bottle of water.

Paklenica Park Office, F. Tudmana 14a, Starigrad-Paklenica. www.paklenica.hr. (*) **023/369-155.** Admission May–Sept 50kn, Oct–Apr 40kn. Apr–Oct daily Mon–Fri 6am–8:30pm; Nov–Mar daily 7am–3pm.

WHERE TO STAY & DINE

Starigrad tourist office (see above) can help find private accommodation. You can also check out the ubiquitous SOBE signs around the park. For hard-core hikers, overnight shelter in a bare-bones mountain hut is available inside the park.

Hotel Rajna ★★ Ideally located at the entrance to Paklenica National Park, this homely 10-room hotel is popular with hikers and free-climbers, many of whom are return visitors. The ground floor terrace restaurant serves fresh seafood dishes, and you have the option of going half board and eating dinner here. Besides the hotel, the owners also manage a complex of three restored 19th-century stone cottages at the foot of Mount Velebit, which come with self-catering facilities and can sleep 12 guests.

Tudjmana 105, Starigrad Paklenica. www.hotel-rajna.com. (*) **023/359-121.** 10 units. Double Jul–Aug 55€. **Amenities:** Restaurant; Wi-Fi (free).

WHERE TO DINE

Hotel Rajna (above) has a good restaurant, and there are lots of pizzerias and grill places in Starigrad itself. In addition, there are several markets and bakeries where you can stock up on sandwich makings and bottled water for hiking.

Pag Island

When you approach **Pag Island** on the ferry from mainland Prizna south of Senj, you'd never guess that it is home to one of the biggest party beaches in Europe. At first glance it looks as if you're headed for a landing on Mars rather than a sojourn on an island awash with nouveau riche villas, condominiums, and a pedigree that goes back to the Roman Empire.

It's difficult to imagine that anything could survive for long on Pag's barren terrain, which appears to be either entirely karst (limestone) or dry dust, but the island once was covered with lush forests. Agriculture thrived on Pag when the Romans settled here in the 1st century, and during the next 1,300 years or so not much disturbed Pag's flora, not even the Slav invasion in the 7th century or Pag's fights over its prized salt fields.

In the 15th century, however, the rulers of Venice and Zadar were in competition for the island and its natural resources. Venice won when it took control of most of Dalmatia in 1409, including Pag and Zadar. Some might say that Pag lost, because once the Venetians had control they used the island's vast tracts of timber as their private lumber yard and stripped the island of its trees to build ships. The hat trick of Venetian deforestation, grazing sheep, and the fierce northwestern wind *(bura)* that frequently hammers the Kvarner and northern Dalmatian coast so traumatized the environment that it has never recovered.

The Venetians engrossed themselves in building, and by the mid-15th century the salt trade on Pag had grown so much that the island's Old Town could no longer handle

THE ZADAR archipelago

Ugljan, Pašman, Murter, and **Dugi Otok** are all part of what is sometimes called the Zadar Archipelago, a group of more than 300 islands. Several of the most popular islands with tourists are detailed below. Each has a distinct personality. All the inhabited islands in the archipelago are accessible by ferry only, with the exception of Murter, which is connected to the mainland by a bridge.

Ugljan is the island closest to Zadar and one of the most populous, though it is never very crowded. It has been inhabited since prehistoric times, and was once the site of Roman habitation, as indicated by the *villa rustica* still found there. Today nearly 8,000 people call it home, including some who work on the mainland. Ugljan's main industries are farming, animal husbandry, and fishing, though tourism is becoming a growing source of revenue.

Pašman, like Pag, has both barren and fertile areas. Most of the sites on Pašman date from medieval times. The only occupied Benedictine monastery in Croatia (Sts. Cosmos and Damian) is behind walls atop a hilltop near Tkon. That and the island's Franciscan monastery in Kraj both keep unreliable hours and don't make great tourist destinations.

Murter is south of Pašman and closer to Šibenik than it is to Zadar. However, it is mostly under Zadar's jurisdiction. Murter doesn't have much to recommend it except that it can be accessed from the mainland by a short bridge, and it's just south of the islands that make up Kornati National Park. Murter's largest and most interesting town, Murter Town, is the site of the Kornati National Park's office. Murter is also the best place to book an excursion to Kornati, as its citizens own 90 percent of the park (see p. 139).

Dugi Otok (www.dugiotok.hr) is the biggest island in the Zadar Archipelago and the farthest from the mainland. It also boasts the most irregular and "wild" coastline, which makes it particularly appealing to those who like adventure and who want to avoid the usual tourist haunts. Eleven villages are strung out along the northeastern side of the island; on the western side, Dugi Otok's cliffs rise almost vertically from the sea. Dugi Otok holds the remains of several medieval churches, as well as a gorgeous white pebble beach on Sakarun Bay at the island's north end. Ferry service reaches Dugi Otok from Zadar, but there is little transportation on the island itself, so if you want to thoroughly explore it, you will need a car. In the southern portion of Dugi Otok lie the cliffs and bays of Telešćica Nature Park (www.telascica.hr). If you want to visit the park you should arrive on the island at the port of Sali (as opposed to Božava). From Sali, several agencies arrange tours of the park by boat.

the population or the business. Consequently, the Venetian administrators hired Juraj Dalmatinac to design a new city, which became **Pag Town.**

Sheep breeding and salt production always have been and still are mainstays of Pag's economy, but it is tourism that now contributes the biggest chunk of revenue to the island. Thanks to that trend, Pag recently has been the site of a building boom that is driving development of other commerce on the island. While tourism is increasing, Pag remains mostly undiscovered and underrated, making it a good vacation opportunity for the knowledgeable traveler.

Pag Island is 60km (36 miles) long and 10km (6 miles) wide at its broadest point. Most of the island's eastern side is barren, or covered with a grid of freehand rock walls that delineate property lines and keep sheep from wandering from one patch of scrub grass to another. However, on the northwest end of the island, from **Šimuni** to **Lun,** olive trees and other vegetation have taken root in large fertile sections.

Pag Island is not densely populated—yet. In fact, most of the time, visitor numbers for Pag's waters and beaches are low, and FOR RENT signs are numerous. The exception is the time from July 15 to August 15, when it seems half of Europe's 20-somethings descend on the island, fill its rooms and apartments, and take over its beaches for wild, scantily clad, nonstop partying.

But most of the year, Pag is a quiet island whose permanent residents produce and promote four products for which the island has become famous—cheese, lamb, lace, and salt. The cheese is known as **Paški sir,** and it is reminiscent of Parmesan, though a bit saltier. It is sold throughout the island by both commercial and home-based producers and usually served sliced and drizzled with olive oil. Paški sir is exported to Croatia's larger population centers, where it goes for a much higher price than it does on Pag.

The second product is **Paški lamb.** Pag is home to many herds of sheep, the meat prized for its high quality and unique flavor, a result of the salt-infused air the lambs breathe and their diet of scrub grass and local herbs that grow wild in the rocky soil. The combination creates lamb that has a singular taste sought after by Croatian gourmets.

The art of making **Paški lace** is a tradition that has been preserved and nurtured on Pag. Once you see real Pag lace (see p. 138), which is incredibly intricate, you'll be able to tell imitations from the genuine article.

Finally, there is the salt once fought over by would-be conquerors. Pag's salt pans are still in production, mostly in the island's central valley. Pag salt is commonplace in Croatian supermarkets, and it is exported as well. Many of the island's souvenir shops sell decorative bottles of pebble-size Pag salt as an inexpensive souvenir.

It's a shame that "the season" on Pag isn't longer than the traditional mid-July to mid-August rush because the climate is still warm in spring and fall, and the island offers lively nightlife, crystal-clear azure water for swimming, and quaint attractions.

ESSENTIALS

VISITOR INFORMATION The **Pag Town Tourist Board** (www.tzgpag.hr; (✆ **023/611-286)** is at Ulica Od Špitala 2 in Pag Town. Novalja's **tourist office** (www.visitnovalja.hr; (✆ **053/661-404)** is at Trg Brščić 1.

GETTING THERE If you are traveling to Pag Island from Zadar and points south, the island is reachable from Posedarje on the mainland via **Pag Bridge,** which takes visitors to the island's south end. **Jadrolinija ferries** (p. 127) make regular runs from mainland Prizna to Žigljen on the island's north end, depositing visitors about 4.8km (3 miles) from Novalja.

Tips: Bura Winds
Check the weather reports before you head out for a weekend on Pag. Ferry traffic (and sometimes bridge traffic) is halted when the *bura* winds are strong.

Backups at the Pag Bridge are rarely more than half an hour, except for weekends during July and August, when they can be much longer. Unless you're coming from Zadar and points south, getting to the bridge involves a few extra driving hours. During the summer, a fast boat (catamaran) runs between Novalja and Rijeka, with stops at Rab Island three times a week. Several daily buses from Rijeka stop in Pag Town and Novalja and go on to other stops along the Dalmatian coast. See "Getting There" under "Essentials" in "Orientation," above, for transportation contact information.

GETTING AROUND   Except for private taxis and intercity buses that run from the mainland and between Pag Town and Novalja, there is little public transportation on Pag. Luckily, both Pag Town and Novalja are compact enough to explore on foot, as are their waterfronts—although most visitors spend just a few hours touring in town before heading to the beach. Travel between the two towns can be time-consuming unless you have your own car, therefore private vehicles are the transportation mode of choice. You'll need a rental car or motor scooter if you intend to explore more than one area of the island or if you want to go beach-hopping. Rental agencies, including Budget, Dollar, Hertz, and Avis, have kiosks at the Zagreb airport and in other major Croatian cities.

WHAT TO SEE & DO

Besides hauntingly beautiful landscapes, clean waters, and deserted beaches in isolated coves, Pag has a nice collection of Roman ruins, medieval walls, churches, and cultural icons. Most of the attractions worth seeing are concentrated in Pag Town and Novalja, which are separated by about 19km (12 miles). **Pag Town** has a partial **15th-century wall** and an **Old Town** complete with the last of four standing **watch towers** that once rose from the town fortifications. The town center is home to two original buildings designed by Juraj Dalmatinac, the prominent Renaissance architect also responsible for Šibenik Cathedral. The **Rector's Palace (Knežev dvor)** is now a cafe; the **Parish Church of St. Mary** stands opposite **Trg Kralja Krešimira IV,** Pag Town's center of social activity. Pag Town is nearly a mile south of the original 14th-century settlement that preceded it, and a few crumbling remnants of the ancient town are still visible and can be visited. There is also a small **Pag Lace Gallery** on the square where you can see what genuine Pag lace (see p. 138) looks like before you consider a purchase. You can also see the town's "wall" of windmills on the hills above Pag, an energy-generating project that takes advantage of *bura* wind power.

Pag Town is where most of the island's locals live and where its salt fields are situated, but it is not as populous as Novalja. If Pag Town is the island's historic center, then Novalja is its New World colony. Novalja is about 19km (12 miles) north of Pag Town and far livelier in summer. The main draw is **Zrće,** a long, curving pebble beach, a little over a mile south of Novalja, and the epicenter of Pag's swinging nightlife. Almost every bar in town (and some from Zagreb, like Papaya and Aquarius) has set up shop on this stretch of coast, which in summer vibrates with nonstop music and tanned bodies during the day, but doesn't *really* get going until 10pm. Zrće draws hordes of the 18- to 29-year-old demographic from as far afield as the U.K., the U.S., and Australia, who come here to attend a succession of commercial dance music festivals from June through August. In a nod to Croatia's strict drinking and driving laws, minivans run partygoers from Zrće to Novalja's harbor throughout the night, although action on the beach usually continues until dawn.

Midway between Pag Town and Novalja, you'll pass through the inland village of **Kolan,** the main center of cheese-making on the island. At Figurica 20, **Sirana Gligora** (www.gligora.com; © **023/698-052**) offers cheese tasting and tours of its dairy. There's also a store where you can buy *Paški sir* (Pag cheese, see p. 136 to bring home.

Pag Watersports

Pag is a favorite of snorkelers and scuba enthusiasts because of its crystal-clear water and the underwater cliffs, caves, and wrecks where remnants of Rome and other eras rest. **Stara Novalja** across the Novalja inlet is a haven for diving schools and suppliers.

Blue Bay Diving ★★   Besides excursions for accomplished divers, Blue Bay offers instruction for beginners, with all necessary equipment provided.

Rupica 17, Stara Novalja. www.bluebaydiving.com. © **091/887-18-10.** May–Oct.

9

UPPER DALMATIA | Zadar Environs

PAG patterns

Pag is best known for its forbidding naked terrain, its salty sheep's-milk cheese (*Paški sir*), its herb-infused lamb, and its wild party beaches. But Pag also has a reputation as the source of intricately patterned lace, produced by local women, who can spend days creating a single 6-inch round. It's used as trim on clothing and tablecloths, as home decorating accents, and sometimes as framed art. Look for elderly ladies dressed in black sitting in Pag Town's center square or near Novalja's market for the best examples of this art. Usually these are the lace makers themselves, who will bargain with you on the price of their wares. Pag lace is quite expensive (a single round can sell for 750kn or more). Each piece of Pag lace is as complex and unique as a snowflake, and makes a wonderful souvenir from this diverse island. Once you've seen the genuine item you won't have trouble recognizing inferior imitations.

WHERE TO STAY

Pag is a popular weekend getaway for Zagrebians, as the island is within easy driving distance of the city. Although there are not many good hotels, there is an abundance of reasonably priced, modern, private accommodations on Pag.

Hotel Boškinac ★★★   This refined family-run boutique hotel, in a stone building with green wooden window shutters, is set in a peaceful garden with pine trees and a pool rimmed by sunbeds. The eight rooms and three suites have wooden floors, quality furnishings, and slick modern bathrooms. The hotel is best known for the adjoining Restoran Boškinac, popular with hotel guests and non-guests alike. The owners also make their own highly esteemed wines, which are served here, and can be tasted (by appointment) in the stone cellar. You'll find Boškinac set amid vineyards and olive groves, 3km (2 miles) from Novalja.

Novaljsko Polje, Novalja. www.boskinac.com. *✆* **053/663-500.** 11 units. Double Jul–Aug from 190€. **Amenities:** Restaurant; konoba/wine cellar; garden; outdoor pool; Wi-Fi (free).

Villa Kaštel ★★   In the village of Povljana, in the southeast of the island, 14km (9 miles) from Pag Town, this modern hotel has eight rooms and three self-catering apartments. The ground floor Restoran Jardin serves fresh Adriatic fish, lobsters, and prawns, and it's possible to go B&B or half board. There's a heated outdoor pool in the garden, plus a front terrace lined with wooden tables and big white parasols that looks onto a pebble beach, with the islands of Olib, Silba, Premuda, and Molat rising from the sea.

Kralja Tomislava bb, Povljana. www.villa-kastel.hr. *✆* **023/692-830.** 11 units. Double Jul–Aug 112€. **Amenities:** Restaurant; outdoor pool; Wi-Fi (free).

WHERE TO DINE

There are plenty of family-style *konobas* and pizzerias on Pag, as well as a few higher-end places where cuisine is taken to an art form.

Konoba Nono ★ DALMATIAN   In the cheese-making village of Kolan, between Pag Town and Novalja, Nono offers a modern take on a traditional Dalmatian *konoba*. The menu includes the classic range of Dalmatian meat and seafood dishes, but with extra attention paid to presentation. Start with the Cold Plate Nono, a platter of prosciutto, cheese, and marinated anchovies, served with olives and honey, then move on to succulent charcoal-grilled lamb with potatoes and salad.

Rudina 1, Kolan. www.konobanono.com. ⓒ **023/698-059.** Entrees 45kn–110kn. Apr–Oct daily 11am–11pm.

Restoran Boškinac ★★★ MODERN CROATIAN   Dining here in summer, on the stone terrace overlooking the surrounding fields and vineyards, is a joy. Boškinac, which is part of a small hotel of the same name, serves creative Mediterranean cuisine, prepared with local seasonal produce. The menu changes several times during the year—for an overview of the chef's skills, opt for the degustation menu, which might include delights such as wild asparagus lasagna with smoked cheese and prosciutto; monkfish with cauliflower, polenta cream, and fennel; and Pag lamb with broccoli cream and potato. The waiters and the sommelier are guaranteed to look after you, and you'd do well to follow their recommendations. Reservations are required.

Novaljsko Polje, Novalja. www.boskinac.com. ⓒ **053/663-500.** Entrees 70kn–160kn. Mar–Dec daily noon–11pm. Closed for vacation Jan–Feb.

Restoran Na Tale ★ DALMATIAN   Hidden away in a courtyard in the historic center of Pag Town, close to the seafront promenade, this quaint eatery makes an ideal spot for a romantic meal. The menu includes traditional local specialties such as *Paški sir,* fresh fish, and spit-roasted lamb, as well as seasonal treats like wild asparagus. It's a little more pricey than other restaurants nearby, but most diners agree that it's worth it.

Radićeva 4, Pag Town. ⓒ **023/611-194.** Entrees 50kn–120kn. Mar–Dec daily 8am–midnight.

Kornati National Park

Kornati National Park is part of a group of nearly 150 mostly uninhabited islands south of Pašman and Dugi Otok. The park's 89 islands, islets, and reefs are scattered across an area of about 78 sq. km (30 sq. miles) of land and 207 sq. km (80 sq. miles) of sea. Kornati's unusual landscape of mostly barren, irregular karst terrain is actually a submerged mountain range; the visible parts are ancient mountaintops and valleys that are now islands and channels. Less than a quarter of the Kornati area is land and the park's underwater landscape is perhaps its most fascinating feature. Kornati is renowned as a diver's paradise, with unusual rock formations where many species of fish and plant life thrive. Both scuba divers and snorkelers will enjoy Kornati, although scuba enthusiasts must be part of a group approved by the National Park if they want to explore any of the seven zones set aside for diving visits.

If you'd rather explore land, don't miss the Kornati "crowns," steep island cliffs that face the sea, a result of a rift caused by a continental collision millions of years ago.

Kornat is the largest of the park's islands and the site of the 6th-century **fortress of Toreta,** an excellent example of Byzantine architecture. The precise history of Toreta is not known, but it's probably safe to assume that the fortress was built to protect navigation on the Adriatic. Near the fortress, you also can see the remains of an early Christian three-nave church from the same period.

SEAFOOD etiquette

In Dalmatia, shrimp (scampi) are almost always served whole in their shells. You'll be spotted as a tourist if you eat them with utensils, but you'll pass for a local if you pick them up with your fingers and suck on their heads.

The islands were sold in the 19th century by Zadar aristocrats to the people of Murter. Today the inhabitants of Murter own 90 percent of the land, and use it to raise sheep or to grow olives and other crops suited to its rocky soil.

There are no permanent residents on the Kornati islands, but some people do have houses that they use when tending sheep or taking care of their crops. It is possible to stay on Kornati with one of the families who have cottages there. To room with a Kornati family, make arrangements with any tourist agency in Murter. Kornati also has 16 bays with mooring areas designated for boaters who want to drop anchor overnight.

ESSENTIALS

VISITOR INFORMATION   For information on visiting Kornati National Park, contact the **park office** (www.kornati.hr; ✆ **022/435-750**) at Butina 2, Murter. The office can direct you to approved dive escorts, and to private agencies approved to run individual tours and accommodations on Kornati.

GETTING THERE   There is no ferry service between the Kornati islands and the mainland, and the only way to get there is by boat. You can book one-day excursions to the islands from Zadar or Šibenik, or you can arrange private boat tours and accommodations at the travel agencies on Murter. You'll have more flexibility if you charter your own boat, but you can't dive unless you are with an approved dive group.

Šibenik

Šibenik fell on hard times after the 1991 war, and the former industrial port town is still suffering from the economic fallout. However, as coastal towns go, Šibenik offers a change of pace from Dalmatia's strong Italianate influences since its origins are pure Croatian rather than Roman.

Situated on a broad bay at the mouth of the Krka River, Šibenik's footprint is sometimes likened to that of an amphitheater as it hugs the slopes that emanate from **St. Anne's Fortress,** a sprawl that began shortly after the city first was mentioned in Croatian historical writings in 1066. Today, much of Šibenik's charm comes from the warren of steep, winding streets and passages, the many sets of stone steps leading up to the center, and the ruins of city fortifications that fan out from St. Anne's to the water. Above the harbor, Šibenik's center is crowded with churches, monasteries, and stone dwellings, clustered on narrow, covered streets that open to a series of interior town squares.

Šibenik's most prominent attraction is the **Cathedral of St. James,** which made the UNESCO World Heritage List in 2000. St. James is a must-see for anyone who comes to town, even the upscale tourists who berth their yachts overnight in Šibenik's harbor. Indeed, the city is a favorite port of call for yachts touring the eastern Adriatic and **Kornati National Park.** It also is within easy access of **Krka National Park,** a region in the Dinaric Alps with karst and waterfalls similar to those of Plitvice, though at Krka you can also swim, which is not allowed at Plitvice.

Immediately offshore, Šibenik has an archipelago of its own, a group of small islands with picturesque coves, blue Croatian sea, idyllic beaches, and few inhabitants. Two of them, **Zlarin** and **Prvić,** once were summer havens for Croatian writers, who retreated there to find their muses. The islands are linked to Šibenik by Jadrolinija ferries on regular runs to the Vodice resort area north of town.

ESSENTIALS

VISITOR INFORMATION   Šibenik's walk-in **tourist information center** (✆ **022/214-448**) is on the seafront at Obala dr. Franje Tuđmana 5, while the **tourist board office** (www.sibenik-tourism.hr; ✆ **022/212-075**) is at Fausta Vrančića 18. The

Šibenik region **tourist office** (www.sibenikregion.com; ✆ **022/219-072**) is at Fra Nikole Ružića bb.

GETTING THERE   There is decent bus service to Šibenik from larger cities in Croatia, as well as from select international locations. The bus station is on the seafront at Draga bb.

GETTING AROUND   The old town is pedestrian-only, and is a joy to explore on foot. Driving in Šibenik is problematic, mainly due to a lack of parking spaces.

WHAT TO SEE & DO

Šibenik remains more low-key than Zadar and Split. Its main attraction is the UNESCO-listed Cathedral of St. James in the old town. Two magnificent national parks, Krka and Kornati, can be done as day trips from here, too.

Cathedral of St. James ★★★   Built in stages between 1431 and 1536, this monumental white Gothic-Renaissance Cathedral brings together various styles and the contributions of multiple architects. However, the design is generally attributed to Juraj Dalmatinac, who was also responsible for Pag Town (see p. 135), though sadly he died before the cathedral was completed. In his absence, one of his pupils, Nikola Fiorentinac, supervised the final stages of the project. Note the trefoil facade, the ornate Gothic portals, the vaulted roof, the splendid cupola, and the exterior frieze made up of 74 carved faces, said to have been local individuals who refused to make financial contributions to the cathedral's construction. Inside, the ornately carved baptistery is also worth a look.

Trg Republike Hrvatske. Admission 15kn. May–Oct daily 8:30am–8pm; Nov–Apr daily 8:30am–noon and 4–8pm. Mass daily 9:30am, 11am, and 6pm.

Krka National Park ★★★   Krka National Park extends from Šibenik bridge to Knin, centering on a deep canyon and several spectacular waterfalls. The park is well signed, with five entrances. The main entrance, and the most convenient one when arriving from Šibenik, is at Skradin (20km/13 miles from the city). From here you can take a national park boat up the river, almost to Skradinski Buk, the park's most impressive falls, which tumble 46m (150 ft.) over a series of 17 cascades. The falls at Krka are similar to those at Plitvice in that they were formed from deposits of limestone sediment (travertine). From Skradinski Buk, where you can swim, a network of footpaths and wooden bridges lead 10km (6 miles) all the way to another thundering waterfall, Roški Slap. Alternatively, you can cover this stretch with another ride aboard a national park boat, which stops en-route at the 15th-century Visovac Monastery, perched on a tiny islet.

Krka National Park Tourism Office, Trg Ivana Pavla II 5, Šibenik. www.npkrka.hr. ✆ **022/201-777.** Admission Jun–Sept 110kn, Mar–May and Oct 90kn, Nov–Feb 30kn. Skradin entrance open Jun–Sept daily 8am–8pm; Mar–May and Oct daily 9am–5pm; Nov–Feb daily 9am–3pm.

WHERE TO STAY

Accommodations in the Šibenik area are mostly in big resort settlements north and south of the city, with a few small hotels and lots of private accommodations in between.

Agrotourism Klapić ★★   Close to Krka National Park, 15km (9 miles) from Šibenik, family-run Klapić is a complex of stone cottages set in a lovely garden, with wooden tables and chairs under the trees. There are eight comfortable double rooms with rustic furnishing and modern bathrooms. Klapić is also a working farm, and there's an excellent eatery serving tasty meals prepared from homegrown organic produce. Many guests opt for half board and eat dinner here.

Klapići 4, Lozovac. www.klapic.com. ✆ **091/584-55-20.** 8 units. Double Jul–Aug 85€. **Amenities:** Restaurant; Wi-Fi (free).

Hostel More ★★ On the road directly above the old town, a 5-minute walk from the bus station, this welcoming hostel opened in 2013. It's run by a friendly Croatian couple, centered on a lovely cobbled courtyard with tables, potted plants, and an outdoor shower. Besides the dormitories, up top there are two cozy private rooms (one double and one triple), both en suite, with sloping beamed ceilings and skylights. The hostel stays open year-round.

Ulica Kralja Zvonimita 40. www.hostel-mare.com. ℗ **022/215-269.** 40 beds. Bed in dorm Jul–Aug 16€. **Amenities:** Courtyard garden; Wi-Fi (free).

Hotel Ivan ★ Within the huge Solaris Holiday Resort, which lies 4km (2½ miles) southwest of Šibenik, Hotel Ivan is one of five big modern hotels. Big is no exaggeration, as the hotel can accommodate over 3,000 guests. Rooms are basic but comfortable, and the public spaces are somewhat impersonal. Most guests are families with kids, who come here specifically to use the resort's expensive sports and recreation facilities (extra surcharge). It is worth paying a little more for a room with a sea view.

Hotelsko naselje Solaris bb. www.solarishotelsresort.com. ℗ **022/361-001.** 372 units. Double Jul–Aug from 120€. **Amenities:** Restaurant; bar; outdoor seawater pool; spa; tennis courts; watersports; Wi-Fi (free).

WHERE TO DINE

Šibenik is home to Pelegrini, one of Croatia's top restaurants. If you plan to really splurge on one meal, you should do it here. In addition, there are plenty of pizzerias, and simple grill restaurants where you can get excellent seafood and pastas.

Konoba Gorica ★ DALMATIAN On a peaceful cobbled square in the medieval old town, on the way up to the hilltop fortress, this informal eatery has just half a dozen outdoor tables and a small dining room. Start with a mixed platter of Dalmatian prosciutto and cheese, followed by fried calamari and a side salad. The service is friendly, the food reasonably priced, and the house wine very palatable.

Frane Dismanića 2. ℗ **098/971-85-39.** Entrees 55kn–110kn. May–Oct daily noon–midnight

Pelegrini ★★★ CONTEMPORAY DALMATIAN Up the steps, on the square in front of the cathedral, this outstanding gourmet restaurant serves creative Mediterranean cuisine made from the finest local ingredients. The owner-chef is a master of surprises—to get an idea of the range of his skills, try the seven-course degustation menu. This might include delights such as pappardelle pasta with black truffles, prosciutto, and fresh basil, or monkfish cooked with zucchini and tomatoes and served with white polenta. The knowledgeable waiters will explain a little about each dish, and the sommelier can recommend wine pairings for each course. With its exquisite food, impeccable service, and romantic setting, Pelegrini reaches perfection. It is a little expensive, but worth it for a special treat (reservations are recommended).

Jurja Dalmatinca 1. www.pelegrini.hr. ℗ **022/213-701.** Entrees 95kn–220kn. Jun–Oct daily noon–midnight; Apr–May Tues–Sun noon–midnight; Nov–Dec and Feb–Mar Thurs–Sat noon–midnight, Sun noon–6pm.

ŠIBENIK AFTER DARK

Vino & Ino ★★ In the heart of Šibenik's car-free old town, this sophisticated little wine bar serves quality Croatian wines, both by the glass and by the bottle. Guests sit at tall wooden tables with stools, arranged on the stone-paved square out front. The bar also does platters of local cheeses and cured meats, and arranges regular wine-tasting evenings.

Fausta Vrančića bb. www.vinoiino.hr. ℗ **091/250-60-22.** Fri–Sat 9am–2am; Sun–Thurs 9am–1am.

LOWER DALMATIA

The skinny strip of land stretching north to south between Bosnia/Herzegovina and the sea presents one breathtaking moment after another. It's almost impossible to zip through lower Dalmatia on a scattershot tour, even though driving from Zagreb to just outside Ploče (21km/13 miles south of Split) is now a high-speed breeze on the country's new toll road. However, once you run out of divided highway, traffic—and life—slows to a languid tempo. Visitors to this rat-race-free zone are forced to go with the flow. The Dalmatian coastal region from Split to Dubrovnik is the inspiration for Croatia tourism's "The Mediterranean as It Once Was" slogan with good reason.

Split is Croatia's second-largest city and home to some of the best-preserved Roman ruins in the world, as well as the main port of departure for ferries to the islands. **Hvar** surrounds visitors in a cloud of glamour and herbal fragrance while Brač puts wind in the sails of board bums off its Golden Cape. **Korčula** draws people through Marco Polo lore, its endless vineyards, and the white stone of its medieval walls. Farther out on the Adriatic, **Vis** and **Biševo islet** beckon travelers to bask in the blue glow of an underwater cave and to explore what was Tito's war room. In between multiple towns, islands and beaches, historic sites, architectural gems, natural wonders, and age-old traditions are the keys that unlock the doors to treasures waiting for anyone savvy enough to seek out this stretch of the Dalmatian coast.

ORIENTATION
Arriving
How you get to Dalmatia's coastal destinations depends on your wallet, time, and whether you want to settle in at a single destination or move around to see as much as possible. Split is the logical northern starting point for any trip along the southern coast, unless you are chartering a private yacht and can pick your ports of call without worrying about traffic, bus schedules, or flight plans. On the mainland coast, a car gives you maximum flexibility, but to do the coast and outlying islands, you're best using a combination of buses and ferries.

SPLIT
Split celebrated its 1,700th birthday in 2005, an anniversary that marked the dual event of the city's founding and the completion of Diocletian's grandiose palace in A.D. 305. Diocletian deliberately chose a tract of land

near ancient **Salona,** thereby securing a location that could provide the best of both country and city pleasures for his retirement years. As emperor emeritus in Split, Diocletian might no longer have had the power of a sitting Roman ruler, but he still had some clout. (It didn't hurt that he claimed to be a descendant of the god Jupiter and had a worshipful following.)

When in Split, Diocletian was just 6km (4 miles) from Salona, close enough for drop-in visits to Dalmatia's provincial center of power. Off duty, Diocletian retreated to his Split palace, where he maintained the illusion of imperial position by receiving heads of state and others, all of whom paid lavish homage to the former emperor.

Today, greater Split is a mostly working-class city of 250,000 and one of Croatia's busiest ports. It has a population of rabid sports fans; it functions as a transportation hub; and it is home to some of the most spectacular Roman ruins in the world.

Essentials

Split is a transportation hub for the Dalmatian coast, which makes it a busy crossroads. Despite the city's spectacular Old Town, whose borders are defined by the walls of Diocletian's 3rd-century palace, Split has never had the exotic cachet of other Dalmatian destinations, though most travelers who head for Dubrovnik or Croatia's islands pass through or make connections here. Today, Split is the source of an extensive transportation network, and it is one of the most accessible cities in Croatia.

VISITOR INFORMATION Split's walk-in **Tourist Information Center** (www.visitsplit.com; © 021/348-600) is on the seafront at Obala Hrvatskog Narodnog Preporoda 9.

GETTING THERE

BY CAR Before May 2005, it took 5 hours or more to drive from Zagreb to Split. That changed when Croatian officials cut the ribbon to open the new Zagreb-Split *autocesta* (highway) that flows through mountains and bypasses country roads. The newer route isn't quite as scenic as the old, but this toll way has cut about an hour from the trip. Except for weekends in July and August, the 364km (226 mile) drive from Zagreb to Split now takes less time than the 217km (135 mile) south-to-north drive from Dubrovnik to Split on the Adriatic Coastal Highway.

BY PLANE Split's **airport** (www.split-airport.tel.hr; © 021/203-555) is 26km (16 miles) northwest of the city center between Kaštela and Trogir. Flights from all over Croatia as well as from many European cities fly in and out on regular routes. Service is more frequent in the summer months than in the winter. An airport bus shuttles passengers between the airport and Split's main bus station for 30kn each way (see www.plesoprijevoz.hr for details).

BY BOAT Split's ferry port lies just a 10-minute walk from the Old Town, opposite the main bus station. International, local, and island ferries and catamarans move in and out of an area that includes Brač, Hvar, Vis, Korčula, Lastovo, and Šolta. **Jadrolinija** (www.jadrolinija.hr; © 021/338-333) runs the majority of local ferry and catamaran routes. Jadrolinija and **Blue Line** (www.blueline-ferries.com; © 021/352-533) also operate overnight ferries to Ancona, Italy, that run all through the year. From June to September, a high-speed catamaran runs daily between Split and Ancona, operated by **SNAV** (www.snav.it; © 021/322-252), an Italy-based company. SNAV also runs high-speed ferries (4 hr. or less) to Ancona from June through mid-September.

BY BUS Split is well served by local, national, and international buses, and the station is conveniently located next to the ferry port. Local bus lines run through Split and

Lower Dalmatia

its suburbs, including Salona, Omiš, and Trogir, while other buses travel many times a day to Zagreb, Zadar, Rijeka, Dubrovnik, and destinations beyond. International buses provide services to Bosnia/Herzegovina, Montenegro, Serbia, Slovenia, Germany, and Italy. Get schedule and fare information at www.ak-split.hr (© **060/327-777**).

BY TRAIN   Split's main train station is next to the main bus station at Obala Kneza Domogoja 10. The only really useful service for visitors is the line between Split and Zagreb, which runs a couple of times per day, and once overnight (couchettes available). Call the **Split train station** (© **021/338-525**) or the **national train office** (www.hzpp.hr; © **060/333-444**) for information.

GETTING AROUND

Most of Split's best sights are within the walls of Diocletian's Palace or nearby. The walled city is limited to pedestrians; even the street skirting the Riva immediately outside the palace walls is closed to motorized vehicles. There are a few sights worth taking in outside the historic core—for example, the **Meštrović Gallery** in Marjan and the public beach at **Bačvice**—and you can reach those on foot. If you need a taxi, the main stands are at each end of the Riva (in front of the town market and in front of the Bellevue Hotel). If you don't see a cab, call © **970.**

City Layout

Split's historic core is bounded by Obala Hrvatskog Preporoda (the Riva) in the south, Marmontova Street in the west, Kralja Tomislava in the north, and Hrvojeva in the east; Old Town's main square, Narodni Trg, is almost in the center of the rectangle.

[FastFACTS] SPLIT

Ambulance Call ✆ **94.**

ATMs & Banks There are numerous ATMs (Bank-omats) in Split's Old Town and on the Riva where you can withdraw cash using American Express, Diners Club, Maestro/MasterCard, and Visa. Most banks are open Monday to Friday 8am to 7pm and Saturday 8am to noon.

Fire Call ✆ **93.**

Holidays Split Summer Festival is from mid-July through mid-August.

Hospitals Firule hospital is located at Spinčićeva 1 (✆ **021/556-111**); it is open 24/7.

Pharmacy There is an all-night pharmacy in the center of town at Pupačićeva 4 (✆ **021/**

533-188) and in the suburbs at Vukovarska 207 (✆ **021/345-738**).

Police Split's main police station is at Trg Hrvatske Bratske Zajednice 9 (✆ **021/307-111**).

Post Office Split's main post office is at Kralja Tomislava 9. Hours are Monday to Friday 7am to 8pm, Saturday 7am to 1pm.

10 What to See & Do

Be sure to stroll down Split's spiffed up **Riva,** one of Croatia's busiest promenades. In the morning, people linger over coffee at the Riva's sidewalk tables before work, after the market, or in preparation for a day of sightseeing. From then on the tables aren't empty until closing time. Never deserted, the Riva is at its busiest in the evening when people dine, stroll the concrete length, or arrive and depart on the late ferries.

Another important point of reference is **Marmontova Street,** a broad, paved pedestrian street that forms Old Town's western border, lined with international clothing shops such as Zadar and Bershka, and mobile phone company stores. West of Marmontova, you'll run into the **Prokurative** (aka Trg Republike), a horseshoe-shaped set of neoclassical buildings, some of which are now cafes and restaurants, with outdoor tables on the car-free square.

Cathedral of St. Domnius ★★★ The main body of the cathedral was originally built in Roman times as Diocletian's mausoleum. An octagonal structure made of massive stone blocks and ringed by 28 granite and marble columns, it was converted into a church by refugees from Salona in the 7th century. The cathedral's massive wooden doors, protected by glass, are the work of 13th-century sculptor Andrija Buvina, who decorated them with carvings depicting scenes from the life of Christ. Inside, the 15th-century altar of St. Anastasius was created by architect Juraj Dalmatinac, who also designed Šibenik Cathedral and Pag Town. The cathedral treasury displays a bewildering horde of gold and silver, including reliquaries containing the body parts of various saints. It is also possible to climb the bell tower for amazing views down onto the Old Town and out to sea. Because of its central location within Diocletian's Palace, the Peristil (peristyle) in front of the cathedral is a popular public meeting place, just as it was in Roman times.

Kraj Sv. Duje 5. ✆ **021/345-602.** All-inclusive ticket to the cathedral and the Temple of Jupiter 25kn; cathedral bell tower only 15kn. Jun–Sept daily 8am–8pm; Oct and May daily 7am–noon and 5–7pm; Nov–Apr daily 7am–noon.

Split

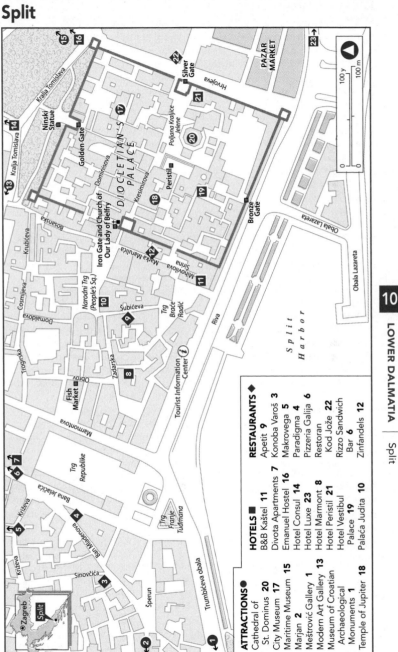

ATTRACTIONS●
Cathedral of
St. Dominus **20**
City Museum **17**
Maritime Museum **15**
Marjan **2**
Meštrović Gallery **1**
Modern Art Gallery **13**
Museum of Croatian
Archaeological
Monuments **1**
Temple of Jupiter **18**

HOTELS■
B&B Kaštel **11**
Divota Apartments **7**
Emanuel Hostel **16**
Hotel Consul **14**
Hotel Luxe **23**
Hotel Marmont **8**
Hotel Peristil **21**
Hotel Vestibul
Palace **19**
Palača Judita **10**

RESTAURANTS◆
Apetit **9**
Konoba Varoš **3**
Makrovega **5**
Paradigma **4**
Pizzeria Galija **6**
Restoran
Kod Jože **22**
Rizzo Sandwich
Bar **6**
Zinfandels **12**

147

There are several access points for entering Split's historic core, but the best place to start your exploration is the **Bronze Gate,** where the sea once lapped at Diocletian's Palace's back walls. Today the Bronze Gate opens outward from the palace's southern flank to Split's Riva and the ferry port beyond. Inside, it leads to the **podrum,** or basement, that meanders under the structure. The underground space was sadly neglected until the mid-1950s, and parts of it have yet to be restored and cleared of centuries of debris. The upper-level *cryptoporticus* (gallery) that runs east-west from the Bronze Gate was an open promenade and probably the site where Diocletian went to catch a sea breeze. Today the promenade can only be imagined from the form of the long corridor beneath it. The part of the *podrum* that extends from the Bronze Gate toward the steps to the Peristil above it is a passageway lined with stalls selling jewelry, leather goods, paintings, and other souvenirs of Split.

At the far end of the aisle that runs through this section of the *podrum* you'll find a staircase that leads up to the *Peristil,* which was the palace's main courtyard and the place where Diocletian received important visitors. Today, the Peristil is one of the busiest spots in the historic city, and home to the cathedral, Luxor Café, and various passages leading to the heart of the Old Town.

Note the **black granite sphinx** standing guard outside the cathedral. It was one of 11 acquired by Diocletian during battle in Egypt, one of only two left (the other sits next to the nearby Temple of Jupiter).

If you are approaching the palace from the **Silver Gate** on the eastern wall, you first must walk through the jumble of stalls that is the **fruit and vegetable market (Pazar).** The Silver Gate leads directly to **Decumanus,** the original east-west street that intersects with **Cardo,** the original north-south artery, at the Peristil. These former thoroughfares sectioned the palace into quadrants, which in turn became districts.

The **Golden Gate** on the north side of the palace was the portal to Salona and the most ornate gate into the palace. It has a guardhouse that contains the 9th-century **Church of St. Martin.** Ivan Meštrović's **statue of Bishop Grgur (Gregorius of Nin) Ninski,** a 9th-century bishop who defended church use of the Glagolitic script and Slav language, towers over visitors approaching the gate. The sculpture is entirely black except for one toe, which is bronze because visitors inevitably touch it for good luck as they pass. To the west, the **Iron Gate**'s guardhouse is the site of the oldest Romanesque belfry in Croatia and the 10th-century **Church of Our Lady of Belfry.**

The **Cathedral of St. Domnius** (above) is on the eastern side of the Peristil. The **Temple of Jupiter** (now the cathedral's baptistery) lies down a narrow alley on the Peristil's western side.

Diocletian's Palace ★★★ Emperor Diocletian (A.D. 245–316) commissioned construction of his palace in A.D. 293 as an imperial retirement home, to which he retreated upon abdicating in A.D. 305. He probably chose this location for its proximity to his birthplace, Salona, and for its natural beauty, between sea and mountains. Built of local limestone (largely from the nearby island of Brač), the vast palace covers almost 3 hectares (10 acres), with walls that are at least 2m (6 ft.) thick and up to 30m (100 ft.) high in parts. Inside were Diocletian's private apartments, overlooking the sea, several temples in the central public area close to the Peristil, plus accommodation for soldiers and servants on the land-facing side. In the early 7th century, refugees from

Salona took shelter here when the Avars and Slavs attacked and destroyed their city, and soon started turning the palace into a settlement in its own right. Through the centuries, building spread beyond the palace walls, and various rulers and peoples, most notably the Venetians, built structures within and around the complex, adding to its fascinating and unique character. The entire old town is now a UNESCO World Heritage Site.

Maritime Museum ★ This museum within the 17th century Gripe Fortress, a 10-minute walk east of Diocletian's Palace, traces Croatia's historical connections with seafaring. One exhibition looks at merchant maritime development, from ancient times up to the advent of the steamboat, while another examines maritime war craft and the numerous battles that have taken place on the Adriatic through the centuries. Displays include model ships, navigational equipment, weapons (including the first torpedo, from 1866, designed by a Croat and manufactured by an Englishman in Rijeka), and paintings of sea battles.

Glagoljaška 18. www.hpms.hr. ℂ **021/347-346.** Admission 10kn. Mid–Jun to mid–Sept, Mon–Fri 9am–7pm, Sat 9am–2pm; mid–Sept to mid–Jun, Mon–Wed and Fri 9am–2:30pm, Thurs 9am–7pm, Sat 9am–1pm; closed Sun.

Marjan ★★ A 15-minute walk west of Diocletian's Palace lies the hillside quarter of Varoš, with its winding alleys and old stone cottages. If you walk uphill through Varoš, you will arrive on Marjan, a nature reserve of fragrant pinewoods crisscrossed by footpaths. Marjan is actually a 3.5km-long (2-mile) peninsula, and if you walk all the way to the end of it you'll come to Bene, a recreation ground with a bathing area, tennis courts, and a cafe on its western tip. If you follow the path along Marjan's south-facing slopes, you get amazing views over the sea to the islands of Brač, Šolta, and Čiovo, and you'll also pass several centuries-old stone churches.

15-min. walk west of Diocletian's Palace. www.marjan-parksuma.hr.

Meštrović Gallery ★★★ The former summer villa of famed Croatian sculptor and architect Ivan Meštrović, this 1930s building is now a gallery dedicated to his creative output, with sculptural works and sketches indoors and more sculpture outdoors in the garden overlooking the sea. Exhibits include pieces in wood, marble, and bronze, with an emphasis on religious themes. Nearby, at Šetalište Ivana Meštrovića 39, is the 16th-century **Kaštelet,** a Renaissance-style summer residence, which Meštrović bought after completing work on his own villa. In Kaštelet's Holy Cross Chapel you can see the artist's enchanting "Life of Christ" reliefs, a cycle of wood carvings that he created between 1916 and 1950. Entrance to Kaštelet is included in the price of the ticket for the main gallery.

Šetalište Ivana Meštrovića 46. www.mestrovic.hr. ℂ **021/340-800.** Admission 30k. May–Sept Tues–Sat 9am–7pm, Sun 10am–7pm; Oct–Apr Tues–Sat 9am–4pm, Sun 10am–3pm; closed Mon and holidays.

Modern Art Gallery ★★ North of Diocletian's Palace, close to the main post office, this fine gallery reopened in 2009. Tracing European art from the 15th century up to the present, it includes religious icons, Old Master paintings, and contemporary sculpture and video installations. Croatian artists make up the larger part of the offerings, with notable names like Dalmatian painters Vlaho Bukovac and Emanuel Vidović and sculptor Ivan Meštrović. There's also a pleasant garden cafe, which is open daily from 8am to 11pm.

Kralja Tomislava 15. www.galum.hr. ℂ **021/350-112.** Admission 20kn. May–Sept Mon 11am–4pm, Tues–Fri 11am–7pm, Sat 11am–3pm; Oct–Apr Mon 9am–2pm, Tues–Fri 9am–5pm, Sat 9am–1pm; Sun closed.

Museum of Croatian Archaeological Monuments ★★ Dedicated to Croatian religious art from between the 7th and 12th centuries, this museum displays some charming stone carvings taken from early churches and decorated with plait-work motifs, reminiscent of Celtic art. Outside, in front of the museum, stand several *stečci*, stone tombstones attributed to the Bogomils, a curious religious sect that was popular in the Balkans in the 10th century, most notably in Bosnia/Herzegovina. The museum is about a 15-minute walk along the coast west of the Old Town, also accessible by bus no. 12.

Šetalište Ivana Meštrovića 18. www.mhas-split.hr. 𝄋 **021/323-901.** Free admission. Mon–Fri 9am–4pm; Sat 9am–2pm; closed Sun.

Narodni Trg ★★ Adjoining Diocletian's Palace to the west lies Split's medieval quarter, built mainly when Dalmatia was under Venetian rule. Here you will find Narodni Trg (aka Pjaca), now regarded as the city's main square. An expanse of white marble paving, it is rimmed with busy cafes and overlooked by the 15th-century Town Hall, with its ground floor loggia comprised of Venetian-Gothic arches.

Narodni trg, center of town.

Split City Museum ★ Housed in the elegant 15th-century Papalić Palace, designed by Juraj Dalmatinac, this museum displays a mish-mash of objects related to the city's proud history, including medieval weaponry, sculpture, paintings, period furniture, and coins.

Papalićeva 1. www.mgst.net. 𝄋 **021/360-171.** Admission 20kn. May–Oct Tues–Fri 9am–9pm, Sat–Sun 9am–4pm; Nov–Apr Tues–Fri 9am–5pm, Sat 9am–1pm, Sun 10am–1pm; closed Mon.

Temple of Jupiter (Baptistery) ★ Down a narrow passageway off the west side of the Peristil, immediately opposite the cathedral, this tiny classical temple, with its richly decorated portal and vaulted ceiling, was built in Roman times but was converted into a baptistery during the Middle Ages. The 11th-century baptismal font is decorated with stone carvings that portray a Croatian ruler (possibly the Croatian king Zvonimir) on his throne.

Kraj Sv Ivana. 𝄋 **021/345-602.** Admission 10kn; also part of the all-inclusive ticket for the cathedral, 25kn. Jun–Sept daily 8am–8pm; Oct and May daily 7am–noon and 5–7pm; Nov–Apr closed.

Where to Stay

Until recently, not much attention was paid to tourist lodging in Split, but that attitude is changing. Hotels of recent vintage are being renovated and upgraded, and small boutique hotels are entering the market.

VERY EXPENSIVE

Hotel Marmont ★ In the pedestrian-only Old Town, a short distance outside the walls of Diocletian's Palace, Hotel Marmont is smart and comfortable, though maybe slightly lacking in soul. Occupying a restored 15th-century building, it opened as a hotel in 2008. All the rooms have king-size beds and oak floors, fabrics in creams and browns, and spacious bathrooms. On the down side, the views are minimal—in the densely packed Old Town, you're basically looking onto neighboring buildings. May 2014 saw the addition of a new ground floor bar-restaurant, with sliding floor-to-ceiling glass that opens directly onto the street in summer.

Zadarska 13. www.marmonthotel.com. 𝄋 **021/308-060.** Double Aug 320€. **Amenities:** Restaurant; bar; smoke-free rooms; Wi-Fi (free).

Hotel Vestibul Palace ★★★ Located in the area that would have been Emperor Diocletian's private chambers in the 4th century, this hotel combines ancient walls with contemporary design details. Guests get sections of exposed 1,700-year-old Roman stonework, polished wooden floors, chic chrome and leather chairs, and slick modern bathrooms stocked with Yves Rocher toiletries. There are seven rooms and suites in the main building, plus an additional four in Villa Dobrić, just a 5-minute walk away. The Diocles Restaurant serves a contemporary take on Dalmatian cuisine at outdoor tables with big white parasols on a peaceful square. The property is a member of Small Luxury Hotels of the World, with extras including a Boston Whaler speedboat for private day trips (with skipper) to the islands.

Vestibula 4. www.vestibulpalace.com. ℭ **021/329-329.** 11 units. Double Jul–Aug from 375€. **Amenities:** Restaurant; concierge; speedboat rental; Wi-Fi (free).

Palača Judita ★★ In a renovated 16th-century Renaissance palazzo on the main square in the car-free Old Town, this romantic upmarket B&B has eight spacious double rooms, all with wooden floors and king-size beds. There's no restaurant, but the house serves a delicious and generous breakfast, with eggs cooked to order. The cost is expensive for an accommodation with no extra facilities, but you're paying for the location, the historic ambience, and the personalized service from a friendly, professional, and accomodating staff.

Narodni trg 4. www.juditapalace.com. ℭ **021/420-220.** 8 units. Double Aug from 300€. **Amenities:** Wi-Fi (free).

EXPENSIVE

Divota Apartments ★★ On the edge of Varoš, a centuries-old neighborhood of fishermen and farm laborers, Divota occupies a cluster of renovated traditional Dalmatian stone cottages. There are six rooms and eight apartments, plus a three-bedroom house, all with minimalist whitewashed interiors, tasteful furnishings, and splashes of color provided by big modern paintings. Each unit has a kitchenette and some even have a private terrace for sitting out. The location is just a 10-minute walk from Diocletian's Palace and the seafront.

Plinarska 75. www.divota.hr. ℭ **021/782-700.** 15 units. Double from 162€, breakfast additional 10€ per person. **Amenities:** Wi-Fi (free).

Hotel Luxe ★★ Luxe stands on the main road directly above the ferry port, ideally located for those with an early morning boat to catch. Opened in 2010, the property has funky minimalist design, with a look that is urban and international rather than Dalmatian. White predominates, with striped turquoise, lilac, and mauve carpets providing the color. Rooms are light and airy, with floor-to-ceiling windows. The best ones have balconies overlooking the port. There's a small wellness center in the basement, with a Finnish-style sauna, whirlpool and gym, plus massage and beauty treatments on request. The hotel can also arrange private motorboat charters, with a skipper.

K Zvonimira 6. www.hotelluxesplit.com. ℭ **021/314-444.** 30 units. Double from 165€. **Amenities:** Bar; wellness center; Wi-Fi (free).

Hotel Peristil ★★ Just inside the walls of Diocletian's Palace, next to the Silver Gate and close to the open-air market, this hotel offers 12 rooms, some with views onto the cathedral. The units are of various configurations, as it's an old building in a UNESCO-protected area and can't be altered, subsequently limiting the room sizes and availability of natural light. That said, the spaces are homey and comfortable, with wooden floors, and some with exposed ancient stonework (pieces of the Roman palace walls). Besides location, the main draw here is the ground floor Tifani restaurant, with outdoor tables on a limestone terrace right next to the palace walls. Yes, breakfast at Tifani is a fine way to start the day, and the creative Mediterranean cuisine served at lunch and dinner is beautifully presented and reasonably priced. The staff is friendly, professional, and full of locals' advice about things to see and do.

Poljana Kraljice Jelene 5. www.hotelperistil.com. ✆**021/329-070.** 12 units. Double Jul–Aug 162€. **Amenities:** Restaurant; bar; Wi-Fi (free).

MODERATE

B&B Kaštel ★★ With windows overlooking the seafront promenade in the Old Town, at the edge of Diocletian's Palace, Kaštel is superbly located if you don't mind some late night and early morning noise from the cafes below. Rooms are clean and modern, most have amazing sea views, and the price includes a hearty breakfast. The staff is friendly and helpful, too. Note that the entrance is a little difficult to find—it's around the back, not on the seafront.

Mihovilova Širina 5. www.kastelsplit.com. ✆**021/343-912.** 12 units. Double Jul–Aug from 135€. **Amenities:** Wi-Fi (free).

Hotel Consul ★ Geared primarily towards business travelers, the Consul nonetheless makes a reliable option for a peaceful and comfortable stay in Split. Lying a 10-minute walk northeast of Diocletian's Palace, it offers spacious rooms, all with bathrooms with Jacuzzis. The restaurant serves surprisingly good traditional Croatian fare on a covered terrace out front; some guests opt to go half board. Limited free parking is available.

Trščanska 34. www.hotel-consul.net. ✆ **021/340-130.** 19 units. Double May–Sept 125€. **Amenities:** Restaurant; bar; limited free parking; Wi-Fi (free).

INEXPENSIVE

Emanuel Hostel ★ This friendly little hostel has just 15 beds, but thanks to clever design, you get plenty of privacy, as each built-in bunk has a curtain and reading light. They're sturdy, too, so you don't feel your neighbors moving around. There's no kitchen or communal space, but you get nice decor and spotlessly clean bathrooms. The price includes towels, lockers, and a breakfast of coffee and croissants. The location is good, a 10-minute walk from the palace.

Tolstojeva 20. ✆**021/786-533.** 2 dorms, total 15 beds. Dorm bed in Aug 22€. **Amenities:** Wi-Fi (free).

Where to Dine

Pizzerias and *konobas* dominate Split's restaurant scene, but the recent influx of tourists and new hotels is spurring more sophisticated restaurant choices.

EXPENSIVE

Paradigma ★★★ CREATIVE MEDITERRANEAN Opened in June, 2014 by the same team that runs Paradox Wine Bar (see p. 154), this sophisticated restaurant has a spacious summer roof terrace that seats 100. The menu features specialties from countries along the shores of the Mediterranean, prepared with contemporary twists, changing to correspond to the season's fresh produce—look for house specialties such as slow-cooked octopus with eggplant, cherry tomatoes, pepperoncini, fresh basil, golden raisins, and almonds. A sommelier is on hand to help with pairings. Round off your meal with Paradigma's signature dessert, a deconstructed baklava.

Ulica Bana Jelacica 3. www.paradox.hr. ✆ **021/395-854.** Entrees 110kn–210kn. Jun–Sept daily 7:30am–11pm; Oct–May daily 11am–10pm.

MODERATE

Apetit ★★ DALMATIAN In the heart of the Old Town, on a side street between the seafront and the main square, you have to walk up several flights of stairs to the second floor of a 15th-century palazzo to find this Dalmatian restaurant. Both the interior design and the menu combine traditional elements with contemporary freshness, so you get medieval stonework and big colorful oil paintings, and classic Dalmatian meat and fish dishes plus pastas and risottos, all presented with creative flair. This is a great find all around, and highly regarded by the locals.

Šubićeva 5. www.apetit-split.hr. © **021/332-549.** Entrees 45kn–110kn. Daily 10am–11pm.

Kod Jose ★★ DALMATIAN   A 5-minute walk north of the palace walls, in an old stone building in a narrow alley, this long-running eatery is a classic Dalmatian *konoba,* with exposed stone walls and heavy wooden tables and benches. The menu is classic Dalmatian, too—*crni rižot* (black risotto made from cuttlefish ink) and barbecued fresh fish served with *blitva sa krumpirom* (Swiss chard and potatoes). The service is discreet but friendly, and the waiters will ensure your carafe is topped up with wine while you eat.

Sredmanunuska 4. © **021/347-397.** Entrees 60kn–120kn, more for fish priced by the kilo. Daily noon–midnight.

Konoba Varoš ★★★ DALMATIAN   Located at the foot of Varoš, a 5-minute walk from the seafront, Konoba Varoš is a long-standing favorite with locals out for a special meal. The house's *frigane lignje* (fried calamari) are served with a delicious garlicky mayonnaise, and the *škampi rižot* (shrimp risotto) is heavenly. Besides seafood, the *konoba* also offers tasty meat dishes, including succulent steaks. The dining room is a tad dingy by day, but cozy when candlelit at night.

Ban Mladenova 7. www.konobavaros.com. © **021/396-138.** Entrees 60kn–120kn, more for fish priced by the kilo. Daily 11am–midnight.

Zinfandels ★★★ CREATIVE MEDITERRANEAN   Opened in summer 2013, Zinfandels is principally a wine bar, with a selection of over 25 wines served by the glass and a sommelier who can explain a little about each one. The bar also does beautifully presented mixed platters, salads, and more substantial dishes such as pasta with truffles, making it the perfect choice if you want to enjoy refined flavors without feeling too full afterwards. In summer the menu is extended to include a champagne breakfast.

Marka Marulica 2. © **021/355-135.** Entrees 60kn–110kn. Jun–Sept daily 8am–1am, Oct–May 10am–midnight.

INEXPENSIVE

Makrovega ★ VEGETARIAN   In Varoš, hidden away in a side alley, this eatery caters to vegetarians, vegans, and those on gluten-free diets. A range of soups, pies, and sandwiches are offered, as well as main dishes based on quinoa, couscous, and tofu. The daily set menu, which can be viewed on the website, is an excellent value for the money. Makrovega closes early evening, so it's a better option for lunch than dinner.

Leština 2. www.makrovega.hr. ©**021/394-440.** Set menu 60kn. Mon–Fri 9am–8pm; Sat 9am–5pm; Sun closed.

Pizzeria Galija ★ PIZZA   Generally regarded as the best pizzeria in town, Galija has expanded over the years, now offering additional outdoor tables on a front terrace. The menu has broadened as well, to include pasta dishes and salads as well as the classic brick-oven pizzas that it has long been known for. The pizzeria is very popular, so you may have to wait for a table. You'll find it between Varoš and the fish market.

Kamila Tončića 12. © **021/347-932.** Pizza 40kn–100kn. Daily 10am–11pm.

Rizzo Sandwich Bar ★ SANDWICHES   Between Marmonova Street and Varoš, behind Pizzeria Galija, this popular little sandwich bar does made-to-order sandwiches, with freshly baked baguettes filled with a choice of cheeses and cured meats, plus fresh tomatoes, cucumber, and lettuce. There's nowhere to sit, but it's a great choice for a takeaway snack.

Tončićeva 4. www.rizzo.com.hr. ✆ **021/348-349.** Sandwiches 14kn–26kn. Mon–Sat 9am–midnight; Sun 10am–midnight.

Split After Dark

Sleepy through winter, Split wakes up with a vengeance in summer, when countless small bars and cafes set up outdoor seating and stay open until 1am. July and August also see a lively program of open-air after-dark concerts, along with the cultural events organized for the Split Summer Festival.

Ghetto ★★   Set in a beautiful candlelit courtyard in the heart of the Old Town, Ghetto does cocktails, music, and art. In summer, when it gets extremely crowded (with foreigners especially), there are special DJ nights; in winter, when the upper level lounge comes into use, exhibitions by local artists are staged. Ghetto is one of the few places in Split that markets itself as gay-friendly.

Dosud 10. ✆ **091/123-45-22.** Daily 8pm–1am.

Luxor ★★   This old-fashioned cafe stands on the Peristil, opposite the cathedral. Open for coffee and snacks during the day, it is also popular for an after-dark glass of wine. In summer the staff puts out red velvet cushions, so you can sit on the ancient stone steps, Roman-style. Luxor also stages occasional live music and impromptu dancing under the stars.

Kraj Sv. Ivana 11. www.lvxor.hr. ✆ **021/341-082.** Daily 8am–midnight.

Paradox Wine Bar ★★   Located behind the theater, at the foot of Varoš, this upmarket wine and cheese bar makes the ideal spot for a pre-dinner aperitif. The staff is professional, but friendly and welcoming as well, and there are several qualified sommeliers who will help you choose wines to satisfy your personal taste. Although the wine list covers the entire country, there is a special emphasis on Dalmatian producers, well-matched to platters of local cheeses.

Poljana Tina Ujevića 2. www.paradox.hr. ✆ **021/395-854.** Mon–Sat 9am–midnight, Sun 4pm–midnight.

Teak ★★   On the south side of Diocletian's Palace, close to the Zlatna Vrata (Golden Gate), Teak has outdoor tables on a tiny square set back from the street. In summer, the bar turns to candlelight after dark, making it a romantic spot for a glass of wine or a whiskey before bed.

Majstora Jurja 11. Jun–Sept daily 8am–1am; Oct–May Mon–Sat 8am–11pm, Sun 5–11pm.

SALONA

Anyone wandering the remains of deserted, windswept **Salona** in the hills above Split will inevitably wonder what it was like to live in the provincial Roman settlement during its prime. The archaeological remains are so spread out and so vast that the city's former status in the empire is unmistakable. There is just enough left of the original ancient structures to paint a good picture of what the city of 60,000 must have looked like, although a depressed economy has left Salona neglected and overgrown.

When you buy your ticket, you will be given a map, but the gravel paths meander—and sometimes disappear—without many signs. Tracts can seem to blend into patches of working farmland. Oddly, these "flaws" don't detract from Salona's appeal.

Salona was originally a sheltered town on the Jadro River that was settled primarily by Illyrians and Greeks from Vis (Issa) who were trading partners. In the 2nd century B.C., the Romans began to infiltrate and eventually Salona was named Colonia Martia Julia Salona and transformed into Rome's administrative center for the province of Dalmatia. It subsequently became the largest city on the eastern Adriatic coast.

During Diocletian's reign, Salona prospered and the Romans undertook extensive building projects, including a theater; a forum with a temple consecrated to Jupiter, Juno, and Minerva; and a three-story amphitheater that could seat more than 15,000 spectators which served as the city's primary sports and entertainment venue.

At the same time, Salona became a magnet for adherents of various spiritual movements of the times. According to scholars examining the ancient city's archaeological traces, these immigrants brought their customs and beliefs with them from such far-flung places as Egypt, Asia Minor, and Persia.

The new Christian faith was also in the mix of emergent religions sprouting in Salona, a situation that particularly vexed Diocletian, who was devoted to his pagan gods and claimed to be a descendant of Jupiter. In A.D. 303, toward the end of his reign, Diocletian solidified his reputation as one of Christianity's most zealous persecutors. He attempted to purge his corner of the empire of the new religion by ordering the churches to be razed and the scriptures to be burned. He warned that high-ranking Romans would lose their places and domestic staff if they continued to profess Christianity, and they would be deprived of their liberty. Other decrees arrived in rapid succession, ordering that "the presidents of the churches in every place should all be first committed to prison and then coerced by every possible means into offering sacrifice."

Bishops Domnius and Anastasius of Aquileia were among the Christian proselytizers of the times and both probably were among those martyred in Salona's amphitheater for their beliefs. Ironically, the bodies of both these martyrs replaced Diocletian's in the **Cathedral of St. Domnius** in Old Town Split after Christianity was legalized and became the religion of the majority in the realm.

At the beginning of the 7th century, the Avars and Slavs invaded Salona, driving the city's residents to nearby islands, from which they later fled to Diocletian's Palace.

Today Salona is a ghost city and little of its former glory remains. The amphitheater's foundation is breathtaking in its scope and size—historians say the arena still was standing in the 17th century when it was deliberately destroyed by Venetian generals who decided it was better to level the structure than leave it for encroaching Turks. After that, Salona was ignored until a Split priest and archaeologist, the Rev. Frane Bulić, began an excavation in the late 19th century.

Essentials

Salona makes a perfect half-day trip from Split or Trogir, but it's not a place you would want to stay in longer. If you brush up on Salona's history so you know what you're looking at when you get there, your visit will be more meaningful. Even so, you will need to use a certain amount of imagination to appreciate the site.

VISITOR INFORMATION Before going to the Salona archaeological site, check with the **tourist office** (www.solin-info.com; ✆ **021/210-048**) of the town of Solin at Ulica Kralja Zvonimira 69 for directions and information. When you arrive at Salona, you will encounter an information/ticket booth at Tusculum, portal to the ancient city.

Tickets are 20kn; maps and other printed material related to the site are also available. Salona is open April to September Monday to Saturday 9am to 7pm and Sunday 9am to 1pm; October to March Monday to Saturday 9am to 3pm; Sunday closed.

GETTING THERE & GETTING AROUND   Salona occupies 156 hectares (385 acres) about 6km (4 miles) from Split. If you are driving, take the Trogir-Split road (D8) directly to the parking lot. If you are using public transportation, the no. 1 bus from Split departs for Salona (stopping at nearby modern Solin en-route) every 20 minutes from 7am to 10pm from the stop across the street from the Croatian National Theater; the trip takes about a half hour.

What to See & Do

Salona is navigable on foot only. You should wear sturdy shoes to tramp around the overgrown fields and gravel paths, and take plenty of water: Except for the arbor near the entrance, there is no shade. The main entrance, **Caesarea Gate,** stands close to the historic house **Tusculum,** the former home of Rev. Frane Bulić, responsible for excavating Salona in the late 1800s. Although the gate is no longer a full arch, you can still see the remains of the octagonal towers that stood to each side of it, attesting to its size and importance.

Manastirine Necropolis ★   The ancients forbade the burial of bodies within the town walls of Solana. From the 4th century onwards, Christian martyrs from Salona and Split, including Salona bishop (and later saint) Domnius, were buried here. Like many Christian burial sites from this period, Manastirine later became a place of worship where Christians would pay tribute to those who had died for their faith. Consequently, in the 5th century a basilica was built over the graves. Rev. Bulić, who died in 1934, was also buried here.

South of Tusculum.

Salona Amphitheater ★★★   At the easternmost part of the site, a 20-minute walk from the Tusculum entrance, this is one of Salona's most impressive monuments. Dating back to the 2nd century, you can clearly make out the circular plan of the amphitheater, built above chambers that are still hidden below. The site has not been fully excavated, and archaeologists believe it may hide more treasures.

East of Tusculum.

Tusculum ★★★   The former home of Rev. Bulić, Tusculum was built in 1898, set in a lovely garden which incorporates several ancient columns and stonework found on the site. Today it is a museum dedicated to Rev. Bulić where visitors can see his personal belongings, photographs documenting his work, and period furniture.

Put Starina bb, Manastirine. © **021/212-900.** Apr–Sept Mon–Sat 9am–7pm, Sun 9am–1pm; Oct–Mar Mon–Sat 9am–3pm, Sun closed.

TROGIR

Trogir is the stuff of fairy tales and one of the most enchanting towns on the Adriatic coast. It was founded in the 3rd century B.C. by the Greeks of Issa (Vis), occupied by the Romans, and a survivor of invading Slavs in the 7th century. Trogir prospered and eventually became part of Venice's portfolio, where it remained until Austria took over in 1797. Today, Trogir's **old town,** with its preserved medieval stone buildings, remains picture-perfect. It was declared a UNESCO World Heritage Site in 1997.

Trogir's historic center is the source of the area's greatest treasures. Almost all houses and structures in the old town are emblazoned with stonework that hints at the past by depicting a coat of arms or some other family symbol over the doorways or windows, some of which are more than 700 years old. Ambling through the town's narrow streets or promenading along the waterfront is almost like walking back in time. At night, the **Riva** comes alive with vendors selling everything from candy by the kilo to lavender oil by the liter. There is also street entertainment in the form of fire-baton twirlers, mimes, and impromptu singing groups. On the mainland, the city market stays open until midnight to give visitors one more chance to buy something before they leave.

Trogir's historic center is actually on an islet on part of Kaštela Bay that flows between the mainland and the island of **Čiovo.** Čiovo was a settlement in prehistoric times, a place of political exile in Roman times, a pariah in the Middle Ages when it served as a leper colony, and home now to a cluster of communities best described as suburbs. Čiovo is connected to Trogir by a bridge, with half-a-dozen settlements made up of closely packed summer houses, pensions, and permanent residences in various stages of construction scattered along the shoreline and in the hills.

Trogir is just 16km (10 miles) from Split and the region's airport actually is closer to Trogir than it is to Split.

Essentials

VISITOR INFORMATION Trogir's **tourist office** is on the main square at Trg Ivana Pavla II/I (www.tztrogir.hr; ✆ **021/885-628**).

GETTING THERE The bus station is just outside the city gate, next to the open-air market and across the street from the Konzum supermarket. Local buses between Split and Trogir run about every half hour; others that travel between Split and Šibenik stop there as well.

GETTING AROUND Trogir's core is a pedestrian zone, so walking is the only option. If you stay outside town, there is a local bus system and a few taxis.

What to See & Do

Trogir is a cheerful little town which has just about everything—history, beaches, harbor, nice restaurants, comfortable accommodations—that a visitor could want. Trogir's cobbled alleys are a joy to wander through, and most will eventually bring you to the main attraction, the magnificent cathedral.

Cathedral of St. Lawrence ★★★ Trogir's undisputed centerpiece is the impressive Cathedral of St. Lawrence. Building began in 1213, with various details added through the centuries, so several styles can be identified here. The magnificent Romanesque portal is decorated with stone carvings, attributed to local sculptor Master Radovan, featuring characters from the Bible, along with scenes from medieval peasant life. Inside, the 15th-century Chapel of St. John was the creation of architect Nikola Fiorentinac, who also worked on Šibenik Cathedral after Juraj Dalmatinac's death. Visitors can climb the Gothic-Renaissance bell tower, which stands 47m (154 ft.), for amazing views over Trogir's old town.

Trg Ivana Pavla II. ✆ **021/881-426.** Daily 9am–noon and 4–7pm.

Where to Stay

There is no shortage of accommodations in the Trogir area, many located on Čiovo, across the bridge. However, the nicest places to stay are in the old town itself. These do get very busy in peak season, so you should book in advance.

Hotel Pašike ★★ In Trogir's car-free old town, this heritage hotel has 13 double rooms of varying size and an apartment sleeping 4. Guests get a pleasing combination of exposed stone walls, antique furniture, and oriental rugs, plus slick modern bathrooms with hydro-massage showers. The ground floor restaurant serves typical Dalmatian cuisine.

Sinjska bb. www.hotelpasike.com. ✆ **021/885-185.** 13 units. Double Aug 135€. **Amenities:** Restaurant; bar; Wi-Fi (free).

Tragos ★★   With an old-fashioned ambience, completely in harmony with Trogir's centuries-old buildings and alleys, this welcoming family-run hotel offers comfortable accommodation and a courtyard restaurant. Rooms have some exposed stone walls, simple pine furniture, and colorful fabrics, adding a cheerful air to the place. The owners are full of local advice, and will collect you from the airport on request. Pets are allowed, too.

Budislavićeva 3. www.tragos.hr. ✆ **021/884-729.** 12 units. Double 110€. **Amenities:** Restaurant; room service; pets allowed; Wi-Fi (free).

Where to Dine

Restaurants are plentiful in the Trogir area, though during the July to August tourist season they can be very crowded.

Alka ★★ SEAFOOD   Founded back in 1966, Alka remains one of the best restaurants in Trogir's old town. The menu includes classic Dalmatian dishes such as octopus salad, scampi risotto and fried squid, and the kitchen also does succulent barbecued T-bone steaks. Tables are arranged in a romantic courtyard, and the service from the tuxedoed staff is professional—attentive but not intrusive.

Bl. Augustina Kažotića 15. www.restaurant-alka.hr. ✆ **021/881-856.** Entrees 70kn–140kn. May–Sept daily 9am–midnight.

Kamerlengo ★★★ CROATIAN   This restaurant in the old town is hidden away on a side alley, at a distance from the busy seafront promenade. There's a spacious terrace for outdoor dining, with a big barbecue in the center so guests can watch the cooks at work. The house specialty is barbecued fresh fish, which comes with a delicious sauce made of olive oil, freshly chopped garlic, and parsley.

Vukovarska 2. www.kamerlengo.hr. ✆ **021/884-772.** Entrees 60kn–150kn, more for fresh fish priced by the kilo. Daily 10am–midnight; early July to end of Aug until 1am.

MAKARSKA RIVIERA

The stretch of waterfront property from Omiš (where you'll find the dramatic **Cetina Gorge,** renowned for rafting) all the way south to Gradac is dedicated to aficionados of sea and sun. Pebbles cover every semi-gentle slope leading into the sea, and in July and August well-oiled bodies cover the pebbles from sunup to sundown along almost the entire length of the 58km (36-mile) strip of coastline. There are six recognized resort towns along the riviera; **Brela, Baška Voda, Gradac,** and **Makarska** are the most notable. The latter caters to families with large, package-oriented resort hotels, while Brela, Baška Voda, and Gradac are low-key resorts composed of small hotels and family-run restaurants. All of them have fine pebble beaches and crystal-clear turquoise-blue sea within walking distance. This entire stretch of coast is backed by the rugged slopes of **Mount Biokovo,** which besides making a dramatic backdrop also shelters the waters from cold winds from the hinterland.

Essentials

VISITOR INFORMATION   The **Baška Voda** tourist office (www.baskavoda.hr; ✆ **021/620-713**) is at Obala sv. Nikole 31; **Brela** tourist office (www.brela.hr;

© **021/618-455**) is at Trg Alojzija Stepinca bb; **Gradac** tourist information center (www. gradac.hr; © **021/697-375**) is at Trg Soline 11; and **Makarska** tourist office (www. makarska-info.hr; © **021/612-002**) is on the seafront at Obala Kralja Tomislava 16.

GETTING THERE It's a 90-minute drive from Split to Makarska along the Adriatic Coastal Highway, a route which is also served by regular regional buses. From Makarska, local buses also cover the smaller towns along the Makarska Riviera. Makarska is connected to Sumartin on the island of Brač by a Jadronlinija ferry (www.jadrolinija.hr).

GETTING AROUND Makarska's waterfront has a palm-lined, pedestrian-only promenade, but the rest of the town is open to traffic, which can become very heavy during July and August. From Makarska, a 14km (8½-mile) path leads along the coast all the way to Brela, passing through Baška Voda (9km; 5½ miles) en-route. It makes a lovely walk or bike ride, passing lots of small beaches along the way, some clothing-optional.

What to See & Do

Although the centerpieces of these towns are the beach and the sea, with a lot of watersports and spectacular scenery, several historic churches and a monastery are sprinkled here and there, too.

Omiš, where the River Cetina meets the sea, is a popular starting point for rafting expeditions, and there are numerous agencies that organize these.

The slopes of **Mount Biokovo** are crisscrossed by marked trails, making this a popular venue for hiking and mountain biking. Makarska is the best starting point for exploring this rugged mountainous scenery. **Biokovo Active Holidays** (www.biokovo. net; © **021/679-655**) at Kralja Petra Krešimira IV 7b in Makarska arranges hiking and biking trips on Mount Biokovo.

Dalmatia Rafting (www.dalmatiarafting.com; © **021/321-698**) in Omiš organizes half-day rafting and canoeing down the Cetina Gorge from April through September. **More-Sub** (www.more-sub-makarska.hr; © **021/611-727**) at Kralja Petra Krešimira IV 43 in Makarska offers scuba diving excursions to several sites, as well as diving instruction at various levels.

GO climb A MOUNTAIN

The majestic peaks of the Biokovo Mountain Range rise about 3km (2 miles) northeast of Makarska and beckon those who want to supplement beach time with aerobic activity. The range is home to the **Biokovo Nature Park** (www. biokovo.com), honeycombed with caves and landscapes, and sporting some challenging hiking and climbing trails. More experienced mountaineers can tackle Sveti Jure, Vošac, or any of 10 other peaks. The rewards are breathtaking views and a sense of accomplishment. You can also drive the 7km (4½ miles) to

Sveti Jure's summit in the summer, but that can be scarier than climbing thanks to lots of hairpin turns. As with any climbing adventure, you should pack emergency gear, check the weather, carry an accurate map and water, and wear good climbing boots.

There is also a small botanical garden at **Kotošina** (open 24/7, with no entrance fee). Kotošina is really more of a rock garden, as the plants are indigenous to the rocky slopes of Biokovo, and nothing is very green or lush. The best time to visit the garden is in spring.

Where to Stay

There are lots of big, impersonal package hotels up and down the Makarska Riviera, but there are also many charming private accommodations and a few small hotels, too. If you are planning on visiting during July or August, when the area is extremely busy, you should book well in advance.

Abuela's Beach House ★★ This converted grandmother's beach house (the *abuela* of the name) has a great waterfront location in Brela, close to some of the region's best beaches. The property has three apartments and one studio, each with a fully equipped kitchenette and a balcony affording spectacular views over the sea and the island of Brač. The hosts are a welcoming young couple, who are full of local recommendations and happy to help you plan your stay. From their house, 220 steep steps lead down to a pebble beach, so you can grab a swim as soon as you wake up in the morning.

Jardula 20, Brela. www.abuelasbeachhouse.com. ℰ **021/695-900.** 4 units. Two-person studio Aug 120€. **Amenities:** Wi-Fi (free).

Hotel Croatia ★★ On a small square set back from the seafront in Baška Voda, this stone building dates to 1911 and first opened as a hotel in 2008 after a complete renovation. The 18 rooms are smart and spacious, with strand-woven bamboo flooring and the possibility of adding extra beds for children. The staff lays out a fantastic buffet breakfast, which guests can eat under the big white umbrellas on the patio out front. Plenty of beaches and restaurants are within easy walking distance.

Baska Voda. www.orvas-hotels.om. ℰ **021/695-900.** 18 units. Standard double Jul–Aug 140€. **Amenities:** Restaurant; Wi-Fi (free).

Hotel Marco Polo ★★ In Gradac, 42km (26 miles) southeast of Makarska at the southern end of the riviera, this welcoming, family-run boutique hotel offers 25 rooms and suites. Facilties include an outdoor pool, sauna, massage and Jacuzzi, and the hotel can arrange excursions, including fishing trips by hotel boat. The excellent a la carte restaurant has waterside tables; besides doing a magnificent breakfast, the staff stages theme nights, highlighting wine tastings, Dalmatian music, or slow food menus.

Obala 15, Gradac. www.hotel-marcopolo.com. ℰ **021/695-060.** 25 units. Standard double Jul–Aug from 130€. **Amenities:** Restaurant; outdoor pool; wellness center; Wi-Fi (free).

Hotel Maritimo ★★ On the promenade overlooking the main beach, a 15-minute walk west of Makarska's old town, this small, peaceful hotel has modern rooms, the best ones with sea-view balconies that catch the magnificent sunsets. There's a ground floor restaurant where breakfast is served on an open-air terrace, and the staff is super-friendly and full of local advice. The hotel also has secure underground parking, although you should make a reservation for it in advance (7€/day).

Put Cvitačke bb, Makarska. www.hotel-maritimo.hr. ℰ **021/619-900.** 20 units. Standard double Jul–Aug from 130€. **Amenities:** Restaurant; pay parking; Wi-Fi (free).

Pansion Batosič ★ A (steep) 10-minute uphill walk from the center of Makarska brings you to this family-run B&B. The 10 double rooms here are basic but comfortable and all have balconies. Breakfast is served on a lovely front terrace with amazing views down onto town and out to sea. Guests have free use of a barbecue in the garden, and the hosts will prepare evening meals on request. They also have bikes for hire and offer yoga classes.

Kipara Meštrovića 25, Makarska. www.batosic.com. ℰ **021/612-974.** 10 units. Double Jul–Aug 56€. **Amenities:** Breakfast terrace; barbecue; bikes for hire; yoga; Wi-Fi (free).

Where to Dine

Makarska is a resort area that lives primarily off of tourism. There are a host of tourist-orientated restaurants and pizzerias that serve decent but unadventurous food. In the smaller towns along the riviera, you'll find more authentic Dalmatian eateries.

Jeny ★★ DALMATIAN   In the village of Gornji Tučepi (a 10-minute drive from Makarska), on a hillside high above the sea, this gourmet eatery makes a fine choice for a special dinner. The chef is noted for his beautifully presented creative cuisine. Diners can start with a dish like smoked venison carpaccio with rocket salad and caramelized pear, followed by a rabbit crépinette with a black trumpet and champignon sauce. The best way to savor the chef's range of skills is to opt for the 5-course degustation menu, which combines both seafood and meat dishes. Terrace dining is available, and the main interior is quietly stylish, with a wood-plank ceiling and white tablecloths. Note that it's dinner-only here (closed in the colder months), and reservations are recommended.

Gornji Tučepi 49, Makarska. www.restaurant-jeny.hr. *©* **021/623-704.** Entrees 70kn–140kn. May–Sept daily 6pm–midnight.

Konoba Kalelarga ★ DALMATIAN   This tiny, traditional wine bar and eatery in Makarska serves up typical local dishes in rustic surroundings, with exposed stone walls and heavy wooden tables and chairs, some made from old wine barrels. There is no menu—each day the cook prepares half a dozen dishes based on the best fresh ingredients found at the market that morning.

Kalelarga 40, Makarska. *©* **098/990-29-08.** Entrees 45kn–70kn. Daily 10am–midnight.

Radmanove Mlinice ★ DALMATIAN   Up the Cetina Gorge, 6km (4 miles) from Omiš, this waterside restaurant occupies an 18th-century mill. It's noted for its excellent freshwater fish, such as trout, and roast lamb, served at tables under the trees next to the river. Many companies that arrange rafting and canoeing down the Cetina begin their trips from here.

Cetina Gorge, Omiš. www.radmanove-mlinice.hr. *©* **021/862-073.** Entrees 50kn–110kn. Apr–Oct daily noon–11pm.

Stari Mlin ★★ FUSION/DALMATIAN-THAI   A pleasant surprise for Makarska, this restaurant serves both traditional Dalmatian seafood dishes and a select choice of Thai cuisine (think shrimp curry or pad Thai). It is set in a romantic 18th-century stone building, its walls decorated with the owner's artworks, with a vine-covered patio at the back. The owner worked for several years on cruise ships, traveling the world, which is how she acquired her knowledge of Thai cooking.

Ulica Prvosvibanjska 43, Makarska. *©* **021/611-509.** Entrees 70kn–120kn, more for fish priced by the kilo. May–Oct, Mon–Sat 10am–3pm and 6pm–1am; closed Sun.

BRAČ

Brač is both a windsurfer's paradise and one of Croatia's least-developed populated islands. It's famous as the source of the stone that built Diocletian's Palace on the mainland and the White House in Washington, D.C. Brač also has a reputation as the source of high-quality Bolski Plavac red wine and delicious locally raised lamb. This rugged land mass, about 1 hour's ferry ride from Split, is the third-largest island off Croatia (Krk is the biggest, followed by Cres). Despite its size, Brač is really just a two-town island. That's because only **Supetar** on Brač's northern shore and **Bol** on the southern shore are frequently visited by the tourists who come for the island's Mediterranean climate and unspoiled countryside. Bol is also home to **Zlatni Rat (Golden Cape)**, Croatia's most famous beach. Tourism currently supplies most of Brač's revenue.

Essentials

VISITOR INFORMATION   The **Supetar** tourist information center is at Porat 1 (www.supetar.hr; ℰ **021/630-551**) and the **Bol** tourist office is at Porat Bolskih Pomoraca bb (www.bol.hr; ℰ **021/635-638**).

GETTING THERE   In the summer, a dozen Jadrolinija car ferries make the daily hour-long journey from Split to Supetar on Brač's northern shore; a once-daily high-speed catamaran runs to Bol on the southern shore. Car ferries from Makarska connect to Sumartin on Brač's eastern shore. Taxi-boats run across the narrow sea channel between Bol on Brač and Jelsa on Hvar.

GETTING AROUND   Buses run from Supetar to Bol six times a day and to several other towns and villages on Brač three times a day, although having to make connections can limit mobility. The best way to explore more than one town per visit is to rent a car or a motor scooter and explore the island independently. If you plan to stay in one place on Brač you can manage everything on foot, although you might consider hiring a bicycle in Bol to get back and forth from Zlatni Rat beach.

What to See & Do

Supetar and Bol are the locations most frequented by visitors to Brač. Supetar is by far the closer landing point from Split, but once you've walked around the pretty horseshoe-shaped harbor, the pebble beach and concrete bathing areas are a little disappointing. In contrast, the former fishing village of Bol is a gem, backed by the rugged heights of **Vidova Gora**, the highest point on all the Croatian islands, with the stunning **Zlati Rat (Golden Cape)** beach just a 20-minute walk west of the village. Bol is also Croatia's top windsurfing destination thanks to the very specific winds that blow down the narrow sea channel separating Brač from the island of Hvar.

SUPETAR

With 3,500 inhabitants, Supetar is the largest town on Brač, and many families from Split have weekend houses here. The ferries landing at Supetar deposit passengers on a dock that sits directly next to the picturesque fishing harbor, around which the old town was built. West from here, the coast curves away from the town, with a succession of concrete bathing areas and pebble beaches running toward an area of modern hotel complexes aimed at the package tourism market.

BOL

Bol is home to Croatia's most publicized beach. Almost every promotion of the country's unspoiled landscapes uses an aerial shot of **Zlatni Rat (Golden Cape)**. From the air, Zlatni Rat does look like a long, inviting tendril of white sand, lazily stretching into the sparkling azure sea. Add a gorgeous sunbather lounging here and there and the shape-shifting strip of land appears to be the perfect place for an idyllic sojourn. The beach is a mini-peninsula made up of fine pebbles, jutting into the sea. It sits a 20-minute walk west of Bol, along a lovely tree-lined promenade, which is laced by several smaller beaches along the way. Three big, modern hotels, set amid pine trees, overlook the promenade. Through July and August, Zlatni Rat is lined with sunbeds and umbrellas for hire, and packed with people from every walk of life, which rather detracts from its romantic image.

To be sure, Zlatni Rat is more upscale and tourist-savvy than the beach at Supetar, its sister to the north, and there is a certain satisfaction in setting foot on this super-hyped playground. But to see it at its best, you should try to visit in either June or September, when the sea is warm enough to swim in but the crowds are not too dense.

WATERSPORTS

Bol has a worldwide reputation as a windsurfer's paradise. It's not unusual to see "schools" of boarders riding the waves in the sea channel between Brač and Hvar, which is exposed to exceptional wind conditions.

Big Blue ★   Big Blue is the largest company for watersports in Bol, both hiring out equipment and giving instruction at all levels, from beginners to advanced athletes. You can rent a board for an hour for 18€, or for a week for 200€. Big Blue also rents out sea kayaks, as well as mountain bikes, and offers mountain biking excursions down the rugged slopes of Vidova Gora, behind Bol.

Near the Hotel Borak btw. Zlani Rat and town, Podan Glavice 2, Bol. www.bigbluesport.com ✆ **091/449-70-87.**

Big Blue Diving ★   Big Blue Diving arranges diving trips to sites that include underwater caves and wrecks in addition to providing instruction at all levels.

Bračka cesta 13, Bol. www.big-blue-diving.hr. ✆ **098/425-496.**

Where to Stay

In Supetar, most accommodations consist of package hotels at the west end of town, though you can secure private accommodations at the tourist office near the dock (see p. 162). You also can inquire wherever you see a SOBE sign. Bol has rooms in well-equipped resort hotels, too, but it also has some charming private accommodations.

Bluesun Borak Hotel ★   The Yugoslav-era Borak stands on the seafront promenade, but its setting back amid pine trees gives it a secluded atmosphere. Standard rooms are in the main hotel building, while family rooms are distributed through six separate pavilions. The hotel has its own pool and fitness room, and guests are welcome to use the Wellness Center Thalasso Bol at nearby sister hotel the Elaphusa (see below). The hotel is just a 10-minute walk from Zlatni Rat beach and a 15-minute walk from the village of Bol.

Put Zlatnog Rata bb, Bol. www.brachotelborak.com. ✆ **021/306-202.** 181 units. Double July–Aug from 144€. **Amenities:** Restaurant; 2 bars; children's program; fitness room; outdoor pool; tennis center; Wi-Fi (free).

Bluesun Hotel Elaphusa ★   Like its sister hotel, the Borak, the Elaphusa lies midway between Zlatni Rat beach and the village of Bol, both of which are within easy walking distance. Excellent sports facilities, including the Wellness Center Thalasso Bol, three pools, a tennis school, and rental bikes, make it popular with families. The buffet breakfast is eaten indoors; in summer many people would prefer to sit outside, but you can always pay a small room service surcharge and eat on your own private balcony.

Put Zlatnog Rata bb, Bol. www.hotelelaphusabrac.com. ✆ **021/306-200.** 306 units. Double July–Aug from 190€. **Amenities:** Restaurant; 2 bars; rental bikes; children's program; 3 pools; tennis center; wellness center; Wi-Fi (free).

Bračka Perla ★★★   This chic but unpretentious boutique hotel lies a 15-minute walk west along the coast from Supetar's harbor. Set in a lovely garden giving onto a small bay, it has an outdoor pool rimmed with sunbeds and big white parasols. The apartments each come with a double room, a living room with a sofa bed (ideal for families with kids), a fully equipped kitchen, and a stone terrace with a table for eating out. In total there are five rooms and six apartments, each one named after a local plant or herb and color-themed accordingly. Extra facilities include a small wellness center and a nearby farm (www.agroturizam-brac.com) where wine and olive oil are made. The hotel is expensive, but it's also very special.

Put Vele Vule 53, Supetar. www.perlacroatia.com. © **021/755-530.** 11 units. Double 335€. **Amenities:** Garden; outdoor pool; wellness center; Wi-Fi (free).

Hotel Villa Adriatica ★★ This friendly family-run hotel in Supetar, a 15-minute walk from the ferry port, offers 23 colorful rooms, all with balconies. The public space centers on a stone terrace shaded by palms trees, with a small pool and cocktail bar; breakfast is served here, too. Additional facilities include a wellness center, offering a sauna, Jacuzzi, and massage. The hotel also offers a 1-week multi-sport island adventure package, with the opportunity to try sea kayaking, windsurfing, rock climbing, mountain biking, and more.

Put Vele Luke 31, Supetar. www.villaadriatica.com. © **021/343-806.** 23 units. Double Jul–Aug from 128€. **Amenities:** Cafe; bar; bike rental; pool; wellness center; Wi-Fi (free).

Zlatni Bol Apartments ★★★ A great alternative to staying in a hotel in Bol, these studios (sleeping 2 to 3) and spacious apartments (sleeping 4) each come with a fully equipped kitchenette. Light and airy, the rooms are tastefully furnished in Mediterranean style, with slick modern bathrooms and private balconies or garden patios for sitting out. The owner is a windsurfing enthusiast and can give you recommendations about local restaurants and adventure sports facilities. You'll find Zlatni Bol a 10-minute walk uphill from the fishing harbor, and a 15-minute walk from Zlatni Rat beach.

Ivana Gundulića 2, Bol. www.zlatni-bol.com. © **091/224-47-00.** 9 units. Two-person studio Jul–Aug 95€. **Amenities:** Wi-Fi (free).

Where to Dine

Restaurants in both Bol and Supetar serve classic Dalmatian seafood dishes in addition to the local lamb for which Brač is renowned. Most of the people who stay in the big resort hotels take advantage of all-inclusive deals or at least half board, though the standard of the food in those complexes is generally rather poor. For meals with accommodations, I recommend B&Bs only.

Bistro Palute ★ DALMATIAN Palute stands on the promenade, with a terrace overlooking Supetar's fishing harbor, close to the ferry landing station. Much loved by locals, favorite dishes include homemade fish soup and the barbecued meat platter, served with delicious fries. Spectacular sunsets, friendly staff, and reasonable prices add to the appeal.

Porat 4, Supetar. © **021/631-730.** Entrees 40kn–60kn. May–Oct daily 8am–1am; Nov–Apr daily 8am–10pm.

Dalmatino ★★ DALMATIAN Formerly known as Konoba Gušt, this old-fashioned eatery changed ownership in 2012. The dining room, decorated with traditional farm implements and fishing equipment, has stayed the same, but the menu now features a wider range of local meat and seafood dishes. You'll find Dalmatino in the center of Bol, 1 block back from the Riva, with an additional six tables in the narrow alley out front.

Frane Radića 14, Bol. © **091/545-57-79.** Entrees 80kn–140kn, more for fish priced by the kilo. Daily noon–2am.

Konoba Mendula ★★ DALMATIAN Hidden away in a residential area of Bol, a few blocks uphill from the seafront, this neighborhood eatery is down-to-earth with no pretensions. Tables are set out on a raised terrace with lots of potted plants. The menu includes meat dishes and local seafood—ask your waiter what fresh fish they have on offer. There's a self-service salad bar with big bowls of chopped lettuce, tomatoes, and cucumber from the owner's garden. The place is popular with locals and visitors alike, so you may have to queue for a table. Note that it's cash only here.

Hrvatskih domobrana 13, Bol. ℂ **021/635-053.** Entrees 45kn–100kn. Daily noon–midnight.

Mali Raj ★★ DALMATIAN Directly behind Zlatni Rat beach, Mali Raj ("Little Paradise") occupies a complex of old stone buildings, set in a garden with stone terraces and lemon trees. The menu covers Dalmatian seafood and meat specialties, plus a few Istrian dishes featuring truffles. It is a bit more expensive than most of the restaurants in the village of Bol, but the setting is enchanting and the proximity to the beach makes it very convenient for a late lunch or early supper.

Put Zlatnog Rata bb, Bol. ℂ **098/756-922.** Entrees 80kn–140kn, more for fish priced by the kilo. Daily noon–midnight.

Vagabundo ★★ MODERN DALMATIAN In the center of Bol, with a lovely raised terrace overlooking the seafront promenade, Vagabundo can feel a little fancy schmanzy, with occasional live piano music. The prices, however, are surprisingly reasonable. The restaurant is run by owner-chef Vinko Marinković, who has spent several years working in the Cayman Islands. Drawing on his experience abroad, he uses local ingredients to create beautifully presented and flavorful dishes. He does a delicious (and enormous) succulent tuna steak, and his menu also includes special choices for children and vegetarians.

Ante Radića 36, Bol. ℂ **021/635-436.** Entrees 60kn–120kn. Daily noon–midnight.

HVAR

St. Tropez, Majorca, Aspen, and other glamour destinations don't have anything on Hvar, the glitzy Croatian playground patronized by celebrities, the idle rich, and the Average Joe tourist who wants to be part of the Hvar hoopla.

Hvar is indeed a lush, sunny Shangri-la, with more hours of sunshine (2,724) than any other place in Croatia, at least according to the literature. But when you're talking just 24 more hours of rays than Brač (2,700) and only 124 hours (5 days) more than most of Croatia's other islands, you're splitting hairs. Ultraviolet rays aside, Hvar is a blissful escape with vineyards, lavender fields, a few interesting sites, a lot of good restaurants, and some über-expensive places to stay.

Hvar's principal towns are Hvar Town, Stari Grad, Vrboska, Jelsa, and Sucuraj, though Hvar Town is most definitely the center of current interest in the island.

Essentials

VISITOR INFORMATION **Hvar Town**'s principal tourist office (www.tzhvar.hr; ℂ **021/741-059**) is on the main square at Trg Sv. Stjepana bb. **Stari Grad**'s office (www.stari-grad-faros.hr; ℂ **021/765-763**) is on the seafront at Obala dr. Franje Tuđmana 1. **Jelsa**'s tourist office (www.tzjelsa.hr; ℂ **021/761-017**) is on the seafront at Riva bb.

GETTING THERE Jadrolinija operates two high-speed catamarans daily from Split to Korčula, which stop at Hvar Town en-route (journey time is approximately 1 hr.). The line also runs several daily car ferries between Split and Stari Grad (journey time 2 hr.). From Stari Grad, connecting buses run to Hvar Town (20km/13 miles). In addition, there's a once-daily Jadrolinija catamaran from Split to Jelsa (a 1 hr., 40 min. ride) on Hvar's north coast, and a several-times-daily car ferry from Dnvenik (just south of Makarska) to Sučuraj, at the extreme southern tip of Hvar. Jadrolinija (www. jadrolinija.hr; ℃ 021/741-132) has an office on the Riva in Hvar Town. Note that in high season, catamarans to and from Hvar Town fill up quickly, so you should buy your ticket at least one day in advance.

GETTING AROUND Hvar Town is closed to motorized traffic from the bus station to the Riva, which is also the busiest thoroughfare until after nightfall, when the long, rectangular main square, Trg Sveti Stjepana, buzzes with open-air cafes. If you want to see anything besides Hvar Town and Stari Grad, a car is a timesaver, but Hvar Town is best covered on foot.

What to See & Do

Hvar Town is St. Moritz with surf instead of snow. It's Hollywood meets Nice, Milan sophistication melded with Mediterranean relaxation, and the Las Vegas Strip transported to Tuscany. Hvar Town is a magnet for film stars, royalty, and business tycoons, as well as your average summertime backpacker.

The uniqueness of the place is that everyone looks rich and famous. It's difficult to recognize even a well-known face because in Hvar Town a pair of Maui Jim sunglasses, designer jeans, and a look of ennui are enough for anyone to blend into the sculpted, perfumed crowd.

Make no mistake, Hvar Town has plenty of culture, much of it in the form of elegant centuries-old architecture. However, it's really the sun, the sea, and the 21st-century social scene that pull in visitors, who make their entrances on everything from sleek yachts to catamarans packed sardine-style. Even if you're here for the beach scene, be sure to check out **St. Stephen's Square (Trg Sveti Stjepan).** Dating from the 13th century, this square is Hvar Town's center of activity. It is bookended by **St. Stephen's Cathedral** at its east end and by a small harbor to the west. The square's borders are lined with restaurants, cafes, and galleries. A 16th-century well sits in the center of the paved space, which was redone in the late 18th century. *Note:* One of the main attractions, the Venetian-era arsenal and the tiny theater above it, are at press time closed for restoration; there is no fixed date for their reopening.

Fortress (Fortica) ★★   Hvar Town is presided over by an imposing 16th-century fortress, built on the site of an earlier medieval castle. It is well worth the hike up steep steps and a meandering footpath for photogenic views over Hvar Town's terracotta rooftops and out to sea towards the scattered Pakleni islets. Within the fortress's Venetian-era ramparts, you'll find displays of amphorae found offshore, a spooky dungeon, and a cafe selling cold drinks. The fortress is stunning from below at night, when it is beautifully floodlit.

North of Hvar Town center. ℃ **021/741-816.** Admission 30kn. May–Oct daily 8am–11pm.

Franciscan Monastery ★★   Southeast of the main square, a waterside promenade snakes its way around a series of bays to arrive at a 15th-century Franciscan monastery. An arched gateway leads into an elegant cloistered courtyard, which hosts occasional classical music concerts throughout the summer. There's also a small museum, displaying a modest collection of sacral art, including a memorable painting of the Last Supper. A peaceful garden affords magnificent views down onto the sea.

Southeast of Hvar Town center. ℃ **021/741-193.** Admission 25kn. May–Oct daily 10am–noon and 5–7pm.

St. Stephen's Cathedral ★ On the main square, Hvar's cathedral is notable for its elegant trefoil facade and 17th-century bell tower. Built on the site of a former monastery, the interior holds a 16th-century wooden choir, several late-Renaissance paintings, and a treasury.

Trg Sv. Stjepana bb, Hvar Town. Admission 10kn. May–Oct daily 9am–noon and 5–7pm, hours sometimes extended during tourist season.

Tvrdalj ★★ In the sleepy port town of Stari Grad, this fortified villa was built in 1520 as the summer residence of local Renaissance poet Petar Hektorović (1487–1572). The villa centers on an internal courtyard with a large fishpond and an adjoining walled garden, which is slightly overgrown but very whimsical and romantic. Hektorović intended that the entire population of Stari Grad be able to take shelter here in the event of an attack by the Ottoman Turks, who were a constant threat at the time.

Priko bb, Stari Grad. ✆ **021/765-068.** Admission 15kn. May to mid-Oct, 10am–1pm and 6–8pm.

BEACHES

All beaches in Croatia are open to the public by law, giving everyone access to the sea. However, the twist in places like Hvar Town is that some businesses are opening beach bars on the coast, complete with sunbeds and umbrellas for hire at a hefty fee. The **Bonj "les bains" beach club** at the Hotel Amfora is a prime example. You have to pay to use the club's stone cabanas and sunbeds, which line a concrete bathing platform affording easy access into the water. In high season, these facilities require booking several days in advance.

From Bonj "les Bains," a 10-minute walk west along the coast brings you to **Hula Hula Beach Bar** (www.hulahulahvar.com; mid-May to late-Sept, daily 9am–9pm), a trendy establishment popular with the younger crowd. Sunbeds are packed close together on wooden platforms built over the rocks and a beach bar plays mainstream commercial music till sunset.

For those who like back-to-nature beaches, the best plan is to hop on a taxi-boat and head for the nearby **Pakleni Otoci,** a cluster of pine-forested, uninhabited islands whose coastlines are alternately rimmed with rocks and little pebble beaches (some of which are clothing-optional). Nowadays even the Pakleni beaches are coming under tight management, however, with venues like **Carpe Diem Beach** (www.carpe-diem-beach.com) in Stipanksa Bay on Marinkovac, which offers sunbeds for hire in a pebble cove, a bar/restaurant, an outdoor pool, massage, and late-night parties with guest DJs.

WATERSPORTS & EXCURSIONS

Away from the glamorous bars and restaurants of Hvar Town, the island of Hvar offers some fantastic back-to-nature experiences. Along the coast, a host of watersports are on offer, while the rugged interior is crisscrossed by hiking and cycling paths.

Hvar Adventure ★★★ This highly respected agency is run by local sports enthusiasts, who arrange adventure-sports activities, including half-day sea kayaking tours, 1-day sailing tours, windsurfing, hiking, cycling, and rock climbing. Cookery classes and wine tasting expeditions are offered as well.

Jurja Matijevića 20, Hvar Town. www.hvar-adventure.com. ✆ **021/717-813.**

Where to Stay

There are no hotel bargains in Hvar Town, and most of the accommodations in Stari Grad are huge, impersonal package resorts. Since the island became all the rage, inn-keepers have been scrambling to expand and renovate, and the result is prices escalating faster than hotel improvements. You still can find modestly priced private accommodations, but in the summer expect to book four days or more just to get a reservation.

VERY EXPENSIVE

Hotel Adriana ★★★ Reopened in 2007, following a complete renovation by British architects, the Adriana's interiors are roomy and full of light, with design details that are slick and contemporary. Guestrooms come with sensual glass-walled bathrooms and suites have the extra indulgence of a whirlpool bathtub. Up top, the vast Sensori Spa offers a host of beauty and massage treatments. The heated seawater pool there has a retractable roof, making it either indoor or outdoor, depending on the season. Also on the roof, The Top lounge bar serves cocktails and finger food, with amazing views over Hvar Town and out to sea. On the ground floor, steakhouse Butchery&Wine, overlooking the harbor, opened in May, 2014.

Fabrika 28, Hvar Town. www.suncanihvar.com. (C) **021/750-200.** 59 units. Double Jul–Aug 412€. **Amenities:** Restaurant; cafe; 2 bars; pool; spa; Wi-Fi (free).

Hotel Amfora ★★★ This vast, Yugoslav-era hotel, originally built in the 1970s, sits on its own bay a 10-minute walk west of Hvar's main square. After 2008 renovations, its rooms and suites are chic and comfortable. The main draw is the landscaped front garden, complete with cascading pools and artificial islets with palm trees, making it a good choice for families with kids. Note that although the Bonj "les bains" beach club appears to be part of the Amfora, hotel guests are still obliged to pay a surcharge for using its facilities.

Majerović bb, Hvar Town. (C) **021/750-300.** 319 units. Double Jul–Aug from 309€. **Amenities:** 3 restaurants; 4 bars; pool; private beach club; spa; Wi-Fi (free).

EXPENSIVE

Hotel Podstine ★★★ Podstine is set in a terraced garden with towering palm trees, which steps down to a rock and concrete beach area lined with sunbeds. Tables are discretely set among the trees, and you can dine here by candlelight at night. Inside, the best rooms have floor-to-ceiling sliding windows opening onto blissful sea-view balconies. Other facilities include a small wellness center with a pool and a scuba-diving center. This hotel is a good choice for couples or older visitors who are not so interested in Hvar Town's notorious nightlife. The setting is on a peaceful bay a 20-minute walk west of town, following the lovely coastal promenade.

Pod Stine bb, Hvar Town. www.podstine.com. (C) **021/740-400.** 40 units. Double Jul–Aug from 270€. **Amenities:** Restaurant; bar; beach; diving center; wellness center; guarded parking; Wi-Fi (free).

MODERATE

Apolon ★★★ This charming heritage hotel in Stari Grad opened in June, 2014. Occupying an aristocratic villa overlooking the bay, it has just three rooms and four spacious suites, all with wooden floors, oriental rugs, and sweeping curtains. A ground floor restaurant serves creative Mediterranean cuisine and offers plenty of gourmet surprises.

Šetališta don Šimuna Ljubića 7, Stari Grad. www.apolon.hr. (C) **021/778-320.** 7 units. Double from 109€. **Amenities:** Restaurant; Wi-Fi (free).

Palmižana ★★★ For a true escape, stay at Palmižana, set in a centuries-old botanical garden on the pine-scented islet of Sveti Klement. There are seven villas and six bungalows here, all with quirky boho-chic furnishings, fully equipped kitchens, and walls hung with colorful contemporary paintings (the owner is an art collector). The complex includes two sublimely romantic open-air restaurants with sea-view terraces, and a narrow

LAVENDER blues

Hvar is sometimes known as "Lavender Island" because the graceful plant with silver-green foliage and a hypnotic, soothing fragrance grows in abundance here. *Lavandula*, as the plant is known in botanical circles, is a native of the dry Mediterranean climate, and is thought to aid peaceful sleep and soothe headaches. On Hvar, lavender is an industry, and you'll pick up the scent as soon as you arrive because the herb is sold up and down the dock at Hvar Town. Locals sell distilled lavender oil in small bottles and lavender bags (filled with dry lavender, to put in the wardrobe) at wooden stands along the seafront. Several Hvar restaurants now serve homemade lavender ice cream as a dessert. Some of the fancy-schmancy Hvar spas (for example, Hotel Adriana's, above) use local herbs, including lavender, in their spa treatments.

curving pebble beach that overlooks a sheltered bay where yachts drop anchor on balmy summer nights. The property is a 20-minute taxi-boat ride from Hvar Town.

Sveti Klement, Hvar Town. www.palmizana.hr. © **021/717-270.** 13 units. Bungalow sleeping 3 persons Jul–Aug from 180€. **Amenities:** 2 restaurants; beach; Wi-Fi (free).

Skalinada ★★ Skalinada is set in a garden planted with pines, fruit trees, and fragrant herbs, and gives onto a lovely pebble beach. Accommodation options include rooms and suites, all with tile floors, beds with wrought-iron bedsteads, and sea-view balconies. There are also three stone cottages, each sleeping 4 to 6 people, complete with fully equipped kitchens, living rooms with open fireplaces, and sea-view patios. A lovely terrace restaurant serves breakfast, followed by local seafood specialties later in the day. Skalinada is a real escape, but visitors might find it a bit too isolated. It's on Hvar's south coast in the sleepy village of Zavala, 30km (9 miles) from Hvar Town.

Zavala, south coast of Hvar. www.skalinada-apartmani-hvar.hr. © **021/767-019.** 15 units. Double Jul–Aug 138€. **Amenities:** Restaurant; beach; Wi-Fi (free).

INEXPENSIVE

Green Lizard Hostel ★★ Hotels in Hvar Town are notoriously expensive, but travelers on a tight budget can still get by if they stay in a hostel. There are only about three proper hostels in town, although several families with a few rooms to rent use the term to attract young guests. Green Lizard stands out as a particularly well-run establishment, overseen by two sisters originally from Hvar. The sisters try to give their guests individual treatment, often going out with them for drinks or a meal, so people traveling alone immediately feel involved and not left out. The hostel has a couple of private doubles with en-suite bathrooms, as well as bunk beds in dorms, and it's nice to have both options. There's a small garden with beanbags, hammocks, and a barbecue, and a friendly atmosphere throughout.

Domovinskog rata 13, Hvar Town. www.greenlizard.hr. © **021/742-560.** 28 beds. Dorm bed Jul–Aug 28€. **Amenities:** Garden with barbecue; laundry; Wi-Fi (free).

Where to Dine

You can eat incredibly well on Hvar, but often at a price, especially if you're in a prime spot in Hvar Town or on the nearby Pakleni islets. Most eateries put an emphasis on local seasonal produce and freshly caught seafood. For a cheaper option, there are

THE REST OF hvar

The glitzy enclave of Hvar Town has become synonymous with Hvar itself, but the island is also blessed with beautiful rugged landscapes and pretty villages that are perfect for lovers of nature and history.

If you hit Hvar at Stari Grad, resist the impulse to cover the 20km (13 miles) between there and Hvar Town as fast as possible, and take the time to see the land between the two. History is on display at **Stari Grad,** the island's main ferry port, as at **Tvrdalj,** 16th-century poet Petar Hektorović's romantic summer home, set in a fine garden.

As you leave Stari Grad, look for signs directing you to **Jelsa,** Hvar's family resort town. Stroll around **Old Town** on the harbor, visit the **Church of St. Ivan,** and stop for *gelato* (Italian ice cream) at any of the cafes that line the harbor. From Jelsa you can detour to any of the villages that dot the hilly Hvar interior for a look at lavender fields, olive groves, grazing sheep and goats, and abandoned stone dwellings. You'll arrive at Hvar Town rested and ready to party.

some very good pizzerias. Alternatively, drive out of town to a more low-key destination like Stari Grad or Milna. *Tip:* For a sweet treat, visit **Nonica** (𝄞 **091/739-23-90**) at Kroz Burak 23 in Hvar Town for irresistible chocolate cakes and cookies, made by the owner-cook, who studied at Le Cordon Bleu London.

EXPENSIVE

Dalmatino ★★ DALMATIAN   Dubbed a "steak and fish house," Dalmatino has earned an excellent reputation among locals and visitors alike. Standout dishes include the octopus carpaccio, shrimp risotto, pasta with truffles, and the excellent châteaubriand. The staff is friendly and professional and will bring you a small glass of *rakija* (a potent local spirit), on the house, either before or after your meal. The interior is modern, and there's candlelit outside seating area under white awnings. Reservations are recommended.

Sveti Marak 1, Hvar Town. www.dalmatino-hvar.com. 𝄞 **091/529-31-21.** Entrees 75kn–150kn. Open mid-Apr to late-Oct, noon–4pm and 6pm–midnight.

Giaxa ★★ CREATIVE MEDITERRANEAN   In a romantic 15th-century stone courtyard in a side alley in Hvar Town, the catchphrase here is "Have you ever tasted art?" The art in question is creative Mediterranean cuisine, including dishes like swordfish carpaccio with wild orange and pistachio, and beef fillet medallions with black truffles. It's all very indulgent and rather expensive, but worth it if you're looking for something different. The interior's ancient arches make a nice contrast with the contemporary furnishings. Reservations are recommended.

Petra Hektorovića 3, Hvar Town. www.giaxa.com. 𝄞 **021/741-073.** Entrees 80kn–160kn. May–Oct noon–4pm and 6pm–midnight.

Macondo ★★★ SEAFOOD   Below the fortress, 1 block back from the main square, Macondo is the restaurant most locals would recommend for authentic Dalmatian cooking and an unpretentious atmosphere. The emphasis is on fresh seafood—try the house's lobster spaghetti, grilled fresh fish, or the island specialty, *Hvarska gregada,* a robust fish stew prepared with potatoes, onions, and fresh herbs.

Groda bb, Hvar Town. 𝄞 **021/742-850.** Entrees 75kn–120kn, more for fish priced by the kilo. Apr–Oct, Mon–Sat noon–3pm and 6pm–midnight, Sun 6pm–midnight.

Toto's ★★ MODERN DALMATIAN   Part of the Palmižana complex, on the islet of Sveti Klement, Toto's is a boho-chic eatery on a stone terrace directly above the sea. Planted with palms, cacti, and exotic shrubs, the mood is cool and unhurried. Come here for cream of shrimp soup, succulent tuna steaks, and creative salads while you watch the yachts put down anchor in the idyllic bay out front.

Sveti Klement, Hvar Town. www.palmizana.hr. ℮ **021/71824.** Entrees 80kn–140kn, more for fish priced by the kilo. May–Oct daily 11am–1am.

MODERATE

Đorđota Vartal ★★ DALMATIAN   Close to the Franciscan monastery, Vartal has a spacious covered terrace, approached up several steps, overlooking a peaceful bay. The owner-chef is a master of Dalmatian cuisine, and his specialties include lobster spaghetti and the local fish stew *Hvarska gregada,* along with delicious barbecued steaks and seasonal salads.

Križna Luka 8, Hvar Town. restoran-vartal.com. ℮ **021/743-077.** Entrees 50kn–130kn, more for fish priced by the kilo. May–Oct daily noon–midnight.

Konoba Lambik ★★★ DALMATIAN   In the village of Milna, 6km (4 miles) east of Hvar Town, this enchanting eatery is set in a lush garden where the owner grows his own tomatoes, cucumbers, peppers, arugula, and fresh herbs. Even the bread, wine, and olive oil are homemade. Order a carafe of white wine and a platter of seafood appetizers, which includes swordfish and tuna carpaccio, octopus salad, fish pâté, olives, and samphire (a coastal green). Tables are set out on a stone terrace beneath olive trees and the experience here is truly authentic and totally unforgettable.

Milna bb, south coast of Hvar. ℮ **021/745-204.** Entrees 50kn–120kn. May–Oct daily noon–2pm and 5pm–1am.

Stari Mlin ★★★ DALMATIAN   This restaurant is hidden away in Stari Grad, a couple of blocks back from the harbor and close to the bus station. It is particularly popular with Italian yachters, who come here to savor delights such as octopus and vegetable stew, or baby-shrimp risotto with tomatoes and capers. There are outdoor tables on a vine-covered terrace, and in winter the dining room, with its exposed stone walls and colorful modern paintings, comes into good use.

Petra Kuničića 3. Stari Grad. ℮ **021-765-804.** Entrees 60kn–110kn, more for fish priced by the kilo. May–Oct daily noon–3pm and 6pm–midnight; Nov–Apr Fri–Sat 6–11pm.

INEXPENSIVE

Alviz ★ PIZZA   Originally founded as a crêperie in 1989, this welcoming family-run eatery now specializes in pizza and barbecued meat dishes. Try the delicious Alviz Pizza, topped with tomato, cheese, prosciutto, mushrooms, artichokes, mild chili, and oregano. The location is central, close to the bus station, and the interior is pleasant, with bright green tables and benches accenting whitewashed walls.

Dolac bb. www.hvar-alviz.com. ℮ **021/742-797.** Pizza 38kn–65kn. Jun–Oct Mon–Fri 6pm–midnight; Sat–Sun 6pm–1am.

Hvar After Dark

Celebrities, royalty, and business tycoons firmly established Hvar as the beautiful-people capital of Croatia a decade ago when they started mooring up their yachts in the island's secluded harbors. Several boho-chic nightlife venues opened to cater to sophisticated tastes, with open-air drinking and chill-out music blending perfectly with the balmy Mediterranean climate and star-filled sky. Start the evening with après beach cocktails at **Hula Hula Beach Bar** (see p. 167), on the coastal path between Hotel Amfora and Hotel Podstine. Later, for the ultimate decadent Hvar cocktail experience, go to **The Top** (www.suncanihvar.com; May–Oct daily 11–2am) lounge bar on the roof of the Hotel Adriana (see p. 168). Or, for after-dark parties and international guest DJs in blissful natural surroundings, hop on a taxi-boat from the harbor and head for **Carpe Diem Beach** (www.carpe-diem-beach.com; June to mid-Sep, daily 10–5am) in Stipanksa Bay on Marinkovac.

KORČULA

There is more to the island of **Korčula** than the walled city of Korčula Town. In the less than 50km (30 miles) between the picturesque walled city at the eastern end of the island and the port town of Vela Luka at the other end, you'll find vineyards and wineries, hills and hiking trails, and quiet towns like **Lumbarda, Smokvica,** and **Blato,** with out-of-the way beaches along the coastal areas between.

Korčula Town

The island of Korčula is a popular day trip from Dubrovnik or Orebič on the Pelješac Peninsula. Medieval Korčula Town is the focus of most tourist activity on the island as well as its main transportation hub. Once you climb the 19th-century Grand Staircase, with its 15th-century Revelin Tower, and walk through the 14th-century Land Gate, Korčula Town will captivate your imagination and take you back through the centuries.

Behind the medieval defensive walls, the Old Town is packed with aristocratic palazzi, built from limestone cut from the island's quarries. Today, these structures accommodate restaurants, museums, and family homes. Steep, dark, narrow streets branch off from the enclave's major north-south thoroughfare (Korčulaskog Statuta) in a pattern that resembles a fish skeleton. The street grid creates the illusion of a central boulevard with a lot of short side streets radiating from it. You can spend hours walking up and down these narrow offshoots and never know exactly where you are in relation to the walled town's exit. Tourists are also drawn by the city's claim that it is the birthplace of legendary explorer Marco Polo. *Tip:* The approach to Korčula Town on the morning ferry from Orebić makes one of the best vacation pictures ever.

The island of Korčula itself, which is just a little over a mile from the mainland across the Pelješac Channel, was once covered with so many pine trees that the sight led the Greeks who settled there around 400 B.C. to dub the island "Kerkyra Malaina" (Black Corfu). As with many of the islands in the southern Adriatic, there is evidence that Korčula was the site of Neolithic settlements. It also experienced much of the same historic string of takeovers and changes of fortune as the rest of Dalmatia's coastal settlements, including long stretches of Venetian rule (the longest being 1420–1797).

Tourists also travel to Korčula to see the traditional **Moreška Sword Dance,** an annual spectacle that recalls a battle between Christians and "infidels" that was fought over a beautiful maiden. In addition, the island is the source of excellent olive oil and wine, most notably white wines (Pošip, Grk) produced from grapes grown on the island's interior.

Essentials

VISITOR INFORMATION The **Korčula Town** tourist office (www.visitkorcula. eu; ✆ **020/715-701**) is on the seafront at Obala Dr. Franje Tuđmana 4.

GETTING THERE   Korčula is linked to Split by speedy catamarans and ferries, each of which makes the round-trip at least once per day, arriving either directly at Korčula Town, or at Vela Luka at the western end of the island. Frequent ferries also serve Korčula from nearby Orebić, with pedestrians landing at Korčula Town and car ferries landing at Dominiče, 3km (1¾ miles) southeast of there. There is also daily bus service from Dubrovnik via the car ferry. For ferry information, contact the Jadrolinija office (www.jadrolinija.hr; ✆ **020/715-410**) in Korčula Town. Bus schedules and fare information can be obtained at the Korčula Town bus station (✆ **060/373-060**).

GETTING AROUND   Local buses make five runs daily from Korčula Town to Vela Luka, covering the length of the island. You can also rent a bike and easily pedal the 6km (4 miles) between Korčula Town and Lumbarda, where the best beaches are. At its widest point, Korčula is about 8km (5 miles) wide and it is less than 32km (20 miles) long.

What to See & Do

Korčula's main attraction is the medieval Korčula Town and its walls, where you will find several historic churches, museums, and other points of interest. Korčula Town likes to promote a once-nondescript stone edifice as the birthplace of Marco Polo, but there is no credible documentation that the great explorer ever set foot on the island.

Cathedral of St. Mark (Katedrala Sv. Marka) ★★   Korčula's Gothic-Renaissance cathedral is notable for its elaborately carved Romanesque portal, which is topped by a proud statue of St. Mark. Statues of Adam and Eve stand to each side of the door, along with various animals and grotesques. Inside, you can see a Pietà by Dalmatian sculptor Ivan Meštrović in the baptistery, and a painting attributed to the highly acclaimed Venetian artist Tintoretto (1518–1594) above the main altar. You can also climb the 30m (98-ft.) cathedral bell tower, completed in 1483, for amazing views over town and out to sea.

Strossmayer Trg. Cathedral 15kn, bell tower 20kn. May–Sept Mon–Sat 9am–7pm; Oct Mon–Sat 9am–4pm.

Land Gate ★★   The main entrance to the fortified old town, the Land Gate is embellished with a stone carving of the Lion of St. Mark's (the symbol of Venice) above its arch. The gate is also guarded by the 15th-century Revelin Tower, which houses a small exhibition dedicated to the Moreška Sword Dance (see box), with unpredictable opening hours. From here, the town's main thoroughfare, Korčulanskog Statuta, runs all the way to the tip of the peninsula.

At Trg Braće Radića.

Marco Polo House ★   Based on local legend rather than reliable documentation, this old stone cottage, to the right of the cathedral bell tower, claims to be the birthplace of explorer Marco Polo (1254–1324). However, historians are still debating whether or not the one-time captain of the Venetian navy even ever set foot in Korčula Town. (What's more, the cottage was built a couple of centuries after Marco Polo died.)

Marka Pola bb. Admission 20kn. Jul–Aug daily 9am–9pm; May–Jun and Sept–Oct daily 9am–3pm.

Town Museum ★★   Opposite the cathedral, the ground floor of the 16th-century Gabriellis Palace houses a curious collection of ancient amphorae and stone carvings, including a copy of the renowned 4th-century B.C. *Lumbardska Psefizma*, a stone tablet recording transactions between Greeks and local Illyrians that proves there was an

SWORD drama

The **Moreška Sword Dance** is a 15th-century narrative in motion that tells the story of two kings who compete for the love of a princess. As the story goes, the Black King kidnaps the young woman after she declares her love for the White King, who retaliates by initiating a battle. The kings and their armies then engage in an intricate "ballet" with swords drawn as they "fight" to musical accompaniment.

The dance is thought to commemorate a real clash between Christians and Moors, precipitated by the Moors' abduction of a young girl. The traditional dance is performed by townspeople, usually outside the town walls, every Monday and Thursday at 9pm in July and August; on Thursdays in June and September; several times on July 29, the town's festival day; and other times when tourist traffic is heavy.

Ancient Greek presence here. Upstairs, you'll find period furniture and household items such as ceramics and glassware.

Trg Sv. Marka Statuta. ℓ **020/711-420.** Admission 20kn. Jul–Sept Mon–Sat 10am–9pm; Oct–Jun Mon–Fri 10am–2pm.

Treasury ★★   Next to the cathedral, this treasury occupies part of the 17th-century Bishop's Palace. Inside you can see religious paintings, gold and silver church paraphernalia, and ancient documents and coins, demonstrating the island's glorious past and former wealth.

Trg Sv. Marka Statuta. Admission 25kn. May–Sept Mon–Sat 9am–7pm; Oct Mon–Sat 9am–4pm.

Where to Stay

Hotels close to Korčula Town tend to be large, 1970s package-type places that haven't been updated since they were built (and are still relatively expensive). However, there are several other interesting options in town.

VERY EXPENSIVE

Lešič Dimitri Palace ★★★   Within the Old Town walls, this outstanding hotel (opened in 2009) is a member of Relais & Châteaux. Comprised of part of the 17th-century Bishop's Palace and a cluster of medieval cottages, it has just five residences (sleeping two to six people), each one themed after a country related to Marco Polo's travels (Arabia, Ceylon, India, China, and Venice are the options). Each residence has self-catering facilities and sensual bathrooms, some with freestanding tubs next to the bed. Besides the highly personalized service, you can enjoy the gourmet restaurant and wine bar, two hotel boats available for private charter (with skipper), and a small spa with a sauna, which employs two ladies from Thailand to give massages.

Ulica don Pavla Pośe 1–6. www.lesic-dimitri.com. ℓ **014/715-560.** 5 units. Two-person residence Jul–Aug 480€. **Amenities:** Restaurant; bar; spa; boats for charter; Wi-Fi (free).

MODERATE

Hotel Korsal ★★   Overlooking the yachting marina, a 10-minute walk from the Old Town, this small, family-run hotel is welcoming and efficient. There are just 10 double rooms, all with sea views and cheerful modern decor. Floors are wooden and interiors feature upbeat color schemes—fabrics in yellows, oranges, and lime green. Although the building is new, it's partly built out of local stone, which is a nice reference. Several rooms are interconnected, making this an ideal option for families with kids. The hotel restaurant has a small terrace down by the sea.

Šetalište Frana Kršanića 80. www.hotel-korsal.com. ✆ 014/715-722. 10 units. Double Jul–Aug 90€. **Amenities:** Restaurant; Wi-Fi (free).

Korčula Waterfront Accommodation ★★   This family house has two apartments and two double rooms to rent, each with its own terrace. The apartments come with fully equipped kitchens. Although the decor is nothing special, the friendly owners make this property stand out, coming to meet guests at the ferry port or bus station, and full of local advice about places to eat and things to see and do. They also have mountain bikes for hire, and can arrange guided wine-tasting excursions. The property overlooks the sea, a 10-minute walk from the Old Town. With just four units, peak July and August reservations may be hard to come by (there are a lot of return visitors), but in May/June and September/October it should be easier to get a last-minute room here.

Šetalište Tina Ukevića 33. www.korcula-waterfront-accomodation.com. ✆ 014/715-085. 4 units. Two-person self-catering apartment with sea-view terrace Jul–Aug 100€. **Amenities:** Bikes for hire; Wi-Fi (free).

Where to Dine

Korčula Town is packed with touristy restaurants, most offering standard Dalmatian fare of moderate quality. However, there are a few memorable exceptions.

EXPENSIVE

Filippi ★★★ CREATIVE MEDITERRANEAN   Filippi holds down a prime waterside terrace on the Old Town peninsula. Opened in 2012, the restaurant already has a firm following of aficionados who come to savor innovative contemporary cuisine like Adriatic tuna served on black beluga lentils with okra, or duck breast with rosemary polenta, red onion chutney, and sour orange sauce. Filippi also does a special children's menu. The smart wine list highlights small producers from nearby Pelješac, Korčula, and Hvar. The results are pricey, but worth it; reservations are recommended.

Šetalište Petra Kanavelića, Korčula Town. www.restaurantfilippi.com. ✆ 020/711-690. Entrees 90kn–180kn. May–Oct daily 9am–midnight.

MODERATE

Konoba Adio Mare ★★ DALMATIAN   Founded back in 1974, Adio Mare stands close to the Marco Polo House, in an old building with exposed stone walls, long wooden tables (you may be expected to sit with other guests), and an upper-level terrace lined with potted geraniums. The menu features old favorites such as bean and pasta soup, *pasticada* (beef stewed in wine with prunes), and barbecued fish. There's an open-plan kitchen, so you can watch the cooks at work. It can get a bit chaotic when it's busy (reservations are recommended), but the atmosphere is fast and fun.

Marka Pola 2, Korčula Town. www.konobaadiomare.hr. ✆ 020/711-253. Entrees 50kn–130kn. Mid-Apr to mid-Oct, Mon–Sat noon–11pm; Sun 5–11pm.

Konoba Mate ★★★ DALMATIAN   For a truly authentic Dalmatian dining experience, visit this informal farmhouse eatery in the inland village of Pupnat, 9km (6 miles) from Korčula Town. Everything is homemade here, and many of the ingredients are home-grown, too. You might start with a platter of mixed appetizers, including grilled zucchini, goat cheese, prosciutto, olives, and eggplant pâté, followed by a hearty lamb stew cooked under a *peka* (a domed metal lid, used to cover casserole pots

THE REST OF korčula

Beaches, vineyards, and history beckon beyond the city walls of Korčula's Old Town. **Lumbarda,** 7km (4 miles) southeast of Korčula Town, was planted with vineyards by the Greeks, cultivated by the Romans, and used as a summer retreat by the island's wealthy citizens. Today, it is a major producer of Grk, the island's signature white wine.

Pupnat Harbor and a lazy pebble beach lie about 9km (5½ miles) west of Korčula Town. Beyond that, there's **Smokvica,** a village set high above a valley planted with grapes used to produce the local Pošip white wine. Keep heading west and you'll run into **Blato** about 10km (6 miles) from Smokvica. The

approach is on a wide road shaded by a canopy of arching trees. Don't miss the town's pilgrimage site, dedicated to Marija Petković (1892–1966), a daughter of Blato who became a nun and devoted her life to helping others. The Roman Catholic Church beatified Petković in 2002 and she is in the Church's pipeline to become a saint.

Vela Luka is the last stop in the trek across the island (or the first if you arrive here by ferry from Split). It is 7km (4 miles) past Blato and it's full of harborside cafes and pizzerias. If you're lucky, you might hear a *klapa* performance while you break for a snack, as Vela Luka is a center of this Croatian a cappella art.

used for slow-cooking over charcoal). Be sure to taste the house's homemade *rakija* (a potent local spirit), infused with wild herbs. Reservations are recommended.

Pupnat bb, Pupnat. ℂ **020/717-109.** Entrees 60kn–110kn. May–Oct Mon–Sat noon–2pm and 7–11pm; Sun 7–11pm.

INEXPENSIVE

Pizzeria Torkul ★★ DALMATIAN   A fine choice for a meal after a day on the beach at Lumbarda, Torkul has tables on a stone terrace overlooking the bay. (There's also a cozy stone house interior.) The pizzeria is known across the island for its friendly service and its delicious, value-for-the-money pizzas, which are expertly cooked in a wood-burning oven.

Uvala Račišće 191a, Lumbarda. ℂ **020/712-129.** Pizza 35kn–75kn. May–Oct daily noon–midnight.

VIS

Vis is the inhabited island farthest from Croatia's mainland, and it has only recently become a destination, having been closed to visitors until 1989 because of its status as a Yugoslav naval military base. Unspoiled and isolated, Vis is short on hotel accommodations and tourism infrastructure, but it is beginning to catch up. The island's two main towns, **Vis Town** and **Komiža,** are particularly popular with yachters who moor up their boats for a couple of days of total relaxation, dining at the island's fine authentic restaurants.

Vis's recorded history dates from the 4th century B.C., when Dionysius of Syracuse founded Issa (Vis), presumably as a strategic base for Greek enterprises in the Adriatic. Issa became a city-state and eventually was taken over by the Romans, the Byzantines, and the Venetians, in that order. Vis attained its greatest notoriety during World War II, when Marshal Tito used a cave on the island as his base for masterminding partisan strategies. Called **Tito's Cave,** the chamber on the south side of Mount Hum makes an interesting visit, even though you have to climb 245 overgrown stone steps to reach it.

Travel routes between the island and the mainland have increased with the introduction of a new fast Krilo catamaran (www.krilo.hr) between Split and Vis Town, on top of existing Jadrolinija (www.jadrolinija.hr) ferry service. There are many secluded bays on Vis (**Rukavac, Stiniva, Milna, Srebrena**), particularly on the island's southern side, but the best way to reach them is by private sailing boat.

Essentials

VISITOR INFORMATION   The **Vis Town** tourist office (www.tz-vis.hr; ℰ 021/717-017) is at Šetalište Stare Isse 5, across the street from the ferry port and adjacent to the Jadrolinija (www.jadrolinija.hr; ℰ 021/711-032) ticket office. The **Komiža** tourist office (www.tz-komiza.hr; ℰ 021/713-455) is at Riva sv Mikula 2.

GETTING THERE   Jadrolinija operate car ferries from Split three times daily in peak season, and twice daily in winter (journey time is 2 hr., 20 min.).

GETTING AROUND   Vis Town is the island's main port, and from here buses to Komiža are scheduled to coincide with ferries. However, if you want to see the inland villages and enjoy the more secluded beaches, you'll need your own transport. There are several sites worth investigating in the rural areas between Vis Town and Komiža, including wineries, caves, and abandoned military installations.

What to See & Do

Vis Town has a permanent population of 1,920 and is the island's largest town and its major center of commerce. It is a combination of two separate settlements: Kut is on the east side of town and Luka is on the west. Kut is a prosperous-looking residential neighborhood, home to several art galleries and the town's best restaurants. One of the most interesting sites on the island is the walled and locked **British naval cemetery** just west of Kut. It dates to the War of 1812 and is the resting place of fallen British soldiers who fought in battles from the Napoleonic Wars through World War II. There is another (unlocked) British burial site along the old road between Vis Town and Komiža.

A seaside promenade connects Kut to Luka, and most of the town's beaches (concrete slabs) are along this path. North of the promenade on Vis Bay, about .5km (¼ mile) from the center of Vis Town, is a pleasant beach in front of the **Hotel Issa.** There are snack huts there where you can get lunch or a cool drink. **Luka** is where you will find the ferry port, the tourist office, and a **Franciscan monastery.**

On the island's southwest coast, the sleepy fishing town of **Komiža** has a population of 1,400, overlooked by the hillside **Church of St. Nicholas.** The main beach there is in front of the **Hotel Biševo,** where you'll also find the **Issa Diving Center** (see box).

Blue Cave (Modra Špilja) ★★   The tiny island of **Biševo** is best known as the home of **Blue Cave,** a sea cave bathed in extraordinary blue and silver lights each day between 11am and noon. The cave, 5km (3 miles) southwest of Vis, is often compared

---

Low-Velocity Vis

Leave your car on the mainland and rent a scooter or bicycle on the dock in Vis from the Ionios Tourist Agency (Obala Sv. Jurja 37; ℰ **021/711-532**). It's more environmentally responsible, better for getting exercise, and cheaper by the day than the fee for transporting your auto on the ferry. Expect to pay about 200kn daily for a scooter and 90kn daily for a bicycle.

to Capri's Blue Grotto. Excursion boats leave Komiža harbor at 9am to make it to the cave in time for the light show, weather permitting. Several agencies in Komiža offer picnic tours, with lunch included—a reliable provider is Darlić & Darlić at Riva Sv. Mikule 13 (www.darlic-travel.hr; (℃ **021/713-760**). Note that to enter the Blue Cave, you have to lie flat in a small boat as you pass through a narrow sea tunnel, an experience that those suffering from claustrophobia might wish to avoid.

Biševo.

Vis Archaeological Museum ★★ In a 19th-century fortress with a grassy moat, built by the Austrians, this museum houses both ancient artifacts and ethnographic treasures. You'll see a display of traditional fishing implements and furniture from houses across the island. The highlights are the ancient finds on the second floor, including a 4th-century bronze head of the Greek goddess Artemis and a horde of amphorae retrieved from the seabed.

Šetalište Viš Boj 12, Vis Town. (℃ *021/711-729*. Admission 20kn. Jun–Sept Mon–Fri 10am–1pm and 5–9pm; Sat 10am–1pm; Sun closed.

Where to Stay

Vis is short on hotels, but private accommodations are plentiful. People with rooms to rent tend to wait for a ferry to pull in and then approach visitors as they disembark.

Hotel San Giorgio ★★ A 15-minute walk around the bay from the ferry landing station, this boutique hotel occupies an old stone building with an adjoining walled garden for open-air dining. All rooms have chic modern furnishings, and the top-floor honeymoon suite comes complete with a Jacuzzi and sea-view terrace. The hotel has bicycles to rent and can arrange wine-tasting tours and scuba diving.

Petra Hektorovića 2. www.hotelsangiorgiovis.com. (℃ **021/711-362**. Double Jul–Aug 152€. **Amenities:** Restaurant; rental bikes; Wi-Fi (free).

Pansion Dionis ★★ This family-run pension in Vis Town has seven double rooms and one triple, all with full modern comforts and slick en-suite bathrooms with showers. The same family runs the ground-floor Pizzeria Dionis, where breakfast is served (there's no fixed time, you can have it whenever you want), with outdoor tables set out on a terrace affording views over the bay.

Matije Gubca 1, Vis Town. www.dionis.hr. (℃ **021/711-963**. 8 units. Double Jul–Aug 70€. **Amenities:** Pizzeria; Wi-Fi (free).

Villa Nonna and Casa Nonno ★★ In a lovingly restored 400-year-old house in Komiža, Villa Nonno has seven comfortable self-catering apartments, all with wooden floors, some exposed stonework, plenty of natural light, and tasteful furnishings. The same family also runs the nearby Casa Nonno, with four double rooms painted in shades of lemon and terracotta. During the season (Apr–Oct) a minimum booking of 1 week is required (Sat–Sat). Also note that it's cash-only here.

Ribarska 50, Komiža. www.villa-nonna.com. ℗ **021/713-500.** 11 units. From 316€/week. **Amenities:** Wi-Fi (free).

Where to Dine

The restaurants on Vis tend to always be good, but some are outstanding. Their proximity to the source of the catch makes just about any fish dish you order a sublime dining experience, complemented by the high quality of the local wines.

Jastožera ★★ DALMATIAN   An unusual dining venue, Jastožera occupies a former 19th-century lobster-pot house, where freshly caught lobsters were kept in cages, still submerged in the sea to keep them alive. The structure, which is wooden, is built on stilts over the sea, with a platform above the water and an internal mooring space where boats could bring in their catch (small boats with no mast can still come in today). It's a special place and beautifully lit at night, although the food is quite pricey, especially for the island of Vis. The ambience is romantic, not touristy, and the service is rather formal and polite. The menu features seafood dishes such as *brudet* (fish stew) and shrimp risotto, but most people come here specifically to eat lobster. The house's signature dish is lobster with spaghetti for two (one lobster is enough to make the sauce for this). Note that lobster is priced by the kilo here.

Gundulićeva 6, Komiža. www.jastozera.com. ℗ **021/713-859.** Entrees 80kn–140kn, more for lobster priced by the kilo. Jun–Sept daily noon–2am.

Pojoda ★★★ SEAFOOD   In a courtyard garden dotted with lemon trees, you don't get a sea view at Pojoda, but you do get an exceptional choice of seafood. The chef is noted for using local ingredients to create sublime dishes, with a few surprises along the way. Start with the tuna in caper sauce appetizer, followed by whole grilled sea bass, which your waiter will fillet for you at the table if you wish. Pojoda stays open all year, evidence of its sound local following.

Don Cvjetka Marasović 8, Kut, Vis Town. ℗ **021/711-575.** Entrees 55kn–125kn, more for lobster and fish priced by the kilo. May–Oct daily noon–3pm and 6pm–1am; Nov–Apr daily 6–11pm.

Villa Kaliopa ★★ SEAFOOD   For the ultimate in romance, dine at this open-air restaurant, where candlelit tables are arranged below towering palm trees in the walled garden of the 16th-century Garibaldi Palace. There's no menu, but your waiter will bring a platter of the day's fresh catch so you can choose your fish at the table before it is grilled. Appetizers include delights such as cream of shrimp soup and tuna carpaccio on a bed of arugula. Popular with yachters, Villa Kaliopa is very expensive (and doesn't take credit cards), but it makes for an enchanting evening.

Vladimira Nazora 32, Kut, Vis Town. ℗ **021/711-755.** Entrees 90kn–160kn, more for lobster and fish priced by the kilo. Jun–Sept daily 6pm–2am.

Vis After Dark

Vis Town's bars are mostly alfresco, concentrated along the waterfront promenade. One place that really stands out is **Fort George** (www.fortgeorgecroatia.com; ℗ **091/883-1093**), set in a fortress built on a wooded peninsula by the British in 1803. A 30-minute walk north of Vis Town, each summer (Jun–Sept) the fort operates as an open-air bar, staging occassional live concerts and art events. The restaurant aspect here remains a work in progress, but Fort George does make a magical wedding venue.

DUBROVNIK

Hollywood's most creative designers would struggle to build a set as perfect as Dubrovnik. In fact, this magnificent medieval walled city (proclaimed a UNESCO World Heritage Site) has been used as a location for filming HBO's "Game of Thrones" and Neil Jordan's "The Borgias."

Yugoslav National Army shells poured down on Dubrovnik during the 1991–92 sieges. But, thanks to extensive restoration, today the walled city is remarkably whole and is as lustrous as it was 5 centuries ago, when Dubrovnik was a major sea power bustling with prosperous merchants and dripping with Renaissance grandeur.

Dubrovnik (née Ragusa) began as a Roman settlement. From the Middle Ages on it was a prize sought by Venice, Hungary, Turkey, and others who recognized the city's logistical value as a maritime port. But *Libertas* (Liberty), the city's motto, has always been uppermost in the minds of Dubrovnik's citizens, and through the ages their thirst for independence repeatedly trumped other nations' plans for domination.

In 1667, another kind of assault leveled Dubrovnik when an earthquake destroyed almost everything except a few palaces and church buildings in the **Old Town.** The city was quickly rebuilt in the Baroque style of the time. Croatia's War for Independence destroyed the tourism industry throughout the country, but Dubrovnik was especially hard hit. Not only was the city physically scarred, it was also economically crushed. Happily, crowds are once again flocking to this charming city nestled between the Adriatic and the Dinaric Alps, and Dubrovnik has regained its status as a vacation destination par excellence. In fact, it is as much loved by international celebrities as it is by student backpackers—recent visitors have included Beyoncé, Tom Cruise, Tina Turner, and John Malkovich (whose paternal grandparents were from Croatia).

Inside protective walls, from Easter through fall the pedestrian-only Old Town is bustling with an international crowd. Here you will find almost all the area's sights worth seeing—historic churches and public buildings; designer shops and homey restaurants; medieval sculptures and modern galleries; fountains and bell towers; monasteries and gardens; and the ancient city wall itself.

However, as property prices within the Old Town have soared, the majority of locals have sold out and now live in modern apartment blocks in the suburbs. Sadly, this wave of depopulation means that Dubrovnik is almost empty in winter, and risks becoming little more than a life-size museum dedicated to its former glory.

West of the Old Town walls, the district of **Lapad** (a peninsula close to **Gruž** port) is packed with hotels and restaurants, all focused on the hordes of tourists clamoring to bask in the city's Mediterranean magic and revel in its citizens' devotion to Libertas.

ORIENTATION

Reaching Dubrovnik by any means except air can be inconvenient and expensive. Even driving there from elsewhere in Croatia is time consuming because of the city's position between the mountains and sea, and the lack of modern roads in the area. Ferry routes to Dubrovnik often include multiple stops at various islands, and train service is nonexistent. Build in extra travel time when you plan a visit to Dubrovnik.

Arriving

BY PLANE Croatia Airlines (www.croatiaairlines.hr) operates regular flights to and from Zagreb and several European cities. Various European budget airlines also serve Dubrovnik through summer. Planes land at **Dubrovnik International Airport/Zračna Luka** (www.airport-dubrovnik.hr), in Čilipi, 18km (11 miles) from the city center.

Atlas (www.atlas-croatia.com) operates shuttle buses to and from Dubrovnik Airport, and they are coordinated with incoming flights, even late ones. Buses supposedly leave the main terminal in Dubrovnik near Gruž Port 90 minutes before each flight, but there is no posted schedule. They also stop at **Pile Gate,** just outside the Old Town. The fare is 35kn one-way and the trip takes about 25 minutes. There is also taxi service to and from the airport—expect to pay around 270kn.

BY BUS Daily buses operate between the Dubrovnik ferry port at Gruž and Zagreb, Zadar, Split, Šibenik, Rijeka, Orebić, and Korčula in Croatia, as well as Mostar and Sarajevo in Bosnia/Herzegovina. For other international service, see p. 219. The main Dubrovnik bus terminal (www.libertasdubrovnik.hr; ✆ **020/357-020**) is in Gruž, close to the port, at Obala Pape Ivana Pavla 44a.

BY FERRY Through the warmer months (mid-Apr through Oct), Dubrovnik is served by **Jadrolinija** (www.jadrolinija.hr) overnight ferry from Bari, Italy. Jadrolinija also operates a summer (May–Sept) coastal service, from Rijeka to Dubrovnik, stopping at Split, Stari Grad (on Hvar), Korčula Town (on Korčula), and Sobra (on Mljet) en-route. However, note that this service is extremely slow—it takes 22 hours to reach Dubrovnik from Rijeka. In addition, Jadrolinija runs local ferries to Dubrovnik from the nearby Elafiti Islands and Mljet. Buy tickets and obtain schedule information at the Dubrovnik Jadrolinija office (www.jadrolinija.hr; ✆ **020/418-000**) at Obala Stjepana Radića 40 in Gruž.

BY CAR The A1 *autocesta* (highway) between Zagreb and Split opened in June 2005, and now extends all the way to Ploče. However, the final section of the road is still under construction, and no reliable completion date has been fixed. If you drive from Zagreb to Dubrovnik using the new highway and the remaining section of the old coastal road, it will take approximately 7 hours.

Visitor Information

You'll find the **Dubrovnik-Neretva County Tourist Board** (www.visitdubrovnik.com; ✆ **020/324-999**) office at Vukovarska 24. The **Dubrovnik City Tourist Board** office (www.experience.dubrovnik.hr; ✆ **020/323-887**) is at Brsalje 5. Walk-in tourist information centers can also be found at the following locations: **Pile Tourist Information Center** (✆ **020/312-011**) at Brsalje 5; **Gruž Tourist Information Center** (✆ **020/417-983**) at Obala Ivana Pavla II; and **Lapad Tourist Information Center** (✆ **020/437-460**) at Kralja Tomislava 7.

Private tourist agencies can be helpful, too—the following represents a partial list. **Adventure Dalmatia** (www.adventuredalmatia.com; ✆ **021/540-642**) is a well-organized and highly professional adventure travel source. Even though it is based in

Split (at Matije Gupca 26), the agency offers an extensive slate of active Dubrovnik excursions, including sea kayaking around the Old Town walls, cycling in Konavle, and hiking on Mount Srdj.

Elite Travel (www.elite.hr; ✆ 020/358-200) at Vukovarska 17 runs one-day excursions from Dubrovnik, such as the agency's "Islands Cruise" (taking in the Elafiti Islands) and "Ancient Montenegro" (visiting the Bay of Kotor). The agency also arranges multi-day tours by bus, covering Croatia, Slovenia, and Bosnia/Herzegovina.

Gulliver Travel (www.gulliver.hr; ✆ 020/410-888) at Obala Stjepana Radića 25 offers a broad range of excursions to Dubrovnik's offshore islands and towns up and down the southern Adriatic coast.

Metro Tours (www.metrotours-dubrovnik.hr; ✆ 020/437-320) at Šetalište Kralja Zvonimira 40A offers daily excursions from Dubrovnik. You can choose from half-day tours to Cavtat, or Trsteno and Ston, or full-day trips to Montenegro or tours like "Fish Picnic Elafiti Islands" and the "Korčula and Pelješac Wine Tour."

[Fast FACTS] DUBROVNIK

ATMs All Croatia's major banks operate Bankomats (aka ATMs) in Old Town and the surrounding suburbs. These are centrally located on the Stradun, in Lapad and Gruž, outside the Pile Gate, and in some hotel lobbies.

Banks Most banks are open Monday to Friday 8am to 7pm, and Saturday 8am to noon.

Credit Cards Credit cards are generally accepted at hotels and larger restaurants, but be sure to ask before you order.

Emergencies Dial ✆ **192** for the police; ✆ **194** for an ambulance; ✆ **193** to report a fire. For road assistance from the **Croatian Auto Club** (www.hak.hr), dial ✆ **1987.**

Hospital **Dubrovnik General Hospital** (www.bolnica-du.hr; ✆ **020/431-777**) is at Roka Mišetića bb.

Internet Access Almost every hotel and hostel now offers free Internet access to guests, as do many cafes.

Pharmacies There are two pharmacies that alternate in working night shifts; if one is not open, the other should be. They are **Kod Zvonika** (✆ **020/321-133**) at Placa 2 in the Old Town and **Gruž** (✆ **020/313-162**) at Obala Stjepana Radića 9 near the port.

Time Zone Dubrovnik is on Central European Time (GMT plus 1 hr.). Daylight saving time starts in late March and ends in late October.

Tipping Tipping is generally not expected, though it is appreciated. High-end restaurants are the exception. Waiters there expect a tip.

Weather The climate in Dubrovnik is typical Mediterranean, with mild, rainy winters and hot, dry summers.

Dubrovnik Neighborhoods

OLD TOWN The area within Dubrovnik's walls is known as Old Town and most of the city's main attractions are there. Besides historic buildings, Old Town is home to restaurants, cafes, shops, and services that line the Stradun—a long (just under .5km/¼ mile) and wide street that runs from Pile Gate (west entrance) to Ploče Gate (east entrance)—and its back streets.

PLOČE Ploče is the neighborhood just outside Ploče Gate, east of the Old Town. Some of the city's classiest hotels are located on waterfront property in this area, as is the city's main public beach, Banje, home to the EastWest Beach Club.

LAPAD There are no big-time historic sites in Lapad, a peninsula west of Old Town. Its main attraction is a wide, leafy, pedestrians-only street lined with hotels and restaurants and backed by a residential area. Lapad abuts Lapad Bay, so it has some beachfront. For accommodations, the neighborhood's draw is several moderately priced hotels—at least moderate compared to the luxury hotels in Ploče and Old Town. Almost every bus that stops in Lapad (nos. 4, 5, 6, and 7) connects with Old Town at the Pile Gate; the ride takes 15 minutes and costs 15kn if you buy on board, 12kn from a news kiosk.

BABIN KUK   On the Lapad Peninsula, at some indeterminable point less than 6.4km (4 miles) from Dubrovnik's center and bordered on three sides by the sea and pebble beaches, the Babin Kuk neighborhood begins. Babin Kuk is home to several hotels in various price ranges. It also is an access point to rocky coves with what optimists call beaches (read: major pebbles/rocks, no sand), as well as restaurants, shops, and services. Babin Kuk is connected to Dubrovnik by the city's bus system.

Getting Around

There are no trains or trams in Dubrovnik, but the Libertas city bus system (www.libertasdubrovnik.hr) is fairly efficient. For those staying within comfortable walking distance of Old Town, everything important is accessible on foot.

BY BUS   Buy one-way bus tickets from news kiosks or hotels in advance for 12kn, or directly from drivers onboard for 15kn; an unlimited full-day ticket is 30kn. All buses stop at the Pile Gate and continue on to outlying hotels, the ferry port, and beyond. Schedules and route maps are available on the Libertas website (see above).

BY TAXI   Taxi stands are at the airport, bus station, and at the Pile Gate. If you need to call a taxi, contact Radio Taxi (www.radiotaxidubrovnik.com; ✆ **0800/0970**). Rides start with 25kn on the meter and go up 8kn per kilometer. If you agree to a meter-less ride, negotiate a price beforehand to avoid rip-offs and unwanted excursions.

ON FOOT   Negotiating the busy streets outside the city walls can be confusing, especially at night. Within the Old Town, you can devise your own walking tour using the suggestions in this book (see below). You can also employ a private guide to accompany you on a walk, or you can book a guided Old Town walking tour through the tourist office or through a private tourist agency.

BY CAR   Congestion and parking make driving in Dubrovnik stressful, and Old Town is pedestrian-only. Cars are best for excursions to nearby Pelješac or Ston; car rental companies at the airport include **Hertz** (www.hertz.hr; ✆ **020/771-568**), **Budget** (www.budget.hr; ✆ **020/773-811**), and **Thrifty** (www.thrifty.com.hr; ✆ **020/773-588**). In addition, **MACK** (www.rent-a-car.hr; ✆ **020/423-747**) is an economical and reliable local company, based at Frana Supila 3, close to the Old Town. Wherever you rent, be sure to reserve a car in advance.

WHAT TO SEE & DO

Dubrovnik sprawls well beyond its city walls, to Ploče in the east and the Lapad and Babin Kuk peninsulas in the west, but just about everything worth seeing is within the walled Old Town.

City Wall ★★★   For many people, the highlight of their visit to Dubrovnik is walking a circuit of the battlements atop the monumental medieval walls. The complete circuit runs 2km (1¼-mile) around the perimeter of the Old Town, affording ever-changing vistas over the terracotta rooftops and out across the glittering blue Adriatic. In places the walls are up to 25m (82-ft.) high and 6m (18-ft.) thick, combining several sturdy fortresses and proud towers along the way. You should allow at least 1 hour to complete the walk, though it may well take longer should you be captivated

Beat the Heat

When Dubrovnik's temperature is above 80°F (27°C)—the average temperature here May through September—tackle the wall when it opens at 8am or wait until after 5pm. During midday visits, besides being atop a high roof, you'll also be standing on an unshaded stone path that absorbs the sun's heat from dawn to dusk, "cooking" you from both above and below. At the very least, wear a hat and take a large bottle of water if you venture out on the wall in the heat of the day.

by the endless photo opportunities on offer here. There are three main points of access up to the walls: just inside the Pile Gate, near the Maritime Museum, and near the Dominican Monastery at the Ploče Gate. To start your walk at Pile Gate, you should turn left immediately as you enter the Old Town and walk up a steep flight of stairs topped by an arch. From here you will proceed in a clockwise direction. The walls date back to the 13th century, but were heavily reinforced during the 15th century due to fear of attack by the Ottoman Turks.

Old Town. 100kn adults. Jun–Sept daily 8am–7:30pm; hours vary slightly to correspond to daylight hours during other months.

Dominican Monastery and Museum ★★★
Off the east end of Stradun, in a high-walled passageway leading to Ploče Gate, you'll see an impressive stairway marking the main entrance to the Dominican Monastery. Inside, there's a charming 15th-century Gothic cloister rimmed by graceful triple arches, designed by the Florentine architect Michelozzo di Bartolomeo, and centering on a garden planted with fragrant orange trees. The monastery also houses a museum, exhibiting religious paintings by members of the so-called Dubrovnik School, as well as a horde of golden reliquaries, one of which is said to hold the skull of King Stephen I of Hungary.

Sv. Dominika 4. ✆ **021/321-423.** 20kn. May–Oct daily 9am–6pm; Nov–Apr daily 9am–5pm.

Dubrovnik Aquarium ★
On the ground floor of Tvrđava Sv. Ivana (St. John's Fortress), this aquarium provides an experience of underwater Adriatic life. A dark, damp, cavernous space with 31 backlit seawater tanks and pools, its charges include indigenous fish, as well as octopuses, starfish, urchins, sponges, corals, and sea horses.

In St. John's Fortress, Damjana Jude 2. ✆ **021/323-125.** 30kn. May–Sept daily 9am–9pm; Oct–Apr Tues–Sun 10am–1pm.

Dubrovnik Cable Car ★★★
An aspect of modern engineering in a city where so much is medieval, Dubrovnik's cable car opened only in 2010. Departing from outside the Old Town walls, it carries visitors to the peak of Mount Srdj (405m/1,330 ft.) in just 3 minutes, providing spectacular views down onto town and out to sea. Amenities up top include a restaurant and a souvenir shop. If you enjoy hiking, you might ride the cable car up, then walk back down following the Mount Srdj Ropeway—the path is rocky and steep, so be sure to wear decent shoes. If romance is more your thing, go up in the early evening and watch the sun set over the sea.

Frana Supila 35a. www.dubrovnikcablecar.com. ✆ **020/325-393.** 60kn (one-way), 100kn (w/return). Jun–Aug daily 9am–midnight; Sept daily 9am–10pm; Oct and Apr–May daily 9am–8pm; Nov and Feb–Mar daily 9am–5pm; Dec–Jan daily 9am–4pm.

Dubrovnik Cathedral ★★★
The town's cathedral stands on the site of a 12th-century Romanesque cathedral, which was destroyed by the 1667 earthquake. The

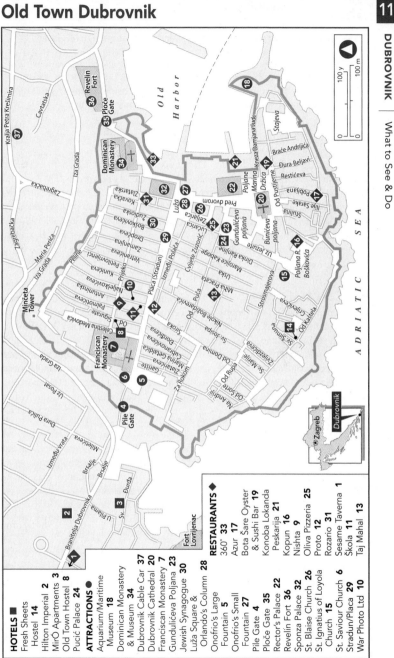

HOTELS ■
Fresh Sheets
Hostel **14**
Hilton Imperial **2**
MirO Apartments **3**
Old Town Hostel **8**
Pucić Palace **24**

ATTRACTIONS ●
Aquarium/Maritime
Museum **18**
Dominican Monastery
& Museum **34**
Dubrovnik Cable Car **37**
Dubrovnik Cathedral **20**
Franciscan Monastery **7**
Gundulićeva Poljana **23**
Jewish Synagogue **30**
Luža Square &
Orlando's Column **28**
Onofrio's Large
Fountain **5**
Onofrio's Small
Fountain **27**
Pile Gate **4**
Ploče Gate **35**
Rector's Palace **22**
Revelin Fort **36**
Sponza Palace **32**
St. Blaise Church **26**
St. Ignatius of Loyola
Church **15**
St. Saviour Church **6**
Stradun/Placa **29**
War Photo Ltd **10**

RESTAURANTS ◆
360° **33**
Azur **17**
Bota Šare Oyster
& Sushi Bar **19**
Konoba Lokanda
Peskarija **21**
Kopun **16**
Nishta **9**
Oliva Pizzeria **25**
Proto **12**
Rozario **31**
Sesame Taverna **1**
Škola **11**
Taj Mahal **13**

185

When you leave St. Saviour Church for the Franciscan Monastery next door, keep your eyes downcast and you'll see a **12×12-inch stone** with a carved face and flat, smooth top protruding about 6 inches above the street. You'll also see a crowd watching people attempting to stand on the stone for a few seconds. Legend says that guys who can stay on "The Mask" long enough to remove their shirts will have good luck. (Girls also try this, but are entitled to the luck without removing their tops.)

current structure was built in the late 17th century in the Baroque style, with an elegant cupola. The interior is quite bare, though of note is Titian's polyptych "The Assumption of the Virgin" (1552), located above the main altar. The adjoining treasury displays an extraordinary stash of golden reliquaries (caskets used to preserve the body parts of various saints), including a gold-plated skull, arm, and leg, said to have belonged to St. Blaise, Dubrovnik's patron saint. The skull, encased in a Byzantine crown decorated with jewels, is outstanding for its intricate craftsmanship.

Poljana Marina Držica. ✆ **020/323-459.** Treasury 15kn. Apr–Oct Mon–Sat 9am–5pm, Sun 11am–5pm; Nov–Mar Mon–Sat 10am–noon and 3–5pm, Sun 11am–noon and 3–5pm.

Franciscan Monastery   At the west end of Stradun, close to Pile Gate, you pass through a lovely 14th-century cloister as you enter the Franciscan Monastery. Rimmed on four sides by late-Romanesque arcades, the cloister opens onto a blissful garden planted with orange trees and palms, provoking the sort of peaceful contemplation that the monks no doubt also seek. From here, you have access to Europe's oldest working pharmacy, founded in 1317, and still in business today, selling herbal lotions and tonics, made to centuries-old recipes. On the shelves, note the medieval laboratory equipment, mortars, and measuring implements. There's also a small religious museum, containing medieval manuscripts and gold and silver church paraphernalia.

Placa 2. ✆ **020/321-410.** 30kn. Apr–Oct daily 9am–6pm; Nov–Mar daily 9am–5pm.

Gundulićeva Poljana   Each morning, stall holders set up their wares for the colorful open-air market held behind the cathedral. You'll find a range of seasonal produce, including tomatoes, zucchini, peaches, and melons in summer, as well as plastic bottles filled with homemade *rakija* (a potent liquor), and handmade table linens. With its old-fashioned local atmosphere, the market also makes a fine place to have coffee and watch the world go by. A bronze statue of Ivan Gundulić, a 17th-century Baroque poet from Dubrovnik and the square's namesake, stands in the middle.

Gundulićeva Poljana. Mon–Sat 8am–2pm; Sun 8–11am.

Jesuit Church of St. Ignatius of Loyola   At the top end of Gundulićeva Poljana, an elegant set of sweeping Baroque stairs, reminiscent of Rome's Spanish Steps, lead up to the Jesuit Church of St. Ignatius of Loyola. Built in Baroque style, the church is the work of Jesuit monk and architect Andrea Pozzo, and is based on the same plan as Rome's Chiesa del Gesu (which inspired the majority of Jesuit churches). Completed in 1725, the church was decorated with frescoes depicting scenes from the life of St. Ignatius. Next to the church stands the 17th-century Jesuit College (Collegium Ragusinum), where many of Ragusa's greatest intellectuals were educated.

Poljana R. Boškovića. Free admission. Daily 9am–noon and 3–7pm.

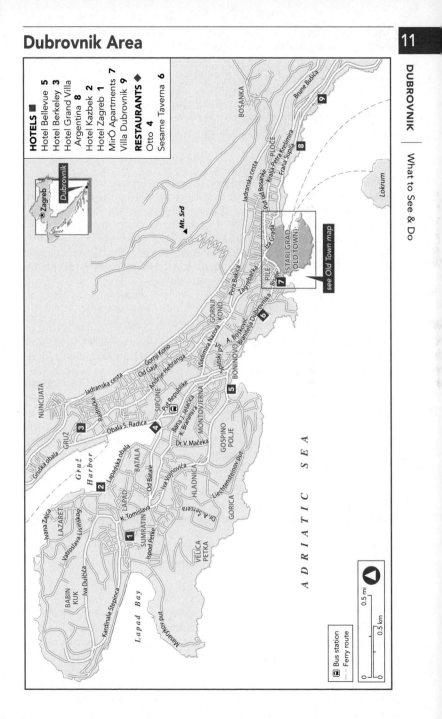

Dubrovnik Area

HOTELS ■
Hotel Bellevue **5**
Hotel Berkeley **3**
Hotel Grand Villa
Argentina **8**
Hotel Kazbek **2**
Hotel Zagreb **1**
MirÓ Apartments **7**
Villa Dubrovnik **9**
RESTAURANTS ◆
Otto **4**
Sesame Taverna **6**

Zagreb
Dubrovnik

Mt. Srd ▲

STARI GRAD
(OLD TOWN)

see Old Town map

Lokrum

BOSANKA

Bruno Bušica

Kralja Petra Krešimira
Frana Supila
PLOČE

Jadranska cesta
put od Bosanke

Iza Grada
PILE
Branitelja Dubrovnika
Pera Bakića
Brsalje

Zagrebačka

GORNJI
KONO
A. Boškovića
Vladimira Nazora
Splitski p.
BONINOVO

Gornji Kono
Od Gaja
Andrije Hebranga

Jadranska cesta

NUNCIJATA

Put Republike

ŠIPČINE

Bana Jelačića
K. Branimira
MONTOVJERNA
Dr. V. Mačeka
K. Branimira

GRUŽ
Radnička
Obala S. Radića

Gruška obala

Gruž
Harbor

Lapadska obala
BATALA
Od Batale
Iva Vojnovića
HLADNICA
Dr. A. Šercera
GORICA

GOSPINO
POLJE
Liechtensteinov put

LAPAD
K. Tomislava
SUMRATIN
Ispod Petke

Ivana Zajca
LAZARET
Vatroslava Lisinskog
Iva Dulčića
BABIN
KUK
Kardinala Stepinca

VELIKA
PETKA

Masarykov put

Lapad Bay

A D R I A T I C   S E A

■ Bus station
-- Ferry route

0.5 mi
0.5 km
0

Jewish Synagogue   You'll find Europe's second oldest continuously functioning synagogue (after the one in Prague) on the north side of Stradun, up the steep-stepped alley of Žudioska Ulica (Jews' Street). Dubrovnik's first wave of Jewish settlers arrived from Spain in 1492, to be followed by Jews from Italy early the next century. This space, on the upper floor of a two-story townhouse, was given to the Jewish community by the people of Dubrovnik. Besides the synagogue itself, which is decorated in 17th-century Baroque style, you can see a small museum dedicated to local Jews. Pride of place belongs to an ancient Torah, brought to Dubrovnik by the earliest Jewish residents.

Žudioska Ulica 5. ✆ **020/321-028.** May–Nov Mon–Fri 10am–8pm; Dec–Apr Mon–Fri 10am–1pm.

Maritime Museum   Historically, Dubrovnik's immense wealth was largely founded upon merchant shipping—in the 16th century, this tiny city-state had one of the largest fleets in the world. In this museum, extending over two floors, you can see an array of objects connected to Dubrovnik's naval prowess: detailed scale models of ships, navigational instruments, ships' equipment, maps, paintings of sea battles, and flags. You'll find the museum in St. John's Fortress, the fortification that once guarded the entrance to the old harbor (the city aquarium is located on the ground floor of the same building, but accessed through a separate entrance).

In St. John's Fortress, Damjana Jude 2. www.dumus.hr. ✆ **021/323-904.** Block ticket 80kn (also valid for admission to the Cultural History Museum in the Rector's Palace). Apr–Oct Tues–Sun 9am–6pm; Nov–Mar daily 9am–4pm.

Onofrio's Fountains   When you enter Old Town through Pile Gate, one of the first things you will see on Stradun is the Great Onofrio Fountain. Similarly, entering from Ploče Gate you will immediately notice the Small Onofrio Fountain. Construction on both commenced in 1438, designed by Italians Onofrio della Cava and Pietro di Martino to bring drinking water into town via an aqueduct from the River Dubrovačka, some 11km (7 miles) away. The larger fountain is domed and rimmed by 16 carved stone heads, which spout water from their mouths. The smaller fountain is decorated with carved dolphins. The water is perfectly good to drink, and on hot summer days, many visitors fill up their empty bottles at the two fountains.

Old Town Dubrovnik.

Orlando's Column   Standing in front of the Sponza Palace, this stone column is carved with the figure of a medieval knight holding a sword and shield. Dating from the 15th century, it is regarded as a symbol of the freedom of Dubrovnik. Legend has it that the knight in question is the mythical hero Orlando, who supposedly helped to liberate Dubrovnik when it was attacked by Saracen pirates in the 9th century. Nowadays, during the Dubrovnik Summer Festival, the column proudly bears the Libertas flag.

Sponza Palace, Old Town Dubrovnik.

Pile Gate   In the days of the republic, both entrances into the walled city were closed at night. At Pile Gate, the busiest entrance into the Old Town (it receives the traffic from the port to the west), the wooden drawbridge would have been pulled up and the wooden doors locked with a key. Now, of course, the gate stays open 24/7. The outer Pile Gate is embellished with a small statue of St. Blaise, the city's patron saint. The inner gate, built in the 15th century, holds a more modern statue of St. Blaise, created by 20th-century Croatian sculptor Ivan Meštrović.

Old Town Dubrovnik.

Ploče Gate   Ploče Gate, the eastern entrance to the Old City, was also built in the 15th century, and is composed of an inner and outer arch, plus a stone bridge. Like Pile Gate, it is embellished with a statue of St. Blaise.

Old Town Dubrovnik.

Rector's Palace   Back in the days when Dubrovnik was an independent city-state, the chief citizen was the rector. As of the 13th century, local government would meet in his palace. The rector himself would reside in apartments on the upper floor (in fact, he was not allowed to leave the building during his one-month term in office). The original palace was destroyed by a gunpowder explosion in 1435. It was rebuilt in Venetian-Gothic style, only to explode again some 28 years later. The building as it stands today is more rehab than redo; its Florentine designer, Michelozzo Michelozzi, grafted his work onto what remained of the previous structure. The design is most notable for its elegant arcaded facade and internal courtyard. The upper floor hosts Dubrovnik's Cultural History Museum, with exhibits including period furniture, costumes, clocks, and oil paintings, giving some idea of how the local aristocracy once lived. During the Dubrovnik Summer Festival, classical music concerts are staged in the courtyard.

Pred Dvorom 3. www.dumus.hr. ✆ **020/321-422.** Block ticket 80kn (also valid for admission to the Maritime Museum). Apr–Oct daily 9am–6pm; Nov–Mar daily 9am–4pm.

St. Blaise Church   Dedicated to the city's patron saint, this church was built on the site of an earlier Romanesque church, which was destroyed by fire in 1706. Approached up a wide set of steps and topped by a dome, it was built in Baroque style between 1706 and 1714. On the altar, note the silver statue of St Blaise, holding a model of the city as it would have looked before the 1667 earthquake—having survived the 1706 fire, the statue came to be regarded as miraculous. Unusual in this part of the world, the church has stained-glass windows, which were added in the 1970s.

Luža Trg. Free admission. Daily 8am–7pm.

Sponza Palace   Looking onto Luža Square, at the east end of the Stradun, this 16th-century palazzo is remarkable for its elegant facade, which combines Renaissance arches and Venetian-Gothic windows. It is one of the few buildings to have survived the 1667 earthquake. In the past it has served as a customs office and the city mint; it now houses the state archives. Most of the palace remains closed to the public, but if you step into the central courtyard you will see the entrance to the small Memorial Room of the Defenders of Dubrovnik, which pays tribute to the people who died (said to be over 300) during the 1991–92 siege of Dubrovnik.

Luža. ✆ **020/321-032.** Free admission, except for some exhibitions. Daily 9am–2pm, though times vary during exhibitions.

Stradun   Running between Pile Gate and Ploc[h]e Gate, through the heart of the pedestrian-only Old Town, Stradun (aka Placa) is Dubrovnik's main thoroughfare. Some 300m (984 ft.) in length, originally it was a marshy sea channel, dividing Dubrava on the mainland from the tiny island of Laus (today the area south of Stradun). Filled in during the 12th century, it was paved with smooth white limestone and lined with ornate buildings. Most of these were destroyed by the 1667 earthquake, and subsequently replaced with the more sober buildings you see today, most of which now house pricey cafes and small shops at ground level. Stradun is the city's main public meeting place, and various major outdoor events are staged here.

Old Town Dubrovnik.

WHO IS st. blaise?

According to legend, St. Blaise once saved a child from choking on a fishbone. For this reason, Roman Catholics everywhere know the Armenian physician and martyr as the patron of people with throat problems. However, the people of Dubrovnik revere St. Blaise (Sv. Vlaho) as the hero who saved their city from a sneak attack by Venetian galleys in the 10th century. When the Venetians dropped anchor off Lokrum, supposedly to pick up fresh water, the fleet actually was surveying the city in preparation for an attack. St. Blaise (who was put to death by the Roman emperor Diocletian in 316 B.C.) appeared to the city cathedral's priest in a dream, wearing a long beard with a miter and staff. He told the priest about the nefarious plot, thus thwarting the attack. Ever since, St. Blaise has been immortalized in sculpture, art, and other media as the city's protector and its biggest hero. To show their appreciation, the citizens of Dubrovnik go all out to honor St. Blaise on his feast day, which the city celebrates with food and festivities every February 3. Reliquaries purportedly containing several of the saint's body parts are carried through the streets in a parade and people line up to have their throats blessed by local priests.

War Photo Ltd ★★★ Distressing but unavoidable, the issue of defense has been an ongoing theme through Dubrovnik's centuries-old history, most recently during the Croatian War of Independence (1991–95). Opened in 2003, this gallery is dedicated to photojournalism from warzones, with an emphasis on the human suffering that wars cause (as opposed to the glorification or vilification of the regimes involved). In summer 2014, War Photo Ltd hosted "Syria's War: A Journal of Pain," featuring the works of Mexican Pulitzer Prize–winner Narciso Contreras. Past exhibitions have included "Purple Hearts," examining the lives of U.S. soldiers after they have been in active service abroad, and "Srebrenica Genocide 11/07/95," recounting one of the most horrific chapters of the Bosnian war.

Antuninska 6. www.warphotoltd.com ⟨📧⟩ **020/322-166.** 40kn. Jun–Sept daily 10am–10pm; May and Oct Tues–Sun 10am–4pm; Nov–Apr closed.

WALKING TOUR: DUBROVNIK'S STRADUN

START:	**Brsalje Square outside the Pile Gate, the west entrance to Old Town.**
FINISH:	**St. Blaise Church/Luža Square.**
TIME:	**Anywhere from 30 minutes to 3 hours, depending on how much time you spend exploring side streets, churches, and museums, and shopping or dining.**
BEST TIMES:	**Mornings from 8am to noon before the sun is overhead; evenings after 6pm and until the last bar closes, when the promenade segues into a fashion show for the young and beautiful.**
WORST TIMES:	**Noon to sundown or whenever the temperature rises above 86°F (30°C).**

A walk up and down both sides of the Stradun is an ideal way to become acquainted with Dubrovnik's charms. Old Town's smooth limestone path originally was a canal separating Old Ragusa from the mainland, and walking its length is a good way to get your bearings and become familiar with the attractions between the Pile and the Ploče Gates. There is a high concentration of important sites on and just off the Stradun, and lots of narrow side streets radiate up and out to intersect with cobbled streets that are packed with religious sites, historic architecture, shops, restaurants, a few courtyards, and even some residences.

Start your tour outside the Pile Gate in Brsalje Square, in front of the Pile Tourist Information Center.

1 Brsalje Square

Rendezvous in this leafy park. Before you enter Old Town, walk away from the street to the low balustrade. You'll have an unobstructed view of the sea and **Fort Lovrijenac** to the right, and the 16th-century **Bokar Fortress** to the left. Lovrijenac is built on a high, rocky peninsula that juts into the sea, and it is Dubrovnik's oldest defensive structure. These days, during the **Dubrovnik Summer Festival,** it is used as a theater for Shakespearean productions and other performances. Daniel Day Lewis and Goran Višjić (Croatian native and TV star of "ER" fame) have performed here. Bokar was used as a prison in the 19th century.

Return to the street, turn right, approach the:

2 Pile Gate

This is the busiest portal to Old Town, really two gates you approach across a wooden drawbridge that once was pulled up each night to protect the city. Note the statue of St. Blaise carved into a niche above the opening of the 16th-century outer gate and another statue of the city's patron (by **Ivan Meštrović**) inside the even older (15th-century) inner gate. Through summer, young men dressed in period costume pose as guards in front of the gate, conjuring up the atmosphere as it would have been during the centuries when Dubrovnik was an independent republic.

Step through the inner gate and stop a moment to orient. Walk through and note:

3 Onofrio's Large Fountain & the Wall Walk Entrance

Walk inside the Pile Gate and immediately to the left you'll see a steep stairway that leads up to the **Minčeta Tower** at the top of the wall. This is one of three access points to the top of the ramparts. To the right is **Onofrio's Large Fountain,** a tall concrete dome that during the Middle Ages was a collection point for water flowing into the city via an aqueduct from the **Dubrovnik River** 11km (7 miles) away. The fountain was more ornate when it was completed in 1444, but the iron embellishments were destroyed in the 1667 earthquake. The fountain also supplied Dubrovnik with fresh water when the city was on lockdown during the 1991–92 sieges.

Stay left. The first building on your left is:

4 Church of Our Saviour

This tiny church was built as a memorial to the victims of a 1520 earthquake, but it became a symbol of strength when it became one of the few buildings to survive the 1667 quake that destroyed most of the city. Today it is used for concerts and exhibits.

Walk on a few steps to:

5 The Franciscan Monastery/Museum

Before you explore this building (see p. 186), with its columned cloister and ancient pharmacy, note the small stone protruding from the bottom left of the church's front (see p. 186) and the people who keep jumping on it.

Exit the monastery and begin your Stradun stroll in earnest to investigate the:

6 Stradun Side Streets

The Stradun (aka Placa) runs to the clock tower and the **Ploče Gate.** All the buildings along the way are almost identical in style, a result of post-quake construction in the 17th century. Note the arches that frame combo doors and windows. The sill was used as a counter over which business was conducted. If you're up for a detour, head up **Žudioska Street** to visit the second-oldest synagogue in Europe and its original 17th-century furnishings (p. 188).

Continue along the Stradun past Zlatarska Street to the:

7 Sponza Palace

As you approach Luža Square, look left and note the graceful Renaissance arches of the **Sponza Palace** (p. 189), which used to be Dubrovnik's customs house. Today it houses the state archives, with a space set aside for the **Memorial Room of the Dubrovnik Defenders.** Multimedia images of destruction and photos of the young people who died while the city was under siege (1991–92) during the War for Independence are moving reminders of the devastation that swept Croatia.

Exit the palace and walk to Orlando's Column in the center of Luža Square. Pause at:

8 Orlando's Column and Onofrio's Small Fountain

Orlando's Column (p. 188) will be in front of you as you exit the Sponza Palace, and the **Clock Tower** will be to your left. Note the statue's forearm, which was Old Ragusa's standard of measurement (512mm/20 in.). The **Clock Tower** features a pair of bronze men who move up to strike the bell on the hour. The **Town Hall** is to the right of the Clock Tower and **Onofrio's Small Fountain** is in front of that.

Turn left from the front of Orlando's Column and walk through the passageway between the Sponza Palace and the Town Hall. Turn left and head to the Dominican Monastery:

9 Dominican Monastery, the Old Harbor, and the Ploče Gate

The Dominican Monastery is a complex that includes a large church, cloisters, and a museum. The original 14th-century church was destroyed in the 1667 quake, and this one was rebuilt late in the 17th century. There are some interesting paintings inside, and the church doubles as a concert venue during the Summer Festival. The cloisters are a must-see, with courtyard gardens and interesting stonework (p. 184).

Exit the monastery and go left onto Svetoga Dominika. Continue on to explore the old harbor, Ploče Gate, and Revelin Fortress, and/or retrace your steps and return to Luža Square:

10 Gradska Kavana & the Rector's Palace

As you return from the Dominican Monastery, the Town Hall and **Gradska Kavana** (Town Café) will be on your left. You can break for a cold drink or coffee and sit at tables facing the square or go inside to the **Gradska Taverna** and grab a spot on the terrace overlooking the **old harbor.** The Venetian-Gothic **Rector's**

Palace (p. 189) is adjacent to the Gradska Kavana complex, fronted by pillars made of marble from Korčula and topped with interesting carvings. The interior is used for summer concerts.

Exit the Rector's Palace and turn left to:

11 Dubrovnik Cathedral

The town cathedral was built in the late 17th century in the Baroque style. Inside, note the minimalist gray marble altar that was installed when Roman Catholicism ruled that the priest should face the people during Mass—its blocky style is incongruent with the Baroque surroundings. Don't miss the **treasury,** which is loaded with priceless relics, including the skull of St. Blaise and a piece of the True Cross (see p. 184).

Exit the cathedral and walk around to the rear. Walk up Androvićeva to the Jesuit Steps and Church of St. Ignatius Loyola (p. 186), or turn left and walk past the Rector's Palace to return to Luža Square.

12 St. Blaise Church

This 18th-century Baroque church (p. 189) is a tribute to Dubrovnik's patron saint. Inside, the altar is the main draw, with its statue of the saint holding a model of the city of Dubrovnik as it was before the 1667 quake. Outside, the church's wide steps are a popular resting/meeting place for tourists.

From St. Blaise you can return to the Pile Gate and inspect the shops along the south side of the Stradun, explore what you've just seen in greater depth, or venture up the steep side streets to discover more sights.

Escorted Walking Tours

Dubrovnik Walking Tours (www.dubrovnik-walking-tours.com; ℂ **020/436-846**) offers a choice of amusing and informative daily guided walks. Advanced reservations aren't required: Just show up at the Great Onofrio Fountain 10 minutes before the walk you want. The agency offers a "Discover Dubrovnik" walk, a "Story About the War" walk, an "Old Jewish Quarter" walk, and a "Game of Thrones Tour." Check the website for days and times. Walks last 1 hour and cost 12€, except for the GoT tour, which lasts 2 hours and costs 24€.

Jungle by the Sea

Escape the city crowds and blazing sun and take shelter in the lush oasis that is Trsteno (ℂ **020/751-019**), a 28-hectare (70-acre), 15th-century villa and garden estate overlooking the sea. Situated 13km (7 miles) northwest of Dubrovnik, Trsteno was once a center of gentility and culture in Dubrovnik. Today it is much more. Besides being a showcase for its Renaissance structures, fountains, and aqueduct, Trsteno serves as a shelter for a wide array of exotic plants, many brought to Ragusa centuries ago by traders from faraway ports. Don't miss the statue of Neptune, which overlooks a goldfish pond and fountain deep in the gardens. Trsteno is open May to October daily 7am to 7pm and November to April daily 8am to 4pm; admission 40kn. You can reach Trsteno by bus (numbers 12, 15, 22, and 35) from Dubrovnik—just be sure to tell the driver in advance that you want to get off here so he doesn't drive straight past.

Beaches

Croatians loosely define beaches as any place the sea meets the land. While some beaches may have names, most are little more than rocks used as platforms for jumping into the water. The coast is considered public property in Croatia, and all beaches must be accessible, free of charge, to anyone and everyone. Nonetheless, several of the hotels east of the port have staked out access routes to sections of the seafront for their guests, making it hard for others to get there.

Dubrovnik's main public beach, **Banje,** lies immediately east of the Old Town walls, close to Ploče Gate. It is managed by the **EastWest Beach Club** (www.ew-dubrovnik.com), which besides running a fancy-schmancy bar-restaurant, hires out the sunbeds and *baldachini* (four-posters with wafting chiffon curtains) that line the golden sand (which, incidentally, is imported). Of course, if you use the facilities you must pay for the privilege; if you forego the sunbed, you can lay out your towel on the sand for free. After dark, EastWest turns into a nightclub, with cocktails, DJs, and a fantastic view of the floodlit city walls across the water.

On Lapad, the main beach is a curving arc of fine pebbles, sitting in the shelter of **Lapad Bay** (www.lapad-beach.com). The beach is lined with sunbeds and umbrellas for hire, and backed by a restaurant and two cafes. It does get busy in peak season, due to the number of big hotels in the area, but the sea is clean and the sunset views are magnificent.

On the west side of Lapad, Babin Kuk's **Copacabana Beach** is a pebble and concrete bathing area with a view of the graceful Dubrovnik bridge and the Elafiti Islands. It has facilities for kids, sports enthusiasts, and swimmers with disabilities. Here you can ride a jet ski, get whipped around on a banana-boat ride, or go parasailing. There are also sea slides for kids. A lift on the concrete part of the beach gives seniors and people with disabilities easy access to the water. There's also a beach bar and restaurant.

Alternatively, you can catch a boat to the tiny island of **Lokrum** (www.lokrum.hr), which sits close to the Old Town. The island is served by water taxis from the old harbor, running every 30 minutes daily in summer from 9am to 6pm. The journey takes about 15 minutes and costs 70kn round-trip. Once on the island, you have your choice of relaxing and swimming, either in the sea or the small saltwater lake, or exploring the woods and the vestiges of an 11th-century Benedictine monastery. In 1859, Lokrum was purchased by Hapsburg Archduke Maximillian Ferdinand and his wife, Charlotte, as a vacation home. However, Maximillian didn't have much chance to enjoy his island escape: He was dispatched to Mexico to be its emperor three years after acquiring the property and never returned to Dubrovnik—he was assassinated in Mexico in 1867. Luckily, the grounds he had started cultivating are now preserved as a botanical garden, replete with peacocks. There's a small seasonal restaurant and cafe on Lokrum. Alternatively, you can bring your own picnic.

Diving

Sometimes the temptation to jump into the deep blue sea around Dubrovnik is just too strong to resist. Get the most out of your plunge with a professional diving school like **Blue Planet.** Rent equipment or use your own for scuba or open-water dives that last from 2 hours to 6 days. No experience? Blue Planet is a certified instruction center and can teach you what you need to know.

In the Dubrovnik Palace Hotel, Masarykov Put 20. www.blueplanet-diving.com. ℰ **091/899-09-73.** Introductory dive (half-day) 495kn; "Discover Scuba" diving (half-day) 720kn; prices include equipment. May–Oct daily 9am–7pm; by appointment the rest of the year.

Sea Kayaking

To explore the coastline in the best way possible (directly from the water), try sea kayaking. **Adriatic Kayak Tours** arranges half-day trips (approximately 4 hr. and 30 min.) around Zaton Bay (northwest of Dubrovnik), departing at either 9am or 3pm. Full-day tours explore around the cliffs and sea caves of Koločep (one of the Elafiti Islands), involving a 15km (9 mile) paddle, departing at 9am. The tour company also hires out equipment to experienced kayakers.

Zrinsko Frankopanska 6. www.adriatickayaktours.com. © **020/312-770.** Half-day sea kayaking tour 280kn; full-day sea kayaking tour 400kn.

WHERE TO STAY

Dubrovnik is the most expensive city in Croatia, especially in summer, when everything from gelato to taxis can be triple the price charged in other destinations. Even moderately priced accommodations are difficult to find unless you opt for private rooms in **Lapad** or **Gruž.** Try the tourist offices or look for signs in windows that say SOBE (room available). If you arrive at the ferry or bus terminal, you'll be greeted (or accosted) by men and women waving photos of lodging options—mainly rooms in private homes. In general, the cheapest are from the seated old ladies asking you if you need a place to sleep. If you choose this option, be sure to inspect the room before you hand over any money. You never know what you'll get—perhaps a dirt-cheap find in the center, or a tiny bed (sharing a bathroom with the owner) on the outskirts of town. All of these latter options take cash only. If you want to be sure of what you're getting, go to a tourist office, which has screened rentals and provides photos and amenity lists.

Very Expensive

Hilton Imperial ★ ★ ★   Dating back to 1897, the Imperial was Dubrovnik's first purpose-built hotel, and it's one of the oldest in Croatia. Standing just outside the Old Town, close to Pile Gate, it has a lovely palm-lined front terrace and a distinctive red brick facade, with wrought-iron balconies painted in Hapsburg-flag yellow. Noted for its highly professional staff, it's popular with businesspeople and international travelers who expect formal service. Inside, rooms are spacious and fully equipped with 21st-century comforts. The hotel's Porat Restaurant has outdoor tables on the leafy front terrace, making it a fine place to enjoy breakfast. There's a fully equipped health club with an indoor pool and fitness room, but no outdoor pool or beachfront.

Marijana Blažića 2, at the Pile Gate. www3.hilton.com. © **020/320-320.** 147 units, including 8 junior suites. Double Aug 324€. **Amenities:** Restaurant; 2 bars; conference facilities; fitness room; indoor pool; sauna; room for those w/limited mobility; Wi-Fi (free).

Pučić Palace ★ ★ ★   To recapture the opulence of Dubrovnik's aristocratic past, stay at this 18th-century Baroque palazzo, overlooking the Old Town square where the morning open-air market is held. The 17 rooms and 2 suites here have parquet floors, elegant antique furnishing, and lavish mosaic-tile bathrooms with both bathtubs and rain showers. The on-site Defne restaurant serves eastern Mediterranean cuisine on an upper level stone terrace with potted jasmine and lemon trees. There's also a ground floor cafe and a wine and tapas bar. The hotel has a yacht for private excursions (with skipper). Beyond the old-fashioned glory here, there are no extra facilities: no pool, spa, or beachfront.

Ulica Od Puča 1. www.thepucicpalace.com. © **020/326-222.** 19 units. Double Aug from 465€. **Amenities:** Restaurant; bar; cafe; concierge; room service; hotel boat; Wi-Fi (free).

Villa Dubrovnik ✦✦✦ This property was totally reconstructed on the site of an older hotel and opened in summer, 2010. Built in a chic, minimalist style, with white concrete and lots of glass affording divine sea views, the hotel has 50 light and spacious rooms, all with wooden floors, glass-walled bathrooms, and private balconies. The 6 suites come with Jacuzzis, too (some outdoor). Facilities include two terrace restaurants with views down onto the turquoise sea through the pine trees, a rooftop wine bar affording stunning sunsets, and a luxurious spa with a pool. The villa is a member of Small Luxury Hotels of the World. It's on the coast, a 20-minute walk east of the Old Town (also served by hotel taxi-boat), commanding fine views back across the glistening Adriatic to Dubrovnik's medieval walls.

Vlaha Bukovca 6, west of the Old Town. www.villa-dubrovnik.hr. ✆ **020/500-300.** 56 units. Double Aug from 510€, a la carte breakfast 30€/person. **Amenities:** 2 restaurants; 2 bars; pool; spa; Wi-Fi (free).

Expensive

Hotel Bellevue ✦✦✦ Built into the cliffs above a deep turquoise bay, midway between the Old Town and Lapad, the Bellevue is modern, chic, and luxurious. The 77 rooms and 14 suites all have wooden floors, earth-tone fabrics, slick white bathrooms, and dreamy sea views. From the street-level reception, a glass elevator descends to the wellness center, with an indoor pool overlooking the bay, and then one level down again, to open onto a secluded pebble beach, complete with sunbeds, umbrellas, and an informal eatery. Come nightfall, there's the more sophisticated Vapor restaurant up top, specializing in creative Mediterranean cuisine, and the Spice Lounge, centering on a huge palm tree, serving champagne and cocktails.

Pera Čingrije 7, east of the Old Town. www.adriaticluxuryhotels.com. ✆ **020/330-000.** 91 units. Double Aug from 268€. **Amenities:** 2 restaurants; 1 bar; pool; spa; fitness room; Wi-Fi (free).

Hotel Grand Villa Argentina ✦✦ Occupying an early 20th-century stone villa, the Grand Villa Argentina is just a 5-minute walk from Ploče Gate, east of the Old Town. Set amid a glorious terraced garden, with orange trees, and rosemary and lavender bushes, it is refined and restful. Rooms come with slightly dated old-world decor, but are perfectly comfortable; the best ones have sea views and balconies. Down below, a spacious waterside stone terrace, lined with sunbeds, features a saltwater swimming pool. It also affords easy access to the sea, for those who prefer to swim away from the coast.

Frana Supila 14, Ploče. www.adriaticluxuryhotels.com. ✆ **020/440-555.** 131 units. Double Aug from 236€. **Amenities:** 3 restaurants; bar; indoor and outdoor pools; spa; Wi-Fi (free).

Hotel Kazbek ✦✦✦ Set in a walled garden by the sea on Lapad, this 16th-century Renaissance stone villa opened as a small luxury hotel in 2008. It has just 12 rooms and 1 suite, all with wooden floors and sweeping curtains. Ancient wooden beams adorn some units; furnishings tend to be sumptuous, to match the historic building. A delicious a la carte breakfast is served in the front courtyard, and there's a heated outdoor pool (with Jacuzzi) in the sheltered garden at the back. There's also a hotel boat, available for private excursions, with a captain provided. Kazbek is a peaceful world unto its own, offering an aristocratic ambience. The personalized service here is welcoming, but never intrusive.

Lapadska obala 5, Lapad. www.kazbekdubrovnik.com. ✆ **020/362-900.** 13 units. Double Aug 250€. **Amenities:** Restaurant; outdoor pool; sauna; hotel boat; Wi-Fi (free).

Radisson BLU ✦✦✦ This sprawling resort on the coast, in the village of Orašac, 12km (7 miles) north of Dubrovnik, opened in 2009. Overlooking the sparkling blue Adriatic, and backed by rocky mountains, it is almost a self-contained village in itself, with everything from shops and restaurants to pools and watersports facilities. Accommodation options cover 201 spacious rooms and suites and an additional 207 sophisticated residences, which are ideal for families, having either one, two, or three bedrooms, plus a lounge, dining room, and fully equipped kitchenette. Rooms and junior suites come with fabrics in cheerful shades of turquoise, royal blue, and pea-green. The bathrooms have big glass windows through to the bedroom, making the bathtub visible from the bed (modesty curtains have been installed for those who are shy). Executive suites are designed with fabrics in more serious, muted, earthy tones—cream, beige, and brown. The entire resort is set amid beautifully landscaped grounds, with a pleasant waterside promenade and magnificent views of the sun setting over the Elafiti Islands. The hotel runs a shuttle bus and taxi-boat to and from Dubrovnik through summer.

Na Moru 1, Orašac. www.radissonblu.com/resort-dubrovnik. ✆ **020/361-500.** 408 units. Double Aug from 290€. **Amenities:** 7 restaurants; pastry cafe; wine bar; children's program; 3 pools; 3 beaches; room service; spa; rooms for those w/limited mobility; sports center; bicycle rental; free parking; Wi-Fi (free).

Moderate

Hotel Berkeley ★★★   Located above Gruž port, this mid-range hotel offers slick contemporary rooms, with wooden floors and modern fitted furniture. Everything feels very new and clean. There are also apartments with basic self-catering facilities, all with balconies. The apartments sleep four persons, so they are ideal for families with children. Breakfast is an expansive continental buffet, with eggs also available on request. The coffee is freshly ground here, a breakfast rarity in Croatia. There's a small heated outdoor pool and Jacuzzi, rimmed by a wooden deck with sunbeds. The property is run by a welcoming Australian-Croatian family, who also organize private boat trips and fishing excursions for guests.

Ulica Andrije Hebranga 116A, Gruž. www.berkeleyhotel.hr. ✆ **020/494-160.** Double Aug from 140€. 24 units. **Amenities:** Breakfast room; pool; bar; boat excursions; Wi-Fi (free).

Hotel Zagreb ★★   Built as a private residence in the 19th century, this structure was converted into a hotel in 1932 and renovated in 2005. The rooms remain basic but comfortable. However, the hotel's old-fashioned elegance and lush leafy garden, complete with a terrace restaurant where breakfast is served, give it a special charm that makes it stand out from the other hotels on Lapad. Sunbeds on the lawn for guests are another nice touch. The property is just a 5-minute walk from the beach in Lapad Bay.

Šetalište Kralja Zvonimira 5, Lapad. www.hotelzagreb-dubrovnik.com. ✆ **020/438-930.** 24 units. Double Aug from 130€. **Amenities:** Restaurant; bar; garden; Wi-Fi (free).

MirO Apartments ★★   Ideally located on a quiet pedestrian street just outside the Old Town and close to Pile Gate, MirO offers seven small, compact, self-catering studio apartments, each sleeping two. The apartments are basically interchangeable, with stylish minimalist white decor and contemporary kitchen facilities. Only one studio, on the top floor, has sea views (note that there is no elevator). There's no extra charge for this unit, but it is rented out on a first-come, first-served basis, so if you want it you should book well in advance and ask if it's available.

Svetog Djurdja 16, Pile. www.mirostudioapartmentsdubrovnik.com. ✆ **099/424-2442.** 7 units. Aug from 140€. **Amenities:** Wi-Fi (free).

Inexpensive

Fresh Sheets Hostel   This friendly hostel in the Old Town has four-bed and six-bed dorms, with lockers and linen provided, plus a cozy private double room with a sea view. Fresh Sheets is a good place to meet others if you're travelling alone; there's a communal kitchen where guests prepare their own breakfasts. It might seem expensive for a hostel, but then you're paying for the privilege of staying in the Old Town, in a prime location close to the seaward walls and Buža bar.

Sv Simuna 15. www.freshsheets.com. ✆ **091/799-2086.** 22 rooms. Dorm bed in Aug from 36€. **Amenities:** Kitchen; lockers; linen; Wi-Fi (free).

Old Town Hostel   In a restored 400-year-old building, close to Pile Gate in the Old Town, this hostel extends over four floors to include spacious dorms and private rooms. There's a common area and kitchen. The kitchen is stocked with a 24-hour self-service breakfast, which includes muesli, milk, juice, tea, and coffee. The prices may seem high, but then you're getting the privilege of sleeping in a piece of history.

Od Sigurate 7. www.dubrovnikoldtownhostel.com. ✆ **020/322-007.** 27 beds. Dorm bed in Aug from 38€. **Amenities:** Kitchen; Wi-Fi (free).

WHERE TO DINE

You won't have to search for a restaurant no matter where you are in the Dubrovnik region. Places like touristy Prijeko Street in the Old Town jam restaurants so close together you can't tell where one ends and another begins—hence the annoying touts who try to lure in passersby. Many serve identical fare, much of it high priced and mediocre, or else high priced and exotic. But there are a few hidden gems. We've listed our take on the Dubrovnik restaurant scene below.

Very Expensive

360°   CREATIVE MEDITERRANEAN   Entered through a discreet arched doorway in the wall close to Ploče Gate, with tables on a terrace high up in the ramparts affording romantic views down onto the old harbor, this is a stylish and unashamedly see-and-be-seen venue. (Beyoncé was spotted here in 2009, when it was known as Gil's). Italian chef Alessandro Martellini works in the open-plan kitchen, turning out fancy dishes like marinated fresh tuna with avocado guacamole, soy sauce, ginger, and sesame, which might be followed by a slow-cooked shoulder of lamb with spinach and red paprika. Reservations are required.

Sv. Dominika 2. www.360dubrovnik.com. ✆ **020/322-222.** Dinner entrees 210kn–320kn; degustation menus, 5-course 780kn, 7-course 970kn. Tues–Sun 6:30–11pm.

Expensive

Kopun   DALMATIAN   You'll find Kopun tucked away in the Old Town, in a lovely peaceful location on the square in front of the Jesuit Church. The atmosphere is mellow and romantic, with terrace dining and an interior space furnished with designed black chairs and tables. The menu features old-fashioned local dishes prepared with fresh seasonal ingredients. Begin with the either the lentil soup or tuna carpaccio, followed by the house's signature dish, *kopun* (capon, or rooster) in orange, figs, and honey. Let the waiter advise you on wine pairings.

Poljana Rudera Boskovica 7. www.restaurantkopun.com. ✆ **020/322-222.** Entrees 90kn–150kn. May–Oct daily noon–10pm.

Proto   SEAFOOD   Founded in 1886, Proto is regarded as Dubrovnik's best fish restaurant—over the decades, it has hosted many well-known visitors, including Edward VIII, former King of England, and his American wife, Wallis Simpson, who ate here in 1938. House specialties include shrimp in saffron sauce; lobster served with truffle and mushroom risotto; and fresh John Dory baked in the oven with potatoes, tomatoes, and zucchini. In winter 2013, the upper level stone terrace was renovated, adding retractable glass, so it's possible to eat there now even when the weather is chilly. Proto is expensive (reservations are recommended), but you're guaranteed a memorable meal.

Široka 1. www.esculaprestaurants.com. ℂ **020/323-234.** Entrees 90kn–160kn, more for fresh fish priced by the kilo. Daily 11am–11pm.

Moderate

Azur ✯✯✯ MEDITERRANEAN-ASIAN   Hidden in a side alley close to the aquarium and the seaward city walls, Azur opened in June 2013 (it has a sister restaurant in Zhuhai, China). The outside seating is especially pleasant, framed by old stone walls. The cuisine is Mediterranean, with an Asian twist. Start with wasabi salmon parcels, followed by either squid ink seafood noodles, or pan-seared swordfish in black curry sauce. All the seafood and vegetables are locally sourced, combining with Eastern spices to produce sublime and beautifully balanced flavors.

Pobijana 10. www.azurvision.com. ℂ **020/324-806.** Entrees 70kn–155kn. Daily noon–midnight.

Bota Šare Oyster & Sushi Bar ✯✯ SUSHI   This slick sushi bar successfully combines both Dalmatian and Japanese influences. From a design standpoint, the old building with exposed stone walls is classic Dalmatian, but the furniture, in minimalist style with clean lines, feels more Japanese. All the seafood is locally sourced, and oysters are served raw with a slice of lemon, in Dalmatian style. The wines are also predominantly Dalmatian, except for the champagne. The menu covers delights such as freshly made shrimp tempura, salmon sashimi, and tuna tartar. (The first **Bota Šare** restaurant was founded in nearby Ston—the family that owns the group still farms their own shellfish there, and are renowned for their exquisite fresh oysters.) The restaurant is in a narrow alley close to the cathedral. No credit cards are accepted.

Od Pustijerne bb. www.bota-sare.hr. ℂ **020/324-034.** Sushi 15kn–50kn/piece, oysters 14kn/piece. May–Oct daily noon–midnight.

Lokanda Peskarija ✯✯ DALMATIAN   This bustling little seafood eatery is perfectly located, overlooking the fishing boats in the old harbor, next to the covered fish market. Dishes are served in black metal pots and include Dalmatian favorites such as *frigane lignje* (fried calamari) and *crni rižot* (black risotto made from cuttlefish ink), as well as an impressive seafood platter for two (comprising swordfish, sardines, calamari, prawns, and mussels). Informal (cash only) and fun, the waterside tables are shaded by big white parasols during the day, and are candlelit come nightfall.

Na Ponti bb. www.mea-culpa.hr. ℂ **020/324-750.** Entrees 60kn–95kn. May–Oct daily noon–midnight.

Nishta ✯✯✯ VEGETARIAN/VEGAN   A real find amid the touristy restaurants that line Prijeko, Nishta is an informal and well-run eatery, specializing in vegetarian and vegan dishes. The menu takes inspiration from Mexico, India, and Thailand, so you get fragrant soups, curries, and salads, with ample use of fresh herbs and spices. There are also several dishes prepared especially for those with gluten intolerance. Note that Nishta only has a dozen or so tables, so it does get crowded.

Prijeko bb. www.nishtarestaurant.com. ℂ **020/322-088.** Entrees 65kn–85kn. Mar–Nov Mon–Sat 11:30am–11pm.

Otto ✯✯✯ CREATIVE MEDITERRANEAN   Overlooking Gruž port, on the landside of Lapad peninsula, Otto occupies an old stone boathouse. It's stylish without being pretentious or overtly expensive. The menu is short, but the choice of dishes is a little different from what you'll find at most Dubrovnik restaurants. Try the much-praised French onion soup (topped with cheese and croutons), followed by succulent tuna steak with mashed white beans and black olive tapenade. For something lighter, the mixed lettuce leaf salad with roast beetroot, goat's cheese, and orange is delicious.

Nikole Tesle 8, Lapad. www.tavernaotto.com. © **020/358-633.** Entrees 85kn–130kn. Mar–Dec Mon–Sat 11am–3pm and 6–10pm; closed Sun.

Rozario ★★ SEAFOOD Located at the far end of Prijeko Street, at the corner where it meets Zlatarska, this charming restaurant has outdoor tables on the stone steps and is one of the few eateries in the Old Town to be favored by locals. For dinner, start with an octopus salad, followed by fillet steak in fig, honey, and wine sauce with potatoes au gratin. Round things off with the delectable homemade orange and almond cake. If you come at lunchtime, the daily prix fixe is a deal at 60kn.

Prijeko 1. www.konoba-rozario.hr. © **020/322-015.** Entrees 70kn–120kn. Feb–Dec daily noon–11pm.

Sesame Taverna ★★ REGIONAL CROATIAN Close to the Hilton Imperial, Sesame occupies a romantic old stone house, with a row of orange trees out front and a vine-covered terrace up top. Highly regarded by locals, the owner-chef offers a contemporary take on Mediterranean cuisine, with dishes such as homemade ravioli stuffed with ricotta cheese and mint, soufflé of goat's cheese and prosciutto, and *gregada* (fish stew). There's a respectable wine list to match. The tavern is a 10-minute walk from Pile Gate outside the Old Town.

Dante Alighieria bb, west of the Pile Gate. www.sesame.hr. © **020/412-910.** Entrees 80kn–150kn, more for seafood priced by the kilo. Daily 8am–midnight.

Taj Mahal ★★ BOSNIAN The name is misleading—this is not an Indian restaurant. Instead, this small and informal eatery specializes in Bosnian cooking, which is strongly influenced by Turkish cuisine. Taj Mahal is best known for its tasty barbecued meat dishes like *čevapčići* (ground meat rissoles) and *pljeskavica sa kajmakom* (homemade beef burgers served with rich, creamy cheese). It's also a sound choice for vegetarians, with staples such as *krompiruša* (filo pastry pies filled with potato and onion) and *shopska* salad (tomato, cucumber, peppers, onion, and a sheep's cheese similar to Greek feta).

Gučetića 2. © **020/323-221.** Entrees 80kn–125kn. Feb–Dec daily noon–midnight.

Inexpensive

Oliva Pizzeria ★★ PIZZA In the Old Town, behind St. Blaise Church, this casual spot serves up delicious thin-crust pizza from a wood-fired oven. The house specialty is the "Pizza Gourmand," topped with fresh mushrooms, bacon, and peppers. There's also a good choice of vegetarian options and salads. Diagonally opposite, sister restaurant Oliva Gourmet (Cvijete Zuzori 2) serves slightly more sophisticated fare.

Lučarica 5. www.pizza-oliva.com. © **020/324-594.** Pizza 55kn–80kn. Daily 10am–11pm.

Škola ★ SANDWICHES In a side alley off Stradun, tiny Škola has just a couple of tables indoors and a couple more out front. An old-fashioned family-run business, sandwiches are all that are done here, but they're exceptionally good ones—thick slabs of freshly baked bread filled with either local *sir* (cheese) or *pršut* (prosciutto) or both. That, and a tasty apple strudel. Most people come here for takeaway, though you're welcome to sit and have a glass of wine or a coffee if you can find a free space.

Antuninska 1. © **020/321-096.** Sandwiches 25kn–30kn. Daily 9am–8pm.

BARS & NIGHTLIFE

Once the sun goes down, Dubrovnik is a hive of humanity, with crowds walking in waves to one restaurant or another and then moving to the Stradun or the Lapad promenade. From about 8 to 11pm, the scene is a diverse mix of families and couples strolling with ice cream cones. Come 11pm, there's a changing of the crowd as the early birds file out and 18-to-20-somethings flow in, dressed in outfits that rival the getups in "Sex and the City." Follow the throbbing music, blaring from jam-packed side streets where nightly block parties convene after the restaurants close, and you'll experience Dubrovnik's cafe society's second shift.

Buža ★★★ Accessed through an arched doorway marked "Cold Drinks" in the seaward city walls, Buža comprises a terrace built into the rocks, shaded by a couple of towering palm trees and several big white parasols. Expect a dozen or so tables, absolutely stunning sea views, and pricey drinks served in plastic cups. The crowd is mainly tourists (it's relatively expensive for locals), varying from young backpackers to couples all the way through to elderly cruise passengers (Buža appeals to everyone because of the amazing view and the utter simplicity of the bar). The soundtrack is mellow jazz around and after sunset.

Od Margarite. May–Sept daily 8–2am, weather permitting.

Club Revelin ★★★ In a 16th-century fortress with an impressive vaulted stone interior, Club Revelin extends over two floors with ultra-modern lighting effects. Often noisy and packed until sunrise, on summer nights it hosts international guest DJs— Boy George played here in 2013. If you need a breath of fresh air, there is a terrace with amazing views over the old harbor. The location is in the Old Town, close to Ploče Gate.

Svetog Dominika 3. www.clubrevelin.com. ☏ **020/436-010.** Jun–Sept daily 11pm–6am; Oct–May Fri–Sat 11pm–3am.

D'Vino ★★★ A great spot to try Dalmatian wines, this relaxed wine bar is run by a knowledgeable owner. You can order by the glass or by the bottle, or opt for a wine flight to sample a variety of either reds or whites (the collection here reaches out beyond Croatia to include vintages from the likes of France, Chile, Spain, and Italy). The location is on a side street off the Stradun.

Palmotićeva 4a. www.dvino.net. ☏ **020/321-223.** Mar–Dec daily 10–2am.

EastWest Beach Club ★★★ A beach bar by day, complete with suntanned bodies and designer bikinis, after dark EastWest turns into one of Dubrovnik's swankiest night spots. Expect pricey cocktails, DJ music, a smattering of celebrities, and lots of showing off.

Banje Beach, Frana Supila 4. www.ew-dubrovnik.com. ☏ **020/412-220.** May–Sept daily 10pm–6am.

Jazz Caffe Troubadour ★★★ The Troubadour is one of Dubrovnik's best known and oldest venues, famous for hosting live jazz on a small stage out front in summer. It has become very expensive, and the quality of the music varies from night to night, but it remains a popular haunt. Breakfast is now served from 8:30am to 3pm, should you wake up late and not manage to have yours before lunchtime.

Bunićeva Poljana 2. ☏ **020/323-476.** May–Oct daily 8am–1am, Nov–Apr 5–11pm.

DUBROVNIK DAY TRIPS
Elafiti Islands

Slow the pace and get away from Dubrovnik's glamor for a day trip to the Elafiti, 14 car-free islands and islets between Dubrovnik and the Pelješac Peninsula. These land masses are the basis for one of the most popular excursions from Dubrovnik. Only the three largest of the "deer islands" (from the Greek *elfos*)—Koločep, Lopud, and Šipan—are populated. They have been inhabited since prehistoric times. During the 10th century, the islands became Dubrovnik territories and were liberally strewn with chapels, churches, and villas designed in a riot of pre-Romanesque, Gothic, and Renaissance styles. Today, the islands' few residents are indifferent to tourists, who mostly are left alone to poke around in the pine forests and crumbling ruins that cover much of the terrain.

If you have the time, you should visit the islands one at a time, travelling independently by local Jadrolinja ferry (www.jadrolinija.hr). However, if time is short, various agencies offer a "Three Islands Cruise," departing from Gruž harbor to take in the three islands above, with a seafood lunch included, for around 400kn per person.

You will find **Lopud Tourist Information Center** (✆ **020/759-086**) at Obala I. Kuljevana 12 and **Šipan Tourist Information Center** (✆ **020/758-084**) at Luka bb, Luka Šipanska. Note that these centers are open in summer only.

WHAT TO SEE & DO: ISLANDS

KOLOČEP Koločep is the island in this group closest to Dubrovnik (3.2km/2 miles away); at less than a square mile, it is also the smallest. The island's fewer than 200 residents live in two tiny villages of stone houses, **Donje Čelo** on the northwest side and **Gornje Čelo** on the island's southwest side. You can cover the distance between the two villages in less than 1 hour on foot, unless you are lured off the path between them to explore Koločep's olive groves and church ruins. In 2014, the Kalamota Island Resort (www.kalamotaislandresort.com), one of the few adults-only hotels in Croatia, opened here.

LOPUD Lopud is the most tourism-oriented of the islands, and has several small B&Bs plus the big, modern Lafodia Hotel (www.lafodiahotel.com). It is just under twice the size of Koločep, and has just one settlement, Lopud Town. Lopud draws more visitors than its sister islands and has the most attractions: the ruins of a Franciscan monastery, several tiny medieval churches in various stages of decay, and the lovely sandy Šunj beach, with an informal restaurant and bar.

ŠIPAN Šipan is the largest of the Elafitis, but it is also the least developed. Ferries from Dubrovnik deposit passengers at Šipanska Luka (Šipan Harbor). From here, an unsurfaced road runs across the island, through a pleasant fertile valley (Šipansko Polje) planted with olive groves and vineyards, to Šipan's second village, Suđurađ. The island has a couple of hotels (one in each village) and several decent seafood eateries.

Mljet

Mljet's background is laced with legends, but its present condition is a real-life experience of nature and history. The ancient Greeks were familiar with Mljet, an island they called Melita ("honey") for the swarms of bees they found there, but except for amphorae in the sea off Mljet, there is no tangible evidence the Greeks ever settled on it. Later settlers—Romans, Byzantines, Avars, Slavs—did leave traces of their time on Mljet; the area around Polače boasts several sites with ruins dating to the 1st through the 6th centuries, including a 5th-century Roman palace and some fortifications.

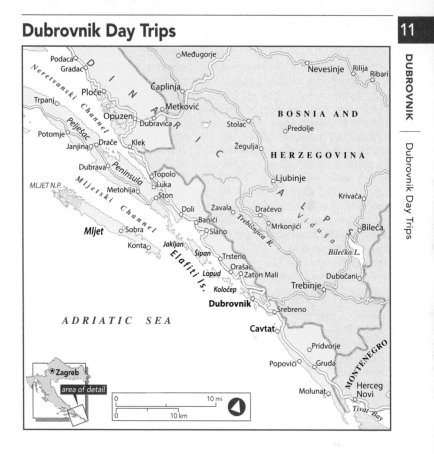

You can visit Mljet independently, traveling from Dubrovnik to the island aboard the **Nona Ana** catamaran (www.gv-line.hr), which runs from Gruž port directly to Polače on the edge of **Mljet National Park.** Through July and August the catamaran departs each day in the morning and returns in the late afternoon, making a comfortable day trip (the ride is a little under 2 hr. each way). Alternatively, you can reach Mljet by Jadrolinija car ferry (www.jadrolinija.hr), departing from Prapratno (close to Ston on Pelješac peninsula), to arrive at the port of Sobra on the island. From June through September, there are five ferries per day. In addition, various agencies offer one-day excursions to Mljet from Dubrovnik, Korčula Town, and Orebić.

On the island, the **Mljet Tourist Board** (www.mljet.hr; ✆ **020/746-025**) is based at Zabrježe 2, Babino Polje; the **Mljet National Park** (www.np-mljet.hr; ✆ **020/744-041**) office is at Pristanište 2, Goveđari.

WHAT TO SEE & DO: MLJET

The western side of Mljet is a national park known as a "green island" because Mljet is heavily wooded (more than 70 percent of the island is covered with forests). Its centerpieces are two saltwater lakes connected by a narrow channel. Water in these lakes is warm: 77°F (25°C) for **Malo Jezero** and 82° to 86°F (28°–30°C) for **Veliko**

Jezero. The lakes' high saline concentration is said to have healing properties, especially for skin diseases and rheumatism.

Most people come here to swim in the lakes, or to hike or cycle around the water and through the island's dense pinewoods. Note that mountain bikes and sea kayaks are available for rent at **Hotel Odisej,** Mljet's only hotel, which lies just under a mile from Pomena and Veliko Jezero.

In the middle of the larger lake, **Veliko Jezero,** rises the tiny **St. Mary's Islet,** capped by a semi-abandoned, fortified, 12th-century Benedictine monastery. The monastery and its **Church of St. Mary** have gone through several incarnations since they were built, including a stint as a hotel during Tito's administration. The 1991 war ended that phase, leaving the monastery and church vacant and neglected. They are currently under restoration—the monastery is closed to visitors, but the tiny church is open, though there isn't much to see. Most visitors end up having a (rather overpriced) snack or drink at **Restoran Melita** (www.mljet-restoranmelita.com), with its tables on a pretty terrace on the quay in front of the monastery. St. Mary's Islet is served by hourly national park taxi-boats from Pomena.

Cavtat

Cavtat (pronounced "*sahvtaht*") is a sleepy fishing town loved by tourists for its beaches and its beautiful horseshoe-shaped harbor, as well as its several sights worth investigating. (The town's proximity to Dubrovnik—just 19km/12 miles to the southeast—makes it an acceptable alternative place to stay when Dubrovnik is full.) Cavtat was originally founded by Greeks from Vis as a settlement called Epidaurum. In the 1st century B.C., the Romans under Emperor Augustus took over, and eventually the town became known as Cavtat. Archaeological finds from those times include underwater ruins in the bay, foundation remains, tombs, and vestiges of a Roman road above the present town. The ancient town was destroyed at the beginning of the 7th century during the invasions of the Avars and the Slavs; it was then that the founders of Dubrovnik fled to the north and established their new city. Cavtat shared Dubrovnik's destiny in the years that followed.

Cavtat is an easy half-hour day trip from Dubrovnik, reachable by bus, water taxi, or organized excursion. Alternatively, with several decent hotels and a low-key atmosphere, Cavtat makes a good alternative base to Dubrovnik. It is near the airport, so you do get some noise from the planes, but nothing excessive.

ESSENTIALS

VISITOR INFORMATION   The **Cavtat Tourist Board of Konavle** (www.visit. cavtat-konavle.com; ✆ **020/479-025**) is at Zidine 6.

GETTING THERE   Cavtat is a short drive from Dubrovnik, but if you don't have your own transportation, the Libertas bus no. 10 runs from Dubrovnik's main station hourly. The trip is less than 1 hour. You also can hop a water taxi from the old harbor three times a day.

GETTING AROUND   As with most towns in Croatia, walking is the best way to see the area's attractions.

WHAT TO SEE & DO

Gallery Bukovac   The highly acclaimed Croatian portrait and landscape painter Vlaho Bukovac was born in 1855 in the house that now holds his namesake gallery. He studied in Paris, spent time in England (where he was commissioned to paint portraits of aristocrats), traveled to America, and then moved to Czechoslovakia, where

The Konavle is a low-key, stress-busting alternative to Dubrovnik's high-powered pace. It's a strip of fertile land flanked by mountains and the sea that stretches southeast of Cavtat and ends at the Montenegro border. A Sunday afternoon drive to watch the weekly folklore show in Čilipi and a stop for lunch at Konavoski Dvori (see below) near Gruda comprise the ideal itinerary for a visit to Konavle.

Dubrovnik Day Trips

he was a professor at the Academy of Fine Arts, Prague. Through his travels he kept this 18th-century house in Cavtat, and returned here throughout his life to paint. It now houses a gallery, exhibiting some of his drawings, paintings, and personal possessions.

Ulica Vlaha Bukovca 5. www.kuca-bukovac.hr. ℗ **020/478-646.** 20kn. May–Oct, Tues–Sun 9am–1pm and 4–8pm; Nov–Apr, Tues–Sat 9am–1pm and 2–5pm; Sun 2–5pm; closed Mon.

Račić Mausoleum   From the center of town, on the west side of the bay, a long set of stairs leads up to the town cemetery, which occupies a small peninsula. Here, on the highest point, you will find this elegant white stone mausoleum, designed in 1921 for the Račić family by Croatia's best-known 20th-century sculptor, Ivan Meštrović. For your stair-climbing trouble, you will also get fine views across the sea, with Dubrovnik visible in the distance.

Admission 20kn. May–Oct daily 10am–noon and 4–8pm.

WHERE TO STAY

Cavtat makes a slightly cheaper alternative to sleeping in Dubrovnik, and it's also much less crowded. You can get leads on available accommodations, including private rooms and apartments, at the tourist office (see above). Cavtat also has several decent hotels—Hotel Croatia is one of the country's largest, with nearly 500 rooms.

Hotel Croatia   Set amid pine trees on a small peninsula, with sea views on three sides, this big, modern, 1980s hotel was totally renovated in 2008. The guestrooms are spacious and tastefully decorated, making for light and airy atmospheres. All have bathrooms with both a rain shower and a bathtub. The seven suites each come with a separate bedroom and living room, plus a furnished terrace for open-air dining. Many guests opt for half-board, and most are extremely satisfied with the quality of the food on offer. Extensive facilities include a spa and two beach areas, with sunbeds and a beach volleyball court. The staff is exceptionally welcoming, friendly, and professional.

Frankopanska 10. www.adriaticluxuryhotels.com. ℗ **020/475-555.** 487 units. Double Aug from 201€. **Amenities:** 5 restaurants; 2 bars; children's programs; beach volleyball; 3 pools; sea kayak rental; scuba diving; spa; fitness room; gift shop; table tennis; Wi-Fi (free).

Hotel Supetar   Superbly located on the seafront overlooking the harbor in Cavtat, this small, old-fashioned hotel is peaceful and relaxing, with a waterside terrace restaurant and a walled garden. It's perfectly adequate and comfortable, but the rooms, despite being spotlessly clean, are a tad dull and faded, and need redecorating. The staff are friendly and professional, and guests have the use of the pools and wellness facilities at the much bigger Hotel Croatia sister property nearby.

Obala A Starčevića 27. www.adriaticluxuryhotels.com. ℗ **020/479-833.** 28 units. Double Aug 113€. **Amenities:** Restaurant; garden; limited access to Hotel Croatia facilities; Wi-Fi (free).

Villa Pattiera   This small, family-run hotel occupies an old stone villa in the center of Cavtat. Welcoming and homey, it has just 12 guestrooms—the rooms on the top floor (no elevator) have balconies and lovely views over the bay. The hotel puts on a hearty and delicious breakfast, which is served on a sunny terrace out front. Guests who opt for half-board have dinner at Restoran Dalmacija across the road (see "Where to Dine," below).

Trubićev put 9. www.villa-pattiera.hr. © **020/478-800.** 12 units. Double in Aug from 200€. **Amenities:** Restaurant; Wi-Fi (free).

WHERE TO DINE

Cavtat and the surrounding countryside have some excellent restaurants, serving authentic Dalmatian fare.

Konavoski Dvori ★★★ DALMATIAN   In the heart of rural Konavle, in an old water mill set amid lush woodlands on the banks of the River Ljuta, this restaurant is well known and much loved throughout the region. It's noted for delicious local dishes such as asparagus soup, barbecued trout with homegrown seasonal vegetables, and spit-roasted lamb, served by waiters and waitresses wearing traditional folk costumes. After your meal, take a walk through the grounds to see the waterfalls and rushing streams, which are lighted at night. The restaurant is 10km (6 miles) from Cavtat.

Ljuta-Konavle. www.esculaprestaurants.com. © **020/791-039.** Entrees 70kn–160kn. Jan–Nov daily noon–midnight.

Leut ★★ DALMATIAN   Founded in 1971, this family-run restaurant is well known for its excellent fresh seafood. Start with the lobster carpaccio, followed by swordfish steak served with grilled Mediterranean vegetables. In summer, tables overlook the sea from the terrace out front—it can get a bit chaotic when it's busy, so order some wine and be prepared to enjoy the lovely view while you wait for your food.

Trumbićeva 11. www.restaurant-leut.com. © **020/478-477.** Entrees 75kn–140kn. Apr–Nov daily 11am–midnight.

Restoran Dalmacija ★★ DALMATIAN   Run by the same family that owns Villa Pattiera (see above), this unpretentious restaurant is noted for its tasty seafood platter (combining sea bream, sea bass, hake, octopus, and prawns) and succulent fillet steak in creamy green pepper sauce. The restaurant doesn't have a sea view, but the food is reasonably priced and the service is friendly and helpful.

Trubićeva 9. www.villa-pattiera.hr. © **020/478-800.** Entrees 65kn–130kn. Daily 7am–midnight.

Pelješac Peninsula

You'll never feel crowded in Pelješac, which is overlooked by most visitors to southern Dalmatia—most tourists make a beeline for glitzier Dubrovnik instead. Their loss is your gain. Pelješac is low-key in every respect, but that doesn't mean it lacks worthwhile attractions: The peninsula is dotted with vineyards and wine cellars (open for tastings in summer), beaches, out of the way *konobas,* and glorious scenery.

OREBIĆ

This town in the southwestern part of the Pelješac Peninsula claims to have one of the sunniest climates in Croatia, thanks to its position at the foot of the 961m (3,153-ft.) **Mount St. Ilija.** Beachgoers take advantage of this in droves, and it isn't unusual to see moms carting picnic baskets to the water's edge for breakfast, lunch, and dinner. Orebić's atmosphere is definitely family-focused. This is where you will find some of Croatia's best beaches and one of the most interesting and congenial promenades anywhere. Orebić is a place where you can settle in and let your mood take you to destinations as varied as the beach, a day trip to **Korčula,** or out to sea on a sailing excursion. Orebić owes much of its cachet to its history as a town of wealthy sea captains, who in the 18th and 19th centuries built many fine stone villas here. Some of these structures are still standing and in use as private residences. **Viganj,** 6km (4 miles) west of Orebić, is a popular windsurfing destination.

Essentials

VISITOR INFORMATION The **Orebić Tourist Information Office** (www. tz-orebic.com; ✆ **020/713-718**) is on the beach at Zrinsko Frankopanska 2. **Orebić Tours** (www.orebic-tours.hr; ✆ **020/714-367**) at Bana Josipa Jelačića 84a can help you find private accommodations and arrange excursions.

GETTING THERE Orebić lies halfway down Pelješac Peninsula, a strip of hilly, fertile land noted for its vineyards. The town is about 1 hour by car from Ston, the peninsula's eastern border, and makes a nice base for day trips to the island of Korčula (served by regular ferry) or to explore the peninsula. There are three daily buses from Dubrovnik to Korčula, which pass through Orebić en-route.

GETTING AROUND Everybody walks everywhere in Orebić, especially in the evening. The Riva is pedestrians-only, of course. To explore the hidden interior of Pelješac, you really need a car.

What to See & Do

Franciscan Monastery   On the hillside above Orebić, a steep 20-minute walk away, this 15th-century Gothic-Renaissance monastery is approached along an avenue of cypress trees. Commanding spectacular views down onto the turquoise sea and the island of Korčula, the site was chosen as a fine vantage point for observing passing ships, at a time when Pelješac belonged to Dubrovnik, while Korčula was ruled by Dubrovnik's archrival, Venice. Inside the monastery, see the display of religious paintings and votive gifts, donated by local seafarers as a way of saying thanks to the Virgin for protecting them through storms and rough seas.

Admission 20kn. Daily 9am–noon and 4–7pm.

Maritime Museum   Historically, Orebić owes its wealth to shipping, several local families having been ship owners and sea captains. Anyone with an interest in nautical history will enjoy a look in this small museum, exhibiting scale models of ships, paintings of sea battles with pirates, and sailing equipment.

Obala Pomoraca.✆ **020/713-009.** Admission 15kn. Jun–Sept daily 7am–10pm; Oct–May Mon–Fri 7am–3pm.

Where to Stay

To rent an apartment, try **Orebić Tours** (www.orebic-tours.hr; ✆ **020/714-367**) at Bana Josipa Jelačića 84a. You can also walk up and down the beachfront and the main drag and look for "APARTMAN," "SOBE," or "ZIMMER FREI" signs.

Hotel Adriatic   Close to the port in Orebić, this chic boutique hotel occupies a 17th-century stone building, which used to serve as the local school. The six rooms here have wooden floors, some exposed stonework, sweeping curtains, and lovely sea views; some have four-poster beds, too. Out front, on a waterside terrace designed to look like a boat, the Stari Kapetan restaurant draws hotel guests and neighbors alike—try the sea platter for two (sea bass, prawns, and tuna) and the excellent house wine, served by the carafe.

Šetalište Kneza Domagoja 8. www.hoteladriaticorbic.com. ✆ **020/714-488.** 6 units. Double Aug from 155€. **Amenities:** Restaurant; Wi-Fi (free).

Hotel Indijan   On Orebić's waterfront, this hotel has 19 rooms and suites, all with balconies affording fine views of Korčula across the deep blue Adriatic. Personally, I prefer the nearby Hotel Adriatic, which is more atmospheric, with antiques and exposed stonework. The rooms here are functional and comfortable, but nothing special, with wooden floors and the sea-view balconies being the absolute highlight. The Korta restaurant serves local fish and meat specialties on a palm-lined waterside terrace, while the Kolona cafe-bar offers local wines and exotic cocktails along with romantic sunsets. There's a small spa centering on an indoor pool with a retractable roof.

Škvar 2. www.hotelindijan.hr. ℰ **020/714-555.** 19 units. Double Aug from 189€. **Amenities:** Restaurant; bar; fitness room; indoor pool; spa; Wi-Fi (free).

Where to Dine

Orebić, especially along the waterfront, has a handful of mediocre restaurants catering to tourists. To really savor local cooking, you should drive a little way out of town, either along the coast or into the hills.

Panorama   DALMATIAN   Run by the Jurković family, this rustic eatery has a big barbecue and outdoor tables on a terrace affording amazing views down onto the sea and Korčula. The house specialty is octopus slow-cooked under a *peka* (see page 102). Other dishes often depend on what's in season. You'll find the restaurant behind Orebić, approached up a steep narrow road on the hillside above the Franciscan Monastery.

Bilopolje, Orebić. ℰ **020/714-170.** Entrees 65kn–130kn. May–Oct daily noon–midnight.

Restoran Vrgorac   DALMATIAN   In Kučište, 3km (2 miles) west of Orebić on the road to Viganj, this family-run eatery serves up authentic local cooking on a waterside terrace draped with grapevines. Everything comes in generous portions: Try the pizza, fresh fish, or barbecued lamb, plus a mixed salad and a carafe of house wine.

Perna 24, Kučište. www.villa-vrgorac.com. ℰ **020/719-152.** Entrees 60kn–120kn. May–Oct daily 10am–11pm.

Wine Bar Peninsula   WINE BAR   In the hills in Donja Banda, 12km (8 miles) east of Orebić, this bar provides an excellent introduction to the region's wines. The house stocks over 60 labels from Pelješac and the island of Korčula, and wine tastings are accompanied by local cheeses and premium olive oils. It's all very well organized and the owners are friendly, welcoming, and very knowledgeable about local wines.

Donja Banda bb, Oskorušno. www.peninsula.hr. ℰ **098/285-824.** May–Oct daily 9am–11pm.

STON & MALI STON

Ston and Mali Ston are adjacent "blink-and-you'll-miss-them" towns at the isthmus where Pelješac meets the Croatian mainland less than 1 hour northwest of Dubrovnik (58km/36 miles). However, both bedroom community Mali Ston and its working-class sister Ston were important strategic locations for the Republic of Dubrovnik, which acquired them in the 14th century. The city-state's officials then built an amazing system of fortified walls and fortresses that still run up the southern slope of Sveti Mihaljo (St. Michael) Hill behind the town, serving to limit enemy access to the rest of the Pelješac Peninsula in medieval times.

You can climb to a lookout point on the wall via stone stairs. Some sets of stairs are overgrown and only appear to lead up from various streets in town to the top of the wall. These are dead ends, so approach from the right.

The town of Ston is a small area scored with a number of very narrow streets designed to flummox would-be intruders. In addition to the walls, the towns prize their salt pans and oyster beds, which still are active today. Stay for dinner at one of the

East of Orebić, about 32km (20 miles) along the main road to Ston, you'll see a turnoff for Trstenik that leads to **Grgić Vina,** the ancestral home of the founders of Grgich Hills, one of America's greatest wineries. Grgić is very modest compared to its American counterpart, but it produces some of Croatia's most sought-after wines. The winery is open daily from 9am to 5pm and takes credit cards. The Bartulović tours include Grgić on their "Three Winery" tour. You can also visit independently, though whether anyone will be available to give an actual tour will depend on how busy it is. I recommend calling in advance, as these are family-run establishments which have somewhat unreliable working hours outside peak season (July and August). You can contact Grgić at Grgić Vina d.o.o., Trstenik 28, Pelješac (www.grgic-vina.com; ☎ 020/748-090).

A few miles past Grgić on the way to Orebić, you'll encounter many signs advertising homemade wine and *rakija.* Stop if you are curious, but be sure to leave time for the **Dingać wine district,** about 16km (10 miles) past Grgić. There are many big names here, including **Matuško** (www.matusko-vina.hr; ☎ 020/742-399) at Potomje 5A and **Skaramuča** (www.dingac-skaramuca.hr; ☎ 020/742-211) at Pijavičino 7. As you approach you'll see a sign for Dingać and a "tunel" [sic] sign on the right. Turn left and you'll hit the 400m (1,312-ft.) "tunel," a dark narrow passage through the mountain that was carved out so vineyard workers wouldn't have to haul grapes up and down the steep hills. Make a left at the end (slow down before you get there because the tunnel leads straight to a cliff and into the sea) for a trip down a character-building road that affords some of the most beautiful coastal vistas I've seen in Croatia. There are many tasting opportunities and apartments for rent the closer you get to the water.

area's good restaurants to feast on oysters taken directly from nearby beds and to drink Pelješac's fine wines.

Essentials

VISITOR INFORMATION Ston's **tourist office** (www.ston.hr; ☎ 020/754-452) is at Pelješka put 1.

GETTING THERE The Libertas no. 15 bus makes three trips daily both ways between Dubrovnik and Ston. In addition, the three daily buses to Korčula and Orebić pass through Ston en-route. Note that local public transportation on Pelješac Peninsula in general is not regular or efficient—if you want to see the exceptional but hidden gems in the hills and valleys of this rarely visited part of Croatia, you'll need a car.

GETTING AROUND The roads through Pelješac are generally narrow and winding, especially the coastal roads as you approach Mali Ston and Ston. The pavement varies from flat through the valleys to heart-stopping hairpin turns in steeper areas. Walking is the best way to explore Mali Ston and Ston. There is a free parking lot outside Ston near the market.

What to See & Do

Mali Ston and Ston are sentries at the entrance to the long and rugged Pelješac Peninsula, which is home to some of the most awe-inspiring landscapes in the country. Even if your objective is to follow Pelješac's wine road to sample its well-respected wines or to head to one of the peninsula's beaches, Mali Ston and Ston should be one of your stops. The monumental Ston Wall and its fortifications are the obvious draw, but if you linger awhile, you'll be able to explore the towns' charming historic buildings and their still-working ancient salt pans before stopping for a sublime meal of oysters or mussels fresh from Malostonski Bay.

Ston Wall and Fortifications ★★ In 1333, the Republic of Ragusa (Dubrovnik) acquired Pelješac Peninsula. To protect its boundaries, Dubrovnik founded the towns of Ston and Mali Ston, one on each side of the peninsula, and connected them with a complex fortification system, effectively closing off Pelješac from the hinterland. Sometimes compared to the Great Wall of China, Ston's walls run 5.6km (3½ miles) up and over the hill between the two towns. The climb up is quite steep, and there are many steps, but from atop the walls you get amazing views over the surrounding landscape. Southwest of Ston, note the vast expanse of salt pans. The Romans were already collecting salt here, but it was under Dubrovnik that the industry really expanded, as salt was in high demand for export and reaped considerable profits. As you walk the walls and cross over to the opposite side of the peninsula, you have views down onto the bay of Mali Ston, with its extensive shellfish farming. Allow 45 minutes to complete the hike, wear good walking shoes, and carry a bottle of water.

Admission to walk the walls 30kn. Jun–Jul 8am–7:30pm; Apr–May and Aug–Sept 8am–6:30pm; Oct 8am–5:30pm; Nov–Mar 10am–3pm.

Where to Stay

Ston makes a good alternative to Orebić if you want a base from which to explore Pelješac Peninsula and the area's wineries.

Ostrea Hotel ★★ This small, old-fashioned hotel by the harbor is a restful and comfortable place to stay. Occupying a renovated stone building, it opened in 1998 and is run by the Kralj family, who also own the nearby Kapetanova Kuća restaurant. The 13 rooms and 1 apartment are individually furnished. Although the units are quite basic (some are rather small), the bathrooms are shiny-new and well-equipped. It's worth asking for a superior room, which costs a little more but comes with a sea view. In addition to the nearby restaurant (a 2-minute walk away), there's a small breakfast room and bar for hotel guests on-site. The hotel's name is the Latin word for oyster, the basis of the local economy.

Mali Ston bb. www.ostrea.hr. ✆ **020/754-555.** 14 units. Double Aug from 110€. **Amenities:** Restaurant; bar; free parking; Wi-Fi (free).

Where to Dine

The area is a popular destination for foodies, who come specifically to feast upon locally grown oysters and mussels, which are served in a handful of restaurants overlooking the harbor in Mali Ston.

Bakus ★ SEAFOOD In the center of Ston, Bakus is informal, unpretentious, and reasonably priced, making it an ideal spot for lunch after walking the walls and visiting the salt pans. Try the *mušule na buzaru,* fresh mussels from the bay, cooked with garlic, white wine, and chopped parsley.

Ston. www.bakus.hr. ✆ **020/754-270.** Entrees 35kn–90kn, more for fresh fish priced by the kilo. Daily 8am–midnight.

Bota Šare ★★ DALMATIAN In Mali Ston, Bota Šare occupies an impressive building with an exposed stone interior, high vaulted ceiling, and a wooden mezzanine. Mussels and oysters feature on the menu, as do local wines. The house specialty is *Dubrovačka porpora* (fish stew with sea bream, grouper, perch, and shark, plus potatoes and fresh herbs). It does get very crowded, especially on weekends, so you'd do well to reserve a table in advance.

Mali Ston bb. www.bota-sare.hr. ✆ **020/754-482.** Entrees 70kn–200kn, more for fresh fish priced by the kilo. Daily 11am–midnight.

Kapetenova Kuća ★★★ SEAFOOD On the small square overlooking the harbor in Mali Ston, this highly regarded restaurant is run by the Kralj family, who also own the Ostrea Hotel (see above). Most people come here to savor the locally produced shellfish—the house specialty is cream of oyster soup with samphire. The wine list features quality Croatian wines, with an emphasis on those from Pelješac Peninsula. Round off your meal with the *makarula* cake, made with pasta and chocolate, which is found only in Ston. Reservations are required.

Mali Ston bb. www.ostrea.hr. ✆ **020/754-555.** Entrees 70kn–220kn, more for fresh fish priced by the kilo. Daily 9am–midnight.

PLANNING YOUR TRIP TO CROATIA

Croatia can be unfamiliar territory for even the most seasoned traveler, but it's no more difficult to put together a dream trip here than with any other European destination. Once you understand that there are no direct flights from North America to Croatia, and that getting here requires a stop in a city with connecting flights, ferry routes, or land access, planning gets much easier. A visit to one or more of Croatia's countless islands requires more precise logistical planning, if only to make sure you don't waste time on long layovers and missed connections. For specific information on planning your trip and for more on-the-ground resources in Croatia, please turn to individual chapters on the regions in question, or the "Fast Facts" at the end of this chapter.

WHEN TO GO

Summer, specifically July and August, is the busiest time on Croatia's coast and islands. This is the country's "season," a time when the sun is the hottest, the sea the bluest, and the traffic at its most endless. The Croatian coast is at its best—and worst—during midsummer. Hotel room rates top out, restaurant tables are always full, and crowds can be overwhelming. This is the period that makes or breaks many businesses that depend on a season's tourism for a year's income, and it can be tough on unsuspecting travelers. Much of the madness is due to traditional European vacation schedules, which coincide with the coast's glorious summer weather. Boating enthusiasts, tour groups, and independent travelers from all over the world make up the rest of the traffic.

Weather

Weather in Croatia can be generally divided into two climates. Northern Croatia has a Continental climate, with average temperatures ranging from near freezing in January to about 77°F (25°C) in August. The coastal areas have more of a Mediterranean climate, with average temperatures ranging from the mid-40s Fahrenheit in January to 100°F (38°C) or more in August. Spring and autumn are pleasant and mild along the coast; winter inland can be cold and snowy.

The bottom line is that in July and August, good weather is almost a certainty and tourism is in full swing, but prices and availability on the coast can be prohibitive. Conversely, in the interior, summer crowds are minimal and prices can reach their lowest levels. Zagreb and other interior cities can be real bargains in summer because many residents will be on the coast, leaving the towns less crowded than usual. (Accordingly, many Zagreb restaurants and shops may be closed.) *A word of warning:* The weather on the coast is usually nice, the sea warm, and the prices lower in May, June, September, and October, but some establishments, especially those on the islands, might be shuttered and some ferry routes might be canceled or on reduced schedules.

Croatia's Average Temperatures (°F/°C)

	JAN	FEB	MAR	APR	MAY	JUNE	JULY	AUG	SEPT	OCT	NOV	DEC
Interior												
HIGH	38/3	43/6	52/11	61/16	70/21	76/24	79/26	77/25	70/21	59/15	49/9	40/4
LOW	29/-2	32/0	38/3	47/8	54/12	58/14	61/16	61/16	56/13	47/8	38/3	31/-1
Coastal												
HIGH	50/10	52/11	56/13	63/17	72/22	79/26	85/29	85/29	77/25	68/20	58/14	52/11
LOW	41/5	43/6	45/7	52/11	59/15	65/18	70/21	70/21	65/18	58/14	49/9	43/6

Calendar of Events

The festivals mentioned in this section, unless otherwise specified, fall on different dates every year. Inquire at the Croatian National Tourist Office (www.croatia.hr) or at local tourist offices for event contact information and for an updated calendar. For an exhaustive list of events beyond those listed here, check Frommers.com, where you'll find a roster of what's happening in cities all over the world.

JANUARY

New Year. Croatians enter the new year with massive firework displays in major cities like Zagreb, Split, and Dubrovnik, followed by partying until dawn.

FEBRUARY

Rijeka Carnival. This pre-Lenten celebration begins in mid-February and ends at midnight on Shrove Tuesday. Although celebrated all over the country, Rijeka has the most lavish event, with parades, masquerades, and merrymaking similar to New Orleans's Mardi Gras. www.rijecki-karneval.hr.

Feast of St. Blaise. Catholics all over the world honor St. Blaise on February 3 with the blessing of throats. In Dubrovnik, where St. Blaise is the city's patron saint, the celebration is more elaborate, culminating with a parade.

APRIL

Easter. In Catholic Croatia, Easter is a major religious celebration. On Hvar, the night before Good Friday locals stage the Procession of the Cross, walking a 25km (16 mile) circular route from village to village following a heavy wooden crucifix, concluding at sunrise.

Music Biennale Zagreb. An international festival of contemporary music, the Biennale is held in April in odd-numbered years in Zagreb. Contemporary classical musicians are the focus. See www.mbz.hr.

MAY

Sudamje. In Split, May 7 is a public holiday to celebrate the day of Sv. Duje (St. Domnius), the city's protector. Stalls set up along the seafront sell wooden handicrafts and a solemn mass is held at the cathedral.

Croatia Boat Show. This annual five-day event sees some of the world's smartest yachts mooring up along the seafront in Split, attracting nautical professionals and amateurs alike.

Contemporary Dance Week. Zagreb is the main stage for this dance and choreography showcase, but parallel events are held in Rijeka and Karlovac. See www.danceweekfestival.com.

JUNE

Animafest Zagreb. This world festival of animated film is a six-day celebration of cartoons. See www.animafest.hr.

International Children's Festival. Šibenik is the setting for this annual festival encouraging creativity in children. Programs showcasing youthful talents are presented in venues across the city from mid-June to early July. See www.mdf-sibenik.com.

Pula Film Festival. The Arena, Pula's ancient amphitheater, hosts this annual two-week festival of film, which was founded way back in 1953. See www.pulafilmfestival.hr.

Valamar Jazz Festival. In Poreč, this five-day event sees internationally acclaimed jazz musicians performing in the atrium of the basilica and on St. Nicholas Island. See www.valamarjazz.com.

INmusic Festival. Staged at Lake Jarun in Zagreb, this three-day fest attracts big names from the worlds of rock and urban music. See www.inmusicfestival.com.

JULY

Motovun Film Festival. The tiny medieval town of Motovun, in the heart of Istria, hosts an annual five-day festival in late July to celebrate independent films. See www.motovunfilmfestival.com.

Musical Evenings of Sveti Donat. From early July through mid-August, this festival stages classical music recitals in the Church of St. Donatus in Zadar. See www.donat-festival.com.

Split Summer Festival. From mid-July to mid-August, this festival takes over Split's historic core with exhibitions, concerts, dance, theater, and opera performed in the Peristil of Diocletian's Palace. See www.splitsko-ljeto.hr.

Dubrovnik Summer Festival. Well-known international artists perform during this annual event, held from early July to late August. Dubbed "Libertas," the festival has gone on every year since 1950, even during the war. See www.dubrovnik-festival.hr.

Jazz Is Back. In the Istrian hill town of Grožnjan, this festival finds world-class jazz musicians playing under the stars. See www.jazzisbackbp.com.

International Folklore Festival. For a week in mid-July, Zagreb comes alive with dancing, song, musical performances, workshops, and exhibitions in celebration of folk culture in Croatia and surrounding countries. See www.msf.hr.

AUGUST

Vukovar Film Festival. Founded in 2007, this annual five-day festival brings European art house cinema to seven locations around the town of Vukovar. See www.vukovarfilmfestival.com.

Avvantura Festival Film Forum Zadar. Held the last week of August, this festival focuses on European film, with projections at open-air locations in Zadar's old town. See www.filmforumzadar.org.

Faros Marathon. On the last Saturday of August, this 16km (10 mile) swimming marathon attracts international athletic stars to Stari Grad on Hvar. See www.farosmarathon.com.

SEPTEMBER

Korkyra Baroque Festival. This one-week event, staged at various locations in Korčula's Old Town, attracts international performers from the world of Baroque music. See www.korkyrabaroque.com.

Varaždin Festival of Baroque Music. Listen to baroque music in one of Europe's most baroque cities from mid-September through early October. Performances are mostly in Varaždin's churches. See www.vbv.hr.

OCTOBER

Marunada (Chestnut Festival). For three weekends in October, the tiny town of Lovran near Opatija celebrates everything chestnut. There's food, merrymaking, and even cook-offs, all in honor of the chestnut and its many culinary uses. See www.tz-lovran.hr.

Zagreb Marathon. A full and half marathon are run each October in Zagreb. See www.zagreb-marathon.com.

Zagreb Film Festival. This one-week movie festival focuses on short, feature, and documentary films, with projections at various indoor locations around the city. See www.zagrebfilmfestival.com.

NOVEMBER

Martinje (St. Martin's Day). Besides being a church feast day, November 11 is also the day in Croatia when the new wine is blessed and "tested" in unlimited amounts. The ceremony is conducted in the grape-growing regions of north Croatia, around Zagreb, and begins with a song in honor of St. Martin. It ends with a prayer for a good year for all. When possible, the blessing is in a vineyard, but wherever it is held, it is followed by a party that includes eating, drinking, and singing well into the night. Most Croatian restaurants mark the occasion by offering special dinners (much as the French do when celebrating the Beaujolais *nouveau*).

DECEMBER

St. Nicholas Day. Komiža, on the island of Vis, honors the town's patron saint on his feast day of December 6 with a huge party that opens with the burning of an old fishing boat in front of St. Nicholas Church in Vis Town. Go to www.dalmatia.hr for more information.

New Year's Regatta. This year-concluding event (December 28 to December 31) features small-boat races off the island of Hvar.

ENTRY REQUIREMENTS

Passports & Visas

E.U. member country nationals can now enter Croatia with just a personal ID. However, all other foreign nationals (anyone from outside the E.U.) need a valid passport for entrance to Croatia. Citizens of the U.S., Australia, Canada, New Zealand, Israel, and Singapore do not need visas for tourist/business trips of fewer than 90 days within a 6-month period. A visa is required and should be obtained in advance for stays over 90 days. South Africans do require visas, even for short stays. As of April 2013, in preparation for E.U. membership, Croatia changed its law regarding Russians, who now need visas, too.

For more information on visas, visit the Republic of Croatia Ministry of Foreign and European Affairs website, www.crovisa.mvep.hr. Here you will find an online visa application form (available in various languages), and if you've already applied, you can check your application status.

U.S. citizens can visit the U.S. State Department website (www.travel.state.gov) and go to the "Foreign Entry Requirement" for an up-to-date country-by-country listing of passport requirements around the world.

Customs

WHAT YOU CAN BRING INTO CROATIA

Visitors can bring 200 cigarettes, 50 cigars, 1 liter of spirits, 2 liters of wine, and 2 liters of liqueur duty-free. Foreign visitors can bring in boats without duty or taxes if the vessels are for private use while in Croatia and if they take them home when they leave.

WHAT YOU CAN TAKE HOME FROM CROATIA

U.S. citizens who have been away from the U.S. for at least 48 hours are allowed to bring back, once every 30 days, $800 worth of merchandise duty-free. A flat duty rate is charged on the next $1,000 worth of purchases. Citizens returning to the U.S. should have their receipts or purchases handy to expedite the declaration process. *Note:* Anyone who owes duty is required to pay upon arrival in the United States, either by cash, personal check, government or traveler's check, or money order; in some locations Visa and MasterCard are also accepted.

To avoid paying duty on foreign-made personal items owned before leaving the U.S., bring along a bill of sale, insurance policy, jeweler's appraisal, or receipts of purchase.

With few exceptions, fresh fruits and vegetables cannot be brought into the United States from another country. For specifics on what is and is not allowed, visit the **U.S. Customs & Border Protection (CBP)** website (www.cbp.gov) and go to "Travel" and click on "Know Before You Go."

For a clear summary of **Canadian** rules, visit the **Canada Border Services Agency** website at www.cbsa-asfc.gc.ca.

U.K. citizens should refer to the **HM Customs & Excise** website (www.hmce.gov.uk).

215

Australian nationals should visit the **Australian Customs & Border Protection Service** website (www.customs.gov.au).

Those from **New Zealand** should check out the **New Zealand Customs Service** website (www.customs.govt.nz).

Medical Requirements

For information on medical requirements and recommendations, see "Health," p. 222.

GETTING THERE & GETTING AROUND

Getting to Croatia

BY PLANE

Croatia Airlines (www.croatiaairlines.com) flies routes between Croatia and Europe's major hubs, among them Amsterdam, Athens, Belgrade, Berlin, Brussels, Copenhagen, Dusseldorf, Frankfurt, London, Munich, Paris, Prague, Rome, Sarajevo, Vienna, and Zurich. **Zagreb** (ZAG) and **Dubrovnik** (DUB) are Croatia's biggest gateways and Lufthansa is the largest international carrier that serves them. Both Lufthansa and Croatia Airlines are members of the Star Alliance, which includes United Airlines. At press time, no U.S. carriers were flying directly into Croatian airports.

Tip: It's wise to book your flight to Croatia on United or other Star Alliance member airline (Austrian, Swiss, SAS, and so on) if only to smooth luggage handling. If your initial carrier is a Star Alliance member, bags will be checked through to your destination, a boon when catching connecting flights. (If you start your trip on a nonmember carrier, you might have to pick up your bag, go through customs, carry your bags through the airport to the connecting gate, and recheck them with Croatia Airlines or other connecting airlines.)

Besides Croatia Airlines, numerous European discount carriers (such as easyJet, Jet2.com, Monarch, and Ryanair) serve Croatia from various European cities.

Departure Tips

In 2003, the Transportation Security Administration (TSA) phased out gate check-in at all U.S. airports. E-tickets have made paper tickets nearly obsolete. Passengers with e-tickets can beat the ticket counter lines by using airport electronic kiosks or online check-in from their home computers. Online check-in involves logging on to your airline's website, accessing your reservation, and printing out your boarding pass—the airline may even offer you bonus miles to do so! If you're using a kiosk at the airport, bring the credit card with which you booked the ticket, or bring your frequent-flier card. Print out your boarding pass from the kiosk and proceed to the security checkpoint with your pass and a photo ID. If you're checking bags or looking to snag an exit-row seat, you will be able to do so using most airline kiosks. Even the smaller airlines are employing the kiosk system, but always call your airline to make sure these alternatives are available. Security checkpoint lines vary in length from country to country and from airport to airport. If you have trouble standing for long periods of time, tell an airline employee; the airline will provide a wheelchair.

If you have metallic body parts, a note from your doctor can prevent a long chat with the security screeners. Keep in mind that only ticketed passengers are allowed past security, except for folks escorting children or passengers with disabilities.

In terms of what you can and can't carry on, the rules keep changing, but in general sharp things such as knives are out, nail clippers are okay, and beverages must be purchased *after* you clear security. Liquids are limited to 3-ounce containers that fit in one, 1-quart plastic bag. Keep this bag outside your suitcase to show screeners as you pass through security.

Note: On Croatia Airlines and most European airlines travelers are allowed only one carry-on bag. Check size and weight requirements for each of the airlines you book with. Limits on carry-on weight and dimensions set by Croatia Airlines and most European airlines are lower than limits on U.S. airlines.

Airport screeners may decide that your checked luggage needs to be searched by hand. You can purchase luggage locks that allow screeners to open and relock a checked bag if hand searching is necessary. Look for Travel Sentry–certified locks at luggage or travel shops and Brookstone stores (you can buy them online at www. brookstone.com). These locks, approved by the U.S.'s TSA, can be opened by luggage inspectors with a special code or key. For more information on the locks, visit www. travelsentry.org. If you use something other than TSA-approved locks, your lock will be cut off your suitcase if a TSA agent needs to hand-search your luggage.

The TSA has issued a list of prohibited items; check its website (www.tsa.gov/traveler-information/prohibited-items) for details.

BY CAR

The highways that connect Croatia to its neighbors (Slovenia, Hungary, Bosnia/Herzegovina, Serbia, and Montenegro) are good and getting better as miles of new pavement are poured. This is especially true of the span between Ljubljana and Zagreb, a route that now takes just 2 hours to complete. The route from Budapest to Zagreb runs across Croatia's northern border and is also popular. It takes about 5 hours to reach Zagreb (362km/225 miles) from the Hungarian capital.

Visitors coming from Italy and Austria must pass through Slovenia to get to Croatia's border, but Slovenia's roads are excellent, too.

Note: If you choose the route through Slovenia, be aware that Slovenia requires tariff stickers for cars using Slovenian roads. In 2014, prices for weekly stickers for motorcycles were 7.50€ and cars were 15€. Even if you are just passing through, you'll have to buy the sticker.

In December 2007, neighboring E.U. countries Slovenia and Hungary joined the Schengen Area, a group of 26 European countries that have abolished passport requirements and other forms of border control at their common borders. Croatia is not yet a Schengen member, but is working to apply to join the group in July 2015. Once it becomes a member, crossing national lines to and from Croatia should be seamless.

Even as European Union border checks disappear, travelers should be sure to carry passports, insurance cards, and any rental car papers (including the car's registration). This is especially true if you are going through Bosnia/Herzegovina, Serbia, or Montenegro, countries that are not yet fully in the E.U. membership pipeline.

CAR RENTAL Car rental in Croatia is expensive, and it can be tricky. Even if you use a global agency like Hertz or Avis, it is best to reserve a car by contacting a local agency in the city where you plan to rent, rather than through the agency's parent company or online. It's also a good idea to take the "full insurance" package offered with your car rental, even though it can add considerable cost. *Warning:* In most cases, liability coverage from your domestic auto insurance policy **will not** cover you on vehicles rented outside the U.S. That is also true of the auto coverage that comes with most major bank cards. Check with your insurance agent and credit card company to be sure.

You will be given a chance to inspect your vehicle with your car rental rep, and you should be certain the rep documents any existing scratches or other damage before you take the keys. Any dings incurred thereafter, not to mention major damage, will be charged to you at full rate.

Note: Most cars rented in Croatia are stick shift. Vehicles with automatic transmissions are scarce and you will pay extra if you need this feature.

BY TRAIN

Trains connect most major Croatian cities north of Split, but there is no train service to cities between Split and Dubrovnik in southern Dalmatia.

Zagreb does have convenient railway links with Austria, Bosnia/Herzegovina, Germany, Hungary, Italy, Serbia, Slovakia, Slovenia, and Switzerland, but the links to and from other European countries can be extremely time-consuming. The train ride from Paris to Zagreb, for example, takes 18-plus hours, while a rail trip from Frankfurt to Split will take almost 24 hours.

If you must get to Croatia by rail from another European city, check schedules, fares, and details on rail passes at **Rail Europe** (www.raileurope.com). For trains within Croatia, check **Croatian Railways** (www.hzpp.hr).

BY FERRY

There is a year-round regular overnight ferry service from Ancona in Italy to Split in Dalmatia. Other less frequent lines include Bari in Italy to Dubrovnik, and Venice in Italy to several coastal towns in Istria. In the Ancona–Split case, you hop aboard the ferry around 9pm and arrive in Dalmatia just as the sun is rising. Routes, fares, schedules, and booking information are available from the respective companies listed below. *Note:* Fares and schedules are subject to frequent change.

BLUE LINE INTERNATIONAL   From April through October, this ferry line has daily overnight service between Ancona and Split. Round-trip deck passage for two without a vehicle starts at 76€ in low season. A deluxe cabin for two with a vehicle runs from 338€ round-trip in low season. See www.blueline-ferries.com.

JADROLINIJA   Croatia's national ferry line has three international routes, which run year-round, though the frequency of service is downscaled in winter. In peak season (Jul–Aug), Jadrolinija ships travel almost every night between Ancona and Zadar, Ancona and Split, and Bari and Dubrovnik. Round-trip deck passage for two adults without a vehicle is approximately 144€ for the overnight trip between Bari and Dubrovnik; the fare on the same route for two and a vehicle plus an external cabin with a toilet is 452€. Note that these are low-season prices. Prices are the same for Ancona–Split and slightly less for Ancona–Zadar. See www.jadrolinija.hr.

SNAV   In addition to the options above, from late April through early October, the Italian company SNAV operates a car ferry between Ancona and Split. A fast "Jet" catamaran used to run as well, but this service was discontinued in 2013. Prices and schedule information are available at www.snav.it.

VENEZIA LINES   This Maltese company runs fast catamarans (foot passengers only) from mid-April through early October between Venice and Rovinj, Poreč, and Pula on Istria's western coast. Current schedule and fare information is available at www.venezialines.com.

Getting Around
BY PLANE

Croatia Airlines has a near monopoly on flights that travel among Croatia's seven airports: Zagreb, Split, Dubrovnik, Rijeka, Osijek, Pula, and Zadar. The best-served routes are Zagreb–Split and Zagreb–Dubrovnik, which both see several flights daily.

BY BUS

Almost every town in Croatia has a bus station, and the network of bus routes makes this form of transportation an excellent, economical option for travel within Croatia. Express routes on updated highways facilitate travel among major cities and buses stop at almost every village in the country, though schedules might be inconvenient for those with limited time.

BY FERRY

Ferry/catamaran travel is a way of life on Croatia's coast. There is no other way to get to the islands (except Pag and Krk, which are linked to the mainland via bridges). Jadrolinija is the major ferry operator. In summer, ferry schedules are beefed up to handle the increased traffic, but not necessarily aligned for the multiple connections necessary for convenient island hopping. Weather is another trip buster: Whenever the *bura* (the fierce northwestern wind that regularly hammers the area) blows, ferries may be delayed, and catamarans sidelined altogether.

Note: When planning your trip, do not underestimate the time it takes to travel by ferry. Besides calculating the water crossing, build in time to get to the ferry port, to wait in line (if you have a car, you might have to queue for hours), and to get from the port to your final destination. Check ferry schedules carefully, as not all routes operate every day.

BY CAR

Driving is the best method for seeing the real Croatia—even the islands. However, between car rental (a subcompact starts at 50€ per day) and gas at unprecedentedly high prices (11kn per liter in the summer of 2014), private transportation can be quite expensive. During July and August, it is important to reserve a rental car well before you arrive.

You will pay extra for each authorized driver besides the primary renter. Every driver must be 22 or older to rent a car in Croatia (some companies stipulate 25 and up for cars more powerful than 80 kW/110 hp).

Local agency **M.A.C.K.** has offices in Zagreb, Split, Dubrovnik, and Cavtat, and offers excellent rates. Reps speak English, provide maps and directions, and are very helpful. Go to www.rent-a-car.hr for more information. Global agencies **Hertz, Avis, Thrifty,** and **Budget** all have offices at the Dubrovnik and Zagreb airports, plus other city locations.

Croatia's main highways (singular, *autocesta;* plural, *autoceste)* are well-marked and well-maintained. Secondary roads vary in quality and can range from excellent to unmarked dirt tracks. Gas stations are readily available on the autoceste, along main highways, and outside smaller towns. These are usually "hyper" gas stations, in that most have attached restaurants, convenience markets, and picnic areas. Gas station restrooms are generally immaculate in Croatia, and some even offer shower facilities. Stations are typically open from 7am to 7pm daily, until 10pm in summer.

Maps that note gas stations across the country are available, and a wise investment if you plan on driving long distances. They're usually available at gas stations. See www.ina.hr and www.hak.hr for details.

Note: Almost every city and town in Croatia seems to be converting intersections with traffic lights to roundabouts with varying rules for entering and exiting, so proceed with caution.

Warning: Police are strictly enforcing Croatia's drinking and driving laws and posted speed limits. If you are a driver under 24 years of age, zero tolerance (0.0 percent blood alcohol) applies. For those 24 and over, a limit of 0.5 percent is the rule.

The speed limit in urban areas is 50kmph (30 mph) unless otherwise marked, 80kmph (50 mph) on secondary roads, and 130kmph (80 mph) on highways. You'll have to pay fines on the spot. If you're stopped for any reason, you will be expected to produce a valid driver's license, car registration papers, a rental contract, and an insurance certificate. Watch for speed traps along the coastal highway and in rural towns and villages.

BY TRAIN

Croatian Railways (www.hzpp.hr) is an efficient way to travel between Zagreb and towns in the northern and inland parts of the country. The overnight train from Zagreb to Split is outfitted with couchettes, meaning you can get a good night's sleep and wake up at your destination. All of Croatia's major cities except Dubrovnik are connected by train service.

MONEY & COSTS

THE VALUE OF THE KUNA VS. OTHER POPULAR CURRENCIES

Cro (kn)	US$	Can$	UK£	Euro (€)	Aus$	NZ$
1	18¢	19¢	11þ	0.13€	19¢	21¢

This guide lists prices in the local currency. The currency conversions quoted above were correct at press time. However, rates fluctuate, so before departing consult a currency exchange website such as **www.xe.com** or **www.oanda.com/convert/classic** to check up-to-the-minute rates.

Currency

The Croatian national currency is the **kuna (kn),** which comes in notes of 10, 20, 50, 100, 200, 500, and 1,000. One kuna equals 100 lipa, and coins with values of 5, 10, 20, and 50 lipa and 1, 2, and 5 kuna are in circulation. To convert prices in kunas to current prices in U.S. dollars, go to www.xe.com/ucc.

Following Croatia's E.U. membership, some Croatian businesses, most notably hotels and tourist agencies, began to express their prices in euros and kuna, though euros are not officially accepted. Foreign currency can be exchanged at post offices, banks, and exchange offices. Numerous hotels and travel agencies also will exchange currency, but beware of the service charges, which can be as high as 3 percent.

Warning: Kunas and euros are very similar in look but dissimilar in value: One euro is worth seven times as much as one kuna. Be sure you separate the two and keep the currencies in separate compartments of your wallet.

ATMs

The easiest and best way to get cash in Croatia is from an ATM (automated teller machine, aka Bankomat in Croatia). The **Cirrus** (www.mastercard.com) and **PLUS** (www.visa.com) networks span the globe; look on the back of your bank card to see which network you're on, then call or check online for ATM locations at your destination. Be sure you know your personal identification number (PIN) before you leave home, and be sure to find out your daily withdrawal limit before you depart. Also keep in mind that many banks impose a fee every time a card is used at another bank's ATM, and that fee can be higher for international transactions ($5 or more) than for domestic ones (where they're rarely more than $3). On top of this, the bank from which you withdraw cash may charge its own fee. To compare banks' ATM fees within the U.S., use www.bankrate.com. For international withdrawal fees, ask your bank.

Credit Cards

Credit cards are a safe way to carry money: They provide a convenient record of all your expenses, and they generally offer relatively good exchange rates. In Croatia, credit cards are accepted by most hotels and restaurants in larger cities, but they generally are not accepted for private accommodations or in rural areas. In addition, some establishments that accept credit cards will offer a discount if you pay in cash.

You can get cash advances on your credit card at banks or ATMs, provided you know your PIN. If you've forgotten your PIN, or didn't even know you had one, call the number on the back of your credit card and ask the bank to send it to you. It usually takes 5 to 7 business days, though some banks will provide the number over the phone if you tell them your mother's maiden name or some other personal information. *Warning:* Credit card companies tend to charge rather large (some might even say exorbitant) fees for providing cash advances.

Keep in mind that when you use your credit card abroad, most banks assess a 2 percent fee above the 1 percent fee charged by Visa or MasterCard or American Express for currency conversion on credit charges. There is also often a service charge on foreign transactions. Even so, credit cards still may be the smart way to go when you factor in things like hefty ATM fees and higher traveler's check exchange rates (and service fees).

Visa, MasterCard, Diners Club, and American Express credit cards are accepted in most Croatian establishments that accept plastic. The Maestro debit card is also widely accepted.

Croatia is an affordable country compared to other European nations, though Dubrovnik stands out as far more expensive than other Croatian destinations. Hotel rooms and rental cars will be your highest expenditures, but in general, food, entertainment, and public transportation costs are a little below those of nearby E.U. countries, such as Austria and Italy.

WHAT THINGS cost IN CROATIA

Airport taxi	150kn–250kn
Cappuccino	10kn–16kn
Coca-Cola	20kn–25kn
Half-liter beer	20kn
Ice-cream cone	7kn per scoop
Pasta dish	50kn–80kn
Pizza	50kn–80kn
Three-course dinner	150kn

Prices outside metropolitan areas in general will be 20 to 40 percent lower.

HEALTH

Staying Healthy

HEALTHCARE AVAILABILITY

Croatia provides its citizens with excellent, all-inclusive healthcare. Foreign tourists do not have to pay for medical services if there is a signed health insurance convention between Croatia and their home country—nationals from E.U. member countries should carry their European Health Insurance Card (EHIC) with them to benefit from this agreement. Healthcare costs for tourists from a country that does not have a signed convention with Croatia are paid directly by the user at the time of service.

No special vaccinations are required to enter Croatia. Contact IAMAT, the **International Association for Medical Assistance to Travelers** (www.iamat.org; © **716/754-4883**, or 416/652-0137 in Canada) for tips on travel and health concerns in the countries you're visiting, and for lists of local, English-speaking doctors. The **United States Centers for Disease Control and Prevention** (www.cdc.gov; © **800/232-4636**) provides up-to-date information on health hazards by region or country and offers tips on food safety. **Travel Health Online** (www.tripprep.com), sponsored by a consortium of travel medicine practitioners, also offers helpful advice on traveling abroad. You can find listings of reliable medical clinics overseas at the **International Society of Travel Medicine** (www.istm.org).

Common Ailments

BITES & STINGS   Mosquitoes found in most parts of Croatia generally do not carry malaria. Use an insect repellent containing DEET. Bees and wasps are commonplace, especially on some islands, and where beekeeping is an industry. Be especially aware of this if you are allergic to bee venom, and always carry an epinephrine autoinjector (EpiPen) for emergencies.

DIETARY RED FLAGS   Croatian food generally is not spicy, so gastric sensitivities are rarely triggered by the national cuisine. However, if you have fish or shellfish allergies, be sure to ask about ingredients, especially when dining on the coast. Restaurants serving vegetarian choices are becoming more commonplace, especially in larger cities, and you can find a cheese *burek* or plain pasta almost anywhere.

SEA URCHINS & OTHER WILDLIFE CONCERNS   Sea urchin needles and sharp rocks pose the greatest health hazards to swimmers in Croatia, especially around rockier beaches. It is best to wear rubber swim shoes both on the beach and in the water. These are available in most resort areas and in towns near the sea. Snake sightings are rare but can occur in wooded areas, especially in spring. If you are bitten, immobilize the area of the bite and get medical help as quickly as possible.

SUN/ELEMENTS/EXTREME WEATHER EXPOSURE   Visitors should be aware that summer in Croatia can be very hot, especially in the southern regions. Air-conditioning is not prevalent in private accommodations or outside of the larger cities. Sunstroke and heat exhaustion can overtake the unwary quickly. Be sure to drink lots of water and get to a shady area or into air-conditioning if you feel dizzy and tired or if you develop a severe headache. These may be signs of heat exhaustion. Sunstroke is more serious and may require emergency medical attention. Symptoms can include fainting and/or agitation. Always carry enough sunscreen with an SPF of at least 15 for all members of your party.

What to Do If You Get Sick Away from Home

Pack **prescription medications** in your carry-on luggage and carry them in their original containers, with pharmacy labels—otherwise they won't make it through airport security. Bring along copies of your prescriptions in case you lose your pills or run out. Don't forget an extra pair of contact lenses or prescription glasses. Carry the generic names of prescription medicines, in case a local doctor is unfamiliar with the brand name. *Note:* In Croatia, *all* medicines, even over-the-counter medications like aspirin, are sold only at pharmacies; other drugs require a Croatian doctor's prescription.

Additional **emergency numbers** are listed in "Fast Facts" below.

SAFETY

Croatia generally is very safe for travelers. Theft and crimes against persons are not commonplace. However, you should exercise caution anytime you're out and about in an unfamiliar area after dark wherever you are.

In some areas, land mines left over from the 1991 war can pose hazards to unsuspecting travelers. According to www.landmines.org, more than 700,000 land mines were buried in Croatia, mostly in eastern Slavonia, around Zadar in northern Dalmatia, with some near Dubrovnik in southern Dalmatia. The government has been demining the country since the end of the War for Independence in 1995, but finding and destroying the ordnance is a slow process. Usually, suspected land-mine areas are marked with red-and-white skull-and-crossbones signs (in Croatian), but you shouldn't tramp around any part of the countryside unless you have a local guide, especially in the above areas. Land mines kill a few Croatians every year. These are mostly hunters who disregard posted signs, or farmers who are impatient to till unswept fields.

SPECIALIZED TRAVEL RESOURCES

In addition to the destination-specific resources listed below, please visit Frommers. com to find specialized travel resources.

Gay & Lesbian Travelers

In Roman Catholic Croatia, gays are tolerated but not celebrated. The country legalized homosexuality in 1977, but overt homosexual behavior is frowned upon in general and may be met with hostility in rural areas. Except for a few places in Zagreb, gay clubs are almost nonexistent, though some nightclubs and discos are patronized almost exclusively by homosexuals. During the summer, many gays frequent FKK (nudist) beaches (p. 235), the city of Dubrovnik, and the island of Hvar. As in many other cities worldwide, the last Saturday in June is Gay Pride Day in Zagreb.

Although many agencies offer tours and travel itineraries specifically for gay and lesbian travelers, few include Croatia on their list of destinations. **The IGLTA/International Gay and Lesbian Travel Association** (www.iglta.org; ✆ **954/630-1637**) is the trade association for the gay and lesbian travel industry, and it offers an online directory of gay- and lesbian-friendly travel businesses and tour operators. For Croatia-specific tips, check out the **Friendly Croatia** website www.friendlycroatia.com, which includes destination guides for gays.

Gay Travel (www.gaytravel.com; ☏ 858/504-7132) is an agency specializing in the LGBT community and helping them find gay-friendly destinations. Zagreb and Dubrovnik are included in the agency's portfolio.

Out Adventures (www.out-adventures.com; ☏ 866/360-1152) specializes in LGBT travel. In 2014, it included a 10-day Croatia Gay Cruise & Tour in its portfolio.

Out Traveler (www.outtraveler.com) is an LGBT travel site that posts occasional articles about Croatia.

British travelers should click on the "Travel" link at **thegayuk.com** for advice and gay-friendly trip ideas.

The following travel guides are available at many bookstores, or can be ordered from any online bookseller: "Spartacus International Gay Guide, 2014–2015" (Briand Bedford; www.spartacusworld.com), and the "Damron" guides (www.damron.com), with separate annual books for gay men and lesbians.

Travelers with Disabilities

In Croatia, as in other parts of Europe, many hotels, restaurants, and sites are not equipped to provide easy access for visitors with disabilities. However, public restroom facilities in train and bus stations, airports, and some hotels usually have been modified to accommodate wheelchairs. In general, museums, churches, private accommodations, ferries, shuttle boats, and local trams have not. There are a few exceptions and those are noted throughout this book. Most disabilities shouldn't stop anyone from traveling. There are more options and resources out there than ever before.

Organizations that offer a vast range of assistance to travelers with disabilities include **MossRehab** (www.mossrehab.com; ☏ 800/CALL-MOSS); the **American Foundation for the Blind** (**AFB;** www.afb.org; ☏ 800/232-5463); and **SATH** (Society for Accessible Travel & Hospitality; www.sath.org; ☏ 212/447-7284). **AirAmbulanceCard.com** is now partnered with SATH and allows travelers to preselect topnotch hospitals in case of an emergency.

Many travel agencies offer customized tours and itineraries for travelers with disabilities. Among them are **Flying Wheels Travel** (www.flyingwheelstravel.com; ☏ 507/451-5005) and **Accessible Journeys** (www.disabilitytravel.com; ☏ 800/846-4537 or 610/521-0339).

Flying With Disability (www.flying-with-disability.org) is a comprehensive information source on airplane travel. **Avis Rent a Car** (☏ 888/879-4273) has an "Avis Access" program that offers services for customers with special travel needs. These include specially outfitted vehicles with swivel seats, spinner knobs, and hand controls; mobility scooter rentals; and accessible bus service. Be sure to reserve well in advance.

Also check out the quarterly accessible-travel magazine "Emerging Horizons" (www.emerginghorizons.com), available by online and by subscription ($16.95/year U.S.).

The "Accessible Travel" link at **Mobility-Advisor.com** (www.mobility-advisor.com) offers a variety of travel resources to travelers with disabilities.

British travelers should contact **DisabledHolidays.com** (www.disabledholiday directory.co.uk; ☏ 0800/993-0796) for a listing of wheelchair-friendly hotels and resorts, including several in Dubrovnik.

Social Etiquette

When entering churches, monasteries, or other religious buildings in Croatia, visitors should dress respectfully. For both men and women, shoulders and thighs should be covered.

Family Travel

If you have trouble getting your kids out of the house in the morning, dragging them thousands of miles away may seem like an insurmountable challenge. But family travel can be immensely rewarding, giving you new ways of seeing the world through younger eyes.

Recommended family travel websites include **Family Travel Forum** (www.myfamilytravels.com), a comprehensive site that offers customized trip planning, and **Family Traveller** (www.familytraveller.com), which offers advice to anyone travelling with babies, children, and teenagers. **TravelWithYourKids.com** (www.travelwithyourkids.com) is a comprehensive site written by parents for parents, offering sound advice for long-distance and international travel with children.

Women Travelers

Women do not face any particular travel difficulties in Croatia They are treated with courtesy and respect in both big cities and small towns. However, female visitors who go out in public looking unkempt might earn a few disapproving looks as Croatian women take great pride in their appearance and what they wear. Women should leave the sloppy p.j. bottoms and flip-flops at home and opt for a put-together look to fit in. If any church visits are planned, remember that women are expected to wear tops with sleeves and bottoms that fall beneath the knees. Churches and some museums post their dress codes and they will turn you away if you are not in compliance (the same applies to men, see below).

For general travel resources for women, go to www.frommers.com/planning.

Senior Travelers

In most Croatian cities, reduced-price admission to theaters, museums, and other attractions is available for "retired persons," generally considered to be those aged 65 and over. Otherwise, there are no breaks for seniors, perhaps because Croatia's senior population is so active and vibrant.

Several reliable agencies and organizations target the 50-plus market. **ElderTreks** (www.eldertreks.com; © **800/741-7956**, or 416/558-5000 outside North America) offers small-group tours to off-the-beaten-path and adventure-travel locations, including Croatia, for travelers 50 and older.

Student Travelers

If you are a student, you should apply for an **International Student Identity Card** (ISIC; www.isic.org), which qualifies you for substantial savings on rail passes, plane tickets, entrance fees, and more. It also provides basic travel insurance and a 24-hour help line. The card is valid for a maximum of 16 months.

You can apply for the card online or from **STA Travel** (www.statravel.com; © **800/781-4040** in the U.S. and Canada). Check the website to locate STA Travel offices worldwide.

If you're no longer a student but are still under 26, you can get an **International Youth Travel Card (IYTC)** from the same people. It entitles you to some discounts.

Travel CUTS (www.travelcuts.com; ℂ **800/667-2887**) offers similar services for both Canadians and U.S. residents.

Single Travelers

On package vacations, single travelers often are hit with a "single supplement" in addition to the base price. To avoid it, you can agree to room with other single travelers or find a compatible roommate from one of many roommate-locator agencies.

The **IndependentTraveler.com** (www.independenttraveler.com) is intended to help those traveling alone to plan their trip, and includes a forum where you can ask for advice from other solo travelers.

Many reputable tour companies offer singles-only trips. **Backroads** (www.backroads. com; ℂ **800/462-2848**) offers "Singles + Solos" active-travel trips to destinations worldwide.

The British company **One Traveller** (www.onetraveller.co.uk; ℂ **0044/1760-722-011**) arranges holidays for mature singles, including the eight-day "Croatia's Dalmatian Coast" tour.

Contiki (www.contiki.com) arranges tours for ages 18 to 35, including a "Croatian Island Hopper," which attracts a mix of nationalities and plenty of singles.

For more information, check out Eleanor Berman's classic "Traveling Solo: Advice and Ideas for More Than 250 Great Vacations, 6th Edition" (Globe Pequot), updated in 2008.

For more information on traveling single, go to www.frommers.com/planning.

SUSTAINABLE TOURISM

The most beautiful countries also tend to be the most conscientious when it comes to taking care of the natural environment. Most visitors to Croatia are immediately impressed by the country's air quality, water cleanliness, and unspoiled landscapes and seascapes.

However, with the rise in the number of supermarkets selling pre-packaged goods, waste management is an ever-increasing problem, especially on the islands. The state is trying to make the public more aware of the need to reduce waste and to recycle.

Bottle Collection

In 2006, Croatia's Ministry for Environmental Protection introduced a policy that has eliminated virtually 100 percent of glass and plastic-bottle litter in the country. Under the plan, people can bring any glass or plastic beverage bottle to any market larger than 200 sq. m. (2,153 sq. ft.) and they'll receive 50 lipa, or half a kuna (approximately 6kn to the U.S. dollar), for each bottle returned, even if they purchased the drink at another store.

It is not unusual to see people searching garbage bins for bottles to return, and collecting them in big plastic bags. In fact, some bottle collectors are so keen they'll watch over as you drink from a bottle so they can take it as soon as you've finished.

The success of the program has been dramatic. Croatia estimates that more than two billion bottles have been collected since the return policy went into effect—that's virtually every bottle sold in the country. Consequently, it is extremely rare to see glass or plastic bottles marring the landscape anywhere in Croatia, with none on the beach, in the rivers, or on the streets. ***Bonus:*** Many new jobs have been created in the recycling industry thanks to the program.

Blue Flag Beaches

The Blue Flag is an exclusive eco-award given to beaches and marinas that meet strict criteria for both water quality and environmental management. It was introduced in 1987 and sets common standards of good management across Europe. Croatia prides itself on the number and quality of its Blue Flag beaches and marinas, which totaled 117 in 2014.

To earn a Blue Flag, a facility has to pass several tests. Water quality is sampled 20 times in summer and must reach the higher of two standards set in the organization's Bathing Water Directive. Beach management criteria include cleanliness, wheelchair access, dog control, first aid, safety, and environmental information. Marina management criteria include provisions for information about the environment, adequate containers for trash and special waste, clean toilets and washing facilities, and safety equipment. Beaches and marinas are monitored both before and during the award year to ensure that all criteria are being fulfilled and that high standards are being maintained. For more information go to www.blueflag.org.

Smoking Ban

In May 2009, Croatia issued a total smoking ban in all public places, including cafes, restaurants, bars, and clubs. (The government backpedaled on the directive four months later, after small business owners complained they were being ruined en masse.) The ban is now optional for smaller establishments; others can accommodate smokers as long as they provide a private, separately ventilated space for them. But in a country where almost everyone smoked just five years ago, this is progress.

Birds & Bees

Croatia fiercely protects its natural resources and wildlife. It maintains eight national parks, and countless arboretums, botanical gardens, wetlands, and animal habitats. Bird-watchers in Croatia delight in multiple opportunities to observe a variety of feathered phenoms.

The **Lonjsko Polje Nature Park** (see p. 66) in north-central Croatia is home to numerous wetlands and bird sanctuaries. The historic settlement of Čigoć and villages in the surrounding area not only comprise habitats for hundreds of species of insects, fish, frogs, and birds (including Čigoć's famous storks), they also protect collections of ethnographic artifacts, including chimney-free houses made of centuries-old timbers.

The **Kopački Rit Nature Park** (see p. 70) in Slavonia on Croatia's eastern border is the country's most fascinating wetland. Besides huge bird populations, the area is beginning to attract cyclists, hikers, and wine lovers thanks to the redevelopment of bike trails, removal of land mines, and a rebirth of the region's vast vineyards.

The **Adriatic Dolphin Project** has research centers on the islands of Lošinj and Vis, working to study and protect the population, ecology, genetics, acoustics, and habitats of bottlenose dolphins and other cetaceous species of the Adriatic. This is an E.U.

GENERAL RESOURCES FOR green TRAVEL

In addition to the resources for Croatia listed above, the following websites provide valuable wide-ranging information on sustainable travel. For a list of even more sustainable resources, as well as tips and explanations on how to travel greener, visit www.frommers.com/planning.

○ **Responsible Travel** (www.responsibletravel.com) is a great source of sustainable travel ideas; the site is run by a spokesperson for ethical tourism in the travel industry. **Sustainable Travel International** (www.sustainabletravel.org) also promotes ethical tourism practices, and manages an extensive directory of sustainable properties and tour operators around the world.

○ In the U.K., **Tourism Concern** (www.tourismconcern.org.uk) works to reduce social and environmental problems connected to tourism. The **Association of Independent Tour Operators** (**AITO;** www.aito.com) is a group of specialist operators leading the field in making vacations sustainable.

○ In Canada, **www.greenliving online.com** offers extensive information on how to travel

sustainably, including a travel and transport section. It also profiles the best green shops and services in Toronto, Vancouver, and Calgary.

○ In Australia, the national body that sets guidelines and standards for eco-tourism is **Ecotourism Australia** (www.ecotourism.org.au).

○ **Carbonfund** (www.carbonfund.org), and **TerraPass** (www.terrapass.org) provide info on "carbon offsetting," for balancing out the greenhouse gas emitted during flights.

○ For information on animal-friendly issues throughout the world, visit **Tread Lightly** (www.treadlightly.org). For information about the ethics of swimming with dolphins, visit **Whale and Dolphin Conservation** (us.whales.org).

○ **Volunteer International** (www.volunteerinternational.org) has a list of questions to help you determine the intentions and the nature of a volunteer program. For general info on volunteer travel, visit **www.goabroad.com/volunteer-abroad** and **www.idealist.org**.

Phare project, and it includes a marine education center on Lošinj with permanent and temporary exhibits, interactive multimedia presentations, lectures, and education programs for visitors. Go to www.blue-world.org for more information.

Eco-conscious Hotels

Hotels are gradually taking steps to protect the environment, not least because claiming to be eco-friendly has become seen as a smart marketing ploy.

Almost all the bigger hotels in Croatia have installed smart rooms with on-demand electricity that works only if you insert your key card in a central slot. In a bid to reduce unnecessary machine-washing, many hotels no longer replace all the bath towels daily. If you want a towel replaced, you should leave it on the bathroom floor—if you hang it up to dry, the maid will presume that you are happy to reuse it.

The **Radisson BLU** in Dubrovnik was built with a green roof and an HVAC system that is cooled by the ocean. The **Kempinski Adriatic** uses nothing but stored rainwater to keep its 18-hole golf course green. The hotel also grows its own herbs for use in its restaurants.

Agritourism (working farms offering accommodation and/or meals) is another growing sector of Croatian hospitality. Travelers can enjoy an eco-conscious experience in a rural environment, with meals prepared from local seasonal produce, much of which is organic.

An excellent resource for booking eco-friendly accommodation is the U.K.-based group **Responsible Travel** (www.responsibletravel.com).

Renewable Energy

During the Yugoslav era (1945–1991), hydroelectric power was developed in Croatia, and it still provides a considerable proportion of the country's energy needs. Since 2004, Croatia has also embraced wind power to produce energy—in Dalmatia, most notably on the island of Pag, you'll see wind turbines dotting the horizon. With its sunny climate, there is also potential for further developing solar power in Croatia.

The sustainable travel industry in Croatia is in its infancy, but conservation and environmental management are not. Croatia always has taken care of its land, water, and air, and all indications are that it will continue to do so.

STAYING CONNECTED

Staying connected with the folks back home is easier than ever thanks to innovations in telecommunications. No matter what kind of hardware you use, you'll need to know (initially) which numbers to punch in and their proper sequence.

TO MAKE INTERNATIONAL CALLS TO CROATIA:

1. Dial the international access code: 011 from the U.S.; 00 from the U.K., Ireland, or New Zealand; or 0011 from Australia.
2. Dial Croatia's country code, 385.
3. Dial the area code, omitting the first zero. For Zagreb, for example, the area code is 01, so you just dial 1.
4. Dial the phone number.

TO MAKE INTERNATIONAL CALLS FROM CROATIA:

1. Dial the access code 00.
2. Dial the country code (U.S. or Canada 1, U.K. 44, Ireland 353, Australia 61, New Zealand 64).
3. Dial the area code.
4. Dial the number.

For example, if you wanted to call the British Embassy in Washington, D.C., from Croatia you would dial 00-1-202-588-7800.

TO CALL FROM ONE AREA CODE TO ANOTHER WITHIN CROATIA   Dial the Croatian area code, including the zero, followed by the phone number.

TO MAKE A LOCAL CALL WITHIN A CROATIAN AREA   Dial the phone number. No codes necessary. Local calls cost about 5kn per minute.

FOR DIRECTORY ASSISTANCE Dial ℂ **11880** or 11888 if you're looking for a number inside Croatia, and dial 11802 for numbers in all other countries.

TOLL-FREE NUMBERS Toll-free numbers in Croatia start with 0800. *Warning:* Calling a 1-800 number in the United States from Croatia is *not* toll-free. In fact, it costs the same as an overseas call.

Croatian SIM Cards

To reduce the cost of calls and text messages during your stay in Croatia, you might consider buying a Croatian SIM card for your mobile phone. All Croatian mobile phone numbers begin with the digits "09."

The main mobile phone network providers each offer special deals to foreign visitors: **Hrvatski Telecom** (www.hrvatskitelekom.hr/visiting-croatia); **Tele 2** (www.tele2.hr/welcome-to-croatia); and **Vipnet** (www.vipnet.hr/tourist-offer/en).

Smartphones

Advances in smartphone technology have fueled a boom in the use and ownership of these one-stop communication-media wonders. However, their services come at a price. Whether your phone of choice is a BlackBerry, an iPhone, or some other brand, you should check how it works with European carriers, so as to avoid nasty surprises when your bill comes in.

SPECIAL-INTEREST TRIPS & TOURS

Special-Interest Trips

Special-interest tours abound in Croatia. Tour operators in and outside the country can arrange tours to suit almost any specification.

ADRIATICA.NET This general tour operator is based in Zagreb and puts together stays in many of Croatia's lighthouses and farmhouses, in addition to arranging sailing vacations (www.adriatica.net).

ARCHAEOLOGICAL INSTITUTE OF AMERICA This archaeology-oriented group offers a 9-day "Idyllic Islands and Majestic Shores of Croatia & Montenegro" tour, and a 12-day "Fabled Sarajevo and the Glorious Coast of Croatia & Montenegro" tour (www.archaeological.org/tours/programs).

MARTIN RANDALL A cultural holiday group that runs art, architecture, archaeology, and history tours, Martin Randall puts on a 14-day "Western Balkans" tour that includes Zagreb and Osijek, and an 8-day "Dark Age Brilliance" tour that includes Poreč. Note that this group's flights leave from London, so U.S. travelers have to make their own way to the U.K. (www.martinrandall.com).

SECRET DALMATIA A Dalmatia-based company run by local experts and enthusiasts, Secret Dalmatia offers signature tours and custom experiences, including gourmet cuisine, wine tasting, historic site and national park visits, and sailing (www.secretdalmatia.com).

SMITHSONIAN JOURNEYS This renowned institution offers several multi-country tours and cruises, taking in sections of Croatia's Adriatic coast, including lectures on the area's culture and history (www.smithsonianjourneys.org).

Sailing

With 1,185 islands and miles of coastline, Croatia attracts a huge number of boating and watersports enthusiasts. Croatia has a large number of charter companies and well-equipped marinas.

Most charters are on a one-week basis, running Saturday to Saturday. You can charter a skippered boat or go "bareboat" (without skipper, although you'll need to have the required boating certifications). You can also join a flotilla (a group of boats under the guidance of one or more skippers). Hostesses can be hired to clean and cook.

EUROMARINE CHARTER This is a reliable charter company dealing in sailing boats, catamarans, motorboats, and luxury yachts. Euromarine (charter.euromarine.com.hr; ℂ 01/555-2200) has bases in Dubrovnik, Split, Pula, and Biograd and Sukošan (both close to Zadar and the islets of Kornati National Park).

SAIL CROATIA This outfit puts together customized floating holidays for experienced sailors and novices alike. Sail Croatia's (www.sailcroatia.net; ℂ 021/494-888) main charter base is in Kaštela (near Split) in Dalmatia.

SUNSAIL A Florida-based international company, Sunsail (www.sunsail.com; ℂ 888/350-3568) has fleets of yachts around the world, including charter bases in Dubrovnik and Marina Agana (near Split).

ULTRA SAILING Based in the ACI marina Split, Ultra Sailing (www.ultra-sailing.hr; ℂ 021/398-578) runs both a summer sailing school (with courses at various levels) and weekly yacht charters (with skipper if required).

Adventure Sports

Croatians are avid sports people with a deep love for the great outdoors, so it should come as no surprise that adventure sports, both sea-based and land-based, are well catered to here.

ADRIATIC KAYAK TOURS Based in Dubrovnik, Adriatic Kayak Tours (www.adriatickayaktours.com; ℂ 020/312-770) arranges half-day, one-day, and one-week tours that combine sea kayaking and cycling.

ADVENTURE DALMATIA Offering one-day and multi-day trips in various parts of Dalmatia, Adventure Dalmatia's (www.adventuredalmatia.com; ℂ 021/540-642) offerings including activities such as hiking, rafting, rock climbing, canyoning, and sea kayaking.

BIOKOVO ACTIVE HOLIDAYS Based in Makarska in Dalmatia, Biokovo (www.biokovo.net; ℂ 021/679-655) is a group that runs one-day guided hikes and mountain biking on Mount Biokovo, sea kayaking near Brela, and rafting down the Cetina near Omiš. One- and two-week tours in Dalmatia that take in a variety of adventure sports along the way can also be arranged.

HVAR ADVENTURE Specializing in half-day, one-day, and multi-day activities on the island of Hvar. Hvar Adventure (www.hvar-adventure.com; ℂ 021/717-813) sports offerings include sea kayaking, sailing, hiking, rock climbing, cycling, and wine tasting.

Windsurfing

Bol on the island of Brač and Viganj near Orebić on the Pelješac Peninsula are Croatia's biggest draws for windsurfing fans. In Bol, go to **Big Blue Sport** (www.big bluesport.com; ☏ **091/449-7087**) for windsurfing lessons and equipment rental. On Pelješac, check with the **Orebić Tourist Office** (www.tz-orebic.com; ☏ **020/713-718**) for information on where to rent boards and get lessons in Viganj.

Cycling

Bicycling for tourists is growing in popularity in Croatia, although currently bike trails are regional and not very well advertised. Istria is leading the way: The Istria Tourist Board has set up an excellent **Istria Bike** website (www.istria-bike.com), offering detailed information on bike trails, accommodation, and bike repair shops in the region.

BLUE BIKE ZAGREB   Offering cycling tours guided by locals, Blue Bike Zagreb (www.zagrebbybike.com; ☏ **098/246-320**) has tours both in Zagreb's city center and up on the green slopes of Mount Sljeme.

CYCLING CROATIA   This professionally run, Zagreb-based company offers one-week guided and self-guided tours in Istria and Dalmatia, with accommodations and meals included (www.cyclingcroatia.com; ☏ **01/580-3770**).

Food & Wine Tours

Increasingly, Croatian entrepreneurs are marketing local products by developing wine and olive roads, as well as special excursions for truffle hunting and wine dinners.

As with many things, Istria is a little ahead of the other regions in terms of developing its potential. The Istria Tourist Board has set up the excellent **Istra Gourmet** website (www.istria-gourmet.com), listing the region's top culinary experiences, such as wine roads and wineries open for tasting, olive oil producers, truffle-hunting providers, and top restaurants.

CULINARY CROATIA   This establishment arranges one-week food tours, as well as one-day wine trips and cooking classes, primarily in Dalmatia, but also in Istria and Zagreb (www.culinary-croatia.com).

DUBROVNIK WINE TOURS   This tour company arranges one-day wine tasting excursions from Dubrovnik and three-day vineyard tours to Pelješac and Korčula with a British–Croatian sommelier (www.dubrovnikwinetours.com).

EAT ISTRIA   This Pula-based company offers one-day wine tours and one-day or weekend cookery classes (www.eatistria.com).

TASTE OF ADRIATIC   This Rijeka-based travel agency specializes in food and wine tours, including agritourism, mainly in Istria (www.tasteofadriatic.com; ☏ **095/894-9735**).

ZAGREB BITES   Specializing in private one-day wine tours departing from Zagreb, this company also offers guided half-day food and drink trails within the capital (www.zagrebites.com).

An excellent website for an overview of Croatia's best food and wine venues (plus news and itineraries) is www.tasteofcroatia.org.

Escorted General-Interest Tours

Escorted tours are structured group tours, with a group leader. The price usually includes everything from airfare to hotels, meals, tours, admission costs, and local transportation.

Despite the fact that escorted tours require big deposits and predetermined hotels, restaurants, and itineraries, many travelers derive security and peace of mind from the structure they offer. Escorted tours—whether they're navigated by bus or boat—let travelers sit back and enjoy the trip without having to drive or sweat the details. Escorted tours will take you to the maximum number of attractions in the minimum amount of time with the least amount of hassle. They're particularly convenient for people with limited mobility, and they can be a great way to make new friends.

On the downside, you'll have little opportunity for serendipitous interactions with locals. The tours can be packed with activities, leaving little room for individual sightseeing, whim, or adventure. They often focus on the heavily traveled sites, so you miss out on many a lesser-known gem.

Countless tour operators offer packages to Croatia. The following are highly regarded and reliable:

ABERCROMBIE AND KENT   This international luxury travel company offers both tailor-made and pre-arranged itineraries. The company's portfolio includes a 9-night "Classic Croatia" tour, taking in Split, Trogir, Salona, Hvar Town, Ston, Dubrovnik, and Cavtat (www.abercrombiekent.com).

ADRIATIC TOURS   A San Pedro–based company founded in 1974, Adriatic specializes in Croatia and offers both escorted and hosted tours to almost all regions of the country. The company also puts together religious tours and cruises (www.adriatic-tours.com; ✆ 310/548-1446).

CROATIA TRAVEL AGENCY   This New York–based company offers a full complement of itineraries for Croatia, running from 8- through 14-day adventures (www.croatiatravel.com; ✆ 800/662-7628).

KOMPAS   A Florida-based company specializing in Central and Eastern Europe, Kompas offers a range of short city stays (Zagreb, Split, and Dubrovnik), escorted tours through Croatia and neighboring countries, and Adriatic cruises (www.kompas.net; ✆ 954/771-9200).

PRIVATE GUIDES   If you have the resources, consider booking a private English-speaking guide who can not only plan a custom itinerary for you, but also arrange transport, transfers, and admittance to otherwise inaccessible sites. The best way to find a reliable local guide is to contact the respective city's tourist board (listed in each section of this guide).

BB, Don't Forget My Number

BB means *bez broja* (without number). This is quite common in Croatia, particularly if the place is a well-known church or restaurant. If you're tracking down an address with a street name followed by bb and you're having trouble finding it, you may need to ask a local for directions.

For more information on escorted general-interest tours, including questions to ask before booking your trip, see www.frommers.com/planning.

TIPS ON ACCOMMODATIONS

Hotel room prices in Croatia vary considerably with location and time of year. Generally, hotel prices in inland cities and towns are the most stable, while hotels in tourist areas along the coast sometimes publish as many as seven rate schedules based on time of year.

In this guide, we have quoted prices for August (or sometimes Jul–Aug), as this is peak season, when the majority of visitors come to Croatia. You can expect prices to be approximately half that in winter (if the hotel stays open all year), and 30 percent lower in spring and fall.

Also note that although the official currency in Croatia is the kuna (kn), most hotel prices are posted in euros (€), so as to make them quickly translatable for foreigners. Croatian hotel rates almost always include breakfast (usually a continental buffet), while private accommodations almost always do not. Private accommodations rented through individuals are the least expensive and can cost as little as $20 per person per night. In a word: *bargain.*

The cost of one night in a double room at a 5-star hotel in central Zagreb will compare favorably with the cost of a similar room in either New York or London. But all the same, bear in mind that Croatia is no longer a cheap option.

Croatia now has more than 600 star-rated hotels that are a combination of '60s and '70s high-rises; stately, ornate, turn-of-the-20th-century buildings; and, more recently, family-run boutiques. Since 2000, Croatia has been in a "renovate and rebuild" mode, and many establishments have completed or are now undergoing updating and upgrading.

HOTELS Most hotels in Croatia carry international star ratings from 1 to 5, which relate primarily to amenities—in some cases, the star ratings can seem a little arbitrary. In reality, 1-star hotels are non-existent and 2-star properties are few and far between. An en-suite bathroom is now a requirement for 2-star hotels, which generally offer basic but comfortable accommodation. A 3-star room has a private bathroom (usually with a shower, not a tub), TV, and perhaps other amenities, though this category is unpredictable and can be a value or a rip-off depending on management. Most 4-star hotels will offer a room with a larger bathroom, possibly with a tub; good-quality furnishings; little extras, such as toiletries; and other facilities like a fitness center, restaurant, and pool. In the luxury category, the number of 5-star hotels has increased since 2000, most notably in Dubrovnik. These of course offer the highest level of comfort, amenities, and contemporary design, and in some cases rival the best the U.S. has to offer.

Almost all rooms and apartments in Croatia now have Wi-Fi, and most have air-conditioning, though this should not be necessary in traditional Dalmatian buildings, where thick stone walls keep interiors cool even in summer.

Croatian chains tend to be local: Arenaturist in Pula, Maistra in Rovinj, Solaris in Šibenik. These generally manage either package hotels in resort areas or former grande dames in various stages of repair that range from crumbling to completely refurbished.

For more information about the small family-run hotels, visit the **Association of Family and Small Hotels of Croatia** website (www.omh.hr).

PRIVATE ACCOMMODATIONS   Private rooms and apartments are found in most tourist destinations in Croatia and generally offer good deals. These are now strictly controlled, and divided into four categories, with star ratings. Some proprietors will refuse to rent for fewer than four nights, or if they do, they will charge extra. Licensed private accommodations are best booked through local tourist agencies, but you can find and book private villas and rooms via www.adriatica.net, too. Alternatively, the international booking site **Airbnb** (www.airbnb.com) lists a host of properties in Croatia.

SOBE   Another tier of accommodations in Croatia is the SOBA (room) or SOBE (rooms) in private homes. These generally are cheaper than those procured through agencies, but they are unregulated and can be anything from a suite of rooms with a private bathroom to a bed in an attic. SOBE signs are often found outside houses in smaller towns. Sometimes they're "advertised," usually by older men and women who await new arrivals at ferry, bus, and train stations, shouting "sobe, rooms, camera!"

CAMPGROUNDS   Camping is very popular in Croatia, with over 300 registered campsites, 90 percent of which are on the coast and islands, close to a beach. Some of the larger campsites include restaurants, sports facilities, laundries, and general stores. Campsites are rated with a star system from 1 to 4. For a full list of registered campsites, visit the **Croatian Camping Union** website at www.camping.hr.

FKK CAMPGROUNDS   Croatia has more FKK campgrounds (nudist camps) than any other European country. Most of these camps are outside cities in the northern Adriatic resort areas (Vrsar, Rovinj, Poreč, and Krk). You will find them on www.camping.hr under "Naturist."

YOUTH HOSTELS   The **Croatian Youth Hostels Association** (www.hfhs.hr) has a network of youth hostels in Zagreb, Zadar, Dubrovnik, Pula, and a few other locations. Most of these are rather basic and usually have check-in and checkout times and rules similar to those enforced in college dorms. Since 2010, an increasing number of boutique hostels have opened, offering a more contemporary approach to design and management, and often including private en-suite rooms in addition to dormitories. Several of these hostels are listed in this guide.

[Fast FACTS] CROATIA

Area Codes   Croatia's country code is **385.**

Business Hours   Banks are generally open Monday to Friday 8am to 7pm and Saturday 8am to noon. The bigger post offices work Monday to Friday 7am to 8pm, and Saturday 7am to 1pm. The smaller ones, for example on the islands, might only operate Monday to Friday 7 to 11am. Public offices are open Monday to Friday from 8am to 4pm.

Shops and department stores stay open from 8am to 8pm and to 2 or 3pm Saturday without a break. Increasingly, stores in malls are open on Sunday, usually from 10am to 6pm. Most supermarkets remain closed on Sunday, as do butchers and bakeries, though in popular resorts along the coast there will often be a few small general stores open for Sunday shopping in summer.

Drinking Laws   The minimum age for purchasing liquor in Croatia is 18, but there is no minimum age for consuming it. Croatia has strict laws regarding drinking and driving; the legal blood alcohol limit is 0.05 percent. In 2003, the country briefly implemented zero tolerance, but found it to be unworkable and amended the law in 2008. Package liquor (wine, beer, spirits) can be purchased in markets, wine stores, and some souvenir shops. Wine can also be bought directly from producers in some rural wine-making areas.

Driving Rules See "Getting There & Getting Around," p. 213.

Drugstores *Ljekarne* are open from 8am to 7pm weekdays and from 8am to 2pm on Saturday. In larger cities, one pharmacy in town will be open 24 hours on a rotating basis.

Electricity Croatian electricity is 220v, 50Hz; the two-prong European plug is standard.

Embassies & Consulates U.S.: Ulica Thomasa Jeffersona 2, Zagreb (www.zagreb.usembassy.gov; ☏ **01/661-22-000.** Australia: Centar Kaptol, Nova Ves 11, Zagreb (www.croatia.embassy.gov.au; ☏ **01/489-12-00**). Canada: Prilaz Gjure Dezelica 4, Zagreb (www.canadainternational.gc.ca; ☏ **01/488-12-00**). Ireland: Trg N.Š. Zrinskog 7-8, Zagreb (www.ie.mvep.hr; ☏ **01/456-99-64**). U.K.: Ivana Lučića 4, Zagreb, and Obala Hrvatskog Narodnog Preporoda 10/III, Split (www.gov.uk/government/world/croatia; ☏ **01/600-91-00**).

Emergencies ☏ **112.** Calls to this number are free of charge. This is the number to call if you need assistance from police, firefighters, mountain rescue, or an ambulance. Roadside assistance is ☏ **1987.** (When calling from abroad or by cellphone, call ☏ **385-1-987.**) The national

headquarters for Search and Rescue at Sea is ☏ **9155.** Weather forecasts are www.meteo.hr and road conditions are www.hak.hr/en.

Etiquette & Customs **Appropriate attire:** Croatians, especially Croatian women, take pride in their appearance. In cities, both men and women usually dress in business casual. On the coast and countryside, the "dress code" is more relaxed. You *never* will see Croatians wearing immodest or sloppy clothes in public places. If you visit museums or churches anywhere, plan to wear tops with sleeves and pants that go to at least the knee.

Gestures: *Dobar dan* (good day) is the way Croatians generally greet each other. Handshakes are appropriate for first meetings and between business associates. Good friends will kiss on both cheeks in the European style.

Avoiding offense: Religion and politics are topics to avoid universally. In Croatia, stay away from discussing Croat-Serb relations or anything related to the War for Independence unless you know who you're talking to, what you're talking about, and have lots of time for debate.

Gasoline (Petrol) Gasoline and diesel are readily available all over Croatia and almost all stations take credit cards. In the summer of 2014, gas was running about 11.08kn

per liter including taxes. One U.S. gallon equals 3.8 liters or .85 imperial gallons. That translates to 42kn or $7.37 per U.S. gallon of gas.

Holidays Croatian shops and banks are closed on public holidays, which are: January 1, New Year; January 6, Epiphany; March or April, Easter Monday; May 1, Labor Day; May (Thurs after Trinity Sun), Corpus Christi; June 22, Anti-Fascist Day; June 25, Croatian Statehood; August 5, Thanksgiving; August 15, Assumption; October 8, Independence Day; November 1, All Saints Day; December 25 and 26, Christmas. For more information on holidays, see "Calendar of Events," earlier in this chapter.

Hospitals Zagreb: Klinička Bolnica "Sestre Milosrdnice" (Vinogradska cesta 29; ☏ **01/378-71-11**). Split: Klinička Bolnica Split (Spinčićeva 1; ☏ **021/556-111**). Dubrovnik: Opća Bolnica Dubrovnik (Toka Mišetića bb; ☏ **020/431-777**).

Insurance Information on traveler's insurance, trip-cancellation insurance, and medical insurance while traveling is at www.frommers.com/planning.

Language Most residents of major Croatian cities speak English. Most movie houses and programs on Croatian TV are in English with Croatian subtitles. For basic phrases and words, see the inside front cover of this book. For more specific vocabulary, see the "Langenscheidt Universal Croatian Dictionary."

Legal Aid Consult your embassy if you get into legal trouble in Croatia. See above for contact information.

Mail It costs 4.60kn to send a postcard to the U.S., and 7.60kn to send a letter weighing up to 50 grams (1.76 oz.). The post office is fairly reliable, but very slow. It takes about 10 days to 2 weeks for postcards to arrive in the U.S. from Croatia and up to a month for regular mail and packages. Other carriers are available (DHL, FedEx, UPS) in major population centers, but the cost is prohibitive.

Newspapers & Magazines English-language newspapers and magazines are a rarity at Croatian newsstands, even in Zagreb. Some of the better hotels supply select U.S. and U.K. publications. Algoritam bookstores in Zagreb, Split, and Dubrovnik are the only common outlets for English-language publications. Look for the "International Herald Tribune" and "The Guardian" if you crave English-language news.

Passports Allow plenty of time before your trip to apply for a passport; processing normally takes three weeks but can take longer during busy periods (especially spring). Keep in mind that if you need a passport

in a hurry, you'll pay a higher processing fee.

For residents of the United States: Whether you're applying in person or by mail, you can download passport applications from the U.S. State Department website at www.travel.state.gov. To find your regional passport office, either check the U.S. State Department website or call the **National Passport Information Center** toll-free number (© **877/487-2778**) for automated information.

For residents of Australia: Applications are available at local post offices or at any branch of Passports Australia, but you must schedule an interview at the passport office to present your application materials. Call the **Australian Passport Information Service** at © **131-232,** or visit the government website at www.passports.gov.au.

For residents of Canada: Passport applications can be made online (www.passport.gc.ca); by post (Passport Canada Program, Gatineau QC K1A 0G3, Canada); or directly at a **Passport Canada Office.**

For residents of Ireland: You can apply for a 10-year passport by referring to www.dfa.ie/passports-citizenship. If you are traveling on short notice (3–10 days) and need a passport urgently, go to www.passportappointments.ie. Once your passport has been processed, you will be able to collect it directly from either

the Dublin or Cork Passport Office.

For residents of New Zealand: Pick up a passport application at any New Zealand Passports Office or download it from the website. Contact the **Passports Office** at © **0800/225-050** in New Zealand or 04/463-93-60, or log on to www.passports.govt.nz.

For residents of the United Kingdom: To obtain an application for a standard 10-year passport (5-year passport for children under 16), visit the nearest passport office, major post office, or contact the **United Kingdom Passport Office** at © **0300/222-00-00** or refer to www.gov.uk/government/organisations/hm-passport-office.

For more information, see www.frommers.com/planning for information on how to obtain a passport.

Police Call © **192.**

Smoking In May 2009, Croatia passed a law banning smoking in all public buildings. However, that was modified four months later to give small bars and cafes the option of allowing or not allowing on-premises smoking. The ban still applies to restaurants and larger bars and cafes. However, it is normal for people sitting at outdoor tables to smoke, especially if they are drinking or have just finished their meal.

Taxes Croatia's PDV (VAT) was raised to 25 percent from 23 percent in March 2012. Refunds of VAT are made to non-E.U. citizens (when they leave the country) for goods purchased in Croatia for amounts over 740kn with a tax check form. Salespeople will provide this form when you make a qualifying purchase. For further information, go to www.carina.hr.

Time Croatia is 1 hour ahead of Greenwich Mean Time, 6 hours ahead of New York (Eastern Standard Time), and 9 hours ahead of Los Angeles (Pacific Standard Time). Daylight saving time is observed from late-March to late-October, when clocks are advanced 1 hour.

Tipping A 10 percent to 15 percent gratuity is expected in upscale restaurants. Otherwise, it is considered polite to leave any coins from your change on the table in cafes and restaurants. A 10 percent tip for other service providers (taxi drivers, hotel personnel, and others) is the norm, as is a tip for anyone who helps you carry your luggage or conducts a tour.

Toilets There are no freestanding public restrooms in Croatia, but most restaurants and public buildings have them and will let you use them if you make a purchase.

Water Tap water is potable throughout Croatia.

USEFUL TERMS & PHRASES

GLOSSARY OF CROATIAN-LANGUAGE TERMS

Most of the natives you'll encounter in Croatia will be fluent in at least one other language besides Croatian, usually English, or German or Italian. However, if you try to learn at least a few rudimentary words and phrases in this Slavic variant, you will be richly rewarded for your efforts. Pronunciation is not as difficult as it looks when you're staring at a word that appears to be devoid of vowels. With a few guidelines and a little practice, you should be able to make yourself understood.

ORDERING A MEAL (& PAYING FOR IT)

English	Croatian	Pronunciation
menu	**jelovnik**	yay-*lohv*-neek
order	**naručiti**	nah-roo-*chee*-tee
waiter	**konobar**	*koe*-noe-bar
I am hungry.	**Ja sam gladan.**	Ya sahm *glah*-dahn.
Do you serve food here?	**Da li poslužujete hranu ovdje?**	Dah lee poe-*sloozh*-oo-yay-tay *ha*-ra-noo ohv-day?
What would you like to order?	**Što bi ste željeli naručiti?**	*Shtoe* bee stay z*jehl*-yay-lee nah-roo-*chee*-tee?
We would like to order . . .	**Željeli bi smo naručiti . . .**	Z*jehl*-yay-lee bee smaw nah-roo-*chee*-tee . . .
Table for two (three, four)	**Stol za dvoje (troje, četvoro)**	Stall za *dvo*-ye (*troe*-ye, chet-*voe*-roe)
We would like to pay.	**Željeli bi smo platiti.**	Z*jehl*-yay-lee bee some *plah*-tee-tee.

BASICS

English	Croatian	Pronunciation
breakfast	**doručak**	*doe*-roo-chahk
lunch	**ručak**	*roo*-chahk
dinner	**večera**	*veh*-chair-ah
knife	**nož**	*noezh*
fork	**viljuška**	vee-*loosh*-kah
spoon	**žlica**	*zhlee*-tsa
plate	**tanjur**	*tah*-nyoor
cold	**hladno**	*hah*-lahd-noe

English	Croatian	Pronunciation
hot	**vruće**	*vrooch*-eh
warm	**toplo**	*toe*-ploe
sugar	**šećer**	*shay*-chair
without sugar	**bez šećera**	bayz *shay*-chair
salt	**sol**	soal
pepper	**papar**	*pah*-pahr
bread	**kruh**	crew
pastry	**pecivo**	*pay*-tsee-voe
meat	**meso**	*may*-soe
I am a vegetarian.	**Ja sam vegetarijanac.**	Yah sahm vay-gay-tahr-ee-*yah*-nahts.

BEVERAGES

English	Croatian	Pronunciation
white wine	**bijelo vino**	bee-*yeh*-lo *vee*-noe
red wine	**crno vino**	*tser*-noe *vee*-noe
(fruit) juice	**sok**	sock
tea	**čaj**	chai
coffee	**kava**	*kah*-vah
coffee with milk/cream	**kava sa mlijekom/vrhnjem**	*kah*-vah sah ml-*yay*-kum/*ver*-nyem
ice	**led**	layd
lemonade	**limunada**	lee-moo-*nah*-dah
milk	**mlijeko**	ml-yay-koe
beer (cold)	**pivo**	*pee*-voe
brandy (usually homemade)	**rakija**	*rah*-kee-yah
water	**voda**	*voe*-dah

SOUPS & STARTERS

English	Croatian	Pronunciation
Swiss chard boiled with potatoes	**blitva sa krumpirom**	*bleet*-vah sa kroom-*peer*-om
sausage	**kobasica**	koe-*bah*-see-tsa
goat cheese	**kozji sir**	*koezh*-yee seer
Zagorje potato soup	**juha od krumpira na zagorski način**	*yoo*-ha ode kroom-peer-ah nah zah-*gore*-ski *na*-cheen
spicy sausage from Slavonia	**kulen**	*koo*-len
bean and veggie soup from Istria	**maneštra**	mah-*nay*-strah
mixed salad	**miješana salata**	mee-*yeh*-shah-na sa-*lah*-tah
hard sheep's cheese with olive oil from Pag	**paški sir**	*pahsh*-kee seer
smoked ham	**pršut**	per-*shoot*

English	Croatian	Pronunciation
stuffed red peppers	**punjene paprika**	poon-yen-ay *pah*-pre-kah
shish kabob	**ražnjiči**	rahz-nyee-chee
spicy seafood/fish stew with paprika	**riblji paprikaš/fis paprika**	*reeb*-lyee *pah*-pre-kash/fish *pah*-pre-kash
hams	**šunka**	*shoon*-kah

FISH/PASTA

English	Croatian	Pronunciation
fish stew	**brodet/brodetto**	*bro*-debt/*bro*-debt-toe
black risotto made with squid ink, olive oil, onion, and garlic	**crni rižot**	*tser*-nee ree-*zhote*
Istrian egg pasta in a special twisted shape	**fuži**	*foo*-zhee

Pronunciation Guide

All letters are pronounced.

c	sounds like "ts" in cats
č	sounds like "ch" in chew
ć	sounds like "tu" in picture
đ	sounds like "dj" in adjunct
g	sounds like "g" in god
j	sounds like "y" in your
š	sounds like "sh" in shut
ž	sounds like "z" in azure
e	sounds like "e" in bet
i	sounds like "ee" in meet
o	sounds like "o" in dog
u	sounds like "oo" in loot
r	is trilled

BASIC VOCABULARY

English	Croatian	Pronunciation
yes	**da**	dah
no	**ne**	nay
good	**dobro**	doe-broe
bad	**loše**	losh-eh
I don't know.	**Ne znam.**	Nay znahm.
I don't understand.	**Ne razumijem.**	Nay ra-zoo-mee-yem.
to	**do**	doh
from	**od**	ode
day	**dan**	dahn
week	**tjedan**	tyay-dahn
month	**mjesec**	myes-ets

English	Croatian	Pronunciation
year	**godina**	*goe-dee-nah*
why	**zašto**	*zah-shtoe*
where	**gdje**	*gd-yay*
when	**kada**	*kah-dah*
how	**kako**	*kah-koe*
early	**rano**	*rah-noe*
late	**kasno**	*kahz-noe*
behind	**iza**	*ee-zah*
in front of	**ispred**	*ee-spread*
turn/go . . .	**vratite se/okrenite/idite**	*vrah-tee-tay say/oh-kray-nee/ ee-dee-tay . . .*
left	**lijevo**	*lee-yay-voe*
right	**desno**	*days-noe*
straight ahead	**ravno**	*rahv-noe*
street	**ulica**	*oo-lee-tsah*
square	**trg**	*tur-ig-ah*
next to	**pored**	*poe-red*
there	**tamo**	*tah-moe*
map	**karta**	*kar-tah*
I would like to buy a ticket.	**Želio/Željela bih kupiti kartu.**	*Zhel-ee-ol/Zhel-yay-lah bee koo-pee-tee kar-too.*
ticket	**(putna) karta**	*(poot-nah) kar-tah*
one-way ticket	**jednosmjema karta**	*yed-nose-myair-na kar-tah*
round-trip ticket	**povratna karta**	*poe-vraht-nah kar-tah*
ticket	**ulaznica** (for movies, museum)	*oo-lahz-neetsa*
Where is the . . . ?	**Gdje se nalazi . . . ?**	*Ga dyay say nah-lah-zee . . .*
bank	**banka**	*ban-ka*
beach	**plaža**	*plah-zha*
church	**crkva**	*tserk-vah*
drugstore	**ljekarna**	*lee-yay-car-nah*
market	**tržnica**	*terzh-nee-tsa*
museum	**muzej**	*moo-zay*
park	**park**	*park*
police station	**policijska postaja**	*poe-leets-ee-ska poe-shta-ya*
post office	**poštanski ured, pošta**	*poe-stan-skee oo-raid, poe-shtah*
tourist office	**turistički ured**	*too-ree-steech-kee oo-raid*
train station	**željeznička stanica/post-aja centra** (if central station in town, then **željeznički kolodvor**)	*zhel-yay-zneech-kee stah-nee-tsa/poe-stah-ya tsen-trah (zhel-yay-zneech koe-loe-dvoar)*
bus station	**autobusna** (if central station in town, then **auto-busni kolodvor**)	*ow-toe-boos-nah (ow-toe-boos-nee koe-loe-dvoar)*

English	Croatian	Pronunciation
airport	**zračna luka**	*zrach*-na *loo*-kah
taxi stand	**taksi stajalište**	*tahk*-see *stye*-ya-lees-tay
exchange office	**mjenjačnica**	myay-nyats-*nee*-tsa
exchange rate	**tečajna lista**	tay-chai-nyah *leest*-ah
Where can I find a (good) . . . ?	**Gdje mogu naći (dobrog) . . . ?**	*Gd*-yay moe-goo *nah*-chee (doe-broeg) . . . ?
dentist	**zubara**	zoo-bah-rah
doctor	**liječnika**	lee-*yaych*-nee-kah
hospital	**bolnicu**	bole-*nee*-tsu

SIGNS

English	Croatian	Pronunciation
entry	**ulaz**	oo-lahz
exit	**izlaz**	eez-lahz
toilets (men)	**toilets/WC (muskarci)**	moosh-*kar*-tsi
toilets (women)	**toilets/WC (žene)**	zhe-neh
police	**policija**	poe-*lee*-tsee-yah
prohibited	**zabranjeno**	zah-brah-nyay-noe

HEALTH

English	Croatian	Pronunciation
I am sick.	**Bolestan sam/bolesna sam.**	*Boe*-less-than sahm/*boe*-less-nah sahm.
I need a doctor.	**Potreban mi je liječnik.**	Poe-*tray*-bahn mee yay lee-*yaych*-neek.
fever	**groznica**	*growz*-nee-tsa
headache	**glavobolja**	glah-*voe*-bowl-yay
stomachache	**bol u trbuhu**	bowl oo *ter*-boo
dentist	**zubar**	zoo-bar
I have a headache.	**Imam glavobolju.**	*Eee*-mom glah-*voe*-bowl-yoo.
I am allergic to . . .	**Alcrgičan/allergična . . .**	Ah-*lure*-gee-chan/ah-*lure*-geech-nah . . .
antibiotics	**sam na antibiotike**	sam *ahn*-tee-bee-oh-teek
antibiotic	**antibiotic**	*ahn*-tee-bee-oh-teek
penicillin	**penicillin**	peh-nee-*tsee*-leen
aspirin	**aspirin**	ah-*spee*-reen
I am on medications for (asthma/diabetes/epilepsy).	**Pijem lijekove protiv (astme, dijabetesa, epilepsije).**	Pee-yem lee-*yay*-koe-vay pro-teev (*ast*-may, dee-yah-*bay*-tay-sah, ep-ee-*lep*-see-yeh).
virus	**virus**	vee-roos

ATTRACTIONS

English	Croatian	Pronunciation
bridge	**most**	most
church	**crkva**	*tserk*-vah
island	**otok**	*oh*-toke
lake	**jezero**	*yeh*-zeh-roe
old town	**stari grad**	*star*-ee grahd
ruins	**ruše vine**	*roo*-sheh *vee*-neh
sea	**more**	*moe*-reh

SHOPPING

English	Croatian	Pronunciation
How much/ How many?	**Koliko?**	*Koe*-lee-koe?
a little	**malo**	*mah*-loe
a lot	**puno**	*poo*-noe
enough	**dosta**	*doe*-stah
(too) expensive	**(pre) skupo**	(pray) *scoo*-poe

GETTING A ROOM

English	Croatian	Pronunciation
room	**soba**	*soe*-bah
Excuse me, is there a hotel nearby?	**Oprostite, da li postoji hotel u blizini?**	Oh-*proe*-stee-tay, dah lee *poe*-stoy-ee *hoe*-tel oo *blee*-zee-nee?
We would like a double room.	**Željeli bi smo jednu dvokrevetnu sobu.**	*Zhel*-yay-lee bee some yay-dnoo dvoe-kray-vayt-noo soe-boo.
I would like a room	**Želio/željela (she) bih**	*Zhel*-ee-oh/*zhel*-yay-lah bee
with a:	**sobu sa:**	*soe*-boo sah:
shower	**tušem**	*toosh*-em
bathtub	**kadom**	*kah*-dome
balcony	**balkonom**	*bal*-koe-nome
air-conditioning	**klimom**	*klee*-mome
telephone	**telefonom**	teh-*leh*-phone-ohm
How much is the room per night?	**Koliko košta soba za jednu noć?**	*Koe*-lee-koe *koe*-shtah *soe*-bah zah *yayd*-noo noech?
per person	**po osobi**	poe *oh*-soe-bee
per week	**za tjedan dana**	zah *tyay*-dahn *dah*-nah
Okay, I will take the room.	**Uredu, uzet ću sobu.**	*Oo*-ray-doo, *oo*-zayt choo soe-boo.
I will stay for 2 nights.	**Ostat ću dvije noći.**	*Oh*-staht choo dvee-yay *noe*-chee.
Can I look at the room?	**Da li mogu pogledati sobu?**	Dah lee *moe*-goo *poe*-glay-dah-tee soe-boo?

Index

See also Accommodations and Restaurant indexes, below.

General Index

A

Abercrombie and Kent, 233
Accommodations. *See also* Accommodations Index
  Baranja area, 70
  best big luxury hotels, 4–5
  best small hotels and inns, 3–4
  Brač, 163–164
  Buzet, 102
  Cavtat, 205–206
  Cres, 120–121
  Dubrovnik, 195–198
  eco-conscious, 228–229
  Korčula, 174–175
  Krk Town/Baśka, 113–114
  Lonjsko Polje area, 66
  Lošinj, 122–123
  Lovran, 111
  Makarska Riviera, 160
  Mali Ston, 210
  Motovun and Livade, 99–100
  Opatija, 108–109
  Orebić, 207–208
  Osijek, 69
  Pag, 138
  Plitvice Lakes, 54
  Poreč, 89–91
  private, 235
  Pula, 78–79
  Rab Island, 117–118
  Rijeka, 104
  Rovinj, 84–86
  Šibenik area, 141–142
  Split, 150–152
  Starigrad Paklenica, 134
  tips on, 234–235
  Trogir, 157–158
  Umag and Savudrija, 93
  Varaždin, 60
  Vis, 178–179
  Vukovar, 72–73
  Zadar, 130–131
  Zagreb, 43–46
Adriatica.Net, 230
Adriatic Dolphin Project, 227–228
Adriatic Kayak Tours, 195, 231
Adriatic Tours, 233
Adventure Dalmatia, 231
Adventure sports, 231
Air travel
  to Croatia, 216
  within Croatia, 218
  Dubrovnik, 181
  Rijeka, 104
  Zadar, 127
  Zagreb, 32–33
Animafest Zagreb, 213
Aquarium, Dubrovnik, 184
Aquarium (Pula), 77

Aquarius (Zagreb), 49
Archaeological Institute of America, 230
Archaeological Museum
  Pula, 77
  Vis, 178
  Zadar, 128
  Zagreb, 41
Arch of the Sergi (Pula), 77
Arena (Pula), 77–78
Art and architecture, 17–18
ATMs and banks, 220–221
  Dubrovnik, 182
  Split, 146
  Zadar, 128
  Zagreb, 35
Avvantura Festival Film Forum
  Zadar, 214

B

Bacchus (Zagreb), 48–49
Balbi Arch (Rovinj), 83–84
Banje (Dubrovnik), 194
Baptistery (Split), 150
Baranja, 69–70
  cuisine, 21
Baranja Wine Road, 70
Baredine Cave (Poreč), 88–89
Baron Guatsch (wreck dive), 23
Baśka, 5, 113, 114
Baśka beach, 113
Baśka Tablet, 113
Baśka Voda, 158
Batana House (Rovinj), 84
Bay of Pula, 74
Beaches. *See also specific beaches*
  best, 5
  Blue Flag, 227
  Dubrovnik, 194
  Hvar, 167
  nudist, 117
Beli, 119, 120
Beram, 94
Big Blue (Bol), 163
Big Blue Diving (Bol), 163
Biking, 232
Biokovo Active Holidays, 159, 231
Biokovo Nature Park, 159
Bird-watching, Kopački Rit Nature Park, 70
Biśevo, 177
Biśevo islet, 143
Bites and stings, 222
Blaise, St., 190
Blato (Korčula), 176
Blue Bay Diving (Pag), 137
Blue Bike Zagreb, 232
Blue Cave (Modra Špilja), 177
Blue Flag beaches, 227
Blue Line International, 218
Boat tours and cruises, Vis, 1
Bokar Fortress (Dubrovnik), 191
Bol (Brač), 161–163
Bonj "les bains" beach club (Hvar), 167
Books, recommended, 18

Bottle collection, 226–227
Brač, 161–165
Breakfast, 19
Brela, 158
Brijuni Archipelago (Brioni), 80–81
Brijuni National Park, 1, 81
British naval cemetery (Vis), 177
Bronze Gate (Split), 148
Brsalje Square (Dubrovnik), 191
Buje (Buie), 96
Business hours, 235
Bus travel, 219
Buźa (Dubrovnik), 201
Buzet (Pinguente), 100–102
Byblos (Poreč), 92

C

Caesarea Gate (Salona), 156
Café Gallery Đina (Zadar), 132
Caffe Uliks (Pula), 80
Čakovec, 61–62
Calendar of events, 213
Campgrounds, 235
Canoeing, Makarska, 159
Cardo (Split), 148
Carpe Diem Beach, 167, 172
Car rentals, 217–219
Car travel, 217, 219–220
Castles, 58
  best, 6–7
Cathedral of St. Domnius (Split), 146, 148, 155
Cathedral of St. James (Šibenik), 6, 140, 141
Cathedral of St. Lawrence (Trogir), 157
Cathedral of St. Mark (Korčula), 173
Cathedral of the Assumption (Katedrala Uznesenja; Krk Town), 112–113
Cathedral of the Assumption (Pula), 78
Cathedral of the Assumption (Varaždin), 59
Cathedral of the Assumption of the Virgin Mary (Zagreb), 36
Cavtat, 23, 204–206
Cellphones, 230
Cetina Gorge, 158
Cherry Days (Lovran), 111
Chestnut Festival (Marunada; Lovran), 111, 214
Church of Our Lady of Belfry (Split), 148
Church of Our Saviour (Dubrovnik), 191
Church of St. Blaise (Vodnjan), 81, 82
Church of St. Germaine (Veliki Brijuni), 81
Church of St. Lucy (Baśka), 113
Church of St. Mary (Beram), 6
Church of St. Mary (Mljet), 204
Church of St. Mary of the Rock, Frescoes at the (near Beram), 95